Urmi Michel Hurd

THE
SUICIDE OF
EUROPE

BOOKS BY PRINCE MICHEL STURDZA

The Suicide of Europe
La Roumaine Peut-elle Combattre sur Deux Fronts?
Avec l'Armée Roumaine
Crise Econimique et Réforme Monétaire
Czecho-Soviet Protectorate or Independent Rumanian Kingdom?
La Bête sans Nom
Katanga: El Occidente al Servicio del Communismo
Open Letter to Their Excellencies
World Government and International Assassination
And You Tomorrow (To be published)
Introduction to a Parabiology (To be published)

THE
SUICIDE OF
EUROPE

MEMOIRS OF PRINCE MICHEL STURDZA,
FORMER FOREIGN MINISTER OF RUMANIA

WESTERN ISLANDS

PUBLISHERS

BOSTON   LOS ANGELES

Direct quotations taken from the following sources have been reprinted in this book with written permission of the respective publishers:

F. J. P. Veale, *Advance to Barbarism* (C. C. Nelson Publishing Company, Appleton, Wisconsin, © 1953)

Hans Rogger and Eugene Weber, eds., *The European Right, a Historical Profile* (University of California Press, Berkeley, © 1965)

Winston Churchill, *The Hinge of Fate* (Houghton Mifflin Company, New York, © 1950)

Winston Churchill, *Triumph and Tragedy* (Houghton Mifflin Company, New York, © 1953)

"Whether you like it or not, history is on our side. We will bury you."

NIKITA KHRUSHCHEV
Moscow, November 16, 1956

Table of Contents

PART FOUR

ANTONESCU, THE INSANE LEADER

PART FIVE

MICHAEL: THE PUPPET KING

Introduction

But who dares call the child by its right name?
The few who knowing something about it
Were foolish enough not to guard it in their hearts,
Those who have shown the people their feeling and their thoughts
Have been since always crucified or burned at the stake.

GOETHE—Faust I

This book is not a history of Europe nor of Rumania nor even of the Legion of the Archangel Michael, but rather the memoirs of one man who has been a witness and a participant in the events which, for hundreds of millions of people, have turned a century so full of promise into an eternity of suffering and slavery. From the first days of the Russian Revolution, this man understood the terrible danger which the Soviet regime represented not only for his own country but also for Europe and the entire world. From that time, his political thinking and activities were unswervingly directed by a growing consciousness of this danger and by the necessity, to which circumstances made him particularly obligated, to inform or to fight those in his nation who were, or pretended to be, blind to the magnitude and the imminence of this peril.

Prince Michel Sturdza, a former Foreign Minister of Rumania, served in the diplomatic corps of his country for twenty-five years without any interruption other than for his tour of duty during World War I, in which he fought first in a squadron of mounted artillery and then as chief of an armored car section, and for a period of service as prefect in Transylvania. During his career, he held posts in Durazzo (Albania), Athens, Bern, Budapest, Vienna, Washington (as Councillor and then Chargé d'Affaires of the Rumanian Legation); he acted as Envoy Extraordinary and as Minister Plenipotentiary in Riga, Reval, Helsinki, and Copenhagen. His time abroad was interrupted several times by periods of service in the Foreign Office in Bucharest.

As a result of violent conflict with King Carol II and his Government, concerning Rumania's internal and foreign policy, Prince Sturdza was forced to leave the diplomatic service for a short time after the outbreak of World War II. In 1940 he was appointed as Foreign Minister in the first cabinet following the abdication of King Carol. In 1945 he belonged, again as Foreign Minister, to the Rumanian Government in Exile, which refused to recognize the capitulation of King Michael to Soviet Russia. Since that time he has continued his fight against the irreconcilable enemy of his motherland and of Western Civilization.

These memoirs center around three basic dramas, all of them interrelated and all, for the most part, unknown to the Western reader: the role of pacts of military alliance between France, Czecho-Slovakia and Soviet Russia in bringing on World War II, the attempts of Germany to avoid a Western war, and the story of the Legion of the Archangel Michael. Prince Sturdza maintains that Rumania was the pivotal point in the events leading to the war. So because Rumania plays such an important part in this book, it is wise to briefly review her history.

The reader should remember that the Rumanians do not consider their nation a Balkan country, but rather a Danubian state, like Austria and Hungary, and with roots deep in Western Civilization. The Rumanians are not Slavs; historically, and in a large part ethnically, the Rumanian people are the heirs of the Dacians. The ancient kingdom of Dacia covered and went beyond the area of the Rumania of 1939; its population, which was an offshoot of the Thracian race, appears to have developed its own particular characteristics from years of isolation in the valleys of Transylvania whence settlers and warriors spread east to the Dniester and west to the vicinity of what is now Vienna, covering the area which was to become Dacia.

The Dacian villages (*davae,* meaning a confederation of villages, may be the origin of *Dacia*) were forged into a real power and an actual empire under the kingship of Burebista. This expansion, combined with her geographical position, soon brought Dacia into conflict with Rome. After years of war and hostilities, the Dacians, led by Decebalus, were defeated in 105 A.D. by the Roman Emperor Trajan. The Dacian prisoners sculptured on the column raised by Trajan to commemorate his victory are, in their physical type, their clothes, and their foot-wear, identical with the Rumanian peasants of the present century. Defeat brought Roman garrisons, Roman colonists, and the Latin language; this occupation went deep enough in its penetration of Dacia to result in Latin becoming the basic element in what has developed into the Rumanian language.

With the withdrawal of the Roman legions in 271 A.D. by the Emperor Aurelian, Rumania was left undefended and open to all attacks. Wave after wave of barbarians passed through the country. All trace of colonial rule would have been obliterated, as happened in Bulgaria, except that the wealth of the country was not great enough or concentrated enough to encourage the marauders to settle down, and, secondly, the inhabitants withdrew into the mountain valleys, particularly those of Transylvania. We do not know when this migration to shelter began, how long it lasted, or at what cost it was undertaken. But late in the Thirteenth Century the process was reversed as a part of the Rumanian nobility, with their followers, left Transylvania and migrated eastward to found what were to become the principalities of Moldavia and Walachia. These two separate states were formed by the merger of the Rumanians from Transylvania with indigenous Rumanian settlements.

From the very beginning, the Walachians under the Bassarab dynasty and the Moldavians under the Mushats had to struggle constantly against attempted encroachments by their neighbors. Hungary had already occupied much of Transylvania, and continually strove to conquer more and more Rumanian territory. The Tartars raided, and even launched full scale invasions against, the principalities until the very end of the Sixteenth Century. Poland maintained pretensions over northern Moldavia. And finally towards the end of the Fourteenth Century, the Turks began their raids which would steadily grow in size and ferocity. Thus the Rumanians were perpetually at war, often with both Christians and Moslems at the same time.

The independence of Walachia was originally secured by the victory of Ivanco (?–1330) over King Charles Robert of Hungary; the Walachian position was strengthened by Vladislav Bassarab's (1360–1374) defeat of an attack by Charles Robert's son, King Louis the Great. Mircea the Old (1386–1418) of Walachia was present with his light cavalry at the battle of Nicopolis in 1396. He urged the French and German leaders of this Western Crusade against the Turks to let him strike the first blow. But the heavily armored crusaders insisted on the honor of making the first charge, the charge failed, and their army was lost. Mircea pulled his troops back over the Danube; the Sultan pursued and the two armies joined in combat at Rovine, where the Walachians cut the Turks to pieces and forced them across the Danube, which the Turks did not recross for half a century.

However the Turks were checked only temporarily. For in the face of the swelling wave of Moslem power, the hostilities among the Christian princes continued to rage, a tragic prefiguration of the situation in Europe before and during World War II. Towards the end of the Fifteenth Century, the two principalities were pressed on all sides, by the Hungarians, the Poles, the Tartars, and the Turks. Walachia was defended by Vlad the Impaler (1455–1462 and 1476–1477); Moldavia, by Ştefan the Great (1457–1504). Vlad earned his nickname from the particular manner in which he dealt with Turkish prisoners. He successfully repelled the Turks, but fell in battle with Matthias Corvinus, King of Hungary and the son of a Walachian nobleman. Ştefan devoted his whole reign to an attempt to rally the West against the Turkish threat. He inflicted a crushing defeat upon the Turks in 1475 at Rahova, and he repelled them at Skeia in 1476. However neither Hungary nor Poland would give him the solid support needed for an attack on the Ottoman Empire. In fact he was forced into war with each country and defeated each army in turn. On his deathbed, believing it hopeless to obtain united action from Christendom, Ştefan advised his son to come to an understanding with the Turks so as to be able to resist Hungary and Poland.

After Ştefan's death, the Turkish advance became a virtual avalanche. Michael the Valiant (1593–1601) of Walachia was able to stop the Turkish progress and even to invade the Ottoman Empire. Yet he was forced to halt his attack in order to repel a raid against Walachia by the troops of Sigismund Báthory, King of Poland and Prince of Transylvania. But before Michael's death at the hands of assassins sent by his ally, the Imperial Commissioner, General George Basta, he succeeded in effecting a brief unification of Walachia, Moldavia, and Transylvania under one crown, thus realizing for the first time, since the fall of the Dacian Empire, the unity of the Rumanian nation.

The centuries of fratricidal wars had taken their toll. Hungary suffered a terrible defeat at Mohács (August 30, 1526); Buda was sacked and burned, and all of Hungary except a fringe of its western and northern borders passed under Turkish domination and remained so until 1686. In 1529 Suleiman was able to march to the very gates of Vienna. Poland's excursions in the south against Christian princes began a fatal weakening in her military power which was later one of the causes of the loss of her independence. By the same token the Rumanian principalities suffered a destruction of their forces of resistance and, during desperate battles, a decimation of the best of their ruling classes. After the defeat at the Prut River, 1711, the Turks replaced the native rulers of the principalities with princes of Greek origin. Some of these were also, by maternal descent, of Rumanian blood and strove to satisfy the best interests of their people, such were the Mavrocordatus who descended by feminine line from the extinct Mushat dynasty, others were completely foreign; all were chosen and imposed by the Turks.

In 1827 the native rulers were restored, with Gregory Ghyka Prince of Walachia and John Alexander Sturdza Prince of Moldavia. The principalities were united, in 1859, under Prince Alexander John Cuza, thus forming the basis of the modern Rumanian nation. After the abdication of Cuza, Charles of Hohenzollern-Sigmaringen was elected Prince. In 1877 after a victorious war, Rumania proclaimed her separation from the Turkish empire, and she became an independent state by the Treaty of Berlin. But the same treaty robbed her of her eastern province of Bessarabia which was ascribed to her Russian ally. In 1881 Rumania was declared a kingdom with Prince Charles becoming King Carol I, and five years later she became a constitutional monarchy with a bicameral legislature.

Despite centuries of wars and of foreign domination, the Rumanian principalities were far from being primitive or backward. Over the many years, the Rumanians had developed a deeprooted and vital national culture. The years between 1827 and 1914 brought the great flowering of this culture and of the nation itself, even though full unification of the Rumanian people was not achieved until 1919. The upper classes practised all the refinements of this most gracious era, and their education in Western Europe permitted them to combine the best of Rumanian culture with the best of France and Germany. From the prospering villages, a vigorous middle class (a class which had not existed in Rumania's social structure until then) was arising and expanding throughout the country and was striving to increase the intellectual level and the economic and industrial resources of the country. The peasantry, satisfied by the first agrarian reform, lived in patriarchal relation with the boyards, the great landowners who by this reform had yielded about one-third of their estates to their tenants. Education was compulsory and was free from primary school through high school up to, and including, the last year of doctoral studies at the universities. Because of the two charitable foundations, Brancoveneasa and Sanct Spiridon, which were profusely endowed through the centuries by the nobility; the numerous public hospitals and clinics belonging to the foundations and to the state; and the corps of state—paid doctors; no one in Rumania was deprived of medical or surgical care for want of money. The Rumanian principalities were among the first nations to suppress the death penalty, doing so as early as 1859.

Such was the state of affairs in Rumania at the outbreak of World War I. Rumania suffered terribly during the war, but when peace finally came, it brought the realization of the centuries old dream of the union of all Rumanians under one crown. Bucovina, which had been seized by Austria in 1773, and Bessarabia, which had been grabbed by Russia in three steps from 1812 to 1878, were restored to the motherland. But most important, Transylvania, which the Rumanians considered the cradle of their nation, was reunited with the rest of the country.

However the war brought great changes in Rumania as it did in all European countries and in the United States. The old order was dead; a new Order now emerged with ever-increasing power. The new order of things was felt at once in Rumania: the Agrarian Reform of 1918–1920 passed into the hands of the peasants ninety-two percent of all Rumania's arable land, but its fraudulent application ruined both the large and medium landowners. The destruction of the landowning class eliminated the Conservative Party which had been the traditional factor of stability, of wise progressive advance, and of integrity and rectitude in Rumania's public life.

World War I was not, as generally believed, the result of only the natural interplay of the ambitions of the Great Powers and of growing nationalism. Generalities and abstractions are not sufficient to cause wars; wars are brought on by the actions of men, and in the case of World War I (and as we shall see with World War II, also) these actions were deliberately calculated to bring on war with all its misery and suffering. The purpose of those who brought on the war was two-fold: first, the war by its own momentum would open huge cracks in the foundation of Western Civilization by destroying the soundest values and most stable institutions in our civilization. Second, the peace conferences following the war would be used to intensify the upheaval and to provide the foundation of a world-wide empire, to be built first on the ruins of all European empires and of the civilization they had spread over the entire globe, and later on the ruins of the United States. Who were these men, and what was their goal?

They were and are a tightly knit clique of conspirators who, with rare exceptions, have been and are made up of, and recruited from, the very top financial, economic, educational, and political levels of each country in which they operate. The ultimate goal of this conspiracy is the absolute domination of the entire world to be accomplished by the destruction of civilization through the merging of all nationalities and races into one people under one government; the abolition of all private property; the destruction of all religion; and the abrogation of all morality. The immediate goal of each generation of these conspirators was the reward, power and wealth and fame, which they received by advancing the final goal. The makeup and purpose of the conspiracy were explicitly defined by its founder, Adam Weishaupt, and embodied in his organization, the Order of Illuminati, founded May 1, 1776. The Illuminati was strong enough by 1789 to play a major role in planning and precipitating the French Revolution, and members of the Order held power in France for about six years. After 1795 the Illuminati went completely underground, and the secret of their existence became the fundamental law of the Order.

But despite the strict secrecy the Conspiracy maintained, we do have a considerable amount of information about its activities between 1795 and 1917 when its principle arm, Communism, erupted in Russia. A chief agent of the Illuminati, Joseph Fouché, was responsible for placing a member of the Order, Jean Baptiste Bernadotte, on the throne of Sweden. It was an agency or ally of the Conspiracy, the League of Just Men, which hired Karl Marx to write the *Communist Manifesto*. This group, which was renamed the League of Communists, was a major factor in bringing about uprisings throughout Europe in 1848. The Conspiracy played a more important role in organizing the Italian Revolution, directed by the American Albert Pike, and also, apparently, the Juarezista Revolution in Mexico in the 1860's. Both the assassination of Czar Alexander II and the Haymarket Riot in Chicago were the work of related agencies of the Conspiracy. In fact throughout the last half of the Nineteenth Century, the Order of Illuminati used Communists, socialists, anarchists, and numerous other groups and subsidiaries to advance its goals and solidify its position in nearly every nation.

By 1914 the conspirators, although still comparatively few, had sufficient power and influence to precipitate World War I. At this point it was not necessary for the Order to be able to control every action in the war. The war itself, by its very nature, served many purposes of the conspirators. They only needed to direct it to the desired conclusion, which they had the ability to do; and when this occurred with the armistice, they held the control of the peace conferences. The war had so weakened Russia that Lenin, Trotsky and their band of vicious criminals, financed and directed by associates throughout Europe and in the United States, were able to seize power, replacing the truly progressive government of Nicholas II with reactionary Bolshevism. The peace conference opened the way for the communization of Europe, and the League of Nations, to which it gave birth, was meant to further the goals of the Conspiracy through the activities of its clique of "illuminated" or Fabian diplomats. (Although the refusal of America to join the League ruined its planned effectiveness, the League still served many useful purposes, not the least being a forerunner of the United Nations.)

These memoirs show the working of the entire, long-developing Conspiracy, which has been, and is, the basis of many separate plots and plans being carried out in every country. In this book the reader will find the names of many of those who, for whatever reason, have carried the thread of a conspiracy, which has run through all human affairs from the time of the French Revolution to the present, and who have helped to nurture and spread Communism—the biggest and most important agency of the Illuminati—throughout the globe. Men such as Léon Blum, Edward Mandel House, Eduard Beneš, Woodrow Wilson, Jean Barthou, David Lloyd George, Winston Churchill, Anthony Eden, Nicolae Titulescu, Carol II, Paul Reynaud, Georges Mandel, Edouard Daladier, and Joseph Paul-Boncour were not members of the Communist Party, yet they served (many of them knowingly, we believe) Communist purposes far better than could have actual members of the Communist *Party*. We believe that Prince Sturdza's memoirs offer conclusive evidence that this deeprooted, centrally controlled and directed Conspiracy, working for the destruction of Western Civilization, precipitated World War II. The members of the Order and its numerous dupes and allies had not the least concern for the welfare of the countries they ruled or were appointed to serve; time and again they sacrificed the interests of their own nation to actions which directly aided Communism. From the end of World War I, these men have not merely taken advantage of every opportunity to foster their plans, but rather they have even created the necessary events on which to build their further advance. This book shows how this strategy was fulfilled in regard to World War II and its outcome. These memoirs show how men of state worked feverishly to push Western Civilization to the brink—and over. They first strove to create, nurture, and firmly establish the Communist beast in Russia; next they introduced it into the system of European alliances; finally, they guaranteed politically and militarily that only Soviet Russia would be the victor and beneficiary in the war they brought down upon the world.

The appearance of Communism in Russia, the treasonous actions of so many men of state, and Communist agitation and infiltration in every country and of every organ of society brought forth in each country of Europe nationalist opposition to this International Conspiracy. These opposition groups varied as greatly in their value, tenacity, and effectiveness as did the reaction of the Conspiracy to their emergence. The Communists organized an international "crusade" in their attempt to crush Spain's revolt against their domination. They arranged for the assassination of King Alexander of Yugoslavia in order to eliminate his opposition to what was in fact the surrender of Europe to Communism. They infiltrated National Socialism and Fascism. They used the most vicious and ruthless means to destroy the national revival in Rumania which was embodied in the Legionary Movement, a group which might have, and almost did, thwart a major part of the plot to start World War II.

The Legionary Movement was founded on June 24, 1927, under the name of the Legion of the Archangel Michael, by one of the truly great men of our era. Corneliu Codreanu was born on September 13, 1899 in Huşi, a town in northern Moldavia, where his father was a teacher at the local lycée. He attended the famous military school Manastirea Dealului and the Infantry Officer's school. The beginning of what was to be his career and mission can be dated from January 1918. After the Bolshevik takeover in Petrograd, the Russian troops which had been fighting alongside their Rumanian allies degenerated into no more than a collection of drinking, looting, raping rabble. During that fateful January, Codreanu organized a group of high school students to fight the Russian marauders, who were menacing the Moldavian city of Iaşi. Shortly thereafter he organized the Guard of National Conscience from among the students and workers of Iaşi.

Codreanu reached what can be considered a point of no return in his tragic life, a life entirely dedicated to the battle for the moral purity and the welfare and the glory of his nation, in 1922 when he organized the Association of Christian Students. He and twenty-six students took a pledge of honor, in a religious ceremony, to continue for the rest of their lives the nationalist fight—a pledge to which many of them remained faithful even unto their deaths. In 1923 he founded the League of National Christian Defense (LANC, which polled 120,000 votes in the election of 1926). When Codreanu returned to Rumania in 1927 after a period of study at Grenoble University, LANC had disintegrated into a collection of feuding splinter groups. From the best of the earlier league, he organized the Legion of the Archangel Michael which came to be called the Legionary Movement. In 1930 a group of hard-core members formed an elite section within the Legion, called the Iron Guard. In time the Legion came to be known by the name of this elite group. Although the two are almost synonymous, the reader should keep in mind that they represent two different aspects of the Movement.

The purpose of the Legionary Movement was the defense of the endangered nation and of all the spiritual and historic values which formed the texture of Rumania's national existence. In many ways the Legionary Movement was unique and singularly Rumanian. But its purity of motivation, its unyielding adherence to the very fundamentals of our civilization and its oneness with all the ideals of Christendom gave it a quality which will endure as one of the great examples of man's fight against evil. The Legion was not a political organization, yet it strove to revive the Rumanian body politic. The Legion was not a religious body, yet Christian belief and Christian principles permeated every level and every tenet of the Movement. Corneliu Codreanu came upon the stage of Rumanian history when all that generations had built and had cherished was being imperiled by the most venal of politicians and the most corrupt of kings. His answer to the problems which faced his motherland was to bring about a rebirth of spirituality, of self-denial, and of responsibility in the soul of every Rumanian. If he failed in his goal, it was not due to any shortcomings in the substance of the Legion, or to any flaw in the nature of the Rumanian people, but to the incredible persecutions of the corrupt governments under King Carol and because of the aid given these governments by the International Conspiracy. The same diabolic forces which destroyed the Legion and Rumania are now threatening the very existence of the United States. If an organization can be judged by its enemies, the quality of the detractors of the Legion, past and present, place it high amongst the champions of Christian Civilization.

Prince Sturdza joined with the Legion because he found in it the links with times gone by and with the essential headsprings of the past, which had been completely lost in his country by the existing political establishment; because he realized that, with the Conservative Party destroyed, the Legion offered the only possible salvation for Rumania. Prince Sturdza's memoirs portray the Legion far better than we can do in this Introduction, but we would still like to quote a few passages from Legionary material. We do so partly because they form the very fabric of the Legionary Movement, but also because we know that these high ideals continued to motivate the Legion through all its history. Furthermore, we believe that these principles still live today in the hearts of Rumanians, both those in exile and those enslaved in their own homeland.

> The Legionary Movement is not founded exclusively on the principle of authority nor on that of liberty, but on the principle of love. Love cannot breed tyranny and injustice, nor sanguinary revolutions and social wars.
> The Legionary Movement will never resort to complot or a coup in order to win. By the very essence of our beliefs we are against conspiracy. This would mean violence of an outward character, while we expect victory from an inner realization of the nation's soul.

We think it is fitting to quote the basic rules of the organization. These are contained in the Manual of Legionary Laws, written for the use of the head of each Legionary group.

> The Law of Discipline: Legionary be obedient; without discipline we will not win. Follow your chief for better or worse.
> The Law of Work: Do your daily work. Work with joy. Let the reward of your work be not any material profit, but the satisfaction that you have

contributed something to the glory of the Legion and the greatness of your country.

The Law of Silence: Talk little. Talk only when you must. Your eloquence is in deeds. Let others talk; you do.

The Law of Education: You must become another man. A hero.

The Law of Assistance: Help your brother in distress. Do not abandon him.

The Law of Honor: Follow only the ways shown by honor. Fight. Never be a coward. Leave to others the ways of infamy. Better fall fighting the way of honor, than to conquer by infamy.

If the Legionary Movement had been just another political party or if it had been an eccentric collection of students, it probably would have been left unmolested. But it was neither. It was a grassroots uprising of the best in Rumania striving to maintain and to perfect the national character and to make Rumania a bastion of Christianity and anti-Communism. Rumania was too important in the plans of the Conspiracy, and the Legion too great a threat, for the conspirators to permit it to survive. Thus they used the most brutal means to crush the Legion—including the murder of Codreanu. With the death of the Captain, as he was called, the Legion was temporarily dispersed, its members either going underground or into exile. Amongst the exiles who gathered in Berlin, a young professor of literature, Horia Sima, soon rose to leadership by the pure force of his personality.

In 1940 Sima secretly re-entered Rumania in order to help end the despotic regime of King Carol. Sima was arrested at once, but the tide of events had so completely turned against Carol that he immediately freed Sima and placed him and some other Legionaries in minor posts in the Government as a last attempt to save his throne. However the Legionaries found it impossible to work with the King, and they resigned almost at once. Shortly thereafter they were able to force Carol's abdication in favor of his son Michael in an almost bloodless revolt. But Carol's last act was to appoint General Ion Antonescu, a non-Legionary and in fact a secret enemy of the Legion, as President. Under Antonescu a National Legionary Government—which the Legion would never control—was formed with Horia Sima Vice President and Prince Michel Sturdza Minister of Foreign Affairs.

When the Legionary Government came to power, Western Europe was already in the throes of a western war—a war that never should have been. The National Socialist State was infiltrated by Communists, some of whom occupied very high positions. Informed people strongly believe Communist or pro-Communist agents had aided the National Socialists in coming to power on the theory that they could use Germany as a foil to enable the Soviets to provoke a war in the West; such a strategy would thus make the Western powers a virtual ally of the Communists before any possible German onslaught against Soviet Russia. And, indeed, what should have been a war, perhaps even a crusade, against the Communist beast, became a suicidal struggle between non-Communist countries. But Prince Sturdza is convinced, together with Professor H. R. Trevor-Roper and so many other students of the origins of World War II, that Hitler himself never wanted a war in the West and that his great goal, as events demonstrate, was the destruction of the Soviet Union. Communism was saved and made victorious in great part because of the Conspiracy's diplomatic successes in 1936.

After the assassination in 1934 of King Alexander of Yugoslavia, the greatest obstacle to the Barthou-Titulescu-Beneš plan to encircle Germany, the balance of power between the anti-Communists and pro-Communists was thrown to the Left. The Western anti-Communist leaders had supported a quadripartite pact proposed by Mussolini which would have been a renewal of the Pact of Locarno and which was, in reality, meant for the common defense of Europe against Soviet Russia. The pact included the Western allies of World War I and Germany, and it would have established an anti-Communist core in Europe. But although all parties signed it, the treaty never came into force because it was not ratified by the French Parliament. It was quite another arrangement which finally triumphed: the pact of military alliance between France, Czecho-Slovakia, and Soviet Russia ratified in 1936 and the major cause of the disaster to come. It introduced Russia into the mainstream of Western diplomacy, perfected the encirclement of Germany, and instead of protecting Europe from the Soviets, it protected the Soviets from Germany's growing military might.

But the pact with Soviet Russia was going to be of absolutely no benefit to France or Czecho-Slovakia, and would probably never have been ratified by the French Parliament unless some passage could be found to enable the Red Army to join in any conflict that might arise between France or Czecho-Slovakia with Germany. Poland and the Baltic states stubbornly refused to permit such passage under any pretext. Thus the worth of the pact depended entirely upon the Red Army being able to cross through Rumanian territory to Czecho-Slovakia without any opposition. It is Prince Sturdza's contention, which he believes he has proven, that it was the secret consent given to this passage, or the secret promise that this consent would be given when needed, by the two men who controlled the foreign policy of Rumania between 1933 and 1940, Titulescu and King Carol, and the servility of their subordinates, that permitted the advocates of the Franco-Soviet alliance to triumph in Paris over those of an anti-Communist federation. It is also his contention that it was the military pacts with the Kremlin which were the *primus motor* of World War II and of its catastrophic consequences. Thus Rumania played a key role in the plans of the Conspiracy, and this explains the reason for the incredible persecution of the Legionary Movement, which could have, and would have, stopped any cooperation with Soviet Russia, thus ruining the plans of the Conspiracy.

The effects of the Franco-Soviet and Czecho-Soviet treaties were immediate. Germany was surrounded and desperately needed to adjust the balance of power, and she needed to protect herself on her western and southern borders. Therefore she reoccupied the Rhineland, on the basis that the Franco-Soviet alliance invalidated the Pact of Locarno. She proclaimed the Anschluss with Austria to the general enthusiasm of the population, and when submitted for approval to the people of Greater Germany, it was approved by 99.08% of the voters. She demanded the return to Greater Germany of the three and a half million Germans, which the Versailles Treaty had incorporated, after the Austrian Empire was dismembered, into Czecho-Slovakia. Contrary to popular belief, sanity won out for a moment at Munich, and after years of harassment and treachery on the part of the government in Prague, what was probably the best possible arrangement was agreed to by the Big Powers. But all was for naught; the conspirators pulling the strings soon had the very men who saved Europe in 1938 destroy it in 1939. Germany had been maneuvered into a trap, which would be sprung by the hopeless Polish problem. The Polish crisis was hopeless not because the disagreement between Germany and Poland was so great (the issue involved was chiefly a matter of border adjustments) or because of an ancient national enmity (Germany and Poland had in recent years enjoyed excellent relations.) The problem was made hopeless by the intervention of Western diplomats, who constantly advised and told the Polish not to negotiate; and by Poles such as Marshal Śmigly-Rydz, who threw their country into a war she could not possibly win. Germany was forced into a war against the West because the leaders of Western Europe made all other courses of action impossible. Germany did not sign the non-aggression pact with Soviet Russia in order to be free to conquer the West. The pact was an expediency and nothing more. Its purpose was to secure her rear position in order to be free to destroy the Soviet Union when the time came. (Hitler abhorred the idea of a two front war. It is ironic, and significant, that he had to conquer the West in order to fight the East.) When war came England and France did nothing to help Poland. Prince Sturdza contends that at no moment were the solicitudes shown by the Western Powers and the vain guarantees they offered Poland motivated by any real intention to save her integrity and her independence. He is convinced, on the contrary, that as far as the Western statesmen were concerned, Poland was sacrificed even before the beginning of the armed conflict.

With the fall of Poland, France was released from any obligation to continue the war (which she had not even fought), and she could have reached a satisfactory settlement with Germany. But the same leaders who had pushed Poland over the brink now threw their own nation into defeat. The onslaught came on May 10, 1940 and by June 14, 1940 the war for France was over. Now Hitler began to prepare his war against Russia; he refused to first eliminate England, and did not consider the United States a threat. When Germany invaded Russia, she could have wiped Communism off the map. That she failed was greatly due to Communist influences in the governments of the West, and also, no doubt, to the Communist agents high in her own government. The final ground work for the destruction of Germany and the victory of Communism was laid approximately between the summer of 1940 and the close of 1941. There were three major reasons for Germany's defeat: Italy's loss of the opportunity to be a mediator between Germany and the West because of Mussolini's cowardly aggression against France, and her disastrous campaign against Greece; Germany's mistreatment of the Russian populations in occupied territory; and Admiral Canaris's treason in conjunction with Communist infiltration of the German Government. The second and third causes are closely connected.

From the beginning of the war, the German Government showed little eagerness or even willingness to cooperate with the truly nationalist organizations which existed in the countries within her sphere of influence. These nationalist groups were willing to help Germany economically in her struggle, but not to the detriment of their own country's vital necessities. Yet, once they were the military allies of the Reich against their monstrous neighbor, they would never have capitulated to the Red Army the moment the tide seemed to have turned against Germany, but rather they would have fought to the last man in the struggle against Communism and for the preservation of their national integrity. In reality the Germans followed a policy of opposing the nationalists, allegedly in order to advance the military and industrial resources of the Reich. It is impossible to state unequivocally that this policy was formulated by crypto-Communist infiltrators. However it did result in the overthrow of the Legionary Government by General Antonescu which ultimately brought the capitulation of Rumania. It ruined the anti-Communist cause in Yugoslavia and brought on an unnecessary war with that nation, tying down troops desperately needed on the Russian front. It reached its climax in the incredibly brutal handling of the

Ukraine—and in this case there are definite indications of Communist hands at work.

Our knowledge of the actual Communist activity in the German Government is still quite sketchy. In most cases we cannot be certain of exactly who the Communist agents were nor where they operated. This is so partly because many, but not all, were never members of the actual Communist Party and because most of the agents were probably in second echelon positions rather than at the top. But what we do know gives a hint of what actually existed. Prince Sturdza relates, from his own experience, the story of Admiral Wilhelm Canaris, head of the German Intelligence Service. Canaris was not subject to the discipline of the Communist *Party* but rather took his orders from the Conspiracy's socialist clique based in Britain—the Fabians. His network riddled the Secret Service and infiltrated the Foreign Office and the Wehrmacht. Two of his confessed co-workers were Baron Weizsäcker, an Undersecretary of State, and General Halder, Chief of the General Staff. The Canaris conspiracy played a major role in bringing about the defeat of Germany and the victory of Soviet Russia.

While the Canaris network was supplying Hitler with false information concerning the Russian military situation, Richard Sorge, a Soviet agent and press attaché at the German Embassy in Tokyo, was keeping Stalin informed of German and Japanese military developments. In 1939 he supplied the date of Germany's planned attack on Poland; in April 1941 he advised Moscow that Germany was concentrating 150 divisions at the borders of the USSR, and he supplied a general scheme of the military operations, including the date for the attack, June 22; and two months before December 7, 1941, he advised Moscow that Japan was preparing for a war in the Pacific and would not attack the Soviet Far East. Thus the German attack against the Soviet Union was not a surprise at all, and Stalin had ample time to prepare his defenses. The Soviet Army was not taken off guard as is often believed. Stalin had massed approximately four and a half million men in the western frontier area—a million and a half more men than made up the German attack forces, but whole Russian units surrendered almost without fighting and thus enabled other units, divisions, and corps to be surrendered and captured. It was only after the Wehrmacht was forced to submit to the orders inspired by Rosenberg to wage a war of extermination that the real Russian resistance began. Also the Kremlin could depend on its friends in the Reich for information. The flow of intelligence data from various sources continued throughout the war. Soviet agent Alexander Rado in Switzerland was able to advise Moscow of decisions of the German High Command within forty-eight hours after they were made. The source was on the German General Staff. Was it General Halder?

Who else was involved? Martin Bormann certainly must be considered. In fact Cornelius Ryan, author of *The Longest Day* and *The Last Battle* relates that "some German generals believe he was a Russian spy throughout the war." (*New York Journal American,* March 19, 1966.) Bormann's influence and power were tremendous and most certainly not used in the best interests of Germany. This, of course, could be explained by the view that he was exactly what he appeared to be—a power hungry fanatic. But it is most significant that doubts can be raised as to whom Martin Bormann was really loyal. And let us not forget that men who knew him believed that he was a Communist agent.

The question of actual loyalty can be raised about another sinister character high in the National Socialist Government, Heinrich Himmler, but in this case any definite conclusion is most difficult to reach. It was under Himmler's command that the great atrocities of the Third Reich were committed. Yet many of his lieutenants found little difficulty in changing uniforms when the Reich fell. One, Heinrich Müller, Chief of the Gestapo, was in contact with the Russian Secret Service at least as early as 1943. He escaped from Berlin, and some of his colleagues believe that he is now in the service of the Soviet secret police. In fact an article in *Die Stern* (January 12, 1964) claimed that Müller had been identified as a captain in the Albanian security police. When Himmler absorbed Canaris's Abwehr, the files were full of the proof of Canaris's treason and of that of his colleagues. Yet Himmler did nothing with this information. When Canaris was finally exposed a year later, it was through sources completely separate from Himmler's apparati. We will probably never know the real reason for his failure to take action in this case or for his many other activities. But let us recall that it was Alfred Rosenberg's advice which caused Hitler to transform the war of liberation, which the Führer had so successfully commenced in Russia, into a war of annihiliation. And it is well known that Rosenberg was Himmler's man.

In this light the outbursts of Hitler to the effect that the war was being lost by treason no longer seem like the ravings of a mad man. He may have become aware that he himself was little more than a pawn. For in his charges of treason, Hitler was correct: Germany's war against Russia was not lost at Stalingrad; it was lost in Berlin.

Despite the conspiracy and brutality which were so rampant in the Third Reich, many Germans and other Europeans still considered the war against Soviet Russia a crusade to save Western Civilization from destruction by Communism. The men who fought and died in the struggle in the East have been condemned, partly because they lost, but the soundness of their fear of Soviet Russia has been borne out by history.

The Legionary Movement and the Rumanian people supported Germany in the war, but the best interests of their country left little other course even considered from the most pragmatic point of view. Cooperation with the West or permanent neutrality was out of the question, for the policies and corruption of Titulescu and Carol had left Rumania unable to defend herself against either Germany or Russia, much less against both as would have been necessary. Such a policy would have turned Rumania, from the very first days of the war, into a huge battleground and then into an occupied appendage of one or the other power. A Soviet alliance would have meant absorption by Russia, or at best, occupation by Germany as a defeated enemy. A German alliance was the only recourse open to Rumania. But in forming this alliance the Rumanians were not simply bowing to expediency; they firmly believed that their national existence and Christian Civilization could only be saved by the destruction of Communism in Russia. The nations of Central Europe chose from the above alternatives in varying manners, yet they *all* fell under the heel of the Soviet Union. Poland fought the joint attack of Russia and Germany, Czecho-Slovakia maintained a solidly pro-Soviet alliance, Rumania and Hungary formed German alliances, Bulgaria maintained a pro-German neutrality, Yugoslavia maintained an anti-German neutrality, and Albania committed no crime but to be occupied by Italy; but all ended under the same tyranny.

The most important point which these memoirs make clear is that World War II was brought on and concluded according to a deliberate plan developed and carried out by a conspiracy of a small, centrally directed group of men high in the governments of nearly every nation. That the Conspiracy intended to deliver all of Eastern Europe to Communism is made clear by its activities as the war came to a close.

After the debacle at Stalingrad, the possibilities of a German victory in Russia were ruined, but the war was by no means over. As the German and allied armies pulled back towards the west, they desperately attempted to form a line of resistance to the Russian onslaught; once such a defensive line was formed two courses of action would become available. The first one, and the one on which Hitler based his strategy, was to hold all possible points in the east in the belief that it was only a matter of time before the United States and Britain would come to see Soviet Russia as their real enemy. Hitler would have then signed a separate peace with the West, and with the aid of his new allies he would have mounted a great counteroffensive which would totally crush the Red Army. As late as March 1945 German troops were ordered to hold, at all costs, bridgeheads across the Oder because they would be needed as launching points for the joint attack. Whether or not the

Allies could have even considered such an arrangement is immaterial. For the second possibility provided by a stabilized line of defense from the Communist hordes offered to the Western powers an opportunity to save Eastern Europe even without accepting Germany as an ally. Those who fought and died to form this line of defense and to permit, thereby, the penetration of Western armies deep into the East fought and died in vain. The Western Powers, conforming to the pre-established plans of the Conspiracy, had decided as early as the conferences at Quebec and Teheran to allow the Red Army to advance up to Berlin, Prague, and Vienna and had consented to abandon eleven European countries as prey for the Communist behemoth. The Western Allies had thus refused to take advantage of this opportunity to save millions of innocent peoples from brutal slavery. Instead they halted at the Elbe.

How complete was the subservience of Washington and London to the wishes of the Conspiracy became absolutely clear in February 1945. Hitler sent a message to Mihailovich, the heroic leader of the Chetniks of Yugoslavia, to be relayed to the British. Hitler offered to withdraw all German troops from the Balkans if the United States and England would agree to start occupying the abandoned area within twenty-four hours; after the West had completely occupied the Balkans, Germany would withdraw from Hungary and Czecho-Slovakia, again on the condition that the West fill the vacuum. The Allies refused even to consider the proposal, telling Mihailovich to have the Germans make their offer to Russia.

The war ended with Germany smashed and half-occupied by the Soviets, with Estonia, Lithuania, Latvia, Poland, Czecho-Slovakia, Hungary, Rumania, Bulgaria, Yugoslavia, and Albania under Communist rule, and with only Soviet Russia victorious. Those military or civilian leaders who had opposed Communism for so long were executed, imprisoned, or forced into exile. But these memoirs provide a stern lesson for those who today believe that they can reach an accommodation with the Communists. For as Prince Sturdza points out, the "Liberals," the appeasers, and the non-Communists, who had opposed the war against the Soviet Union, had sabotaged the war effort, and had betrayed their own country into Communist hands, were among the first to be victimized by the beast. They too were executed, imprisoned, or forced into exile—not with the knowledge that they had fought to the end against their nation's implacable enemy, but with the indelible stain of having helped in the defeat of their own motherland.

The publishers of this book do not necessarily agree with all of the opinions expressed by Prince Sturdza, nor are they necessarily in agreement with all of his interpretations of the events and actions which led to World War II. However the publishers do believe that Prince Sturdza has a responsibility to express his views and that the public should have the opportunity to consider them, particularly since Prince Sturdza's lifelong experience and activity in the diplomatic field have given him a tremendous insight into the events of the Twentieth Century. Furthermore, histories of World War II, as a rule, have been written from the Western point of view. This book presents for the first time the true Eastern point of view, and the publishers believe that it is a major addition to the literature dealing with Europe between the two wars. A reviewer of the French preview of this book has stated an opinion shared by the publishers: It is now impossible to write a history of World War II without referring to the memoirs of Prince Michel Sturdza.

Critics who have never opposed the Conspiracy which has murdered untold millions, and who still refuse to take cognizance of its existence may be tempted to justify their complacency and ignorance by trying to find fault with the views and actions of Prince Sturdza and the Legionary Movement. But such play will not change the history of this century nor will it prevent the impending destruction of our whole Civilization.

Prince Sturdza had the foresight to realize that the Communist Conspiracy was the greatest danger ever faced by his motherland and by Western Civilization itself, and he had the courage to sacrifice all in his fight against the beast. Rumania fell because too few people in Europe and the United States were willing to recognize the threat from Communism. Since that time the Conspiracy has enslaved a third of the globe and is rapidly approaching its final goal. Prince Sturdza has continued his battle, and he offers these memoirs in the hope that others will learn the lessons of history. The warning is clear and, if it is not heeded, the United States too will suffer the fate it allowed to befall so many millions. But this time there will not even be a place of exile.

Thomas J. Haas

Note to the Reader

The reader is urged to refer frequently to the sequence of time and dates listed in the Analytical Chronology which follows for a clear understanding of the events as they took place.

We wish also to call your attention to the Index of Persons in the back of the book which gives a biographical sketch of the political and historical personalities presented in these memoirs.

Analytical Chronology

Collective security, indivisible peace . . . this means simply a pro-Soviet crusade in the event of a Russian-German conflict.

SAINT-AULAIRE
Ambassador of France
(*Genève contre la Paix*)

PART I

1917

March 12–16. Prince Georgi Lvov heads a Russian Provisional Government. Alexander Kerensky is Minister of Justice. Czar Nicholas II abdicates in favor of his brother Michael. Michael abdicates in favor of the Provisional Government.

April 17. Lenin, Zinoviev, Lunacharski and other Bolsheviks, the majority of them from New York, arrive in Petrograd where Trotsky and other New York Bolsheviks have already settled.

May 16. Kerensky becomes Minister of War and starts immediately the systematic disintegration of the Russian Army with the famous Prikase No. I.

July 16–18. Bolsheviks make a premature attempt to seize power in Petrograd.

July 20. Prince Lvov resigns. Kerensky Prime Minister.

September 8–14. Kerensky prevents General Kornilov from saving Petrograd. Arrests him, but releases from prison Trotsky and other terrorists.

November 6 (O. S. October 24). The Bolshevik Revolution. Kerensky escapes to Finland then to Paris. Eleven years later we will find him in New York where Governor Lehman will convince him with irresistible arguments, the very day of his arrival, to give up any idea of campaigning against the Soviet Government.

November 7. A new Government in Petrograd, headed by Lenin. Including Trotsky as Commissar for Foreign Affairs and Stalin as Commissar for Minorities. Majority of the Government of New York origin. They assume the name of Council of the People's Commissars. Russian troops in Rumania, in full anarchy, roam the country menacing Iași, the seat of the Government. They are either disarmed or beaten back. There is fighting in Bessarabia.

1918

January 1–15. In Rumania, in the woods of Dobrina, the young Corneliu Codreanu gathers his first followers in order to resist the mutinous attacks of the Russian troops.

July 16–17. Murder of Czar Nicholas and the Imperial Family.

1919

January 7. President Wilson orders William H. Buckler, a troubleshooter attached to the United States Embassy in London, to proceed "at the earliest possible moment to Stockholm" to confer with representatives of the Bolshevik Government.

January 14, 15, 16. Buckler confers with Maxim Litvinov in Stockholm.

January 21. Wilson submits Buckler's report of the Stockholm meeting to the Big Five in Paris. The "conciliatory attitude of the Soviet Government is unquestionable," wrote Buckler. Furthermore, "agreement with Russia can take place at once, obviating conquest and policing and reviving normal conditions as disinfectant against Bolshevism."

February 22. William C. Bullitt, accompanied by radical journalist Lincoln Steffens, leaves Paris for Russia and a meeting with Bolshevik officials.

March 10. Bullitt arrives in Petrograd and is accompanied to Moscow by Grigori Chicherin and Maxim Litvinov.

March 14. Lenin presents Bullitt with a Soviet peace plan drafted by Litvinov.

May 4. Slovak General Milan R. Štefánik dies in a mysterious airplane crash over Bratislava. Czech Eduard Beneš supplants him not only in the history of Czecho-Slovakia but also in that of Europe.

August 4. Rumanian troops occupy Budapest. Despite the violent opposition of the Supreme Council, the Rumanian Army liberates Hungary from the Béla Kun Communist terror after two weeks of fighting the Red rabble.

1920

January 14. French General Maurice Janin, Commander-in-Chief of the Allied troops in Siberia, orders the Czecho-Slovak Legion to kidnap Admiral Aleksandr Kolchak, Supreme Ruler of Russia and leader of the anti-Bolshevik resistance, and to hand him over to the Bolshevik Political Centre at Irkutsk in exchange for one-third of the bullion of the Russian Imperial Treasury which was under Kolchak's control. This bullion went to form the first national treasury of the newly invented country of Czecho-Slovakia where 7,000,000 Czechs held sway over 8,200,000 non-Czechs.

February 7. Admiral Kolchak and his Prime Minister, Victor Pepeliaev, are executed. General Janin was never court-martialled, arraigned, or even blamed.

February 11. In Rumania, Corneliu Codreanu and the labor leader Constantin Pancu forcibly take a factory from the hands of the Communists.

April 25. Beginning of the war between Poland and Soviet Russia.

September 30. In Rumania, Corneliu Codreanu and his followers forestall an attempt by the Rector of the University of Iași to open the academic year without the traditional religious ceremony.

October 5. Moscow asks for an armistice.

October 12. Preliminary treaty of peace between Poland and Russia signed in Riga

1921

March 3. Signing of the Rumano-Polish Treaty of Alliance, the only safeguard Rumania ever had against a Soviet onslaught.

March 18. Definitive Treaty of Riga signed. Polish-Russian frontier defined.

March–June. Negotiations and conclusion of the Little Entente between Rumania, Yugoslavia, and Czecho-Slovakia, strictly limited to controlling Hungary's irredentist aspirations. Masaryk and Beneš stubbornly oppose a larger coalition including Poland and the Baltic States proposed by Rumania as a guarantee against Soviet territorial and messianic ambitions. Czecho-Slovakia is the only beneficiary of the Little Entente, Rumania and Yugoslavia being more than a match for Hungary. The Prague Government always refused to guarantee or even to acknowledge the frontiers of Soviet Russia's neighbors.

March–June. Great Britain and France recognize *de facto* the Soviet Government as the legitimate Government of Russia. (Consolidation under the invisible control of the Anonymous Forces, of the unholy alliance of the Western Powers–Soviet Union which will lead the world to World War II and to its fateful and still unpredictable consequences.)

1922

April 6. The Soviet delegation headed by Grigori Chicherin arrives in Genoa to meet the British, French, North American, Italian, and German delegations.

April 10. Beginning of the Genoa Conference with Soviet Russia's participation.

April 15. Secret negotiations between the German and the Soviet delegations begin at two o'clock a.m.

April 16. Surprise conclusion of the Treaty of Rapallo between Germany and Soviet Russia. "A bomb in the sky of the Conference. It will upset the world," said U.S. Ambassador Richard Washburn Child. This happened seventeen years later.

May 19. Genoa Conference collapses over the insistence of France that Russia recognize its pre-war debt.

October 15. In Rumania. Coronation in Alba Iulia of King Ferdinand and Queen Marie, in the same city where three centuries before Michael the Valiant was proclaimed Sovereign of all Rumanians.

923

March 4. In Rumania. Formation of the League of National Defense by Professor Alexandru Cuza and Corneliu Codreanu.

March 24. Codreanu arrested for the first time by the Liberal Government.

November 8–11. Hitler-Ludendorff *Putsch* in Munich.

1924

April 2. Breaking up of Rumano-Soviet negotiations, which had started one week before in Vienna upon insistence of our French allies.

May 31. Codreanu arrested again with fifty other students, boys and girls. Beginning of what has been called the Manciu Terror, under a Liberal Government. In prison the students are submitted to the most cruel tortures and abject humiliations. They are liberated after the intervention of a group of university professors and important citizens. Manciu, the Police Prefect of Iaşi, and his deputies, promoted and decorated by the Government.

October 25. Codreanu shoots Manciu in self-defense when Manciu attempts to arrest him again.

October 28. Following the example of Great Britain (February 1), France extends *de jure* recognition to the U.S.S.R. Rumania and Yugoslavia refuse recognition.

1925

January 5. In Rumania. Great manifestations of sympathy for Corneliu Codreanu throughout the whole country. The Government changes the venue of the trial from Iaşi to Focşani.

May 20. The manifestations of sympathy and admiration growing in intensity, the Government changes once more the venue from Focşani to Turnu Severin at the other extremity of the country.

May 26. Codreanu acquitted by the Turnu Severin court. General manifestation of enthusiasm throughout the country.

December 1. Signing of the Locarno Treaties. Agreement of guarantee between France, Great Britain, Germany, Italy, and Belgium.

1926

January 20. As a result of his scandalous conduct, Prince Carol of Rumania is deprived of his rights of inheritance. His son Prince Michael proclaimed heir to the throne by Act of Parliament.

April 24. Treaty of German-Soviet friendship and neutrality. Extends the Rapallo Treaty of 1922.

September 8. Germany admitted to the League of Nations. Permanent seat on Council.

1927

May 26. Temporary rupture of diplomatic relations between Great Britain and Soviet Russia due to friction caused by Communist agitation. Violation of treaty agreements.

June 24. In Rumania. Founding of the Legion of the Archangel Michael.

July 20. Death of King Ferdinand of Rumania. Michael proclaimed King. Constitution of a Regency headed by Prince Nicholas, brother of Carol.

August 21. Congress of the National Socialist Party in Nürnberg. Twenty thousand Storm Troopers present.

November 30. A Soviet delegation arrives in Geneva to take part in the deliberations of the preparatory commission on disarmament.

1928

August 27. Kellogg-Briand Pact signed at Paris. Russia concurs on September 6. Renunciation of aggressive war. No provision for sanctions.

November 25. Communist trouble in Bucharest.

1929

February 9. Signing in Moscow by Soviet Russia, Poland, Rumania, Latvia, and Estonia of the Litvinov Protocol giving immediate validity to the Kellogg-Briand Pact between those five countries. Next day an article in *Pravda* reminds the Rumanian plenipotentiary of Soviet Russia's pretensions upon Rumanian territory.

April 7. Communist trouble in Timişoara. Several dead.

August 17. Communist trouble in Lupeni: twenty-five dead.

October 7. Death of Gheorghe Buzdugan, the most important personality in the Rumanian Regency.

December 15–25. Two important Legionary rallies in Braneşti and Lugoj. Illegal intervention of the authorities. The Movement takes on greater proportions every day. Many adherents in the working classes.

1930

January 20–March 25. Intensification of the Legionary activities with anti-Communist accent. In Kagul 20,000 peasants come to listen to Codreanu. Great anti-Communist manifestation in Bucharest March 25.

June 6. Carol's return to Rumania with Magda (Élèna) Lupescu. Betraying the promise he had made to all his supporters during his exile, to the writer of these pages among others, he refuses to resume, at least ostensibly, conjugal life with Princess Hélène and to proclaim her Queen. Starts living in open concubinage with Magda Lupescu.

June 20. Codreanu creates a new organization to defend Rumania against Communism, in all its disguises, on the home front and against Soviet undertakings on the outer front. He calls this new force the Iron Guard which will later become identified with the Legionary Movement.

July 25. Codreanu arrested again, under a National Peasant Government, and tried in a fraudulent case. Acquitted after two months in prison. There were still at that time judges in Rumania.

November 14. Communist trouble in Bucharest.

PART

1931

January 11. The Legionary Movement dissolved for the first time, by a National Peasant Government. Mass arrests, new persecutions. Another fraudulent case against the Movement. Unqualified acquittals from the lowest to the highest courts for all Legionary leaders. Carol's corruption has not had time yet to penetrate all of the State institutions.

April 18. King Carol forms an Iorga-Argetoianu Government.

June 1. New Elections. Codreanu elected to Parliament.

December 3. Codreanu's speech in Parliament. Cardinal points of the policy of the Legionary Movement: God, Country, King, Ownership, Army, Relentless Fight against Communism.

1932

March–April. Rumano-Soviet negotiations in Riga for a pact of non-aggression. The French Government has asked its allies Rumania and Poland to try to come to a non-aggression agreement with their Russian neighbor, in order to further its purpose to conclude a military alliance with Soviet Russia; a purpose which was shared by Beneš and Titulescu. The negotiations are broken off by the Rumanian negotiator when, at the moment of signing the text agreed upon, the Russian delegate pretends to introduce a clause alluding to Soviet Russia's pretensions upon a part of Rumania's territory. France, the middleman, had given the Rumanian Government the assurance that the Soviets will not raise any territorial question.

March 13. Presidential elections in Germany. Hitler receives 11,339,446 votes (30.1 percent). President von Hindenburg fails to receive an absolute majority.

March 15. The Legionary Movement dissolved for the second time, by the Iorga-Argetoianu Government. The most arbitrary and unconstitutional measures are taken against its members. Mass arrests, beatings, and tortures.

April 10. Hindenburg is reelected. But Hitler receives 13,418,547 votes (36.8 percent).

May 6. Murder of Paul Doumer, President of the French Republic, by Dr. Paul Gourgoulov, a Russian émigré.

May 31. The Iorga-Argetoianu Government resigns. Replaced by a National Peasant Government, headed by Alexandru Vaida-Voevod.

July 31. Reichstag elections. Hitler's National Socialists win 230 seats; Socialists 133; Center 97; Communists 89. Total National Socialist vote is 13,745,000.

September 12. Reichstag dissolved.

October 10. Nicolae Titulescu, Minister of Foreign Affairs. Convokes immediately the French and Polish Envoys, thanks their governments for the support they have given during the Riga negotiations, but asks those governments to negotiate their agreements with Soviet Russia without any consideration for the Rumanian position towards Moscow. As a consequence France and all of Soviet Russia's neighbors, *except Rumania,* have pacts of non-aggression with Soviet Russia before the end of 1933.

November 6. Election in Germany fails to break parliamentary deadlock.

1933

January 23. Molotov speech announcing ratification of non-aggression pacts with all of Soviet Russia's neighbors except Rumania. The Franco-Russian Treaty of Non-Aggression ratified one month later.

January 30. Adolf Hitler becomes Chancellor of the German Government.

June 7. In Rome the four Big Powers, France, Great Britain, Italy, and Germany sign the Quadripartite Pact of Guarantee proposed by Benito Mussolini, a reinvigoration of the Locarno Pact with the new Germany. (The signature was ratified by all parliaments concerned except that of France, where the partisans of the military alliance with Soviet Russia succeeded in rejecting it. *It never came, therefore, into force.*)

July 4. Pact of Definition of Aggression signed in London, between Soviet Russia, her neighbors, and other countries. Rumania participating, Pact contrived by Titulescu, pretending to substitute it for the Pact of Non-Aggression that had not been signed in Riga because of Soviet Russia's insolent pretensions concerning Rumania's territory.

July 10. A National Peasant Government begins what will become the first Călinescu terror against the Legionary Movement.

October 10. Franklin Delano Roosevelt's letter to Mikhail Kalinin, proposing the establishment of diplomatic relations between the United States and the Soviet Union.

November 13. Interview between Hitler and Lipski. Hitler tells Lipski: "Any war could bring Communism to Europe. Poland is at the forefront of the fight against Asia. Poland's destruction would be therefore a universal misfortune. . . . The other European governments ought to recognize Poland's position."

November 14. Liberal Party leader Ion Duca forms a cabinet.

November 16. Roosevelt recognizes the Soviet Government as the legitimate Government of Russia.

December 10. In order to prevent the Legionary Movement from participating in the electoral campaign, Ion Duca, the Prime Minister, under the pressure of his French sponsors and of Titulescu, dissolves for the third time the Legionary Movement and starts the biggest period of terror the Movement has undergone until then. More than 20,000 Legionaries are arrested, Legionaries are assassinated by Duca's police. Hundreds are tortured and beaten. A wave of indignation and horror sweeps the country.

December 20. The Duca Government wins at the polls.

December 29. Duca murdered by three Legionaries who surrender immediately to the police.

1934

January 26. A ten-year pact of non-aggression between Germany and Poland.

February 9. The Balkan Pact between Yugoslavia, Greece, Turkey, and Rumania. Without any significance for Rumania which is not a Balkan country. Another of Titulescu's inventions to calm apprehensions provoked in Rumania by his pro-Soviet policy and his anti-Polish attitude.

April 4. The military court, before which Codreanu and all the Legionary leaders have been arraigned, discharges them all and condemns only the three murderers of Duca to hard labor for life.

June 9. A Titulescu triumph: Resumption of diplomatic relations between Rumania and Soviet Russia.

August 2. Feldmarschall Paul von Hindenburg's death. Hitler now Führer, Chancellor, and Commander-in-Chief of the Reichswehr.

August 19. Plebiscite approves (88 per cent) Hitler's assumption of full power.

September 13. Poland denounces the Minorities Agreement, which was a part of the political and territorial status established at Versailles and guaranteed by the Covenant of the League of Nations. Germany, directly interested, prefers not to protest.

October 9. King Alexander of Yugoslavia and French Foreign Minister Jean Barthou are assassinated in Marsailles on their way to Paris.

October 22. General Hermann Göring, talking in the name of Hitler, sets forth for the first time to Petrescu-Comnen, our Envoy in Berlin, Germany's offer to Rumania: A guarantee of all our frontiers, those with Soviet Russia and Hungary included, complete rearmament with the most modern weapons for our military forces. Germany does not ask Rumania to abandon any of her alliances. The only thing Germany asks in exchange is a pledge to oppose any attempt of the Soviet troops to cross our territory. Titulescu, Rumania's Foreign Minister, who had already promised his French and Czecho-Slovak friends to let the Soviet troops cross Rumania's territory, in case of a European conflict, conceals Petrescu-Comnen's report, intending to keep our Foreign Office and our Government in ignorance of it until the moment he could make it impossible, by a *fait accompli* on the diplomatic field, for Rumania even to consider the German proposals.

November 20. Informed by this author, of Titulescu's treachery,

Gheorghe Brătianu, chief of the Liberal Dissident Party, goes to Berlin and has an interview with Göring. Göring repeats Germany's offer insisting upon the fact that Rumania is not asked to abandon any of its alliances. Germany's desire, of having the assurance that Soviet troops could not attack her through Rumanian territory, was so earnest that those proposals will be repeated again and again, by Hitler and by Göring, to our Envoy in Berlin and to Rumanian statesmen until the very eve of World War II. It will be a last Rumanian rebuff that will force Hitler to change, momentarily, his attitude towards Soviet Russia and bring about the Ribbentrop-Molotov Agreement.

1935

January 13. Plebiscite in the Saar Basin, supervised by the League of Nations. Ninety percent of the electors vote for union with Germany. Ten percent vote for union with France.

January 24. Interview between Hitler and Lipski. Józef Lipski, the Polish Ambassador in Berlin, reports to Józef Beck, the Polish Foreign Minister: "The Chancellor talked lengthily about the Russian question. According to him the moment would come when Poland and Germany will both be forced to defend themselves against Soviet aggression. In his opinion the policy of the former German Governments and of the Reichswehr to play Russia against Poland was the greatest possible political mistake."

February 8. Agreement between the Soviet Union and Rumania concerning re-establishment of direct rail communications.

February 10. Note of Count Jean Szembeck, Polish Undersecretary for Foreign Affairs, for Beck's information: "Mr. Lipski told me that Göring was very frank with him in his conversation at Bialystok and in Warsaw. Talking to the generals he developed great plans for the future, suggesting almost a German-Polish alliance against Soviet Russia."

May 2. Signing of the Franco-Soviet Pact of Mutual Assistance, obviously directed against Germany.

May 16. Signing of the Czecho-Soviet Pact of Mutual Assistance. Both this and the Franco-Soviet Pact would not mean anything for France and Czecho-Slovakia if Rumania's consent to let Soviet troops pass across her territory were not secretly implicit in the resuming of diplomatic relations and railway and road communications between Rumania and Soviet Russia.

May 23. Lipski's report to Beck: "Later Hitler amplified his policy towards Poland. . . . Even before coming to power he tried to convince General Schleicher to have no relations with the Soviets.

... Hitler said that the Reichswehr considered Soviet Russia as a danger only for Poland and not for Germany. This was a policy of shortsighted people."

October 3. Italian troops enter Ethiopia.

October 7. Titulescu orders Petrescu-Comnen to declare to the German Foreign Office that our geographical position forces Rumania to take into consideration the implications in Russia's vicinity. In certain circumstances, therefore, Rumania could be brought to sign also a pact of mutual assistance with Soviet Russia, like France and Czecho-Slovakia.

1936

January 29. King Carol in London on the occasion of the funeral of King George V. Very cold reception. Queen Mary refuses to see him.

February 24. Following Titulescu's orders, additional provocative declarations by Petrescu-Comnen at the Auswärtige Amt.

February 27. The French Parliament ratifies the Franco-Soviet military alliance.

March 7. The ambassadors of the signatories to the Locarno Treaties convoked at the Auswärtige Amt by Baron Konstantin von Neurath, who informs them that Germany considers the Treaties have been violated by France, through the conclusion of a military alliance with Soviet Russia, obviously directed against Germany. Consequently Germany will reoccupy the demilitarized territory along the Rhine. At the same time Germany offers to sign a pact of nonaggression with France and Belgium, to sign an Air Force Convention with all the Western Powers, and to reenter the League of Nations if it should be admitted that its Charter is independent of the stipulations of the Versailles Treaty. None of these proposals was taken into consideration by the Western Powers.

Night of March 7 to March 8. In Rumania, the Liberal Government orders the Rumanian Railways to group as much rolling stock as possible at the Rumano-Russian frontier, which meant obviously to put this stock at the disposition of the Soviet Command in case the reoccupation of the Rhineland would provoke World War II. (The gauge of the Rumanian rails is narrower than the gauge of the Russian rails.)

March 8. Informed about this fateful measure Corneliu Codreanu, the leader of the Legionary Movement and General Cantacuzene, the second in command, decide that the Movement will oppose by force any attempt of the Soviet forces to cross Rumanian territory. Preparatory measures are immediately taken.

March 12–18. Britain's, Italy's, and Belgium's declarations in Paris and in London at the Council of the League of Nations make France to understand that even if the reoccupation of the Rhineland by Germany must be considered as a violation of the Versailles Treaty it will not be considered as a *casus foederis* or a *casus belli* by any of the cosignatories of the Versailles Treaty or of the Locarno Pact.

May 30. Codreanu issues a proclamation concerning Titulescu's machinations and any attempt of alliance with Soviet Russia: "It will be an act of treason against God, against Rumania and against the moral order of this world."

August 14. Count Jean Szembeck reports his conversation with Joachim von Ribbentrop: "Ribbentrop insisted upon the necessity of German-Polish collaboration. Both Poland and Germany are under the threat of a very great danger. . . . Bolshevism intends to destroy all the fruits of Western Civilization. . . . The Chancellor [Hitler] could not consent to any compromise in his relations with Soviet Russia. . . . He is himself convinced of this necessity [of German-Polish collaboration] and is one of the most ardent advocates of the idea of such a rapprochement."

August 29. Rumanian Foreign Minister Titulescu dismissed by King Carol. Titulescu's policy remains however fundamentally the policy Carol has decided to follow.

PART III

November 5. Codreanu's Memorandum addressed to the King and Rumania's political leaders, concerning Rumania's foreign policy. The Little Entente and the Balkan Alliance have absolutely no practical value for Rumania. They will both crumble to pieces at the moment of any European conflict. The whole of the Rumanian people will rise and oppose those who prepare Rumania's death by trying to associate her with the Soviets in case of a general conflagration.

November 13. German Military Attaché in Bucharest, Colonel Schunke, visits Petrescu-Comnen. He renews Germany's offer to Rumania. Insists again upon the fact that Germany does not expect us to abandon any of our alliances. All that is asked from us is our promise to oppose any Soviet attempt to cross our territory. If Bucharest continues to reject Germany's friendship, Germany may be forced to look for friends in other directions.

November 16. Second visit to Berlin of Gheorghe Brătianu, chief of the Liberal Dissident Party. Interview with Hitler and with Göring. Both insist upon the necessity for Germany to be assured that no Soviet attack could come through Rumanian territory without opposition from Rumania. Both renew their proposal to arm our forces with the most modern equipment. We are not asked to abandon any of our alliances.

November 24. A group of Legionaries leaves for the Spanish Civil War. Join Franco's troops.

1937

February 13. Funerals in Bucharest of the Legionaries killed in the Spanish Civil War fighting on the side of the Nationalists. Impressive manifestations of sympathy on the part of 300,000 who follow the cortege.

February 16. Göring's friendly declarations to Marshal Edward Śmigly-Rydz in Warsaw. Poland and Germany equally menaced. Necessity to adjust their policy.

February 20. New interview: Göring-Petrescu. Göring renews offer of guarantee of all our frontiers and of rearmament. One condition only: That we promise to defend our frontiers against any Soviet attempt. Petrescu-Comnen answers that he is not allowed to discuss politics but only economic questions. Göring tells him that he is invited by Hitler who wishes to confirm personally Germany's proposals. Petrescu never responds to this invitation.

February 29. New measures of suppression against the Legionary Movement. Codreanu's proclamation: "The Legionary Movement will never resort to violence and conspiracy. It will not answer to these new provocations. Our victory will come with an inner transformation in the soul of every Rumanian. We refuse to soil this victory with plots and violence."

March 20. Last interview between Göring and Petrescu. The former renews Germany's offer and promises to arm our forces with the most modern and even the most secret equipment. Only one condition: that we pledge to defend our frontiers. Petrescu declares in the name of his Government that Rumania will never enter into an agreement which might bring her into difficulties with the Soviets.

June 12. Execution of Marshal Mikhail Tukhachevski in Moscow. During a visit to London and Paris, Tukhachevski committed the imprudence of confiding to some military people his plans for a coup against the Communist regime. Moscow was immediately informed.

November 30. New proclamation of Codreanu about Rumania's foreign policy: "I am against the policy of the great Western democracies. I am against the Little Entente and the Balkan Alliance. I have not the slightest confidence in the League of Nations. I am with the countries of the National Revolution. Forty-eight hours after the victory of the Legionary Movement, Rumania will be allied to Rome and Berlin, thus entering the line of its historical world-mission—the defense of the Cross, of Christian culture and civilization."

November–December. Kidnaping in the streets of Paris and assassination in Moscow of General Kutiepov, chief of the former Nationalist Russian Army in exile.

December 21. Legionary triumph at the parliamentary elections. Sixty-six seats in Parliament.

December 28. King Carol appoints Octavian Goga Prime Minister. Goga and Armand Călinescu, as Minister of the Interior, form a National Christian Government. Goga's National Christian Party was an insignificant extremist right group which received only 9.15 percent of the vote in the last election.

1938

December 1937–January. General Miller, Kutiepov's successor, is kidnapped in the streets of Paris and assassinated in Moscow.

February 6. Beginning of the new electoral campaign in Rumania in an atmosphere of terror and murder.

February 9. Goga, profoundly affected by the turn the electoral campaign has taken under Călinescu, comes to an agreement with Codreanu.

February 10. King Carol, informed of this agreement, dismisses Goga.

February 12. Carol's *coup d'état.* Suppression of the Constitution. Suppression of political parties. Patriarch Miron Cristea, Prime Minister. Armand Călinescu, Minister of the Interior. New Constitution places all powers, even the judiciary, in Carol's hands.

February 21. Codreanu's proclamation announcing the dissolution of the Movement: "We will not answer the Government provocations. We will not transform Rumania into another Spain." He announces his decision to leave Rumania for a couple of years and settle in Italy.

March 5. The Government orders the dismissal of every Legionary from every state office and from every private enterprise. All Legionary establishments, commercial and industrial, are closed. The greatest anti-Legionary terror known until then begins with thousands of arrests.

April 7. Codreanu arrested. He will never be free again.

April 19. Codreanu sentenced to six months in prison for having "offended" Professor Iorga.

April 22. Trouble in the Sudetenland. Beginning of the Czecho-Slovak crisis.

May 27. In one of the most monstrous judiciary crimes, with Professor Iorga's collaboration and complicity, Corneliu Codreanu is sentenced to ten years at hard labor. This meant also, as everybody guessed, his death.

September 13. Open insurrection in the Sudetenland. Martial law is proclaimed.

September 15. First meeting between Neville Chamberlain and Adolf Hitler at Berchtesgaden.

September 22–23. Second Chamberlain-Hitler meeting at Godesberg and general mobilization in Czecho-Slovakia.

September 29–September 30. Munich Agreement. Over three and a half million Germans allowed to live free.

September 30. Chamberlain speaks to the crowd from the window of No. 10 Downing Street: "My good friends, this is the second time in our history that there has come back from Germany to Downing Street peace with honor. I believe it is peace for our time. We thank you from the bottom of our hearts. And now I recommend you to go home and sleep quietly in your beds."

October 13. To everybody's amazement, the first of Chamberlain's warlike speeches in the Commons: "The Munich Agreement does not permit us to diminish our efforts towards the realization of our military program."

October 24. Friendly interview in Berchtesgaden between Ribbentrop and Lipski, the Polish Ambassador. Invitation to Polish Foreign Minister Beck to visit Berlin: "A standing invitation to our Polish friends." Ribbentrop's suggestions are: 1) Danzig a German city; 2) Free port for Poland in Danzig with communications assured by extraterritorial railway and highway through Danzig; 3) Extraterritorial zone one kilometer wide for a railroad and highway across the Polish Corridor uniting the two portions of Germany carved out at Versailles; 4) Both nations recognize and guarantee their frontiers; 5) An extension of the German-Polish treaty of friendship, complete with a consultative clause, by from ten to twenty years. (These proposals were standing and open from Germany's side until August 10, 1939, when Poland rejected them and declared that "any intervention by the Reich Government [would be regarded] as an act of aggression."

October 31. Polish Foreign Minister Beck instructs Lipski on how to reply to Ribbentrop's proposals on Danzig and the Corridor. Answer entirely negative.

November 7. On the eve of Ribbentrop's visit to Paris, Hershel Grynszpan, a seventeen-year-old Jewish refugee, assassinates Ernst vom Rath, Third Secretary of the German Embassy in Paris.

November 13. King Carol receives an unexpected invitation from the British Government to visit London.

November 14. President Roosevelt recalls Hugh Wilson, the American Ambassador in Berlin.

November 19. Lipski confers with Ribbentrop in Berlin. He informs the German Foreign Minister that "any tendency to incorporate the Free City in the Reich must inevitably lead to conflict." However, Poland would be willing to replace the League of Nations' guarantee of Danzig with a German-Polish agreement. Ribbentrop asks the Polish Government to think about the German proposals in terms of centuries and of a permanent friendship between the two countries.

November 22–28. Clandestine publishing and diffusion of a series of Legionary manifests concerning the question of Rumano-Soviet relations. Student trouble at the University of Cluj.

November 28. Carol's return from London. In Paris, according to Paul-Boncour's memoirs, Carol promises to come to an understanding with Soviet Russia about the passage of Soviet troops across Rumanian territory in case of a European conflict. He asks, however, for a necessary respite in order to prepare Rumania's public opinion.

November 29–30. By order of King Carol, Codreanu and thirteen of his followers are garotted. Beginning of the promised "preparation."

December 6. Declaration of non-aggression and friendship between France and Germany. Mutual guarantee of common frontiers.

1939

January 5. Beck confers with Hitler at Berchtesgaden. In regard to Danzig, Hitler declares that he is thinking about a formula that would make it politically German and economically Polish. He is ready to give formal and clear guarantee for the German-Polish frontiers. (A strong Poland was absolutely necessary for Germany. Any Polish division in front of Soviet Russia was as good as a German division.)

January 6. Beck confers with Ribbentrop at Munich. Ribbentrop asks the "reunion of Danzig with Germany" and proposes to guarantee "in the most generous manner" Polish economic interests. Ribbentrop also proposes that if Poland would agree to a German "extraterritorial motor road and railway across the Corridor," Germany would "guarantee the Corridor and all Poland's present positions."

January 23. Chamberlain's new war speech. Announcing the introduction of the National Service: "It is a project that must make us prepared for war."

January 25. New arrests, assassinations and tortures of Legionaries in Rumania, in connection with the discovery of a "Legionary conspiracy." The young Lucia Grecu, having been savagely tortured, is killed by jumping from the third floor of the Police Prefecture in Bucharest when she feels she can resist her tormentors no longer.

January 25-27. Ribbentrop in Warsaw. Renews Germany's proposals: Danzig politically German, economically fully Polish. Extraterritorial railway and highway connection, of one kilometer width, between the two Germanies. Same extraterritorial connections for Poland through Danzig territory towards her free port in Danzig. Reciprocal guarantee of frontiers. Sincere and earnest desire of Hitler to achieve with Poland, permanent friendship by "an appropriate working agreement."

January 28. Chamberlain's speech in Birmingham. Great Britain must prepare herself to defend not only her territory but also "the principle of liberty."

February 8. Six Legionaries arrested in Bucharest and immediately murdered by Armand Călinescu's police.

February 22. Chamberlain's speech in Blackburn: "Ships, guns and ammunition are produced by our shipyards and factories with an increased acceleration. . . . Even if the whole world be against us we will win." All of these provocative demonstrations on Great Britain's side (there were also the speeches of Churchill, Eden, Duff Cooper, etc.) went on while Berlin reiterated incessantly its generous and friendly proposals to Poland.

March 6. Armand Călinescu becomes Prime Minister on the death of Patriarch Cristea.

March 14. Monsignor Josef Tiso proclaims the independence of his country, Slovakia. (After General Štefánik's murder, the Pittsburgh Agreement between Czechs and Slovaks, promising autonomy to the latter, was torn to pieces by Beneš. Monsignor Tiso was kept in prison for years by the Prague Government.)

March 15. German troops enter Prague. Bohemia a German protectorate. Contrary to the still prevailing information, it was not this German move that provoked the abandonment by the Western Powers of their peace-minded Munich attitude, but the other way around.

March 15. From Count Ciano's *Diaries*: ". . . German troops began their occupation of Bohemia. . . . It is useless to deny that all this concerns and humiliates the Italian people. It is necessary to give them a satisfaction and compensation: Albania."

March 21. Sir Howard Kennard, the British Ambassador in Warsaw, offers Poland, in the name of his Government, a Pact of Consultation and Resistance to include Great Britain, France, Poland, and the Soviet Union.

March 24. The German Ambassador in Warsaw tells of great activity between the Polish Foreign Office and the British Embassy. Miroslav Arciczewski, the Polish Undersecretary of State, complains to the German Ambassador about British and French intrigues in Warsaw, that do not take into consideration the dangers to which Poland is exposed.

March 26. Ambassador Lipski brings to Ribbentrop Poland's answer to Germany's proposals of October 1938. Poland rejects them totally. Beck will not go to Berlin in answer to Hitler's invitation and in exchange for Ribbentrop's visit to Warsaw, so long as Germany will not abandon explicitly the idea of a German Danzig and of an extraterritorial strip of 1,000 meter width across the Polish Corridor. Should Germany insist, it would mean war.

March 31. Chamberlain announces in the House of Commons that the British Government considers itself bound to come immediately to Poland's aid the moment the Polish Government feels that it is to its interest to resist any action, *that in its estimation,* would put Poland's existence in danger. The unconditional guarantee given to Poland, by France, and Great Britain, which later will be given to Rumania, concerns only the western borders of the country, not the frontiers with Soviet Russia. A detail to which the governments of Poland and Rumania gave no great importance.

April 6. Italian ultimatum to King Zogu I of Albania.

April 7. Italian occupation of Albania.

April 13. Paris and London inform Bucharest that in answering King Carol's demand they guarantee Rumania's western borders. As opposed to Germany's offer (which will be repeated once more) these guarantees leave us open to Soviet aggression; they constituted somehow an invitation to such an aggression.

April 18. Grigore Gafencu, new Minister of Foreign Affairs of Rumania, invited to Berlin. Before contemplating a fateful change of policy towards Soviet Russia, Hitler decides to renew once more his offer to guarantee the borders and to rearm Rumania's forces. Both Hitler and Göring warn Gafencu that "Rumania will be abandoned to the covetousness of her neighbors," if she persists in her hostile policy towards Germany. (In Paris and London Gafencu receives instructions and gives assurances to the respective governments. In Rome he tries to persuade Ciano to join the Western Powers.)

July 10. Niculeta Nicolescu, head of the Legionary Women's Organization, arrested by Călinescu's police seeking information regarding an alleged Legionary conspiracy. She is tortured and violated. After her breasts are cut off, she is put to death.

July 12. Chamberlain's fateful declarations in the House of Commons which deprive him and his Government of any possibility of being an impartial arbiter, or even an intermediary, between Germany and Poland in the Danzig question. Fully adopting Poland's intransigent attitude he states that: "The present status of Danzig could not be considered as illegal or unjust. . . . We hope that the Free City will prove once more that different nationalities can collaborate when their interest demands it."

August 4. Upon uncontrolled and mistaken information the Polish Government sends a wanton ultimatum to the Danzig Senate.

August 9. Germany warns Poland that any further comminatory note to Danzig would result in strained Polish-German relations with Poland being responsible.

August 10. In a strongly worded note the Polish Government warns Germany that "any future intervention by the latter to the detriment of Polish rights and interests at Danzig would be considered as an act of aggression."

On or about August 12. Fabricius, the German Envoy in Bucharest, phoned Gheorghe Brătianu that he had been instructed by Marshal Göring to ask him to try once more to convince King Carol and his Government of the necessity to give without delay to Germany the guarantee that Rumania will not permit Soviet troops to pass across her territory. If this guarantee were not given there would be a change in Germany's foreign policy very detrimental to Rumania's interests. The warning was transmitted. Carol and his ministers did not pay it any attention.

August 15. German State Secretary Baron Ernst von Weizsäcker warns Sir Nevile Henderson, the British Ambassador in Berlin, that the situation is extremely serious. Sir Nevile suggests a new German initiative in Warsaw. Weizsäcker answers that a German initiative is unthinkable in view of Beck's speech declaring that Poland was prepared to talk only if Germany would first accept the principle he had laid down; in view of the senseless ultimatum to the Danzig Senate and in view of the comminatory note of August 10 to the German Government. The same warning was repeated three days later from the same quarter to the British and the French Ambassadors.

August 19. Trade and credit agreement between Germany and the Soviet Union.

August 22. Chamberlain's letter to Hitler:

"Your Excellency will have already heard of certain measures taken by His Majesty's Government, and announced in the press and on the wireless this evening.

"These steps have, in the opinion of His Majesty's Government, been rendered necessary by the military movements which have been reported from Germany, and by the fact that apparently the announcement of a German-Soviet Agreement is taken in some quarters in Berlin to indicate that intervention by Great Britain on behalf of Poland is no longer a contingency that need be reckoned with. No greater mistake could be made. Whatever may prove to be the nature of the German-Soviet Agreement, it cannot alter Great Britain's obligation to Poland which His Majesty's Government has stated in public repeatedly and plainly, and which they are determined to fulfill. . . ."

August 23. Hitler's reply to Chamberlain:

". . . Germany was prepared to settle the questions of Danzig and of the Corridor by the method of negotiation on the basis of truly unparalleled magnanimity. The allegations disseminated by England regarding a German mobilization against Poland, the assertion of aggressive designs towards Rumania, Hungary, etc., as well as the so-called guarantee declarations which were subsequently given had, however, dispelled Polish inclination to negotiate on a basis of this kind which would have been tolerable for Germany also.

". . . The German Reich Government has received information to the effect that the British Government has the intention to carry out measures of mobilization which, according to the statements contained in your own letter, are clearly directed against Germany alone. . . . *I therefore inform your Excellency that, in the event of these military announcements being carried into effect, I shall order immediate mobilization of the German forces."*

August 23. Ribbentrop-Molotov Agreement of Non-aggression and Economic Collaboration for ten years. The British and French Special Military Missions leave Moscow.

August 24. Anglo-Polish Military Agreement.

August 25. Suicide of Colonel Slawek with two bullets in his body. Slawek was a stubborn and influential partisan of Pilsudski's policy towards Germany.

August 25. Hitler-Henderson meeting. The British Ambassador reports Hitler's declarations: "Poland's provocations have become intolerable. He has decided to put an end to these macedonian situations. But he has no intention of being small-minded in an arrangement with Poland. Nor has he the intention of asking Great Britain to break her commitments with Warsaw." Hitler makes new proposals to Great Britain whose friendship he has always sought. Hitler asks Sir Nevile to leave the same day for London with his proposals.

August 27. Birger Dahlerus, a Swedish businessman and friend of Göring, who had seen Hitler the day before, lands in Croyden in Göring's personal aircraft and hands Lord Halifax Hitler's proposals for a peaceful conclusion of the Danzig and Corridor affairs. These proposals are substantially the same as those which will be proposed by Germany August 30.

August 28. Henderson back from London. Chamberlain asks precisions concerning Hitler's intentions towards Poland.

August 29. Hitler's answer is affirmative on all counts. Renews his friendly sentiments and intentions towards the British Empire. "Germany has never intended to endanger Poland's vital interests." Germany accepts Britain's offer to intervene for the presence in Berlin of a Polish plenipotentiary. Sir Nevile asks if this diplomat would be assured of a courteous reception and if negotiations would be conducted on a basis of perfect equality. Hitler answers, "Of course!" Henderson observes that the short term of thirty-six hours seemed like an ultimatum. Hitler and Ribbentrop observe that it was not an ultimatum at all, but had the purpose of stressing the urgency of a situation where two armies completely mobilized were confronting each other. What Hitler and Ribbentrop could not tell Henderson was their anxiety about the precarious situation on the Western Front where five German divisions manned the Siegfried Line in front of the whole French Army and possibly quickly-transported British reinforcements.

August 30. Upon Britain's insistence Germany agrees to an extension of twenty-four hours to permit a Polish negotiator, who naturally might have been Lipski, to present himself at the Wilhelmstrasse. At midnight Sir Nevile Henderson hears Germany's proposals for a basis of negotiations; early next morning Göring sends Henderson the full text. "Those proposals are in general not too unreasonable," says Sir Nevile in his *Final Report*. Pierre and Renée Gosset in their rabid anti-German book *Hitler* declare: "It was a proposal of extreme moderation. It was in fact an offer that no Allied statesman could have rejected in good faith." They, however, rejected it. Why?

August 31. Henderson informs Lipski of neither the first term (August 30, Midnight) nor the second (August 31, Midnight). Instead of stressing the deadly necessity of seeing the German Foreign Minister before midnight the 31st, he dissuades him from doing it at all. In his *Final Report*: "I suggested that he recommend to his Government an interview between Marshal Śmigly-Rydz and Göring. I felt obliged to add that I could not conceive of the success of any negotiations if they were conducted by Herr v. Ribbentrop." Henderson is aware that this dilatory recommendation means war. In fact he recognizes it implicitly in the same *Final Report*.

August 31. From a telegram of Lipski to Beck: "Mr. Coulondre, the French Ambassador, has told me that Nevile Henderson has been informed through German contacts, that the German Government had the intention of waiting until midnight August 31st. Coulondre advises me to inform the German Government, *only after midnight,* that the Polish Embassy was always at its reach." Coulondre, it seems, was no more eager than Henderson to see a fruitful meeting between Ribbentrop and Lipski. This meeting, on the other hand, had been condemned days ago to a tragic end because of the orders sent to Lipski by the Polish Government.

August 31. From the telegram of Sir Howard Kennard, British Ambassador in Warsaw, to Lord Halifax, received in London at 7:30 a.m.: "I have asked Mr. Beck what would be the attitude of the Polish Ambassador in Berlin if Herr v. Ribbentrop will communicate to him the German proposals. *He answered that Lipski has been forbidden to receive such a document."*

August 31. Telegram to Beck from Lipski who days before has been strictly forbidden to accept any written proposals from Ribbentrop or anybody's hands, even if it were only for reading them: "I have been received by Mr. v. Ribbentrop at 6:30 p.m. I have obeyed instructions received and told him that I was not empowered to negotiate. Mr. v. Ribbentrop repeated that he believed I had such powers. He told me that he would report my visit to the Chancellor."

September 1. Hostilities begin between Germany and Poland. From Sir Nevile Henderson's *Final Report*: "The Wehrmacht asked YES or NO, as the success of its plan depended largely on the rapid occupation of Poland, and on the conclusion as rapidly as possible of the operations on the Eastern Front. Bad weather could start at any moment and was one of the best defenses of Poland against the German Army which was almost entirely motorized. However, because of Hitler's hesitation, one week had already been lost." Each day increased the possibility of a Franco-British attack on the Western Front, an attack that never took place despite the Franco-British guarantees given to Poland.

September 1. Danger of peace! Mussolini's proposals: Suspension of hostilities, immediate convening of a Conference of the Big Powers,

Poland included, to discuss terms for a peaceful agreement. Immediate acceptance of Mussolini's proposals by Germany, France, and Poland. Categorical British rejection, asking withdrawal of the German troops from the part of Polish territory (thirty kilometers deep) which they had already occupied. Remarkable fact: The British Government does not consult Warsaw before taking this fateful decision. Acceptance by London of the Italian proposals would have spared Poland the Soviet onslaught.

September 2. Coulondre's telegram to Daladier: "Stay firm, Hitler will knuckle under [*se dégonflera*]." Intrigues of Reynaud, Mandel, and Léger; pressure by Great Britain. Subordination of Daladier to the Anonymous Forces. France revokes her acceptance of the proposals of Mussolini which would have saved Poland and her independence and spared the world World War II. *Count de Saint-Aulaire's predictions, made eight years before, come true:* "Collective security, indivisible peace . . . this means simply a pro-Soviet crusade in the event of a German-Russian conflict."

September 3. Great Britain and France declare war on Germany.

September 4. Göring's speech. A last effort, with Hitler's consent, to reach a settlement with Poland. This speech backed by Hitler's meaningful visit to Pilsudski's grave countered by fiery British, French, *and American* pressures in Warsaw. (No historian of those fateful days has, to our knowledge, ever mentioned this fact.)

September 6. The German Command asks the Polish Command to evacuate the non-combatants, especially women and children, in case it intends to defend Warsaw. Poland's answer: "Warsaw will be defended, nobody will be evacuated."

September 17. The Red Army invades Poland.

September 21. Execution of Armand Călinescu, the murderer of Corneliu Codreanu and of so many Legionaries, young men and girls, by a group of nine Legionaries. They give themselves up immediately at the first police precinct. They are immediately executed after routine torture, their bodies left for days where they had fallen.

September 21–22. Massacre of four hundred Legionaries. Their bodies left at the country's crossroads for several days.

September 27. After a prolonged bombardment Warsaw is taken. The Western Powers neither break their diplomatic relations with Moscow nor declare war on her. *FINIS POLONIAE!* (When General Kazimierz Sosnkowski, Supreme Commander of the Polish troops fighting on the Western Front in 1944, reminded his soldiers that "Poland entered this war four years earlier because of the urging of Great Britain" at Churchill's insistence Sosnkowski was deprived of his command for having recalled what had to be forgotten.)

September 28. Germany and Soviet Union divide Poland.

October 6. Hitler's peace offer rejected by France and Great Britain.

November 30. The Red Army attacks Finland. The Western Powers do not react. Later Churchill will declare war on Finland.

December 14. Soviet Russia expelled from a defunct League of Nations. The Western Powers maintain their diplomatic relations with Russia.

1940

March–April. Massacre in Katyn and in the Arctic of 15,000 young Polish officers. Fitting preface to Teheran and Yalta.

April 9. German invasion of Norway, beating the Franco-British invasion by twelve hours. Naval battle of Narvik.

May 6. Horia Sima, the young Legionary leader, leaves Berlin with a group of comrades and secretly enters Rumania.

May 11. Great Britain starts indiscriminate bombing of civilian population, a purely terrorist rather than a military action, a thing that had until then not occurred in this war.

May 19. Horia Sima is arrested. Meanwhile Carol starts negotiations with other Legionary leaders. Carol is impressed by Germany's victories. The Legionaries would like to save Horia Sima's life.

May 28–June 22. German Blitzkrieg in the West. Armistice between France and Germany. At the Armistice ceremony, as Feldmarschall Wilhelm Keitel and the French General Charles Huntziger face each other with tears in their eyes, Keitel declares: "I cannot, as a soldier, let this occasion pass by without expressing to you my sympathy for the sad moments you have experienced as a Frenchman. You can be comforted however by knowing, as I state it here expressly, that your soldiers have fought with their usual gallantry." Both soldiers exchanged a long handshake. Six years later in similar circumstances Feldmarschall Keitel was hanged in Nürnberg.

May–June. German military authorities warn our Military Attaché in Berlin of Soviet Russia's military preparations at our frontiers. Grigore Gafencu, the Rumanian Foreign Minister, refuses to believe the warnings of Colonel Vorobchievici and accuses him of alarmism.

June 1. After eighteen months as Foreign Minister, Gafencu resigns.

June 10. Mussolini declares war on already-defeated France and on Great Britain.

June 13. Horia Sima liberated. Audience with the King.

June 25. A new Government in Bucharest. Some Legionaries participating as undersecretaries in secondary departments.

June 26. Soviet ultimatum. Rumania to start evacuation of Bessarabia immediately and to terminate in four days. Carol complies.

July 3. In consideration of the new dangers at the Rumanian frontiers, Horia Sima consents to participate in a new Government.

July 7. Realizing that Carol's attitude, in front of these new dangers, will be as cowardly as in the Bessarabian affair, Horia Sima resigns.

July 27. Gafencu appointed Rumanian Envoy to Moscow.

August 3. Horia Sima with Legionary leaders in audience with Carol. Sima states that only a Legionary Government can save Rumania from new territorial mutilation and asks for full responsibility. No understanding is reached.

August 29–30. Arbitration of Vienna. The work of the anti-Rumanian Ciano. Half of Rumanian Transylvania given to Hungary. Meanwhile a part of the Dobruja province has been retroceded to Bulgaria.

September 1. Horia Sima broadcasts a manifest demanding Carol's abdication.

September 3. At 9 p.m. the Legionary Revolution breaks out. Fighting in Bucharest, Braşov, Constanţa. The army does not react with conviction. Nine Legionaries killed. The public buildings are occupied. The Palace is surrounded. General Coroama, Commander of the Bucharest Army Corps, refuses to order his soldiers to fire upon Legionaries.

September 5–6. Triumph of the Legionary Revolution. King Carol abdicates in favor of his son Michael and leaves Rumania with Magda Lupescu, passing a part of his royal powers to General Ion Antonescu. In Berlin: Sturdza-Canaris and Sturdza-Ribbentrop interviews.

September 14. Formal understanding between the Legionary Movement and General Antonescu, sanctioned by King Michael. Proclamation of the National Legionary State. Formation of the National Legionary Government: General Ion Antonescu, President (*Conductorul Statului*—the Head of State); Horia Sima, Vice President and Commandant of the Legionary Movement; Prince Michel Sturdza, Minister of Foreign Affairs; General Petrovicescu, Minister of the Interior; General Pantazi, Minister of Defense; Mihai Antonescu, Minister of Justice; Vasile Iasinschi, Minister of Health and Labor; Professor Braileanu, Minister of Public Education; Gheorghe Cretzianu, Minister of Finance; Ion Protopopescu, Minister of Public Works; Cancicov, Minister of Industry and Commerce.

November 14. Rumania being absolutely deprived of armored defense and under the constant menace of the Red Army, the National Legionary Government asks Germany for two tank units. They are immediately sent with the necessary instructors in order to train Rumanian crews. Thanks to the squandering of government funds by Carol and his Governments, these few tanks will be the only modern weapons with which Rumania will enter World War II. Mussolini protests, and suggests that Rumania also ask for the presence of Italian troops. His wish cannot be granted.

(October 28. Obsessed by the idea of doing no less than Hitler and considering that Rumania has been "occupied" by Germany, Mussolini attacks Greece unexpectedly and without any visible reason but in order also to occupy something.)

November 14–16. Antonescu and Sturdza visit Rome. Courteous but strained reception.

November 20. Antonescu and Sturdza visit Berlin. Rumania's adhesion to the Tripartite (intended to be Quadripartite) Pact, signed by Antonescu, not by Sturdza. Antonescu leaves Berlin on November 24; Sturdza six days later.

November 29. The second night in Jilava.

December 15. Antonescu-Sturdza conflict. Sturdza forced to resign.

1941

January 15. Antonescu visits Hitler in Salzburg. Hitler announces impending war with Soviet Russia; asks for Rumania's collaboration. Antonescu pretends that he must first liquidate the Legionary Movement which is "an element of trouble," but forgets to ask for more than a promise of modern war matériel for the Rumanian Army. The condition *sine qua non* ought to have been the prior delivery of this matériel. All through the campaign in Russia, the Rumanian troops were completely deprived of adequate matériel.

January 19. Conflict between General Antonescu and General Petrovicescu, the Minister of the Interior and a friend of the Legionary Movement. Petrovicescu forced to resign.

January 21. The district prefects, all Legionaries, called to Bucharest by Antonescu for an alleged conference. In the absence of the prefects, the colonels with the highest grade in each locality are ordered to occupy and take charge of the prefectures. (It was under colonel-prefects, during Carol's regime, that four hundred Legionaries were massacred.)

January 21. Antonescu coup against his own government. Passive but stubborn resistance of the Legionaries. Barricaded in the buildings they are lawfully occupying, they fire over the soldiers' heads. Legionaries are killed. No Rumanian soldier is killed or wounded.

January 21. Antonescu asks for Hitler's advice and help. Hitler's answer: "Liquidate the Movement." The German forces in Rumania ordered to help Antonescu crush the Movement.

Night of January 22–23. Dr. Neubacher, the German Chargé d'Affaires, is received by Sima. He is the bearer of a solemn promise from both Antonescu and Hitler of complete impunity for Legionaries, and suggests participation of the Movement in a new Government, if resistance ends before noon, January 23rd.

January 23. Legionary resistance ceases in Bucharest before eight o'clock and in the provinces before eleven o'clock. Nevertheless Antonescu's forces start massacre of peaceful crowds on Bucharest's central avenue. According to Antonescu's official statistics there are 360 dead among whom many are women and children. No Legionaries among them; they had already peacefully withdrawn, conforming to Horia Sima's orders.

January–June. Arrests, summary trials, condemnations, and many executions of Legionaries by Antonescu, under the protection of the German forces and with the approbation of the new German Envoy, Baron Manfred von Killinger. Legionaries who succeed, with the help of the National Socialist Party, in reaching Germany or Austria are immediately interned by German authorities.

February 10. Great Britain severs diplomatic relations with Rumania.

March 1. Bulgaria adheres to the Tripartite Pact. German troops begin crossing Rumanian territory in order to help the Italian Army in full route in the Balkans.

March 27. Italy's insensate ambitions over Croatia and other Yugoslav territories; her unexplainable attack on Greece, and Western intrigues in Belgrade, result in the coup of General Dušan Simović, Chief of the Yugoslav General Staff, and the beginning of Yugoslav-German hostilities.

June 11–12. Antonescu visits Hitler in Munich. Full agreement concerning the cooperation of the two armies against Soviet Russia. Promise of massive armaments to Rumania. (This matériel was not delivered until the last weeks of the war.)

June 22. Germany, Rumania, and Finland at war with Soviet Russia. Finland's gallant army limits its operation to the recovery of her former frontiers. Italy and Hungary join with token contingents. (Later Danish, Norwegian, Dutch, Belgian, French, and Spanish legions of volunteers will enter the anti-Communist crusade. This will be the first and perhaps the last and unique joint effort of defenders of Western Civilization to crush the Nameless Beast before being devoured by it. These volunteers attempting to oppose the Great Design of the Anonymous Powers, when back in their countries, will everywhere, except in Spain, be sentenced to long prison terms or be executed.)

June 22. All Legionaries in Antonescu's prisons or in German concentration camps ask to be sent to the front. Their demand rejected by both the Rumanian and German Governments.

July–November. Victorious advance of the German and Rumanian troops on the Southern Russian Front.

July 30–31. Harry Hopkins in Moscow.

August 21. Antonescu promotes himself to the rank of Marshal.

October–December. Battle and retreat from Moscow.

October 16. Odessa taken by Rumanian troops after some of the bloodiest combat of the Eastern War. Antonescu's increasing insanity causes him to refuse Germany's offer of heavy artillery, armored units, and bombers, which the Rumanian troops are totally lacking. These troops suffered 75,000 casualties. Four divisions had to be sent home for reorganization and replenishment.

December 7. Pearl Harbor! "The day of infamy" that permitted Franklin Delano Roosevelt to trample over every solemnly repeated promise he had given to the mothers and wives in the United States. It gave him the opportunity to ask the United States Senate to authorize sending an expeditionary corps to Europe, an opportunity he and his mentors had looked and worked for since September 1939. Britain declares war on Rumania.

December 12. The German Minister Manfred von Killinger and the Italian Minister Bova Scoppa force Mihai Antonescu, the Rumanian Foreign Minister, to declare war on the United States, a mistake Finland refused to make.

1942

May–July. Difficult but continuously victorious advance of the German and Rumanian Armies on the Southern Russian Front. Kerch, Sebastopol, and the whole of Crimea taken. Hundreds of thousands of prisoners and enormous amounts of war booty taken. After the capture of Rostov, half of the German and Rumanian troops that were destined to encircle and take Stalingrad are sent to the Caucasus in order to conquer the oil producing territories. (This was a fatal mistake—opposed vainly by the Rumanian command. Otherwise Stalingrad would, very likely, have been taken by surprise. Once more it was forgotten that the destruction of the enemy forces is the purpose of war and that economic or other interests are cared for after victory.)

August 6–September 3. Crossing of the Don. The Fourth Rumanian Army takes its position along a line 100 kilometers south-west of Stalingrad, without any armored or motorized units, with horse-drawn artillery and with no possibility of building a significant reserve for this sector with only 180,000 men to cover it. High and low-ranking Rumanian officers signal the danger of the situation to the German command: Weakness of the line and insufficient armament to hold the front against continuously increasing masses of enemy troops and armament.

October 1–11. The Rumanian Third Army takes position along the Don, north of Stalingrad: Seven divisions no better armed than the Fourth Army in charge of a front of 120 kilometers and facing countless Soviet divisions provided with the best, modern and abundant armament by Russia's Western allies. The German command opposes the Rumanian suggestion to liquidate immediately the bridgehead the Red troops had kept on the right shore of the Don. This front must be kept quiet. No maneuvering. Stalingrad will be taken by frontal attack.

November 19. Beginning of the great Soviet offensive on the Don and the Volga, against the Rumanian Armies north and south of Stalingrad. The front pierced by Soviet tank divisions. Five Rumanian divisions lost. The Italian and Hungarian contingents included in the debacle.

November 19–20. After one month of sterile frontal attacks by the German troops, retreat from Stalingrad.

End of November. First secret contacts between Antonescu's Government and the Western Powers. The contact between the enemy and the politicians led by Iuliu Maniu, chief of the National Peasant Party, had already started in the very first days of Rumania's war against Soviet Russia, when Maniu organized a secret system of information for the Western Powers which was sending this information to the Soviet command. Repeated Legionary warnings in Berlin and in Bucharest to the German Envoy are totally discounted

1943

January 2. Antonescu visits Hitler. Reconciliation after crisis of reciprocal incriminations concerning the Stalingrad disaster.

January 19. Mihai Antonescu, the Rumanian Foreign Minister, asks Mussolini to take the lead of a Latin League including the minor belligerents and to start negotiations with the Western Powers.

February 1–15. Contact between the emissaries of Mihai Antonescu in Bern with the Western Powers, through the Papal Nuncio Bernardini; and in Bucharest through the Turkish Ambassador.

February 2. The German General Hansen reports to Hitler concerning the Rumanian troops in the Crimea and the Caucasus: "All the Rumanian units show an indomitable will to resist the Red Army's advance; distinguished among them are the First and Second Divisions of the Mountain Corps and the Ninth Division." It is not at the front that betrayal is prepared.

July 1. Mihai Antonescu again in Rome, suggests that Mussolini begin immediate negotiations with the Western Powers.

July 25–26. Mussolini kidnapped by King Victor Emmanuel; abandoned by the majority of the Fascist leaders, but not by his Black Shirts.

July–August. Renewed warning by Legionary leaders in Berlin and in Bucharest. Killinger, the German Envoy, absolutely ignorant of what is going on around him, disregards them all.

September 23. Antonescu visits Hitler. Hitler asks him not to receive an anti-Mussolini Italian Envoy, and to dismiss Mihai Antonescu. Marshal Antonescu refuses to comply. Hitler, deceived until then by the reassuring reports from his Envoy in Bucharest, begins to understand the real attitude of Rumania's leaders.

November 28–December 1. Teheran Conference where Roosevelt is a guest, not of the United States Embassy, but of the Soviet Embassy. Joins the murderers of Katyn in recommending the assassination of 40,000 German officers after victory. Admits all the territorial pretensions of Stalin in Europe. Asks only that this arrangement be kept secret until after the Presidential elections in the United States. In Ankara, Eden tells the Foreign Minister of Turkey that Soviet Russia will be given a free hand in the Balkans after the war.

December 24. Beginning in Stockholm of secret negotiations between Marshal Antonescu's emissaries and members of the Soviet Embassy. (Not even Antonescu had fully realized the implacability of the Communist Beast and the impossibilities of any arrangement, between Soviet Russia and her neighbors, which would not finally engulf them in Communist-dominated territory.)

PART V

1944

March 17. Barbu Ştirbei in Cairo sent by Iuliu Maniu and Dinu Brătianu, chief of the Liberal Party, with the approbation of King Michael, in order to discuss secretly conditions of a separate peace or an armistice with the Western Allies. (The error of the King and of the politicians was as great as that of Marshal Antonescu: In the policy and the intentions of the Western leaders there was no trace of anti-Communist solidarity, a situation which prevails even today in the Western chancelleries.)

March 18. Ştirbei is informed that the subject of discussion can be only about "operational details concerning the overthrow of the Antonescu regime and its replacement by a Government prepared to accept unconditional surrender." The conditions of this surrender, already established between the Western Powers and Soviet Russia, are imparted to the Rumanian emissaries only towards the end of August.

April 18. Harriman's telegram from Moscow to the United States Secretary of State: "In my talk with Molotov last evening he told me that the Rumanian troops were still fighting the Red Army and that those who surrendered had done so only after battle. In the Crimea the resistance was particularly stubborn as the Rumanian divisions there consisted of better trained troops." Meanwhile Maniu, Brătianu, and King Michael were asking for a powerful Soviet offensive, for a Soviet debarkment in Dobruja and for the bombing of various Rumanian localities.

May 12. Roosevelt's "Dear Peter" letter to the young King of Yugoslavia, ordering him most affectionately to dismiss General Draža Mihailovich, the legendary hero of the Yugoslav resistance, as Minister of National Defense, and to replace him by Broz-Tito, the Communist leader, hated by the Yugoslav people and without military value as an ally.

June 1. The Rumanian emissaries in Cairo are informed that "further negotiations would serve no purpose" and that Mr. Maniu "should follow the advice already given him by sending an officer to make direct contact with the Red Army on the front."

June 6. Invasion of France.

June 29. A certain Constantin Vişoianu, Maniu's new emissary who arrived in Cairo on May 25, has authority which prevails over Ştirbei's. Contrary to what was occurring in Stockholm, and in a certain measure until then in Cairo, Vişoianu abandons any effort to secure desirable guarantees for Rumania. He accepts, in Maniu's name, unconditional surrender, expressing only Maniu's hope that the conditions finally imposed will not be too severe. He also transmits Maniu's plans and proposals: "The change of government shall take place simultaneously with a massive Soviet offensive." Maniu also asks for a debarkment in Dobruja, for Allied bombing raids, for three airborne brigades, and two thousand parachutist troops: "Whether these Allied contingents are to be Anglo-American or Russian is left to the decision of the Supreme Allied Command." King Michael, and the Patriotic Democratic Front, which has been formed with the Communists, are in full accord with those proposals.

July 2. United States Political Adviser Robert Murphy to Washington: "The Allies are warned against any illusion that any understanding is possible with Antonescu." The Marshal is negotiating with the Rumanian Army behind him whereas the politicians are preparing the disarmament of our troops and the kidnapping of their Commander-in-Chief.

July 9–August 7. Between those two dates Maniu reiterates, four times, his proposals without receiving any answer from the Allied representatives other than that those proposals have been transmitted to their respective Governments.

August 5–6. Last meeting between Hitler and Antonescu.

August 20. Beginning of the great Russian offensive in northern Moldavia.

August 21. Observing the failure of his negotiations with the Soviets in Stockholm and in full agreement with General Fiessner, Commander of the German troops on the Rumanian Front, Marshal Antonescu decides to organize a powerful resistance on the Focşani-Nămoloasa-Galaţi Line. Betrayed in his intentions by the Generals Aldea, Racovitză, Sănătescu, and Şteflea.

August 23. Antonescu and his Foreign Minister are summoned by King Michael. They are kidnapped in the Palace and delivered to the Communist agent Bodnăraş.

August 23, ten p.m. King Michael's proclamation broadcast to his troops, declaring that an armistice has been signed with the Russian command. Consequently he orders his army to cease any resistance. (No armistice had been signed and the result of this deceit to his soldiers was the capture and transfer to Russia and Siberia of sixteen Rumanian divisions and the abandonment of Antonescu's orders regarding the occupation of the Focşani-Nămaloasa-Galaţi Front.)

August 24. Considering that the Bucharest Government had committed an act of treason against the Rumanian people and their destiny by the arrest of Marshal Antonescu, the head of the Rumanian Army, and by handing him over to Soviet agents, Horia Sima and the Legionaries who were then in Germany, or free in other countries, decided to continue the fight against Rumania's implacable enemy with every means at their disposition. They start immediately the formation of the Rumanian National Army with all the Legionaries and all Rumanian volunteers then in Germany and with all those who succeeded in joining them by crossing into Hungarian and Austrian territory.

August 30. Rumania's new Government, including numerous Communists following Italy's shameful example, declares war on its former ally.

August 31. Plundering, destroying, murdering and raping, the Soviet hordes occupy the whole of Rumania's territory and enter Bucharest. No Convention of Armistice having been signed or even discussed, the Red troops behave as on enemy territory.

September 13. The Convention of Armistice falsely announced twenty-one days before is finally signed on the dotted line in Moscow by the Rumanian delegates. It is an unconditional capitulation that put Rumania entirely in Soviet hands.

September 12–December 5. Under the pressure of the Red Army, the successive Governments in Rumania are more and more of a Communist character. General Rădescu, last non-Communist Prime Minister, attempts a timid resistance to this disastrous flow of events.

December 9. U.S. Representative Burton Y. Berry cables Washington that Iuliu Maniu told John Le Rougetel, the British Representative in Bucharest, and him that "if he [Maniu] had known the Soviets were to be given a free hand in application of armistice terms he would not have advised the King to sign the armistice. He argued that his pressure and the Rumanian action which resulted from it had actually advanced the Focşani-Galaţi Line, which might have been held a long time, to the very gates of Budapest." That was the line upon which Antonescu and the loyal military leaders wanted to organize the national resistance when the Marshal, on Maniu's advice, was kidnapped by King Michael and delivered to the Communists.

December 10. Formal constitution in Vienna of the Rumanian National Government. Five Legionaries: Horia Sima, Prince Michel Sturdza, Vasile Iachinschi, Corneliu Gheorghescu, Professor Manoïlescu; and three non-Legionaries: General Chirnoagă, Professor Singheorghe, Wladimir Christi.

1945

February 7–11. Stalin, Roosevelt and Churchill meet in Yalta. The Western Powers' side of the Conference is entirely controlled by Harry Hopkins and Alger Hiss, the latter convicted for *denying* under oath, and contrarily to testimonies and evidence produced, that he was a Soviet agent. Poland sacrificed. Europe is dismembered. Ten European countries and one-third of Germany is left in Soviet hands, while from the Baltic States, from Poland, from East Germany, and from Rumania, millions of human beings are torn from their ancestral homes and sent to Siberian Arctic extermination camps. To Maniu and Brătianu who complain to Roosevelt and Churchill about these barbarous proceedings, these statesmen who proclaimed the "Three Liberties" and signed the Atlantic Charter, answer that Soviet Russia has been allowed "to use manpower" as partial payment of war indemnities.

February 11. After a few verbal patriotic capers, General Rădescu, the Rumanian Prime Minister, takes refuge in the British Legation. After a few months of hibernation he flees in disguise to Cyprus and Portugal.

February 13. After Hamburg, Berlin, Frankfort, and many other cities, the terrorist bombardment of Dresden. Estimated casualties: About 300,000 victims. The greatest authenticated war crime, "the greatest cemetery in the world and in history." Nobody hanged for it.

March 6. The first regiment of the Rumanian National Army takes position along the Oder, where it is inspected by General Platon Chirnoagă, Minister of Defense in the Rumanian Government-in-Exile.

March 8. Vyshinsky forces King Michael to appoint Communist Petru Groza as Prime Minister of Michael's now purely Communist Government. The King, Maniu, and Dinu Brătianu ask vainly for Allied support.

April 12. Death of President Franklin Delano Roosevelt.

April 28. Murder of Benito Mussolini.

April 29–30. Suicide of Adolf Hitler.

May 7. Germany's unconditional surrender.

May 7. End of the activities of the National Rumanian Government. Retreat of the troops engaged on the Oder. The rest of the First Division of the Rumanian National Army, in training in Austria, surrenders to Anglo-American troops. (The Rumanian Government-in-Exile was a logical reaction to the treacherous behavior in Bucharest of the Palace clique and of the power-hungry, panicky, faithless politicians; and a desperate attempt to prevent the unavoidable consequences of this behavior; suppression of any liberty for the Rumanian people, suppression of any independence for the Rumanian State.)

June 26. In San Francisco, end of the United Nations Conference, over which Alger Hiss presided as Acting Secretary General. Soviet Russia admitted as a partner, with three seats instead of one as in the case of every other member, into an association supposed to defend the rights of man and the independence of nations.

July 17–August 2. Potsdam Conference. Soviet Russia senselessly invited to participate in the war against an already defeated Japan which two months before had offered to negotiate through Moscow. Prelude to the delivery of the whole of China to the Communist empire.

August 6–August 9. Wanton atomic bombing of Hiroshima and Nagasaki, killing 170,000, injuring and maiming countless others for life. Nobody is hanged for this.

December 21. U.S. Army General George S. Patton dies in Germany as a result of injuries suffered in an automobile-truck collision on December 9. (Patton's untimely death is followed by that of former Secretary of Defense James V. Forrestal, who plunged to his death on May 22, 1949, from the sixteenth floor of Bethesda Naval Hospital.)

1946

March 13–July 17. Communist Josip Broz (Tito) kidnaps, summarily judges, and assassinates Serbian General Draža Mihailovich. Tito, the murderer of tens of thousands of Mihailovich's followers, was imposed as ruler of the Yugoslav people by the British and American Governments without any reason other than their submission to the Anonymous and Omnipotent Powers who decided that the hammer and sickle should replace the Cross where it has reigned for about two thousand years. Another move in the astounding game of the systematically directed suicide of the Western World. Duplication of the Kolchak episode, but this time with Churchill on the side of the kidnappers.

March 17. Marshal Ion Antonescu is sentenced to death by one of the kangaroo courts whose pullulations will be a sad characteristic of the Western Powers' victory. (King Michael could have exercised his right of mercy, but to Rumania's astonishment and humiliation he did not do it.)

October 15. Reichsmarschall Hermann Göring commits suicide two hours before he would have been hanged.

October 16. At 1:11 a.m., crowning the horrors of six years of war, Foreign Minister Joachim von Ribbentrop, Feldmarschall Wilhelm Keitel, General Alfred Jodl, and seven other National Socialist leaders are executed in Nürnberg followed by an orgy of similar outrages in Europe and in Japan. This is the beginning of a new era in Western justice where all the basic principles of law established through centuries of maturation in countries of both Roman and consuetudinary traditions will be forsaken and where judges and hangmen will belong to the same fraternity.

1947

December 30. Abdication of King Michael under the pressure of the enemy army which he and the Rumanian politicians had helped to take possession of their country. *FINIS DACIAE!*

PART ONE

Prelude

A wind of reaction was blowing at that time over the whole of Russia against the devastating furors of Bolshevism. The struggle for emancipation in the Urals, in Siberia, in the Donets and in the northern provinces, had torn from the authority of the Soviets a great part of Russian territory. Bolshevism seemed to be on the verge of collapse.

It was saved by the intervention of the allied powers, and principally by the untoward intervention of President Wilson [who] secured the survival of the Communist regime. The Bolsheviks themselves were convinced that the experiment of Communism had reached its end; they were more surprised than anybody else at the unexpected turn of events.

Joseph NOULENS

Ambassador of France
Mon Ambassade en Russie Soviétique, 1917–1919
(My Embassy in Soviet Russia)

Hungary's capital, an excellent base for the conquest of Central Europe by Bolshevism, had become its headquarters. Some of the most eminent strategists of revolution had settled there under the cover of commercial, financial and even humanitarian missions. The majority of them had kept their posts after the occupation of the city by the Rumanian Army. The liberators of Hungary had not turned them out in order to avoid provoking the remonstrations of the Supreme Council, whose thunders, in those circumstances, were hurled not against the Bolsheviks but against the Rumanian soldiers, who in smothering this furnace of bloody anarchy, had saved Western Civilization despite itself in that part of Europe. . . . Many revolutionaries, expelled from Hungary, had come back after the armistice in U.S. uniforms, and it was their reports to Wilson that inspired the policy of the Supreme Council in Central Europe.

In 1919, it was Wilson, godfather of the League of Nations as well as master of the Supreme Council, who forced it to adopt a scandalous partiality in favor of Bolshevism.

Collective security, indivisible peace. . . . This means simply a pro-Soviet crusade in the event of a German-Russian conflict. [*Roman added.*]

SAINT-AULAIRE

Ambassador of France
Genéve contre la Paix
(Geneva against Peace)

CHAPTER

I

The Past in Us

Chateaubriand, the famous French author and statesman, narrating in his *Mémoires d'Outre-tombe* the past and the glories of the Chateaubriand family, informs us that he does it only for the sake of his nephews who might be interested in such futile things. Less pharisaical than he, I confess that I do it for the contentment of my own predilections.

I believe that every race, every country, every province, every hamlet even, has not only the right but also the duty to cherish and respect its history, and that the forgetting of a country's past by its leading class is one of the greatest misfortunes that can occur to it. A nation that has been mentally severed from its past is like an army whose line of communications has been cut off by the enemy. This is what happened in Rumania after World War I with the disappearance of the traditional Conservative Party.

It is also what brought me into the Legionary Movement, in which I found and recognized the links with times gone by which had been lost by our political sects.

At the origin of the oldest Rumanian families, of the Rumanian *uradel*, history always finds a *kneaz*,[1] military chieftain and administrator of high and low justice in the territory over which he rules. A. D. Xénopol, the well-known historian, in his *Histoire des Roumains de la Dacie Trajane* quotes a chart of King Béla II of Hungary dated 1230, which mentions the Kneaz Vlad Sturdza and his sons John and Lirthuon

---

[1] *Boyard* means "warrior," and was the title of every member of the landowning nobility. *Voevod* means "war-leader," corresponding to the Western "duke," and was the title of the reigning princes of Moldavia, Walachia, and Transylvania. *Kneaz* and *kneazina* were titles belonging only to the Rumanian *uradel*—the descendants of the old rulers of the independent or semi-independent *kneazate* or *judete*.

3

in relation to some military services rendered and to the confirmation of certain land ownership.

The Sturdza name has been woven into the history of Moldavia—one of the two principalities that, with Walachia and later Transylvania, form Rumania of today—since the birth of that East European state. Kneaz Nan was the companion of the founder's grandson. Baliță, his grandson, fought the Turks in the fifteenth century under Ștefan the Great, the Moldavian hero. The Polish historian Orehovius mentions the Great Hetman John Sturdza Burgrave of Hotin coming to the rescue of the Polish troops at the head of the Moldavian cavalry: . . . *quorum principes erant Sturdza et Movilae* (". . . whose princes were Sturdza and Movilae"). Kneaz Barboi and his son were defeated by the Turks and the Tartars at the battle of Corn-Luncei. Barboi was impaled, his son hanged, on the spot where their widow and mother had erected, toward the end of the sixteenth century, the still-existing Barboi Monastery.

Mathew Sturdza, the son-in-law of the Voevod ("Reigning Prince") of Moldavia, Gheorghe-Stefan—who was known as the Wandering Prince and whom Louis XIII of France addressed as "mon bon frère"—waged all the wars of his father-in-law. His young children, pursued by the Turks, the eternal enemy, had to take refuge at the court of Hungarian Prince Michael Apaffy of Transylvania. Maurus Jokai, the Hungarian Walter Scott, records in one of his novels how Apaffy's wife, Anna Bornemisza, saved them at the last moment from being delivered to their persecutors by her husband. Anna-Maria Sturdza, one of those children, who later reigned in Walachia with her husband Gregory Ghyka, kept up a long friendship and an abundant correspondence with her neighbor and savior, of which a few letters were once in my possession. *Soror nobis Domina Vicina* ("to our sister the neighbor princess"), reads the mutual address.

It was her brother Elie Sturdza, last Voevod to be elected at that time by the Moldavian boyards according to the traditional national rules, who abdicated almost immediately and threatened to behead half of the nobility if they forced him to the throne once more, as they intended to do.

Alexander Sturdza, the great Chancellor of Prince Demetrius Cantemir, one of the most learned men of his time, was caught by the Turks. Also captured was Peter the Great of Russia and his ally Prince Cantemir, but all three escaped thanks to the cleverness of Czarina Catherine. Alexander lived for a long while as an exile in Russia. Another Alexander Sturdza, his great-grandson, was a favorite adviser of Czar Alexander I, Napoleon's contemporary. He earnestly warned the Czar against the secret societies and especially against the Illuminati of Adam Weishaupt. It was about him and his family that Joseph de Maistre had said: *La famille Stourdza est à elle seule toute une Academie* ("The Sturdza family is by itself a whole academy").

About two hundred years after Elie Sturdza's election and abdication, John-Alexander Sturdza was proclaimed Reigning Prince of Moldavia, the first to be elected again according to the traditional rules after a long period of foreign interferences. He was soon followed on the throne by Michel-Grigory Sturdza. Both were hard but excellent rulers who reestablished law and order in their troubled and agitated country.

Basil Sturdza, the Regent, was my grandfather. He belonged to a new generation of boyards who were influenced by new ideas born of the French Revolution and the Napoleonic wars, and in the mid-nineteenth century they were ready to renounce all their privileges without even being asked to do so. He was, with his brother-in-law Constantin Negri, the principal factor on the Moldavian side in the historical union of Moldavia and Walachia. This union gave birth to the Rumanian state. They declined with a smile and a thank-you the crown that was unanimously offered to them. Both served with unshakable fidelity the man on whose head this crown was finally placed: Prince Alexander John Cuza, later victim of a plot organized by the Liberal Party, whose members were already called "the Reds" in Rumania.

My grandmother on my father's side and my great-grandmother on my mother's side were both the sisters of Constantin Negri, the great patriot and idol of his generation, and one of the purest figures of Rumanian history. His other sisters were Princess Ruspoli di Pogio Suaza; Helen, who died young and beautiful but still lives in the immortal stanzas of her fiancé, the great Rumanian poet Vasile Alexandri; and Eugenia, Abbess of the Convent of Varatic, which was situated in one of the prettiest regions of the Moldavian Carpathians, and where we spent many summers of our childhood. The distance of about fifty miles was covered by four-in-hand carriage with a stop at Tescani, the country seat of my mother's sister, where we were generally joined by her children, our beloved cousins and playmates.

It was in Tescani that I saw one afternoon, stopping before the stairs of the white mansion, a team of four nimble ponies, masterfully driven by a young girl of fourteen. The girl was to become my wife ten years later. She had come with her mother for an afternoon visit from Comanești Court, the huge mountain estate of her grandfather, Prince Dimitri Ghyka-Comanești.

It was in the same nook of the Carpathians that my wife and I spent our childhood and adolescence. It was between Tescani and Comanești that we spent the months of our betrothal. It was in Comanești that we were married. We shared the same love of life in the open, of riding, hunting, and fishing. We spent part of our honeymoon camping in the mountains, and never lost an opportunity to spend weeks and even months under tents and before campfires, a taste shared later by our son.

At Varatic, Abbess Eugenia told us more than once the story of her ordination, which haunted our imagination when we were children. It happened that Eugenia's parents, having found that there were too many girls in the family, had brought Eugenia and her sister Helen, aged ten and twelve, to the Monastery of Varatic. Upon seeing their mother leaving them there, the two girls in their despair started running alongside the carriage, trying to climb into it. Their mother, after entreating them to go back, repeatedly slapped their grasping hands with her fan, until they had to abandon their attempt. This was the terrifying side of the story; but then came the redeeming part. At the death of their father, their brother Constantin, then studying in Paris, hastened to Varatic where his young sisters were still postulants, offered them a substantial part of their father's inheritance, and insisted that they return to the outside world. Helen yielded easily to her brother's request, but Eugenia preferred to stay in her peaceful seclusion. We were so spoiled, pampered and happy whenever we visited the nunnery of Aunt Eugenia that we were almost inclined to forgive those cruel slaps on the hands of the two little girls.

Regarding those long, horse-driven journeys, which were a normal practice at the time of my youth—there was a railway system plying between the principal cities, but the country houses of kin and friends, which were so often the object of our trips, were generally far enough from the nearest railway station to make a shortcut by road and carriage the better solution. Being invited to a relative's or a friend's house was a powerful incentive to go; but in the Rumania of my youth an invitation was not at all necessary. One arrived and was welcomed and stayed as long as one felt, until the time had come to call on others or to go home. There were some very well-known, impoverished gentle people whose most valuable property was four horses and a carriage, or if necessary a sledge. Their annual journeys around the Moldavian countryside were as regular as that of the Earth around the Sun. When those cyclic guests were also great hunters, as was the case with the person I have in mind, one was certain to see them coming at the right time for the fall and winter hunting seasons.

My mother, whose maiden name was Jora, was the daughter of my father's first cousin. Such weddings were not unusual in Moldavia in our family circle where marriages occurred almost always among the same dozen or so families. The Joras had been fighting men who enlivened our old chronicles with their adventures. The ford where one of them, pursued by some rival chieftain, was drowned with his horse when trying to cross the Prut, is still called Vadul Jorei, the Jora Ford. Fleeing in hot pursuit must also have been Antioche Jora who was caught half hanging from the drawbridge of the castle of Neamtz. The bridge had been hastily drawn up by a too cautious bridge guard. However, a seventeenth-century chronicler says that Jora escaped "with only a pike sting in his buttocks." Dafina Jora, who lived about the same time, was the wife of Voevod Dabija, Reigning Prince of Moldavia. Each time that hunting, the passion of my life, brought me to the four-centuries-old Monastery of Secul, I would read upon the portals of its church the names of the founders—the Great Vornic Nistor Ureche and his Kneazina, Maria Jora. In the monastery's archondaric (guest room) where I spent many nights, I was never able to hear, as others did, the suppressed breath of unfortunate Brother Ghidion, who had been bricked in, says the legend, by the cruel Nistor for having dared to look at the Kneazina with an unmonastic gaze.

Indeed, many a Banquo haunts the tragic chronicles of Moldavia. My childhood was spent in castles and courts where wary maids walked (or rather, half-ran) the corridors at night, crossing themselves, a candle in their hands. I have climbed expectantly the staircase of Ruginoasa, where the young and handsome Constantin still crawls, I was told, at the appointed hour, bloody and ashen-faced, to die at the feet of his mother, killed by the bullets of her guardsmen. I have looked from the proper rooms and in the proper moonlight for the hanged monk to come airily from the old elm tree in the park of Tescani and knock with his muddy boots at the windows of his persecutors. Also in Tescani as a child, clad in my nightgown, I had often peeped through the keyhole of my safely bolted door, hoping to see the little red man striding up and down the echoing corridor. I sat in the huge armchair in the servants' quarters in Dumbraveni, where the old housekeeper awoke from her slumber to feel and see, to her horror, a paw "like that of a goose" firmly gripping her ankles. I never saw, heard, or felt any such thing.

The Rumanian past was made by boyards and peasants, the continuators, by direct blood inheritance or by substitution—as has been the case with a certain part of the ruling class of foreign origin—of the old Dacian kingdom, which fought and sometimes defeated the Roman Empire more than two thousand years ago.

There has been also in the Rumanian past a middle class of traders and shopkeepers, mostly of foreign extraction. More recently, since the union of the principalities of Moldavia and Walachia in 1859, a bourgeois class with healthier relations to the Rumanian permanent background had started to form. It was well on its way for the greater community's benefit, but it was cruelly smitten after World War I by specifically Rumanian post-war factors—the fraudulently conducted agrarian expropriation, the catastrophic fall of the national currency, and the dropping of wages and salaries to the lowest level known in Europe—three basic factors which had transformed a country where everybody had known *la joie de vivre* into one where only the profiteers of the general misery and restricted political camarillas lived far removed from what was almost starvation.

The relations between boyards and peasants had been the subject of the wildest assertions, which were generally a planned part of the hostile publicity that had always been aimed at Rumania.

The origins of and the reasons for this circumspect but systematic anti-Rumanian propaganda were multiple. A substantial part of it can be traced to the propaganda of covetous or apprehensive neighbors. Hungary's hostility was understandable, as Rumania represented a real danger to her. But the hostility of Russia had only one explanation: We were an indigestible non-Slavic obstacle upon the road to Constantinople (Tzarigrad). However, the principal source and motives of the subtle and permanent anti-Rumanian campaign were of international origin and of ultra-political character.

For his good or for his harm, the Rumanian is strangely impenetrable. He juggles away, absorbs or capsulates the scanty foreign elements that have succeeded in entering his habitat. That goes for ideas, for groups or for individuals, and has nothing to do with racism or lack of hospitality. There is no country where the stranger is received more heartily into the house of the humblest or the wealthiest; and if you were to talk of racism to a Rumanian peasant, he would ask you what you meant. The would-be conquerors of the world have, from this point of view, found a much harder nut to crack in little Rumania than in gigantic Russia, and they have always hated us for that. Even now, when foreign ruling cliques and foreign ideologies have been superimposed by force on the Rumanian structure, the Rumanian people are farther from a Communist mental and spiritual conquest than the peoples of the Western "democracies."

The relations between the former ruling class and the peasants have also been the subject of a flow of incorrect information from an inside origin—from the Liberal Party and its publicists and pseudo historians, the foes of the Conservative Party. The leaders of the latter belonged generally to the ruling class of yore and succeeded in keeping, in the newly created circumstances, a wise, moderating, and incorruptible influence on Rumania's public affairs. The echo of this disparaging campaign of incorrect information vibrates today in many "twistorical" efforts, as for instance in those of Messrs. Hans Rogger and Eugen Weber in *The European Right*. "The Conservative party," Weber says, "loved

Rumania like a prey." [2] To reach this conclusion, the two learned professors of history had to deprive their readers of the benefit of a series of conclusive facts, and had to proceed very unscientifically by unsubstantiated affirmations. We will try to fill those gaps and rectify those errors, common also to other biased parties, in the very short space we have here for this task.

The landowners in Rumania were leaving the benefits of the cultivation of a certain percentage of their land to the landless peasants in exchange for a certain number of days of work. The land reform bill of 1860, voted by a Parliament the membership of which was comprised almost entirely of landowners (all of them boyards), declared the peasants full owners of the lot they were then cultivating as tenants, thereby liberating them from any obligation toward their former landlord. In the course of the sixty following years, and terminating with the big agrarian reform of 1917–1921, ninety-two percent of the arable land of the country was passed into the hands of the peasants. The landowners, the majority of whom were members of the old ruling class, with an important minority of the newly formed bourgeoisie, received as compensation one-third of one percent of the value of the expropriated property, thanks to a fraudulent application of the law of expropriation —a law that had been passed without any opposition from the landowners during World War I. This fraudulent application had of course as an objective the liquidation of the Conservative Party. One does not find any mention of this agrarian reform of 1917–1921 in the writings of the majority of the commentators of Rumanian modern social history; or if it is mentioned it is alluded to in such a way, as in *The European Right,* as to hide completely the importance of the distribution and the greatness of the sacrifice.

It is generally pretended that the contacts between landowners and peasants in Rumania were more remote than in any other European country. This time, the misinformers chose not to alter the truth but to effect its complete reversal. Rumania's feudality was a paternal feudality, the character of which seems to have escaped many superficial Western observers, who base their facetious impressions quite often on the old Rumanian custom of hand-kissing. Hand-kissing in Rumania's social life of yore had absolutely no servile significance. In my time girls and boys kissed the hand of their elders, men or women; in a former generation even the younger boys kissed the hand of their elder brothers. We kissed the hand of our old nurses and they kissed ours. It was an expression of affection. Our peasants kissed our hands as they would

[2] Eugen Weber, "Romania," in Hans Rogger and Eugen Weber, eds., *The European Right, a Historical Profile* (Berkeley and Los Angeles: University of California Press, 1965), p. 515.

have kissed that of their father or of their elder brother, of their protector, because we *were* their protectors. Nobody died of hunger, of cold or of misery in the villages of the boyards.

Help was always to be found at the court, as our homes were called, where the church of the village was also to be found. Every newly married couple received as a present a pair of oxen and a plough. Marriages and christenings, at which the boyards often played the part of godfather and godmother, created a real spiriutal relationship between the landlord and the villagers. It was in the home of one of her spiritual daughters that my wife found refuge with our grandson at the worst time of the Communist persecution. The friendly and familiar relations between the peasants and the boyards are borne out by Rumanian folklore. The *haiduc,* the beloved Robin Hood of our legends and of our history, is never represented as hostile to the boyards, but only to the *ciocoi,* the *parvenu* (newcomer), generally of foreign origin. Haiducs and boyards often in popular ballads, and sometimes in reality, coordinated their activities.

But it is not the ceremonial aspects of Rumania's social life which any serious historian should take into account when appraising the merits or the demerits of the old Rumanian ruling class; it is rather the fact, also never mentioned by our "twistorians," that toward the middle of the nineteenth century our grandfathers and great-grandfathers, doing what no other ruling class has ever done in any other country—and without being forced to it by any revolution, or even pressed to it by a rural population uncontaminated by any Illuminati penetration—gave up privileges freely enjoyed by them for centuries in the old code known as the *obiceiul pamantului* (custom of the soil) and accepted a modern and liberal constitution and civil laws so docilely copied from the Belgian Civil Code that they provided for indemnification of damages caused by rabbits, an animal that has never lived in our country.

It was the large land bequests of the ruling class exclusively that had built up for centuries the two big charitable foundations, Brancoveneasa and Sanct Spiridon. These foundations had covered Walachia and Moldavia with hospitals and infirmaries where the poor were cared for, absolutely free, by the best available practitioners. (Few Western "democracies," we note, have solved so thoroughly the problem of medical care for the poor.)

It is with veneration and pride that we remember those forefathers who loved their country and their people well enough to give up their prerogatives and power, not because they were asked to do so but because they believed it was the right thing to do. But seeing those who have replaced them in the national and political life of Rumania, especially after World War I, we wonder whether these same forefathers would do it again, and whether it was not the few old bearded, water-pipe smoking boyards, irreverently called "the ghosts" by their offspring, who were right in wanting to keep at least a part of the traditional establishment, which in that convulsed and embattled part of the continent had saved the Rumanian national life during the hardest and most involved circumstances.

Early Posts and World War I

Prince Alexander John Cuza, who had signed the historic Act of Appropriation (1859–1861) involving the Rumanian peasantry, was dethroned by a conspiracy of a small group of officers, affiliated with the Liberal Party, who surprised him in his palace on the night of February 11, 1866. Prince Carol Hohenzollern, who followed him on the Rumanian throne, did not, as he was asked by the rest of the army, punish the conspirators. As a consequence, sixty of the most distinguished officers resigned immediately. In our family such was the loyalty we held to the memory of the dethroned prince that almost half a century after that unpunished act of treason, my brother John and I did not choose a military career, for which we felt a great inclination, because we found also that the stain on our flag had not yet been washed away; we later regretted very much this romantic attitude.

I was brought up in a home where memories and events of the times gone by were told and retold to the children, often by very old relatives who had witnessed some of them, or had known their protagonists when they were themselves children. We listened with the eagerness and fascination of our age and *this* explains in part, no doubt, the deep interest I have felt since my early years in all matters concerning the life, the vicissitudes and the dreams of my nation, and my growing desire in later years to play my part in this life and to help those dreams come true.

But there was in me a strong inhibition towards the fulfillment of such ambitions: It was the repulsion I felt for all the political and electoral comedy through which one had to pass in my country, as in so many "democracies" of our era, in order to be able to exercise any influence on public affairs. It was this inner conflict that made me choose the diplomatic career as a final orientation for my activities.

My career almost ended without laurels before it really began. In

January 1914, I was a young attaché at the Rumanian Legation in Durazzo, then the capital of the new Albanian State. I had chosen Albania for my first post because of its medieval character and because of the presence of a Rumanian population in its southern provinces. Living in Albania at that time was like living in the fifteenth century, with all the enchantment of an incomparable tradition of chivalry, of courage, and of unshakable fidelity for the recognized leader.

I could not relate more concisely the reprehensible facts that brought me to the threshold of a well-deserved and inglorious dismissal than by quoting the French newspaper *Le Temps*:

> The troops of Prenk Pacha Bib Doda under the command of the Rumanian Military Attaché, Colonel Sturdza, have stormed the Ishmi castle after a fierce battle and are marching toward Durazzo.

It was not Colonel Alexander Sturdza, who at that time was the Rumanian Military Attaché in Berlin, but the Reserve-Lieutenant and Attaché to the Rumanian Legation in Durazzo, Michel Sturdza, who at the head of about three thousand warriors, Mirdites and Malissores, was trying with variable results, to break the siege of Durazzo, which was under attack by various tribes of insurgents.

The truth is that, completely enraptured by Albanian magic and lore, I had abandoned to Mr. Burghelea, my chief, the premises of our Legation and attached myself to the corps of hard-working, hard-fighting Dutch officers who were in charge of the Albanian militia, and who were facing a foreign invasion in the south and an insurrection in the north. Colonel Thompson, the defender of Durazzo, had been killed in a recent battle, and Major Kronne, who was asked to take his place, had left me in command of his troops, with whom I was trying to do my best.

The trouble was that neither Mr. Burghelea nor Mr. Porumbaru, our Minister of Foreign Affairs, had any real appreciation of my military initiatives. After playing truant for about five months I finally felt obliged to part with my gallant companions and to answer a last and comminatory summons from the Ministry of Foreign Affairs. Back in Bucharest, where normally a well-deserved punishment would have awaited me, I was saved by the important events of the moment—the assassination of Archduke Francis Ferdinand in Sarajevo (June 28, 1914) and the beginning of World War I, which gave good Mr. Porumbaru the opportunity to speak Latin: *De minimis non curat pretor* ("the praetor doesn't worry about small things"), and to appoint me to the cipher department of his Cabinet.

Between the beginning of the war and Rumania's entering it—and with some interruption of my diplomatic activities by various periods

of military service with my unit, the first squadron of mounted artillery
—I was moved from our central administration to our Legation in
Athens, and ultimately to our Legation in Bern. It was there that my
wife and I learned that Rumania had declared war on the Austro-Hungarian Empire. A few weeks earlier I had published my book *La Roumanie Peut-elle Combattre sur deux Fronts? (Can Rumania Fight on
Two Fronts?)*, which recommended the evacuation of a part of our territory and the erection of a strong line of defense from the Carpathians
to the Danube that would cover Bucharest and the oil-producing regions.[1] After the declaration of war, I left for Rumania without delay,
leaving my wife in Bern, who followed me a short time later, and our
newborn son, whom we left with an aunt of ours in Nice. We were not
to see him again until two years later.

The battle of Bucharest, in which I was wounded, could have been
won, perhaps even without the line of modern fortifications I had been
suggesting, but for the treacherous immobility of the Russian troops
that were supposed to attack on our left flank. In my book *Avec l'Armée
Roumaine*[2] dedicated "To the heroic memory of my brother, Lieutenant
John Sturdza, and of my brother-in-law, Lieutenant Alexis Mavrocordatu, killed by our allies the Russians," I have already recorded my war
experiences. I will mention here, therefore, only one significant episode
because of its direct connection with one of the principal themes of this
book, and also three incidents of a more personal character, the details
of which became known to me after the mentioned publication.

In the summer of 1917 we were aligned along the Siret with the Second Cavalry Division; I was in command of a section of armored cars.
We were expecting at any moment the order to attack. Our troops,
finally armed in terms of modern warfare, had been victorious at Mărăşti
and Mărăşeşti. Their morale on this eve of a meticulously prepared offensive was higher than ever. A few moments before the impatiently
awaited signal, the Russian troops started abandoning their positions.
The order of retreat had been unexpectedly given by Alexander Kerensky, the man who was busy at that time making Russia safe for Communism. All our efforts, all our preparations, were brought to nil and
soon we were forced to defend ourselves against our former allies, the
soldiers of the glorious Imperial Russian Army, transformed into a
drunken and incontrollable rabble.

Real life is sometimes stranger in its surprises than anything the most
fanciful writer could imagine. Toward the end of World War I my

[1] The Central Powers included, in addition to Germany and Austria-Hungary, both
Bulgaria and Turkey. Rumania, a member of the Allied Powers, had to fight Austria-
Hungary on the northwest and Bulgaria on the south.

[2] Michel Sturdza, *Avec l'Armée Roumaine*, preface by G. Lacour-Gayet of the French
Academy (Paris: Hachette, 1918).

elder brother Constantin was located with his cavalry squadron close to
the demarcation line of the cease-fire agreement, which had been signed
shortly before with the German and Austrian armies. The Austrian general in command on the other side of the line had complained to my
brother's chief, General Schina, that during that night a troop of unknown origin had attacked one of his squadrons, killed some of its soldiers and stole all the horses. After that, said the Austrian general, these
troops passed the line of demarcation and rode into Rumanian territory. The Austrian general asked for explanations and appropriate
measures. General Schina sent my brother to reconnoiter with his squadron. Nearing the border of the village in question, Constantin dismounted, posted his men, and sent one of his sergeants to offer a halfway
meeting place to the officer in command of the mysterious troop. The
offer was accepted, and the officer who cantered to the rendezvous upon
one of those Austrian horses was our brother John.

John, impatient, had taken service in the Russian Army one year before Rumania entered the war. He had fought on both the European
and Asiatic fronts, and when the Imperial Army started disintegrating,
thanks to Kerensky's activities, John, as did many of his comrades, along
with the loyal elements of his unit, formed a troop of volunteers with
which he intended to join one of the generals of the Nationalist Russian
resistance. My brother Constantin urged him to stay with our troops.
General Schina insisted also and very understandingly offered John a
command in his division. John could not bring himself, however, to
leave his companions. He crossed the Dniester next day not far from
Hotin, where four hundred years earlier another John Sturdza had
battled with other heathens. John was killed two days later in an am-
bush and his troops were nearly exterminated by much superior Bolshevik forces. Some survivors related the happenings to Constantin.

It was by the same enemy that my brother-in-law, Lieutenant Alexis
Mavrocordatu, was attacked at night in the village in which he was
camped with his platoon. The fight lasted a few hours, and the troops
that came too late to the rescue were Austrian soldiers commanded by
Captain von Hambar, the brother-in-law of the Rumanian Colonel
Diculescu-Botez, who, as commander of Alexis' regiment, was killed in
the first days of the war. Hambar told us much later in Vienna that
Alexis and his men had fired their last rounds before falling on the
spot where they were later buried.

In our childhood we discriminated among our uncles according to
the game that came out of their woods during the autumn and winter
drives. There were the wolf-uncles and the bear-uncles. Our beloved
uncle George Donici was a bear-uncle. I described in *Avec l'Armée
Roumaine* the death of that seventy-two-year-old boyard at the head of

one of the last cavalry charges of modern warfare. One of the German officers who was looking at the body of the old warrior exclaimed in Rumanian to Captain Filiti, lying wounded among his fallen soldiers: "But this is George Donici of Valea Seaca!" In civilian life this officer was one of the German technicians who were taking care of the woods in our province.

The German colonel in command of the regiment with which the squadron of Captain Filiti had collided, in a gesture of military courtesy completely forgotten today, sent over the lines to my family in Bucharest the row of medals won by George Donici in the 1877 war against the Turks, during which he served in my father's squadron. How different from the Nürnberg travesty and from General Eisenhower's opinion, expressed in his memoirs, that chivalry toward the adversary is a deplorable medieval inheritance from the time when soldiers were paid mercenaries and not patriots.

Toward the end of the hostilities with the troops of the Central Powers, I passed through Petrograd at the moment General Lavr Kornilov appeared at the gates of the city. He was feverishly expected because he represented the only possibility of saving Russia's capital from the repeated murderous attempts of Lenin and Trotsky's ignoble rabble. Kerensky forbade the general to enter the city, arrested him, and thus removed the last obstacle in the way of the Bolshevik Revolution—a foreign revolution, prepared and directed from those dark recesses in New York and other Western cities where Mob and Money collaborate in their sinister schemes.

CHAPTER
III

The Beast and Its Friends

The last days of the war found me in Italy where I was organizing a volunteer Rumanian Legion comprised of the prisoners of Rumanian nationality taken from the Austrians by the Italian Army. Officers and soldiers were enlisting with the greatest enthusiasm. The difficulties I encountered came from the intrigues of the Rumanian political cliques in Paris. Each group had a favorite general in mind for the command of a combat unit which they had helped me in no way to organize.

It was at this time that I had my first experience with what I have come to call "convenient deaths." I had struck up a great friendship with General Milan R. Štefánik, a Slovak, and therefore a man extremely wary concerning Russia's intentions towards his homeland. Besides, he was an inveterate anti-Communist. In the team of three—Tomáš G. Masaryk, Štefánik, Dr. Eduard Beneš—militating for an independent Czecho-Slovak State, he was number two in importance, representing the conservative element, and was the advocate of Slovak semi-autonomy within the Czecho-Slovak State.[1]

[1] In 1916 the Czecho-Slovak National Council was established in Paris with Tomáš Masaryk as President, Josef Dürich and Milan Štefánik as Vice Presidents, and Eduard Beneš as Secretary General. Dürich was soon expelled from the Council for his pan-Slavism. Masaryk served as President of the Czecho-Slovak Republic from 1918 to 1935. Beneš was Foreign Minister from 1918 to 1935 and President from 1935 to 1938 and again from 1945 to 1948. The anti-Communist Štefánik was an astronomer who, after coming to France in 1905, became a French citizen and served in the French Air Force on the Western Front and in the Balkans. He supported a Swiss-type organization for the multinational Czecho-Slovak State as stipulated in the Pittsburgh Agreement of May 30, 1918: "Slovakia shall have its own administration, its diet [parliament], its own courts, and Slovak shall be the official language in the schools, state services, and public life." With Štefánik, and not Beneš, guiding the foreign affairs of Czecho-Slovakia, the history of that country would have taken a different turn—one for the greatest benefit of Europe and the cause of peace. After Štefánik's death, the Masaryk-Beneš establishment totally ignored the Pittsburgh Agreement; and the defenders of Slovak interests were thrown into prison, where some of them lingered for eight years.

His prestige was enormous, as he had been the organizer of the Czecho-Slovak volunteers, had fought with them on all the various fronts, had been wounded several times, and besides had one of the most alert thinking apparatuses one could hope, or fear, to come across. I had seen Beneš in the waiting room of Vittorio Orlando, the Italian Prime Minister, holding Štefánik's brief-case—indicating Beneš's subservient position.

On May 4, 1919, General Štefánik left Udine, Italy, by airplane for Prague, the capital of the country he had done so much to put on the map. He never reached it. He was shot down over Bratislava, Slovakia, by an anti-aircraft battery that had absolutely no business being there. It was thus that Beneš replaced Štefánik not only in the hierarchy of Czecho-Slovak statesmen, but in that of the few personalities who were to play a decisive part in forging the tragic destiny of our present world. I thought of foul play at the time of Štefánik's death, and my suspicions were fully confirmed, years later, when Grand Duchess Olga, who was living in Slovakia as a refugee from Bolshevik terror, told me there had never been any hostilities around the area of Bratislava and that nobody understood the reason for that sudden and fateful burst of shrapnel.

In Petrograd I had had the opportunity to see the first signs of the existence of certain Anonymous Forces; forces which were the organizers, the protectors, and the bankers of the host of foreign agitators who —with the help of a few thousand workers from the Putilof factories (rapidly and thoroughly organized under the protection of Kerensky's imposture)—had undertaken the conquest of the Russian Empire. I had not failed to observe also that it was very likely those same forces that had prevented United States participation in the hostilities as long as this participation would have benefited Imperial Russia. A short time after the signing of the Treaty of Versailles, two series of events removed my last doubts concerning the existence of an anonymous, patient, omnipotent influence to which the Russian people owed their present troubles and for which the conquest of Russia was only a beginning—a prelude to more extended conquests. Indeed, today these conquests encompass more than one-half of the surface of this planet and include more than one-third of its population.

Up to the beginning of the last century, history was very difficult to ignore, or to forget. As paradoxical as it may seem, it was the multiplication of the means of information that made the neglect of history possible. When thousands of newspapers and magazines, when the radio broadcasts, the tribunes, the chairs and the pulpits, seemingly at a sudden and mysterious command, unanimously stop talking about a certain event, *it is as if this event did not happen,* however notorious, however significant it may have been.

That is why I do not think it superfluous to recall the way those Anonymous Forces provoked the defeat of the Russian nationalist armies, and the effort they made to perpetuate the Communist regime of Béla Kun in Hungary, a regime equally as bestial and demented as Lenin's in Russia.

Mr. Joseph Noulens, the French Ambassador to Moscow, has told us in his book *Mon Ambassade en Russie Soviétique, 1917–1919* that, alarmed by the growing sympathy shown by President Woodrow Wilson for the Bolshevik gang, which at that moment was being pressed on every side by the Nationalist Russian troops, Premier Georges Clemenceau of France and Prime Minister David Lloyd George of England asked President Wilson whether or not he intended to continue helping the Nationalist forces in association with France and Great Britain. The President answered that his decision would depend upon Masaryk, whose advice Wilson always took, he told them, in matters concerning Russian affairs. The President's final decision was to allot not a dollar, not a rifle, not a round more, for Nationalist Russia.

Mr. Noulens also states that the Trotsky-Lenin enterprise was on the eve of a complete collapse and was saved by the new attitude adopted suddenly by President Wilson:

> President Wilson secured the survival of the Communist regime. The Bolsheviks themselves were convinced that the experiment of Communism had reached its end; they were more surprised than anbody else at the unexpected turn of events.

One can understand perhaps forgetting even such an important fact as the President of the United States saving the Bolshevik horror from imminent destruction; but how could man's memory have forgotten the unbelievable treason of French General Maurice Janin and of his Czecho-Slovak accomplices, an unmistakable counterpart in the decision of Wilson and Masaryk.

General Janin was the man picked by the French Government (or by the hidden hands behind it) and by Mr. Masaryk to command all the Allied forces (including the Czecho-Slovak Legion) that were fighting in Siberia under the orders of Admiral Aleksandr Kolchak, the Supreme Ruler of Russia and leader of the anti-Bolshevik forces. The Admiral's divisions were engaged in fierce fighting with the Bolshevik forces, which had been liberated by Wilson and Masaryk's decision.

At six p.m. on January 14, 1920, two officers of the Czecho-Slovak Legion, acting under orders from General Janin, kidnapped Admiral

Kolchak and his staff (his Government) in the Glaskov railway station at Irkutsk and handed them over to the Bolshevik Political Centre in exchange for one-third of the 650 million rubles in gold and platinum bullion that formed the Imperial Russian Treasury which Kolchak was transporting toward Vladivostok. On February 2 the Bolsheviks executed Kolchak and his Prime Minister, Victor Pepeliaev. General Janin was never court-martialled, arraigned, or even blamed.

The Czecho-Slovak share of the bullion, the price of blood and treason, became the basis of the Czecho-Slovak Treasury—a strange foundation, along with Štefánik's assassination, for Dr. Beneš's ill-fated state. For the nauseating details of this horrible episode, which was at that time unique in the military history of civilized countries, we refer the reader to Winston Churchill's *The World Crisis, V, The Aftermath*.[2]

The continuation of Béla Kun's Government in Hungary in 1919 would have meant—besides the mortal danger it represented for Rumania caught in a Communist claw—the end of heroic Poland (then in the pangs of her rebirth); the spreading of Communism in Germany and Italy, where subversive forces were already in motion; and perhaps the end of Europe—a Europe that had seen traitors like Captain Jacques Sadoul and André Marty triumphantly elected to the French Parliament by millions of voters;[3] and the Labour Party in Great Britain identify itself entirely with Red Russia's interests.

Nevertheless, the Allied and Associated Powers tried everything in order to save Béla Kun's regime, starting with a long and friendly visit by Jan Christiaan Smuts of the Union of South Africa to the Communist tyrant's headquarters. The advance of the Rumanian troops in Hungary against Kun's regime took place *in spite* of the violent opposition of the Western Powers. And if it was Europe and not Béla Kun's regime that was saved, this was only due to the high sense of responsibility of Rumania's King Ferdinand and of his Government, and to the fortitude of the Rumanian soldiers.

We quote the former Ambassador to the Court of St. James, Count de Saint-Aulaire, in his book *Genève contre la Paix*:

> All the reprobation of the Allies' Supreme Council was not for the Hungarian Bolsheviks but for the Rumanian soldiers who saved Western Civi-

[2] General Draža Mihailovich, the Yugoslav hero of World War II, was betrayed under almost identical circumstances into the hands of the Communist Tito. This time Great Britain was the responsible party.

[3] Sadoul was a Captain in the French Army, and Marty was a Seaman-Machinist in the French Navy. Objecting to orders received to support the anti-Bolshevik White Russians, they instigated the 1919 mutiny of French forces operating in the Black Sea area. Upon their return to France, instead of being shot, they received only token punishment. They were subsequently elected to the French Parliament on the Communist ticket.

lization, despite itself, by cleaning this focus of bloody anarchy in that part of Europe.

In my country, public opinion and many of the principal leaders of the political parties were well aware at that time of the continuous menace represented by the Soviet proximity. There were some of them however, belonging mostly to the National Peasant group, who could not hide their sympathies for the Kremlin gang of murderers. For instance, Mr. Bujor, Rector of the University of Iași, declared in the Rumanian Parliament without much originality: "A new light comes from the East." In conformity with this new illumination, he tried to suppress the traditional religious ceremony and the hoisting of the flag at the beginning of the academic year, provoking a violent reaction among the students led by the young Corneliu Zelea-Codreanu, who later was to become the symbol, the hero, and the martyr of the fight against the international conspiracy in Rumania. He was the true representative of the popular instinct, which in our country often has been more perceptive and independent than that of the majority of the political leaders.

Few, indeed, were those leaders who understood the real meaning of the latest international events—Mr. William C. Bullitt's *first* mission to Moscow (1919), the Western-Soviet negotiations in Genoa (1922), and the anti-Polish declarations of the Czecho-Slovak statesmen—and who realized that among the Western leaders, besides those who continued to believe in the necessity of crushing the Bolshevik monster in its cradle, an opposed force and influences were growing from day to day. This force and these influences friendly to the Soviets did not content themselves with recognizing the existence of the new Russia, but dreamed of her incorporation into a belligerent system of European alliances, similar to that which faced the Central European Powers at the beginning of World War I. This system, absolutely foreign to Rumanian interests, endangered our very existence. Its advocates in France, our principal ally, extended from certain right-wing groups represented by Mr. Jean Barthou, through Mr. Édouard Herriot, Mr. Paul Reynaud, and Mr. Léon Blum on the extreme left.

The continuous progress in Western political life of the pro-Soviet doctrine already had made me reach, at that time, the conclusion that the moment would soon come when our existence as an independent state could not further be ensured by our Western alliances, but only through a political and military association with Poland and Hungary, directly menaced, as we were, by the Communist monster. It was this conviction that made me abandon the diplomatic service, for a few months in 1920, and take over a governorship in Transylvania, where I believed that more suave and tactful methods could win us the friendship of the Hungarian population. Following the same line of thought I arranged later to be sent to Budapest as First Secretary to our Legation there.

After the collapse of the Austrian Empire and the subsequent Rumanian annexation of Transylvania (which had been for a long while a part of the Kingdom of Hungary) several Hungarian statesmen (among them Count Pál Teleki and Count István Bethlen) thought of offering the Hungarian crown to King Ferdinand of Rumania. Count Miklós Banfy, whom I had known during my administrative activity in Transylvania, and whom I met again in Budapest when he was Hungarian Minister of Foreign Affairs, also supported the creation of such a new Danubian state. His reasons were however of a much deeper and more historical character than those of Bethlen and Teleki, who probably thought mainly of the possibility of Hungarian predominance in a Rumanian-Hungarian federation.

Count Banfy was thoroughly convinced that because of the chaotic situation in which the disappearance of the two Germanic empires had left this part of Europe, and because of the apparition on its menaced borders of the formidable and pestilential entity whose name was Soviet Russia, only an organic union of our two countries, a merger of their political and military means, could in the long run ensure their survival.

When I left Budapest I hastened to communicate to King Ferdinand, and to Queen Marie, Count Banfy's views on the future and destiny of our two countries. Both the King and Queen had been very receptive to the proposals of Bethlen and Teleki, which were energetically opposed, however, by the chiefs of our various political parties, who worried only for their electoral problems.

I do not know if Count Banfy has passed away in some Communist prison or some Allied concentration camp, but if he is, as I hope, still free and alive, I am certain that he wonders, as I do, if the destiny not only of our two countries but of Europe would not have been a happier one if his dreams, which were also mine, had come true.

The insistence of the French and Czecho-Slovak political circles, which considered the existence of Soviet Russia as a happy complement in the political life of Europe, had brought the Rumanian Government to agree reluctantly to negotiate with Soviet Russia the possibility of establishing diplomatic relations between the two countries. The negotiations took place in Vienna in 1925 where I had been transferred to our Legation as Counsellor.

The most promising assurances had been given us by the French and Czecho-Slovak middlemen. Our delegation recognized too late the trap into which it had fallen. The Soviets had asked for those negotiations only in order to transform them into a vociferous propaganda platform for their insolent pretensions to a part of our territory.

Little did I know at the time that I would myself have to face, as Rumanian Representative, a similar Soviet attempt, but this time with my own Minister of Foreign Affairs as my adversary and as the Kremlin's associate.

I arrived in Washington at the roaring end of the Roaring Twenties —the Washington of yore where the streets were safe by day and night for women and children, where everybody knew everybody, where whiskey was served at the Mayflower Hotel in innocent looking tea cups, where there were always enough diplomats at a reception to justify a flow of Veuve Cliquot, where the Misses Patterson, who had never consented to climb into an automobile, ruled the social set from the height of their brougham seats and regularly stole all the White House guests the night of the annual diplomatic reception.

I arrived in the capital of the United States in time to participate, with a delirious crowd, in the enthusiastic reception granted to the gallant Lindbergh. I signed with a flourish and a disrespectful smile the ineffable Kellogg-Briand Pact.[4] Later on, as Rumanian Chargé d'Affaires, I helped float for my country a loan of some three hundred million dollars on the New York market.[5] This gave me the opportunity to learn a lot about that kind of operation. Among other things, I realized with amazement that before a single dollar could enter the Rumanian treasury we had to leave in the hands of middlemen and French bankers about thirty-three percent of the loan's nominal value.

It was in Rock Creek Park, in Washington, that I had my first, but not my last, experience with American helpfulness of the old pioneer brand. I somehow had a breakdown with my new Nash in the middle of the creek and could do no less, nor more, than wade in water up to my knees, lift the hood, and look desperately at all the machinery. Seeing

[4] The Kellog-Briand Pact was signed in Paris on August 27, 1928, and entered into force on July 24, 1929. Sixty-two nations, including the Soviet Union, ratified this Pact which outlawed war "as an instrument of national policy." To say that it had the slightest influence upon the policy of the signatories or that it promoted the cause of peace in the most imperceptible way would be exaggerating.

[5] From several sides I had been advised that Mr. Louis Marshall's cooperation could be a decisive influence for our project. Mr. Marshall was the lawyer of important New York banks including, if I remember well, the Otto Kahn, the Warburg, the Jacob Schiff, and Kuhn-Loeb institutions. I called on Mr. Marshall, and although our meeting started in a rather agitated atmosphere, it ended very peacefully. When taking leave of the famous lawyer, he showed me that part of New York that could be seen through his Wall Street window, and told me: "Look what we can do for a country we love, *in Russia we have shown the world what we can do to a country we hate.*" Mr. Marshall felt obliged to repeat this statement to our Financial Attaché, Mr. Gheorghe Boncescu.

my distress, a passing motorist stopped, alighted from his automobile, and after a moment's hesitation, jumped into the cold water with no regard for footgear and trousers, and quickly helped me out of my quandary.

We availed ourselves, my wife and I, of the opportunity of my first leave of absence on the North American continent, to go for a five-week hunting trip in northern Alberta, Canada. Broad then were the ranges, generous the bag limit, and game was everywhere. We came back with six excellent head of bighorn, wild goats, and moose. We hiked along the Smoky River, with our two Indian guides, our Canadian cook and our twenty-eight packhorses, to the Eagle Nest Pass—a spot of unforgettable grandeur—without meeting any other hunting party or even any other human being; a situation that would be hard to duplicate in the crowded hunting grounds of today.

Back in Washington, it was on our early morning cavalcades in Rock Creek Park that we satisfied our enjoyment of life in the open and our love of streams and woods. Idaho Senator William E. Borah, on a sturdy palomino, was almost always an earlier rider than we.

It was from the United States that the tailor Trotsky and his cosmopolitan companions set out for the conquest of the world, well-financed by New York bankers with that indispensable lubricant for making wars and revolutions. And it was an American President who by his attitude and his decisions saved the Soviet regime from a gory still-birth. Yet the United States waited until 1933 to recognize this regime. While in Washington I had the opportunity to find out that this contradiction in the United States policy toward the Soviets was only an apparent one.

Indeed, it was about that time that Washington made the fateful decision to send technicians, engineers, and workers by the hundreds to help the Soviet Union build up her heavy and semi-heavy industry on the most modern footing and with the most modern material; this material was sold of course by American industrialists. The argument invoked was that of the financial benefit not only to those big industrialists but also to the hundreds of technicians and workers who were sent into Soviet territory.

Sallust once said: "For the vile metal for which the plebeian was as avid as the rich speculators, the greatness of Rome collapsed, her blood was defiled, her glory and her honor were lost."

The European Right and Professor Weber's Special Assignment

To provide the reader with a better understanding of Rumania's position between World War I and World War II, and to enable him to understand not only what the Rumanian Legionary Movement was but also what part that band of patriots played in Rumanian affairs during that trying period, a short examination of selections from a book entitled *The European Right, a Historical Profile*, seems now to be in order. Specifically I will discuss those parts of the book that deal with Rumania in general and the Legionary Movement in particular.

Edited by Professors Hans Rogger and Eugen Weber of the University of California, *The European Right* attempts to examine in ten essays the Rightist movement in England and on the Continent. Mr. Weber wrote the "Introduction" and the essay entitled "Romania." Mr. Rogger contributed a piece called "Afterthoughts" in which he tried to explain what he and Weber mean by "Right":

> "Without wishing to impose our views and preferences," we wrote to our contributors, "we have yet had to make certain assumptions in order to delimit the meaning of 'Right' for present purposes, and hope that these assumptions will be shared. They are that the Right is a phenomenon of fairly recent history (i.e., the last sixty to eighty years), that it is characteristically a postliberal (or postdemocratic) and postindustrial phenomenon, that as a reaction to the liberalization of political life it was more violent or radical than the conservative wish to preserve privilege or the status quo, and that it implied a readiness to conduct politics with some or all the techniques and appeals introduced by the mass parties of democracy and the Left, as well as some novel ones." [1]

[1] Hans Rogger, "Afterthoughts," in Hans Rogger and Eugen Weber, eds., *The European Right, a Historical Profile* (Berkeley and Los Angeles: University of California Press, 1965), p. 575.

Actually the Rightist movements studied in *The European Right* by ten university professors under the sponsorship of the University of California and other educational institutions all have one trait in common: They were first of all anti-Communist movements. There is no doubt that if Communism had not conquered Russia, if Moscow had not suddenly become the spiritual and temporal Mecca of a monstrous faith and of a subtle, poisonous, insinuating and conquering power, those movements either would not have been born, or would have followed quite another evolution; provoking less virulent hostilities, they would have been themselves less violent in their expressions and reactions.

Anti-Communism being the common characteristic of the movements under study, it would have been, we think, logically and intellectually necessary for this characteristic to be emphatically present in their definition. However, by carefully chosen timing—"sixty" or "eighty" years ago, in 1965—the editors and contributors have at the onset excluded not only from their definition, but also from their whole learned investigation, multiple, fundamental, and essential elements of truth. For instance:

1. The post-World War I Rightist movements have been, first of all, a spontaneous reaction against the Communist danger in all its forms and disguises.

2. Those movements owed their popularity, and sometimes their existence, to the inability of the established powers, on both domestic and foreign policy fields, to meet the Communist danger with appropriate force and decision.

3. It was the strange and unexplained collusion between those established powers and the Communist world—on both domestic and foreign fields—that brought the major clashes between those powers and the young nationalist movements, and also brought the final clash between non-Communist countries.

4. The solidarity between the young nationalist movements of various European countries was based principally on their identical reaction to the Communist danger and to this unexplainable collusion, rather than on any absolute sameness of doctrines.

Without taking those elements of truth into consideration even an unbiased investigator could only have failed in his research. Take for instance Corneliu Codreanu's declaration of November 30, 1937: "Forty-eight hours after the victory of the Legionary Movement, Rumania will be allied to Rome and Berlin, thus entering the line of its historical world-mission: the defense of the Cross, of Christian Culture and Civilization." The conclusion of the two connected pacts of military assistance between France and the Soviet Union and Czecho-Slovakia had occurred a year before Codreanu made that statement. These new instruments of European diplomacy, and the obvious acquiescence of the established powers in Rumania to them, had suspended the Damoclean sword of a Soviet invasion over the country's very existence. Against such an invasion Rumania had no allies other than those governments and nations for which Soviet Russia and Communism were also the preeminent danger and recognized enemies.

It has been objected that it was almost hypocritical for Codreanu to invoke the defense of Christian Civilization in order to explain his readiness to conclude an alliance with National Socialist Germany and Fascist Italy. For Codreanu, Christian Civilization and Western Civilization were one and the same thing; the thing that Germany and Italy had helped Franco in Spain to defend and save against the allied forces of the Communist parties of all European countries, and against the coalition of the Soviet Union and the Western Powers, the United States included.

A definition of the Legionary Movement could not limit itself, of course, to the Movement's anti-Communist character. But reflection will show that the source of most of its other traits is to be found also, if less visibly, in the sudden emergence of the Communist atrocity in the political, social, economic, and spiritual structure of Europe and of the world; an emergence which created totally novel problems and situations or greatly accentuated some of those already existing. The profound damage and lasting convulsions which afflicted this structure after World War I were not to be attributed principally to the unavoidable consequences of all wars. We had the instances of the Napoleonic wars and of the war of 1870 between France and Germany quickly followed by long periods of prosperity and tranquility for all the countries concerned. The source of the economic damage and social disorganization of the Continent was the appearance on its Eastern borders of a menace the equivalent of which it had never known before.

Among those damages one of the most destructive was the deterioration, sometimes to almost nothingness, of the worth of so many European currencies. If gold was fleeing from Europe, it was for fear of contagious and conquering Communism. For the countries involved the disappearance of the metal coverings meant inflation, paralysis of the economic exchanges, insolvency of governments, reduction of the salaries of state employees to an unbearable minimum, rampant speculation and profiteering, unavoidable corruption of moral standards, fateful devaluation of social and patriotic values. But for Rumania it meant also something else: the disappearance of the Conservative Party, an historical element of wisdom and morality. This fact radically influenced her political and social life, a circumstance to which we have already alluded in a preceding chapter.

The agrarian reform that had been presented to the Rumanian Parliament during World War I by a coalition government of Liberals and Conservatives provided a reasonable indemnification for the landlords based on the minimum worth of comparable arable land in the last ten years. The enforcement of this reform between 1917 and 1921 brought ninety-two percent of Rumania's arable land in the hands of the peasants. But at that time devaluation of our currency had brought it to one-fiftieth of its nominal gold value. Moreover, the landlords were not paid in this already almost worthless *lei,* but in bonds which quickly fell to one-third of their nominal value in worthless *lei.* This reduced the landlords' indemnification to $\frac{1}{150}$ of that intended by the original legislator. This fraudulent implementation of the agrarian reform was carried out enthusiastically by the Liberal Party and by the newly hatched political groups, the Populist and the National Peasant groups, eager and happy to get rid of a rival and a censor.

This enormous fraud ruined indeed the very base and *raison d'être* of the Conservative Party: the complete independence of the material means of its leaders from political pursuits and from other worries than those for the public welfare and for the security and greatness of the fatherland. It was, therefore, quite another Rumania that Corneliu Codreanu and his young companions had to deal with than that of a few years before. The sacrifice of hundreds of them would not have been necessary in order to prevent servile governments from promising free passage over our territory to Soviet armies, or in order to make a quick end to the Carol-Lupescu regime of corruption and iniquity, if men like Lascar Catargi, Petru Carp, Titus Maiorescu, Gheorghe Cantacuzene, Ion and Jack Lahovary, Nicholae Filipescu, and Delavrancea had still been at the head of a powerful party with deep roots in the country's past and a strong and natural attachment to the rural classes.

It is interesting to remark that it was Petru Carp, one of the most distinguished leaders of the Conservative Party, who, in an almost prophetic vision, foretold the emergence of a new movement under the leadership of a young chief, that would not be a copy but a continuation, adapted to changed situations, of the Conservative Party. Corneliu Codreanu's Movement would have been just that if fate had permitted it to be born in less tragic circumstances.

By deciding to start their investigation of the postwar nationalist phenomenon at a date prior to the end of the war and the birth of Bolshevik Russia, the learned editors of *The European Right* decided by the same token to ignore the difference which was strikingly and painfully obvious to any person who had known both the pre-war and the post-war Rumania. This permits Mr. Weber to vent his antipathy, or perhaps his hate, toward Rumania with a greater semblance of veracity.

> In the meantime, it should be observed, Codreanu's mysticism did not exclude a very hard-headed appreciation of the situation. *From a mendacious people* he demanded honesty, *in a lazy country* he demanded work, *in an easy-going society* he demanded self-discipline and persistence, *from an exuberant and windy folk* he demanded brevity and self-control.[2]

It is from the same position of hostility that Professor Weber repeatedly insists on a pretended similarity in the relations between "masters" and working classes in Algeria and Peru, and those in Rumania, where the two social groups "belonged figuratively and sometimes literally to two different nations." [3] He is silent about the enormous sacrifice in land and fortune made by the Rumanian "masters" for the benefit of the Rumanian peasant (eighty percent of the Rumanian population), a sacrifice which has had no equivalent among any other group of "masters" in the social history of any other country.[4] Very characteristically Professor Weber invokes as principal authority for his metaphors, and his silences, the novels of the foreign-born Penait Istraiti, heinous enemy of all that was Rumania; a slum-dweller completely ignorant of Rumanian country life and Rumanian history; a notorious Communist and homosexual, whose works published in French (a language he did not know) were in a large measure ghost-written by French writers of the same ilk.

Concerning the Legionary Movement, Professor Weber also shows a fondness for extra-European comparisons, appealing to "students of African history" and invoking the "messiahs of the Ba-Congo" and of other dark recesses of darkest Africa in order to explain Corneliu Codreanu's prestige and the fidelity of his followers.[5] When such similes do not appear convincing enough, the learned professor falls back on Freud, throwing around such phrases as "transfer-wish fulfillment" and other psychoanalytic gibberish.

Brasilach, the enthralling writer murdered ten years after Codreanu by the same hidden forces, the idol of those of the French youth for whom "the most natural human society was the nation," and for whom

[2] Eugen Weber, "Romania," in *The European Right*, p. 537.
[3] *Ibid.*, p. 504.
[4] The agrarian reform carried out in Japan under the reign of Emperor Mutsuhito was comparable, in regard to the extention of arable land expropriated, to the last Rumanian agrarian reform, but it was soundly conceived and honestly applied and one of its consequences was the astonishing Japanese industrial development in the following century.
[5] *Ibid.*, p. 523.

Communism represented the decay and disintegration of any human society, was able in a few lines to go far deeper and more accurately into this subject matter than Professor Weber was able to do in eighty-two pages:

> Before the universal Communist menace, from the frozen Norwegian fiord to the red flatlands of Castille and the arid escarpments of Greece, all the peoples of Europe were awakening from a listless slumber to the cry of "Nations, arise!" In Rumania, Corneliu Codreanu was addressing his Legionaries in rugged speeches full of picturesque poetry, appealing to their honor and their spirit of self-sacrifice and discipline, trying to conjure that state of inner enlightenment, present in all religious experiences, that he called "the national unity" and upon which he was founding the original, the monastic, the military movement of the Iron Guard.

We quote here also a letter from Pastor Richard Wurmbrand, who gathered his information and his impressions from more reliable sources than Professor Weber, addressed to a representative of the Legionary Command:

> If you are like the Legionaries, whom I have seen dying with a last word of love to God and to their fatherland upon their lips, you are my friends. God looks at the heart and even if you did not have the privilege to die a martyr as they, God appreciates your willingness to give your life whenever it might be necessary for . . . our oppressed country. I have seen Legionary children like Gavrilaş and Ciubotea die as heroes. My wife was in prison with Mrs. Codreanu and Mrs. Moţa. We know how many very valuable elements are among you. Mocked by everybody, continue to believe and to love and God will reward you. . . . Who could forget men of a legendary grandeur like Gafencu,[6] Ianulidi, Tetea, Gavrilaş, and others who won our respect—the respect of those who were not Legionaries and were not in agreement with the Legionaries in many ways. Some of them saved my life. . . .

It would be unjust, perhaps, to ask from this new crop of intellectuals —victims, it seems, of a contagious brain-corroding pestilence that has already suffused Western universities with its materialistic, utilitarian and Marxist philosophy, to understand fully the notion of sacrifice for a principle, or for one's country, or of fidelity, even unto death, toward the leader who incarnates this principle or represents better than anybody else the interests and destiny of that country.

For this new generation of "educators" and public opinion builders, religion is no better than magic; love and fear of God is superstition; patriotism is an error; nationalism is a crime; self-sacrifice is masochism;

---

[6] No relation to Grigore Gafencu the former Minister of Foreign Affairs.

The author as an artillery captain in the Rumanian Army.

Aimez comme lui votre Pays, par dessus tout au monde!

The author's parents.

Constantin Negri, the great Rumanian statesman, with the following dedication from the author's mother: "Love, like him, your country above anything else."

Prince Nicolas Ghyka-Comanesti, Princess Sturdza's uncle, was decidely a "bear uncle."

Comanesti Court, the estate of Princess Sturdza's grandfather.

eneral Prince Léon Mavrocordatu, Princess
turdza's father.

Prince Eugene Ghyka, the grand-uncle of
Princess Sturdza, fought with the Union
Army during the American Civil War. His
wife, Princess Jeanne Ghyka, who died in
1954 at the age of ninety, was a sister of
Queen Nathalie of Serbia.

Prince John Sturdza (left), the author's brother, and Prince Alexis Mavrocordatu (right), Princess Sturdza's brother. They were both killed in fighting Trotsky's armies.

Tescani, the colonial style estate of the author's aunt, Alice Rosetti-Tescani. This was a second home for the author and his brothers, where in the winter drives many wolves were killed, and where a library of more than ten thousand volumes helped the author, from his early years, satisfy his intellectual curiosity.

Four generations: Prince Dimitri Ghyka-Comanesti; Princess Marie Mavrocordatu, his daughter; Princess Zoé Sturdza; and Prince Elie Vlad Sturdza, her son.

Princess Sturdza with her son.

Wedding in Comanesti, Prince and Princess Michel Sturdza.

Princess Sturdza with the head of a moose shot on a trip to Canada.

A typical Rumanian peasant family, from a painting by Miklós Barabás.

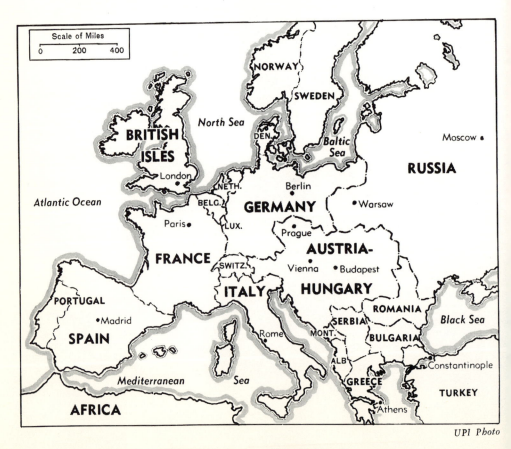

Europe on the eve of World War I.

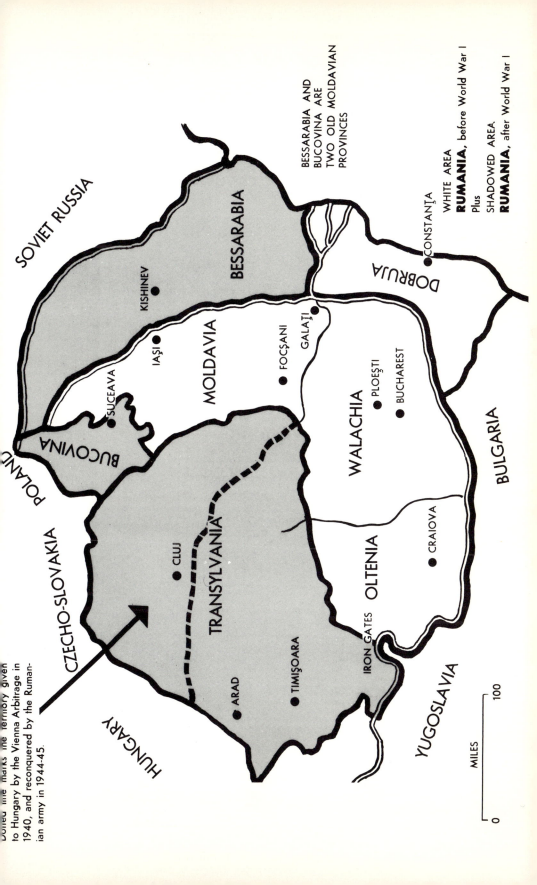

SOVIET RUSSIA

BESSARABIA

KISHINEV

BESSARABIA AND
BUCOVINA ARE
TWO OLD MOLDAVIAN
PROVINCES

WHITE AREA
RUMANIA, before World War I
Plus
SHADOWED AREA
RUMANIA, after World War I

CONSTANȚA

DOBRUJA

MOLDAVIA

IAȘI

SUCEAVA

FOCȘANI

GALAȚI

BUCOVINA

POLAND

WALACHIA

PLOEȘTI

BUCHAREST

BULGARIA

CZECHO-SLOVAKIA

TRANSYLVANIA

CLUJ

OLTENIA

CRAIOVA

IRON GATES

HUNGARY

ARAD

TIMIȘOARA

YUGOSLAVIA

MILES

0   100

Dotted line marks the territory given
to Hungary by the Vienna Arbitrage in
1940, and reconquered by the Rumanian army in 1944-45.

Princess Zoé Sturdza with her dog, Haiduc, a present from an American friend. Haiduc died when he and Princess Sturdza were in prison together.

Prince Elie Vlad Sturdza, the son of the author, with Haiduc in Riga in 1934.

Riga: In front, the President of Latvia; at his left, Princess Zoé Sturdza; back center, the author with other members of the diplomatic corp.

love of the past is necromania; an obeyed leader is a medicine man; and discipline is a dark cult. Those people are, no doubt, sincere in their disbeliefs and in their beliefs also, when they care to exhibit them; one cannot, therefore, berate them for the one or for the other. But we are allowed to be surprised when university professors, in a book which assumes the form and the aspect of a methodical and didactic investigation and which concerns itself with a highly controversial and angrily disputed debate, instead of confronting opposing documentation, use only material furnished by the declared adversaries of the political movement being studied. The result could not have been any other, regarding Rumania and the Legionary Movement in any case, than to add another stratum to the accumulation of slander and deliberate misinformation upon which condemnatory judgment have already been passed, and to give new luster and credit to testimonies which have long ago been totally disproved. In this category, for instance, fall all the "official documentation" furnished by General Antonescu against the activity of the Legionary Movement during the National Legionary Government and under Horia Sima's leadership. It is exclusively upon this "documentation" that Professor Weber based his final conclusions with the simple qualification that the official data "were perhaps inflated," when, indeed, they were entirely fabricated or perverted.

Horia Sima, the Commandant of the Legionary Movement, is alive. Professor Weber spent long hours with him asking and listening with apparent great interest. He might have taken into account Sima's first-hand and abundant information about so many controversial events, situations and attitudes, expressing, of course, his own dissent or his doubt if he felt it necessary. Not one line in Professor Weber's elaborate composition records or reflects such important data or statements; there is not one quotation from Sima's works, in English, Spanish, or Rumanian in a production in which even African sorcerers are quoted! Is that honest academic research? Is that what the professor's sponsors, who no doubt paid for his special trip to Spain, expected from him?

A Legionary text says that all great changes in human history are provoked by the simultaneous occurrence of two events: a paroxysm in the collective aspirations of some human group, and the appearance of a creative personality, essentially representative of those aspirations, with enough spirituality to bring them to life, and with enough discernment to steer their course toward lasting realization.

Such a person for Rumania was Corneliu Zelea-Codreanu. What the text did not say, but what the Legionary Movement learned from bitter experience, is that almost by definition such a personality is fated to disappear violently, long before he sees the outcome of his toils and of his calvary.

> Wer darf das Kind beim rechten Nahmen nennen?
> Die wenigen die was davon erkannt
> Die töricht genug ihr volles Herz nicht wahrten.
> Dem Pöbel ihr Gefühl, ihr Schauen offenbarten
> Hat man von je gekreuzigt und verbrannt.[7]

For Rumania, two factors determined the paroxysm and the necessity for fearless spiritual and realistic leadership: 1. The realization of a centuries-old dream—the reconstruction almost in its entirety of the Dacian empire and the reunion of all Rumanians under the same crown; a realization that conjured in the soul of every young Rumanian all the spirit and the glories of the past. 2. The sudden emergence at our eastern borders of a deadly menace to this miraculous reconstruction—a menace more repugnant, perhaps, to Rumanian mentality than to that of any other nation.

It was in January 1918 that for the first time a group of Rumanian young people gathered around Codreanu, then nineteen years old. The purpose then was the same as that of all of Codreanu's later efforts: the defense of the endangered country and of the spiritual and historic values which composed the texture of Rumania's existence. The Bolshevized Russian Army was roaming around Moldavia and menacing Iași, the provincial capital, then the seat of the Court and of the Government. Codreanu and his young comrades of high school age decided to organize a guerrilla war against the Communist enemy if serious hostilities should break out between Rumanian troops and their former allies.

In the following years, Codreanu while a student at the University of Iași continued among students and workers his fight against insidious Communist ideas and infiltration. This time the fight was not against foreign troops but against some of his own professors, against professional agitators, and also partly against the authorities of the province. Helped by his friend, the workman Constantin Pancu, he founded the Guard of the National Conscience. In March 1922, before graduating from the Iași Faculty of Law, he organized the Association of Christian Students. Codreanu and twenty-six comrades in a solemn religious ceremony bound themselves by what has been called the *angajamentul de onoare* ("pledge of honor")—to continue for the rest of their lives the nationalist fight they had started on the benches of the university—a pledge to which many of them remained faithful even unto their deaths.

---

[7] But who dares call the child by its right name?
 The few who knowing something about it
 Were foolish enough not to guard it in their hearts.
 Those who have shown the people their feelings and their thoughts
 Have been since always crucified or burned at the stake.
 —Goethe, *Faust I*

We think March 27, 1922, must be considered as the point of no return in Codreanu's life and destiny.

After graduation Codreanu left for Berlin in order to complete his studies in political economy, but he returned hurriedly to Rumania to establish some order among the numerous nationalist movements that had sprouted in the country in his absence. He had to overcome great difficulties but finally succeeded in forming the League of National Christian Defense, LANC (Liga Apararei Nationale Crestine) from forty-two sporadic nationalist movements whose forty-two banners were solemnly blessed at the Iaşi Metropolitan Cathedral. LANC was no more a limited student movement but a national organization. The League elected Professor Alexandru C. Cuza as president, who delegated to Codreanu the mission of further organizing the movement throughout the whole country.

For Codreanu and LANC there followed three years of continuous and often violent agitation, caused in part by the mass naturalization of more than 500,000 Jews suddenly introduced by law into the organism of the nation, and in part by the corruption that had started to infect Rumania's public life. Against LANC activities the most brutal and unjustified official reprisal was hurled. This was a time when independence of the judiciary, strength of character, and civic courage still dwelled in Rumania. Public sympathy, public support, and incorruptible courts sided with the young nationalist movement against the iniquities and the cruel repression of the various Governments.

Between 1923 and 1925 Codreanu established an indissoluble friendship, fateful for the destiny of his Movement, with Ion Moţa. Codreanu also organized the first working camp and the first "Brotherhoods of the Cross" among the younger of his disciples. It was also during this time that he and his followers met with one of the cruelest chapters of the reign of terror to which they were to be continuously submitted. This chapter of the Legionary calvary has been called the "Manciu Terror," named for the police commissioner of the city of Iaşi to whom the direction of the operation had been entrusted by the Liberal Government then in power.

Young men and young girls were imprisoned for no reason and without any trial. They were humiliated, beaten, and tortured. One of Manciu's favorite performances was to hang his victims by their feet and submerge their heads in a bucket of water until they nearly drowned and then to repeat this treatment. Freed from such atrocities by the intervention of a group of influential people, the victims asked for the punishment of Manciu and his accomplices for their criminal activities. The result was the criminal's promotion and decoration with ribbons and orders. Let us hear Professor Weber himself on the subject:

The first task which Codreanu set for himself and the members of his brotherhoods was to build their own student center with bricks they made themselves and money they raised by working in a market garden. *But the authorities suspected that their intentions were less specific than they seemed,* and the prefect of Iaşi himself led the police and gendarmes to break up the group with great brutality. Arrested without *apparent* reason while at their work, they were tied up with ropes, dragged through the streets, spat on, beaten, humiliated, and released only on the intervention of Cuza and other leading citizens. *Arbitrary beatings and arrests were hardly unusual in Romania,* but this was Codreanu's first experience of sheer injustice. An official inquiry which established the unwarranted arrests, beating, and torture of the schoolboys led only to the decoration of the prefect, Manciu, and the promotion of his principal assistants. . . .

Denied a hearing for his griefs, let alone any sanctions against the guilty, Codreanu now took the law into his own hands and shot Manciu down.[8]

Let us observe Professor Weber's clever attempts at extenuating as much as possible Manciu's sadistic activities, and also the fact that he fails to mention that Codreanu's gesture of revolt was also an act of self-defense. When Manciu and his stooges came to arrest him again Codreanu drew his gun and fired. Despite the persistent and illegal efforts of the authorities (who twice changed the seat of the trial in order to find a more pliable court), Codreanu was acquitted by twelve jurymen who returned to the courtroom "sporting on their lapels the LANC emblem. . . ."[9] "Codreanu was not only acquitted but vindicated,"[10] relates Professor Weber. "On the way back to Iaşi, the peasants gathered to cheer him . . . priests blessed him, and in the cities great crowds filled the railroad stations with flowers and songs."[11] Rumania at that time was still Rumania, and not what years of corruption and submission to the orders of the Unnamed Powers were to make her. However much Manciu had deserved his fate, however much Codreanu was supported in his action by his compatriots, those who knew Codreanu knew also that he never justified to himself the shooting of Manciu, whose death left an ineradicable shadow upon his thoughts.

About 100,000 persons gathered in Focşani to attend Codreanu's wedding, and in a neighboring village one hundred newborn peasant children were gathered to be baptised with him as godfather. Back in Iaşi he took the necessary measures in order to complete the building interrupted by his arrest. But eager to have some time elapse between his future activities and what had just happened, he left with Moţa for the University of Grenoble in order to continue his studies, and after two years there he graduated in political economy.

[8] Weber, *op. cit.*, p. 525. Italics added.
[9] *Ibid.*, p. 526.
[10] *Ibid.*
[11] *Ibid.*

Once again in Rumania, Codreanu tried to reconstruct the LANC, which had disintegrated after his departure. He failed in his efforts and asked Professor Cuza for authorization to leave the League and to found his own organization. On June 24, 1927, the Legion of the Archangel Michael was founded. The Legion was organized into *cuibi* ("nests") of not less than three Legionaries but not more than thirteen. When a nest seemed sufficiently strong, three of its members would start the formation of another. The spreading of nests all over the country followed and the Legion grew rapidly in the following years. To his Legionaries Codreanu was the Captain, and his authority was unquestioned. This is what the Captain says about it: "The Legionary Movement is not founded exclusively on the principle of authority nor on that of liberty, but on the principle of love. Love cannot breed tyranny and injustice, nor sanguinary revolutions and social wars."

The educational methods of the nests are clearly stated by the six fundamental laws written in the manual of the nest-chiefs:

1. The Law of Discipline: Legionary be obedient; without discipline we will not win. Follow your chief for better or worse.
2. The Law of Work: Do your daily work. Work with joy. Let the reward of your work be not any material profit, but the satisfaction that you have contributed something to the glory of the Legion and the greatness of your country.
3. The Law of Silence: Talk little. Talk only when you must. Your eloquence is in deeds. Let others talk; you act.
4. The Law of Education: You must become another man. A hero.
5. The Law of Assistance: Help your brother in distress. Do not abandon him.
6. The Law of Honor: Follow only the ways shown by honor. Fight. Never be a coward. Leave to others the ways of infamy. Better fail fighting the way of honor, than to conquer by infamy.

From the field of student agitation, the Legionary Movement in June 1931, passed for the first time to that of the electoral conflict, a field upon which it encountered in an unequal and cruel fight an enemy with which it had had until then only skirmishes: the politician. From prison to prison, from torture to torture, from illegal dissolution to illegal dissolution, the Legionary Movement reached the election of 1932 more powerful and more antagonized than it had ever been. It now had an alternate designation, the Iron Guard, which reflected the increase in the amount of fortitude and steadfastness asked from the Legionaries in order to face the new wave of persecutions. Indeed, by decree of the Liberal Government presided over by Ion Duca, "the political group known under the name of the Legion of the Archangel Michael, or the Iron Guard, or the Group Zelea-Codreanu" was dissolved on December 10, 1933.

Meanwhile a new and invaluable partner had joined the ranks of the Iron Guard, General Gheorghe Cantacuzene, the most admired, the most beloved, the most heroic of the leaders of the Rumanian Army during World War I. It was with the General at their side that Codreanu and the Legionary Movement faced the Duca terror; the cruelest the Movement had had to endure up to that point. By the thousands Legionaries were arrested, beaten, and tortured. Twelve of them were killed by Duca's police before three of their comrades took the law into their own hands and on December 29, 1933, killed Duca in the Sinaia railway station and then immediately gave themselves up to the police.

The Government brought all the Legionary chiefs before a military court, together with the three murderers, and asked that all of them be sentenced as accomplices. The prosecutor for the State was General Petrovicescu, a man who had at that time absolutely no connection with the Iron Guard, but who eight years later was to share with it another part of its calvary and was to die in prison for its cause. Refusing to take into account all the pressures to which he was submitted— including an order from King Carol—Petrovicescu limited his indictment to the three murderers and declared that after careful investigation he was convinced that none of the leaders of the Legionary Movement were aware of the murderers' intentions nor had any responsibility concerning the murder in the Sinaia railway station.

Professor Weber thinks he knows better. Here is his account of this drama:

On December 10, 1933, at the height of yet one more electoral campaign, the ruling Liberal government, responding to its western allies' fears of a fascist agitation, again dissolved the Guard. In the ensuing persecution, *half a dozen* legionaries were killed and hundreds were imprisoned until the *elections had been held* and the Liberals had secured the desired majority. On December 29, three legionaries "punished" I. G. Duca, the premier responsible for this, by shooting him down at point-blank range on a railroad station platform, and then gave themselves up. [There were twelve, not half a dozen, killed. Thousands were imprisoned and tortured, not hundreds. They were kept in prison for several months.]

When Duca had signed the decree that dissolved the Legion and kept it from the polls, General Gheorghe Cantacuzino [Cantacuzene] (1869–1937), an old follower of Averescu's Popular Party who had since joined Codreanu, had written him, "You have signed your will." Although Duca's murderers seem to have planned their coup alone, they were encouraged to do it— if not put up to it—by the General. Codreanu, though he endorsed their act post facto, always claimed he had no knowledge of it. *Even if that were true, the moral responsibility for this and other acts of murder and mayhem must be placed at his door.*[12]

[12] *Ibid.*, p. 547. Italics added.

Regarding General Cantacuzene's supposed participation in Duca's murder, Professor Weber has given us a perfect instance of quotes cleverly isolated from their context. General Cantacuzene was an old and good friend of Prime Minister Duca, toward whom, as toward many of his friends, he was inclined to assume a blunt fatherly attitude. The letter quoted by Professor Weber was, of course, one of the principal exhibits at the trial, where it was read *in extenso* and correctly interpreted as a pressing warning to a friend from one who knew at first hand the intensity of the indignation raised among the Legionary masses by the assassination of their comrades and the increasing cruelty of the Duca terror.

Concerning Codreanu's supposed complicity in the Duca crime or in the "other acts of murder and mayhem [which] must be placed at his door," Professor Weber could have easily avoided the fault of misinformation (remembering that Codreanu had never lied or tried to fool anybody) by reading in its original text the precept of non-violence on which the Captain had based the Legionary Movement *after his departure from the LANC* and his farewell to the period of student agitation that had preceded the Manciu murder and trial. We quote from *Pentru Legionari*, the book in which Codreanu had determined the way of life and the way of action for the new movement he had created:

> The Legionary Movement will never resort to complot or a coup in order to win. By the very essence of our beliefs we are against conspiracy. This would mean violence of an outward character, while we expect victory from an inner realization of the nation's soul.
>
> We have walled ourselves inside a framework of perfect order and legality, so as to be above any reproach. We will follow the line of the country's laws without provoking anybody, without answering to any provocation. But do not believe that this will be of any avail. The way our governments think is this: "We cannot destroy you under the pretext that you have violated our laws; therefore, we will violate our laws and destroy you. You have decided not to be 'illegal'? Well, we will be illegal for you." So, we have been locked up in a purely diabolical system: We are accused by the press and all the official media of propaganda, of violating the law, and it is just because we maintain ourselves unshakenly in the framework of the law that our adversaries are able to crush us in the most cruel way.
>
> They try to throw us out of that state of legality into one of violence. But we won't allow ourselves to be pushed into that position. We have decided to act in the framework of the law. We do not want to use force. We do not want to use violence.

At a later time, in February 1938, in a circular to the members of his Movement, which had presented itself at recent elections under the name of the All for the Country Party, Codreanu stated:

To all concerned: the All for the Country Party does not exist any more. All those presently belonging to the Legionary Movement are released from their bonds. All the offices of the Movement are abolished.

We do not want any more of the experiences of the past, when contrary to our will we have been pushed onto the road of violence. We won't answer violence any more. We will accept any brutality even if the whole nation is treated as a herd of livestock. We won't revolt, because we have the conscience of our mission and of our responsibility. We won't, through irrational action, make of our country another bleeding Spain.

Our generation sees the gauntlet that has been thrown before it. We won't take it up. The hour of our victory has not yet struck. This is the hour of others. If the generation of our predecessors think that they are doing right, we won't try to prove them wrong. They have the responsibility of their actions before God and before history.

It was after the Captain had thus disbanded his organization, and on the eve of his departure for Italy, that he was once more arrested. Before leaving for another prison, the soaked casemates of Jilava, where a few months later his tortured body would be brought back and buried under several tons of concrete, the Captain had the opportunity to pass to his family a few sheets from which we extract these following lines:

Wednesday, June 15, 1938—When I had finished the reading of the Gospel, I understood that I was in this prison by the will of God, that however innocent I was according to human justice, he punished me for my sins and put my faith to test. I calmed down; serenity descended upon the torments of my soul, as the serenity of the evening descends upon the agitation and the passions of this world. For, I have been cruelly tortured. My poor flesh has suffered much. I don't think that I have ever suffered so much. I have not lost faith and love, but I felt at one moment that I had lost any tie with hope. Physically tortured like a beast, my clothes are filled only with aches. For sixty nights I have been sleeping on these planks. Sixty days and nights, that my bones absorb like a sponge the moisture that oozes from floor and walls.

For two months I have not exchanged a word with anybody, as everybody here is forbidden to talk to me. Manacled and stricken, without any possibility to defend myself. I am declared foreign to my nation, and an enemy of the state. With my heart oppressed, thinking of the sufferings of my family and of so many of my comrades, I felt that in me one of the links between man and God had broken: hope. . . .

Friday night, June 17, 1938—Half an hour ago my lawyers came and told me that my appeal to the court of cassation had been denied. All of them were mournful and dispirited. I stayed with them about fifteen minutes. I asked them about the court hearings. They answered with a few words, and we parted.

I went back to my cell, sat on the planks of my bed and prayed: Our Father Who art in Heaven, Thy will be done.[13]

[13] "It is hard to tell whether, with Codreanu once put away, the King and his premier, Calinescu, really intended his death," says Professor Weber (*op. cit.*, p. 554). He

If one remembers that, with the Captain, hundreds of leaders of the Movement had been arrested in the capital and in the provinces, and when one tries to realize the turmoil and anger that had broken loose in the souls of the Legionary masses, deprived momentarily of any leadership, one can only wonder that more disorders had not occurred at the time of the last arrest and of the iniquitous verdict that sent Codreanu to his last prison—than the limited happenings in Cluj, amplified and used by many commentators, and by Professor Weber also, to explain and even excuse the murder of the Captain. The readers of this book will have the opportunity to form their own opinion about the subject.

A few words more about those commentators. It has been their practice to grant a certain measure of understanding and compassion for the Legionary leaders who have passed away, generally victims of violent deaths. Professor Weber followed the routine concerning Codreanu. But this indulgence toward the dead is often only a way to win more credit for the denunciation and slander of those alive, especially of the leaders.

Denunciation is directed very naturally today to the present Commandant of the Movement, Horia Sima, as it had been directed to Codreanu, Moţa, and others when they were alive. And here Professor Weber's insinuations are sometimes qualified as in the case of the trouble in Cluj, where he admits somewhat reluctantly, that Horia Sima tried to prevent it. They are sometimes even contradicted by his own text, as in the case of the pretended Legionary insurrection against General Antonescu. "The Legion's 'rebellion' was actually its resistance to a coup by its governmental partner [General Antonescu] to eliminate it from power," [14] says Professor Weber. That throws the burden of this tragedy in Rumania's history and of all its consequences where it belongs: upon the shoulders of General Antonescu. That the learned pro-

---

discreetly prepared this attempt at minimizing Carol's and Călinescu's infamy by the utterly misleading information that Codreanu had "refused . . . to leave the country" (*Ibid.*, p. 552). Far from refusing to leave the country, Codreanu, who had announced that he was leaving for Italy with the intention of spending several years there, already had his passport visaed by the Rumanian authorities and by the Italian Consulate, and his tickets and that of his family booked, when at the last moment his passport was confiscated by Călinescu's police and he was arrested, never to be free again. If Carol and Călinescu had only wanted him "put away," to use Professor Weber's words, it would have been easy enough for them to let the Captain leave. It is not hard to understand why Professor Weber omits this important episode, one pebble among the avalanche of misinformation by omission and commission in his script, *for this one instance suffices by itself to show what exactly was the task assigned to Professor Weber by his generous sponsors—the American Council of Learned Studies, the John Simon Guggenheim Memorial Foundation, and the Research Grants Commission of the University of California.*

[14] Weber, *op. cit.*, p. 566.

fessor adds: "There is every reason to suppose that legionaries had considered a coup of their own, but Antonescu beat them to it," [15] without giving any of those reasons, is too much in the natural line of the "twistorians" of every epoch to chide him for it.

The same contradiction between facts and Professor Weber's allegations might be often detected by anyone just from Weber's own text, as for instance when Professor Weber suggests that, contrary to what was occurring under Codreanu's leadership, under Sima the Legion was "a conscious agent" of National Socialist Germany. Under Codreanu, as well as under Sima, the Movement had always jealously kept its independence from any foreign influence. But it was under Sima that this attitude of independence provoked the greatest difficulties between the Movement and Germany, difficulties which reached the point of open conflict, even according to Professor Weber's narrative itself, and led to the imprisonment in Germany of about four hundred Legionaries, among whom were Sima himself and the principal leaders of the Movement. They were "held in gentle confinement by the Germans," says Professor Weber, which is a deliberate falsehood. As everybody knows, it was in the concentration camps of Dachau and Buchenwald that these Legionaries were confined until the last months of the war. It was from there that they surged to take arms against the Communist enemy, to save at least the honor of a betrayed army and a betrayed country.

This book is not a history of the Legionary Movement, although I might be tempted sometime to write it, even without the generous sponsorship of a "liberal" university or of the Guggenheim Foundation; but a history of the part Rumania played in the events that have led the world to the last great war between non-Communist powers. What will follow will unavoidably bring Codreanu and his Movement into the focus of this narrative and to the attention of the reader. I would like, however, to try to answer here a question that has often been asked me: *What now?* Does the Movement still exist as an operating organization? Has it not been completely annihilated by the fierce new repression to which it has been submitted by the Communist regime?

We are not concerned here with what is left in Rumania of the Legion of the Archangel Michael. What we are anxious to see is the hour at which it will become evident that every Rumanian has become a Legionary. For we firmly believe that as long as such a transformation has not occurred, in Rumania and the other enslaved countries, and even among the masses of all Western non-Communist countries, the

[15] *Ibid.*

danger of a universal Communist victory is constantly around the corner.

In what concerns more specifically Rumania and the Legionary Movement, I cannot do better than quote the following words of the Captain:

> Then, we will accept death. Our blood will run. We have lived with death as a thought and a decision and we have always had thereby the certitude of victory. Our victory will not be *life* but *resurrection!*

PART TWO

Titulescu,
the Enemy's Agent

The catalogue of his acquaintances . . . would throw a curious light on those subterranean agencies of which the world in general knows so little, but which exercise so great an influence on public events.

. . . .

"So you see, my dear Coningsby, that the world is governed by very different personages from what is imagined by those who are not behind the scenes."

DISRAELI

Coningsby

I strive not to throw Europe into this criminal adventure. But the states, even the British crown, are not the masters of their destiny. Powers that elude us are promoting in Great Britain, as in other countries, special interests and an aberrant idealism.

Stanley BALDWIN

From a speech in the House of Commons

Mount Vernon, October 24, 1798

Reverend Sir:

It was not my intention to doubt that the doctrine of the Illuminati, *and the principles of Jacobinism, had* [sic] *not spread in the United States. On the contrary, no one is more satisfied of this fact than I am.*

The idea I meant to convey was that I did not believe the Lodges of Freemasons in this country had, as societies, endeavored to propagate the DIABOLICAL tenets of the former, or the PERNICIOUS principles of the latter, IF THEY ARE SUSCEPTIBLE OF SEPARATION. That individuals of them may have done it, or that the founder, or instruments employed to found the DEMOCRATIC societies in the United States may have had this object, and actually had a separation of the people from their government in view, IS TOO EVIDENT TO BE QUESTIONED.*

With respect, I remain, Sir, etc. . . .

George WASHINGTON

From Washington, The Man and the Mason, *by Charles Callahan 1913.*

---

* Capitals added by Callahan.

Riga and the Pacts of Nonaggression

When I took over the direction of the recently created Rumanian Legation in Riga, Latvia, in November 1929 and for two years thereafter, Rumania was in the happy situation of not having diplomatic (nor any other) relations with the Soviet Union and no rail or road contact with her. We were the only neighbor of Soviet Russia that had kept untouched the barbed-wire barrier which, had it become a general policy of the Western Powers, would have promptly put an end to the existence of this apocalyptical apparition. News from Sovietland reached us only through the diplomatic and intelligence services of our allies, especially France and Poland.

The chief mission of our new Legation in Riga was to make up for this important and detrimental lack of information. In order to simplify my task I had been accredited to the Estonian Government and later to the Finnish Government, simultaneously. The choice of the Baltic capitals as watchposts for what was happening and brewing in Soviet Russia was most appropriate. These regions had been a part of the Russian Empire; their statesmen, their intelligentsia, their civilian and military officials, were familiar with the ambiance and the mentality of their former country. Although the Baltic states had been for a short but tragic period occupied by murderous Soviet gangs, they maintained diplomatic relations with Soviet Russia, toward which they had the same apprehensive and mistrusting attitude as we.

During all my activity in Riga, Reval, and Helsinki, I had the benefit of the great mass of information of the three Governments and of their intelligent and experienced interpretation of the reports that reached us. Another interesting source of information was the legation of the United States. This country, like Rumania, having at that time no diplomatic relations with Soviet Russia, was in an especially favorable situation regarding its intelligence service. Indeed, hundreds and even thousands of American technicians and workers, placed at the disposal of Soviet Russia by Washington, in order to build up her heavy industry and therefore her military potential, were passing through the Baltic ports when leaving or entering Soviet territory. Each of these travelers had something to tell, even if it was only about the atmosphere which surrounded him in a Communist country.

Concerning my own reports to Bucharest, I will mention only that they insistently and repeatedly mentioned the Soviets' enormous efforts to build up their military capacity at the price of any sacrifice from their unhappy people.

Because Rumania's diplomatic personnel were forbidden to give out press releases or statements, it was my son, then fifteen years old, who translated and annotated for the Rumanian public a German book that was extremely informative regarding the increasing Soviet military possibilities. This book was all the more interesting because at that time German military experts at the military academy in Moscow were establishing the military doctrine of Stalin's budding armies. When a scandalous affair, involving embezzlement, temporarily deprived our armies of the heavy and light artillery that the Czecho-Slovak Skoda factories were building for us, I could not resist the impulse of informing not only our Foreign Office but also the Rumanian public of the increasing possibilities of action by our gigantic neighbors; and I passed, over my initials, two articles to the Rumanian press entitled, if I remember correctly, "Shall We Be Caught again without Arms?" [1]

It was about that time that a false alarm of not well-identified origin was spread concerning an imminent Soviet surprise attack. A wired circular from our Foreign Office to all our diplomatic agencies abroad asked us for all the information we could gather on that subject. In a considered answer I reassured our Government that I was convinced that Soviet intentions toward their neighbors were not of an immediate impulsive nature but were developed over a long period of time and called for, besides, a long political and diplomatic preparation, upon which the Soviets had just embarked.

Mr. Gheorghe Mironescu, our Foreign Minister, who had summoned me to Bucharest, informed me that the alarm of our Government was all the greater since Russian aggression would have caught us—thanks to the Skoda scandal—in a dangerous state of unpreparedness. He suspected the Skoda industry of having spread the misleading alert in order to induce us to accept their faulty material. He informed me also that King Alexander of Yugoslavia had spontaneously offered to us the

[1] I have described in my book *Avec l'Armée Roumaine* the state of complete disarmament into which the Rumanian Army was thrown during World War I.

excellent artillery material that the same company was about to deliver to the Yugoslav Army. Our War Department, for motives unknown, declined King Alexander's offer.

It was, I think, my reports about the situation in Soviet Russia and about the likely unfolding of their next diplomatic activity which prompted the new Rumanian Government in 1931 to select me as its Representative at the Rumanian-Soviet negotiations, concerning a pact of nonaggression.

Before relating the story of those negotiations and of the subsequent events in Rumania, I would like to recall to the reader's memory how extensively the friendly relations between the Western Powers and Soviet Russia had developed at that time.

The present apostles of coexistence as a newly publicized way of reaching a real and durable peace between the Communist and the non-Communist world choose to forget the attitude of benevolent tolerance practiced almost without interruption by the Western Powers toward the Communist monstrosity since the first years of the USSR's existence. They take particular care to forget the first experience in proclaimed friendly coexistence, which will be described in this and following chapters, with all its fatal consequences.

Two very simple directives had governed Soviet foreign policy from 1918 until 1939: 1. There could not be a more favorable climate for the cause of the world revolution than a war between bourgeois countries; 2. In order to keep alive the possibility of such a war, the Soviets must always fall in line with the nation which without Soviet assistance would have felt unable to resort eventually to arms.

Lenin had given us fair warning:

> In the pursuit of our aim we can afford, with our power of destruction, to collaborate with some capitalist governments. . . . We can even conclude alliances with them in order to lure them into a false feeling of security. When their government, relying upon our support, throws itself into I do not know what mad adventure, we will let them fall, and we will build our empire upon their ruins.

It is in keeping with those principles that we have seen the following Soviet diplomatic maneuvers:

1. After Versailles and the disintegration of Germany's military establishment, the USSR signed the surprise Rapallo agreement with Germany; and thus began the Chicherin-Rantzau policy.[2]

---

[2] The Allied and Associated Powers met with Soviet delegates in Genoa in April 1922 in order to discuss the possibilities of economic exchanges between East and West. The Soviet delegates showed no special interest in these talks, but meanwhile they were secretly negotiating with German delegates in a neighboring city, Rapallo. These latter negotiations came to a quick conclusion: the Treaty of Rapallo between

2. When the efforts of National Socialism, an Italian alliance, and Polish friendship had made again of Germany the first military and political power on the continent, Russia inaugurated what Dimitrov called the Trojan Horse policy—she entered the League of Nations, signed a pact of nonaggression and friendship with her neighbors, and made a pact of mutual military assistance with France and Czecho-Slovakia.

3. Finally, when the combination of the rupture between Berlin and Warsaw, the reluctance of Mussolini, the opposition of Göring and the Generals of the Reichswehr, plus the unmistakable stand taken by the United States, might have prompted Hitler to a milder or slower course of action, Russia signed the Ribbentrop-Molotov Agreement—with World War II as a consequence.

Panic struck, therefore, the diplomatic and military circles in Moscow, at the growing possibility during the first years of the Thirties of a new four-power pact between France, Germany, Italy, and Great Britain which might reassert and complete, with the successors of Stresemann,[3] the Locarno Pact.[4] These memoirs will show how close Europe and the world came to getting the priceless benefits of such a diplomatic instrument, which would have been the best guarantee of a durable peace between non-Communist powers; they will also show all the exertions made by some Western quarters in order to help the Soviets avoid such an impasse.

Potemkin, one of the Kremlin's official historians, wrote in his *History of Soviet Diplomacy*, "The new attitude of the Soviet Government (the pacts of nonaggression, the entrance into the League of Nations, etc.) . . . had as motives the necessity to thwart the project of a four-power pact." The first tactical aim of this new policy was the renewal of the Franco-Russian alliance of the pre-World War I period, a master-

Germany and Soviet Russia. This was a bitter surprise for the Western negotiators in Genoa—a prefiguration of the Ribbentrop-Molotov Agreement of 1939.

The Treaty of Rapallo provided for a reciprocal renunciation of all financial war claims, resumption of diplomatic and consular relations, and the application of most-favored-nation economic exchange. It also provided for "mutual feelings of good will." As a result, Germany was allowed to produce, in Soviet factories, the types of armament forbidden to her by the Versailles Treaty, thus probably putting the blueprints of these arms at the disposal of the Soviet High Command.

[3] Gustav Stresemann was the German Foreign Minister who negotiated the 1925 Locarno Pact. Moscow feared a renewal, either in fact or in spirit, of the Pact.

[4] This treaty was the result of meetings of Germany, France, Great Britian, Italy, and Belgium in Locarno, Switzerland. There these powers came to an agreement which maintained the territorial *status quo* created by the Versailles Treaty, gave Germany certain moral satisfaction and prestige, and established a solidarity concerning the respect of treaties and preservation of peace. It was guaranteed by the League of Nations and came into effect September 14, 1926. It was by this treaty that the Rhineland was demilitarized.

stroke that was sure to preclude any further rapprochement between Germany and France and even to provoke an explosive reaffirmation of their traditional hostility.

The principal difficulty for Russian diplomacy, besides the general distrust among the rightist and centrist members in the French Parliament, lay in the terms and spirit of Franco-Polish and the Franco-Rumanian military and political arrangements, which practically forbade not only a military alliance but even any radical change in the status of the Franco-Soviet relations without Poland and Rumania's consent. Very influential leftist circles in France, headed by Édouard Herriot and Premier Léon Blum, were fighting violently against the new four-power pact proposed by Mussolini and openly favored by Great Britain and Germany.

*   *   *   *

Writing memoirs was for Sir Winston Churchill what plucking the lute was for Nero on that fabulous night. We wonder if sometimes his mind took him back to that turbulent session in the British Parliament when Ramsay MacDonald, the Prime Minister, returned from Rome, and Sir John Simon, Minister of Foreign Affairs, presented to the House the text of the four-power pact on which they had agreed with Mussolini. Sir Winston rose in wrath at that session and opposed with his well-known eloquence, a diplomatic instrument that might have spared the world from the war that brought the disintegration of the British Empire.

The forces in France that opposed a new Franco-Russian alliance argued very naturally the incompatibility of such an alliance with the interests of Poland and Rumania—France's principal allies on the continent—at least as long as an improvement in the relations between those two countries and their big neighbor had not been reached. With such an alliance a possibility and with the thesis of the leftist circles prevailing in France, Poland was asked by France to start discussing with the Soviets the terms of a nonaggression pact. Marshal Józef Pilsudski accepted reluctantly the French suggestion, but with the condition *sine qua non* that the Soviets should first come to a similar agreement with Rumania.

Such was the situation at the first attempt of coexistence when in the winter of 1931–1932 I was unexpectedly informed in Riga, Latvia, by Prince Dimitri Ghyka, our Minister of Foreign Affairs, that discussions regarding a Rumanian pact of nonaggression would start forthwith and that I was in charge of the Rumanian side of the negotiations. I say "unexpectedly" because a short time before, in Bucharest, I had reached with King Carol and Dimitri Ghyka the conclusion that the best relation we could have with our Communist neighbor was no relation at all.

I was informed also that Mr. Maxim Litvinov had solemnly promised Hervé Alphand, the French Ambassador to Moscow, that the question of Bessarabia would not be in any way discussed by the Soviet negotiator. Bessarabia, the eastern half of Moldavia, had been forcibly taken from us by Imperial Russia in three successive operations, in 1812, 1856, and 1878. We had recovered it at the end of World War I.

A few hours after his arrival in Riga, Ambassador Stomoniakov, the Soviet delegate, came to the Rumanian Legation and our negotiations began. I had already prepared in a text of six articles a paraphrase of other pacts of nonaggression and of the Kellogg Pact—a pact that I had signed with the same skepticism with which I was starting these Rumanian-Russian discussions.

Mr. Stomoniakov, after a long examination of the proposed text, informed me that even if only for esthetic reasons every pact should have a preamble. An admirer, myself, of well-balanced diplomatic literature, I approved the idea and asked him to make his suggestions.

The following dialogue ensued:

STOMONIAKOV: "You do not ignore, my dear colleague, the fact that the Soviet Government has never recognized your eastern frontiers nor the conquest of Bessarabia by your troops. . . ."

STURDZA (Interrupting abruptly): "I have never heard that such pretensions existed from the side of your Government. I don't know what you mean by Bessarabia;[5] if such a province existed I would certainly have been informed about it. But what I know very well is that without a solemn promise given by Mr. Litvinov to Mr. Alphand we would not be here negotiating, you and I."

STOMONIAKOV: "I know what you mean. But it is just in compliance with that promise that I wish to insert in the preamble that the question of your eastern frontiers won't be mentioned."

STURDZA (Trying to hide his great admiration for that piece of Soviet casuistry): "Mr. Ambassador, any insistence in that direction would force me to interrupt immediately our negotiations. I have, however, a proposal to make. Let us forget for now the preamble, to which we can come back later, and start discussing the text of the pact proper."

After a delay of twenty-four hours, and contacts with his Government, Stomoniakov accepted my suggestion. I had a very definite plan: It was necessary to show the French and Polish Governments that we were doing our best to comply with their wishes and that the impossibility

---

[5] "Bessarabia" means the country of the Basarabs. The Basarabs were the oldest Rumanian dynasty. It was a name given by the Tartars and the Turks to what was eastern Moldavia, *but the term was not used by the Moldavians themselves.*

of coming to an understanding with the Kremlin was entirely due to the crookedness of its policy.

In five sessions, each of which ended with a protocol signed by both negotiators, I succeeded without any great difficulty in establishing a perfect pact of nonaggression with my Soviet partner. But when at our final meeting Mr. Stomoniakov reminded me that we had also to agree upon the text of a preamble, I refused further discussions and suggested that we send to our respective governments for approval the text on which we had agreed.

Stomoniakov left the Rumanian Legation in a rage, and half an hour later I received a letter from him dealing fully with the question of Bessarabia and of our eastern frontiers. After making a copy of it for the use of my Government, I returned it to the Soviet Legation with the comment that I had not found any place for it in my files.

Russia's Trojan Horse venture was at a stalemate—all the more so as both the French and the Polish Governments, whose representatives in Riga, Jean Tripièr and Miroslav Arciczewski, had backed me loyally during my boresome palaver with the Soviet mouthpiece, continued to assure us of their unfaltering support and of the fact that they would not accept any new commitment with Soviet Russia as long as she did not give us an unqualified guarantee of her peaceful intentions.

I must confess that I was rather satisfied with myself. I had left my Government in the strongest possible position, under the circumstances, and the Soviet Government in the position of either having to accept our uncompromising terms or to give up, at least for a while, its new fraudulent policy in which I saw a mortal danger for my country.

My optimism had not taken into account certain very special circumstances in our domestic political life and the imminent conjunction of the interests and ambitions of two rather notorious personalities: the matrimonial ambitions of Madame Magda Lupescu, the slightly overfed Pompadour of Rumania's decadence; and the political interest of Nicolae Titulescu, who was Rumania's Ambassador-at-Large—the fair haired boss of the League of Nations and a high-priced international "call girl." [6]

[6] Crown Prince Carol, after having married the charming Princess Hélène of Greece, suddenly abandoned her and their son Michael and eloped with a woman of uncertain reputation—Magda or Élèna Wolff alias Lupescu—with whom he lived until his death. As this was not Carol's first escapade, his parents, King Ferdinand and Queen Marie, backed by the responsible statesmen, decided to proclaim Carol's son Michael Crown Prince. At the death of King Ferdinand, Michael was proclaimed King, with a Council of Regency to control Rumania's affairs until his majority. Many people in Rumania had kept their sympathy for Carol, hoping that he would return to Princess Hélène, his wife, who was well loved by everybody. Carol returned, proclaimed himself King and demoted his son to the rank of Voevod; but it was Magda Lupescu, not Princess Hélène, who *de facto,* shared the throne with Carol.

Titulescu to the Rescue

The Trojan Horse policy—the tactic newly adopted by the Kremlin in order to ward off the danger of a reinforced coalition of the non-Communist powers—had been stopped in its tracks, at least for a while, in Riga.

Indeed, the conclusion of a Rumanian-Soviet pact of nonaggression was the obligatory prelude to any similar arrangement between the Soviets and their other neighbors: Poland, the Baltic States, and Finland. And without such an arrangement, the conclusion of any military understanding between the Soviets and France—the final goal of the Kremlin's new policy—would have been unthinkable.

It was Mr. Titulescu who helped Soviet Russia out of this predicament.

From Riga I had sent to our Minister of Foreign Affairs, Dimitri Ghyka, who at that time was attending a session of the League of Nations at Geneva, together with a copy of the rejected Stomoniakov letter, the endorsed proceedings of our sittings with the Russian delegate and an almost word-by-word rendering of my discussions with him. All those documents and especially Stomoniakov's letter were classified as highly confidential. Ghyka, too much of a gentleman to imagine even the possibility of one of his subordinates feloniously using those official, confidential files, put them into Titulescu's hands. Titulescu had as one of his numerous residences two suites at the Hotel des Bergues in Geneva. One suite he lived in, and the one above he always kept empty to avoid noises that could have interfered with his sleep or his cogitations.

Titulescu surreptitiously copied those parts of the confidential literature that could serve his purpose, and sent them to his friend André Geraud, alias Pertinax, the foreign policy commentator of the *Echo de*

Paris. Geraud immediately reproduced from the Stomoniakov letter—a letter which, remember, did not exist for us because we had rejected it— and from my discussions with the Soviet delegate, enough to proclaim to the world at large that there *was* a Bessarabian question and that Soviet Russia did not recognize our eastern frontier—the very things that the Kremlin would have liked to have publicized, but could not, through the Riga negotiations. Pertinax rounded off his last article with criticism about the "young, light-headed Rumanian negotiator."

I quickly went to Paris and obtained from Mr. Geraud the following declaration: 1. It was Titulescu who had sent him the confidential literature; 2. Both articles had received the approbation of Mr. Titulescu before being printed. From Paris I rushed to Bucharest and had a very serious talk with Mr. Titulescu, who meanwhile, thanks to his intrigues, had taken the place of Ghyka as Minister of Foreign Affairs. I demanded full personal satisfaction. It was given to me before the Rumanian Parliament where Mr. Titulescu completed his criticism of his predecessor's activity by declaring, "Our Minister in Riga saved all that could have been saved." A very unjustified censure of Ghyka, whose behavior, in the difficult position in which Rumania had been placed by France's exigencies, followed the most proper and patriotic course, his only fault having been his failure to bring Titulescu before the courts for an infraction that in Rumanian penal law was punishable by up to five years' imprisonment.

The second step in Titulescu's program was to regain the favor of King Carol—favor he had lost because of certain declarations of a transparent anti-monarchist character. Titulescu realized immediately the advantages to be had from the existing crisis in the royal family. King Carol had tried through every possible means of persuasion to induce Princess Hélène—the wife he had abandoned when he ran off with Madame Lupescu, and the mother of his son Crown Prince Michael— to leave Rumania, where her presence was a permanent reminder of his turpitude and cynicism, and greatly embarrassing for his pseudo-matrimonial frolics. Carol's efforts had been backed without visible result by those politicians who wanted to please him.

Titulescu offered King Carol a very interesting barter: If he (Titulescu) were given the Foreign Affairs portfolio, he would pledge himself to prevail upon Princess Hélène's resistance. And, using his well-known and insinuating eloquence by appealing to Princess Hélène's patriotism and arguing for the necessity of calming the agitation in our public opinion, he succeeded in convincing her to leave for Italy, despite my respectful insistences and those of others who understood what the Princess's departure meant for our country.

Hardly established at the Palais Sturdza (the Rumanian Foreign Office)[1] Titulescu, with the obvious approval of King Carol, took a decisive step concerning our policy toward Soviet Russia that changed its course completely. He convoked, without delay, the French and Polish Envoys in Bucharest, thanked them warmly for the loyalty with which their Governments had backed our position during the Riga negotiations, but let them know that from then on Rumania intended to carry on alone any discussions with her eastern neighbor. Far from having any objection to France's and Poland's concluding pacts of nonaggression or of friendship with the Soviet Union, he said that such diplomatic instruments could only reinforce Rumania's position.

As a direct consequence of Mr. Titulescu's declarations, pacts of nonaggression were immediately concluded between Soviet Russia and all her neighbors *except Rumania*. Thanks to Mr. Titulescu, the Trojan Horse had successfully jumped the first hurdle, and was comfortably trotting toward its next goal: the Franco-Soviet and Czecho-Soviet military arrangements. This was the policy announced by Lenin when he recommended a fake alliance with some bourgeois countries—a policy that in the long run destroyed every possibility of a standing reconciliation between the adversaries of World War I. Concerning Rumania's domestic affairs, it was this policy also that provoked the greatest tragedy of her history.

The cruel persecutions of the Legionary Movement by almost all the governments that ruled in Rumania between the two World Wars has been wrongly attributed to what has been called the Legion's anti-Semitism. There were, however, in Rumania political parties and organizations that were flagrantly anti-Semitic; but at no moment were they ever treated with the brutality and the sadism that were used against Corneliu Codreanu, the young leader of the Legionary Movement, and his companions, of whom about six hundred, including Codreanu himself, were to be assassinated by Carol and his stooges.[2]

Codreanu never tolerated the slightest physical violence against Jews or Jewish properties. Any act of indiscipline in that direction would have been punished immediately by the expulsion of the culprits from

---

[1] The Palais Sturdza was an old Sturdza possession which was bought by the Rumanian Government and was used for more than half a century as the Rumanian Foreign Office.

[2] Codreanu's first organization of young people took place in 1918 and was directed against Russian Bolshevik troops then stationed in Rumania. Codreanu's political formations were known successively by the names of the League of Christian Defense, the Legion of the Archangel Michael, the Iron Guard, the All for the Country Party, and the Legionary Movement. The Iron Guard and the Legionary Movement were organized in small units of a maximum of thirteen Legionaries called *cuibi* ("nests"). Corneliu Codreanu was for his partisans "the Captain" (*Capitanul*).

the organization. It was a former Jew, Father Botez, who officiated at Codreanu's wedding. There were always one or two Jews in the Movement, and the only trouble they gave was due to their sometimes too extreme devotion to the Legionary cause. One of Codreanu's most beloved lieutenants, Vasile Marin, who fell in the Spanish Civil War, had married, with Codreanu's approval, a Jewish girl. Mrs. Marin became a Legionary heroine when she was sentenced to death by one of General Antonescu's courts for having helped two comrades avoid capture.

The Legionary Movement represented the most powerful, the most irreducible opposition in Rumania to the Anonymous Powers that wanted to introduce the Kremlin gang as comrades-in-arms in the drama of European rivalries. The greater and more intimate grew the collusion between the Soviets and those powers—of which Titulescu was the proconsul in Rumania—the greater grew also the campaign of slander and the persecutions against the Movement and its chief, Codreanu.

This fact was verified again with Titulescu's seizure of the Foreign Affairs portfolio. This event coincided with the beginning of the febrile activity of Mr. Jean Barthou, the French Minister of Foreign Affairs, which aimed at nothing less than an encirclement of Germany, *and coincided also with President Franklin D. Roosevelt's letter of October 10, 1933, to Russia's President Mikhail Kalinin, offering to resume diplomatic relations between their two countries.* None of the periods of violence and persecutions of which the Legionary Movement had been the victim until then could be compared with the brutality and the ferocity of the onslaught that broke out in the fall of 1933 under the Liberal Government of Ion Duca, whose Foreign Minister was Titulescu.

We do not intend to describe in detail the series of murders, tortures, beatings, imprisonments, and assorted atrocities perpetuated by Duca's police, gendarmerie, and rowdies; but we will quote a passage from Mr. Henri Prost's book *Destin de la Roumanie*. Mr. Prost is a grim enemy of the Legionary Movement and is one of its most vociferous critics.[3]

> Codreanu could not participate in the electoral campaign. A decree of December 11 once again—it was for the third time—dissolved the Iron Guard. But the Government did not stop there. It made wholesale arrests of Guardists, closed their meeting places, and confiscated their archives. Some Guardists were killed. According to certain information there were ten victims; according to other information, thirty. The Iron Guard answered without delay. On the evening of December 29, on the platform of the Sinaia railway station, Duca, fresh from an audience with the king,

[3] We will refer often to Mr. Henri Prost's *Destin de la Roumanie* and to Mme. Denise Basdevant's *Terres Roumaines contre vents et Marées*, both hostile to the Legionary Movement.

was shot and killed by three Guardists as he prepared to board the train for Bucharest.

The circumstances of this assassination have been the subject of animated controversy. There is no doubt that Duca had acted brutally or that his police went further than his instructions. But who had taken the initiative in the dissolution of the Iron Guard? We know that Duca had thought about it before forming his Government. Titulescu had made this dissolution a condition *sine qua non* to his collaboration with the Liberal cabinet, asserting that the nationalist agitations gravely endangered his policy.[4]

The answer to Mr. Prost's question is very simple: The initiative in this earlier attempt to destroy the Legionary Movement had been taken by Léon Blum, the chief of the French Socialist party.

When visiting Paris before his appointment as Prime Minister, in order to secure the investiture from those Anonymous Forces that under King Carol had supreme control of Rumanian affairs, Duca had bound himself to outlaw the Legionary Movement if given the Presidency of the Rumanian Government. He was tarrying with the fulfillment of his promise. His hesitations and his misgivings were told to me by Baron Guillaume, the Belgian Minister in Bucharest, and by Miroslav Arciczewski, the Polish Minister. To both gentlemen Duca confided that he did not like at all what he was doing but that he could not do otherwise. Asked for some explanation by both diplomats, Duca answered with manifest irritation, "It is Titulescu! He threatens me with his resignation and with the collapse of all our systems of alliances if the Legionary Movement is not liquidated. I could not leave my country without allies." The final impetus to the fulfillment of the promise which Duca had made to outlaw the Legionary Movement was given by one of Titulescu's bosom friends. Léon Blum, through his scandalous irruption in a French Government Council—to which he did not belong—demanding vociferously that the greatest pressure be applied to Duca, the Rumanian Prime Minister, to force him to abide by his promise.

It was this irruption and this pressure that helped Titulescu in forcing Duca to keep his tragic promise to outlaw the Legionary Movement. The cooperation between Titulescu and the French leftist circles from Socialists to Communists, his cooperation with all those who yearned for a Franco-Soviet alliance, has been a permanent feature of European policy. I think that Duca's murder, on December 29, 1933, served the interest of those circles in two ways: 1. Despite the military court's acquittal of Codreanu and all the Legionary chiefs of any complicity or responsibility in Duca's murder, this tragedy forced the Legionary Movement into a long period of inactivity; 2. Duca, too weak to resist out-

---

[4] Henri Prost, *Destin de la Roumanie (1918–1954)* (Paris, Éditions Berger-Levrault, 1954), pp. 66–67.

right the pressure of the Anonymous Powers, would not have submitted to them on their most important demand—the free passage of Soviet troops through Rumanian territory in case of a new European war.

Temporarily subordinated to those powers by political opportunism, Duca was not, like Titulescu, their agent.

CHAPTER

VII

A Strange Railway Agreement

It would be difficult to understand Rumania's foreign policy following the Riga negotiations without being acquainted with Nicolae Titulescu's personality, with the man into whose hands this policy had been entrusted; the man who, with Eduard Beneš, the Czecho-Slovak Foreign Minister, was the most instrumental factor in helping Lenin's dream of the "mad adventure" come true in Europe.

Let Mr. Prost introduce him to you:

> Titulescu is a very strange person. He has a Mongoloid mask, a hairless face, a body with awkward rotundities abnormal in a man. He looks like one of those former Bucharest cabmen who belonged to a sect that constrained them to castration after the birth of their first child. His nervousness, his sensitivity, his flusters of temper, his jitters before the smallest danger, his luxurious tastes—are all betrayed by a feminine temperament, which explains many of his attitudes.[1]

Titulescu was, in the history of Rumania, a tragic and fantastic apparition. Tragic because of the influence he had upon the destiny of his country, fantastic not only because of the physical aspect and the strange traits of his personality, *but also because of the mysterious origin of the powers that dominated him and controlled his conduct.* Rapacious and extravagant, millions poured into his hands and out again. Corrupt and corruptor, a French deputy once said of him, "Titulescu: he would pay you to buy him!" He felt at home only in Geneva, in Saint-Moritz, at the Lido, at the Côte d'Azur, and at other luxurious resorts. He hated the soil of his country, from which he fled in haste after the shortest possible visits, visits motivated by his financial and political interests. Born in Rumania, a Rumanian citizen, he was

[1] *Destin de la Roumanie,* pp. 17–18.

living like a high priced odalisque a life of opulence and extravagance
—thanks to the money and the influence with which Rumania provided
him—but he was not a Rumanian.

Moreover, we must not forget that Titulescu's enigma was only a part
of a greater mystery. How could it be explained that all the leaders of
a country, unanimously conscious of the danger represented by Soviet
Russia's proximity and intentions, chose to be blind to that danger and
deaf to all warnings, until the moment that Soviet troops invaded our
territory?

* * * *

My first contact with Titulescu was of an epistolary character; I had
written him from Washington to suggest a practical and rapid solution
of the "optant" [2] problem, which I must admit, had no relation at all
to my official activities in the United States. Without knowing it I had
blundered upon a most sensitive area in Mr. Titulescu's activity. This
problem was at that time for him the lifeblood of a not negligible in-
come, and he had no interest in any rapid and practical solution of it.

I blundered once more, I believe, when several years later I advised
my Government, from Helsinki (where I was serving as Rumanian Envoy), to adopt Finland's honest attitude toward the question of debts to
the United States. Titulescu, who remembered the not very flattering
reception he had received in Washington in 1926, was on the contrary
entreating our Government to repudiate them. But I had not been in
any direct conflict with him until the moment I realized, without any
possible doubt, that the interests that had provoked his intrusion in the
nonaggression discussions were not Rumanian interests, and that this
intrusion was not motivated solely by the fact that someone other than
he had been entrusted with an important Rumanian foreign policy
affair.

A short time after Titulescu's statement to the French and Polish
Ministers, concerning his approval of new pacts of friendship between
their countries and the Soviet Union, I was informed of the imminent
conclusion of pacts of nonaggression between Soviet Russia and all her
neighbors except Rumania. I went to Bucharest to communicate to
King Carol and some responsible statesmen my worries about the new
political and military situation brought upon us by those fateful declara-

[2] After the Kingdom of Rumania annexed Transylvania, the inhabitants of that
province were allowed to choose between a Hungarian and a Rumanian nationality.
They were given a right of option. Those who chose a Hungarian nationality were,
for the Rumanian Government, the "optants." The question in dispute was that of
their indemnification for the land properties they were losing through the agrarian
reform.

tions. Without yet fully realizing that this breach in the common defensive barrier, maintained until then by Russia's neighbors, represented the designs of Mr. Titulescu, I took the liberty of also telling him of my anxieties. He answered me with a pacifying smile, "Just wait and you will see." I had not long to wait, and what I saw did not please me at all.

During his ministry Mr. Titulescu followed with all his cunning and all his unmatched faculty of dissimulation the same fixed idea: *The building of a contractual international situation that would oblige Rumania to open her frontiers to Russian troops in the event of a new European war. This was an indispensable complement to the Franco-Soviet and Czecho-Soviet pacts of mutual assistance, for which, with his friend Beneš, he relentlessly worked until their adoption in May 1935.*

Seen from the point of view of the inevitability of an armed conflict between Germany and France—a faulty point of view, I believed—Titulescu's activity agreed with French and Czecho-Slovak interests. Indeed, how could the Soviet armies reach the Central European battlefields to comply with their part of the bargain except through Rumanian territory? Especially since Poland and the Baltic States had firmly decided to resist with all their might such an attempt.

From a Rumanian point of view, however, Titulescu's maneuvers represented nothing less than an act of treason—treason toward his own country, which the Soviet troops would never abandon after a victory; treason toward our ally Poland, whose defensive system would unexpectedly be outflanked; and treason toward another ally, the Kingdom of Yugoslavia, which was the object of Russia's aggressive pan-Slavism and of Communist hatred.

In order to attenuate the sentiment of profound anxiety provoked by the deterioration of our relations with Warsaw and Belgrade, Titulescu offered Rumanian public opinion some artificial and deceptive securities such as the Balkan Pact, concluded in Athens on February 9, 1934, which had no practical significance for Rumania; and recommended Rumania's adhesion to a pact of definition of aggression—a remarkable product of the collaboration of Messrs. Titulescu and Litvinov—worded in such a way that Russia would have no legal trouble invading a few years later the territory of all her neighbors.

But even this last fallacious security would not have been procured from the Kremlin had Titulescu not given the Russians in exchange, in a dissimulated but perfectly effective way, what they could not get at the Riga negotiations: the admission by Rumania of the disputability of our eastern frontiers and of our rights to our eastern provinces. This satisfaction was given to the Soviet Government, through the unprecedented wording of a railway agreement, immediately after the opening for the first time, on June 9, 1934, of diplomatic relations between Bucharest and Moscow.

Before narrating the story of this treaty and analyzing its terms and significance, it is interesting to relate the following incident, which occurred toward the middle of 1934.

I had received from the respective services of the League of Nations in Geneva the first volume of a diplomatic directory which was sent to every embassy and legation. Looking under the heading "Bessarabia," I found that the history of that Rumanian province had been written in a fraudulent way, detrimental to our interests, and favorable to Russia's insolent pretensions. I therefore sent the directory back with the comment that I saw no reason to buy and keep among my books such an inaccurate document. The editor's answer was that they were doubly surprised since the passages in question had been previously approved by a highly placed Rumanian personality. There is no doubt in my mind that this person was Mr. Titulescu, the permanent Rumanian delegate in Geneva.

Let us go back now to the revealing document of the agreement for the reopening of railway and highway connections between Rumania and Soviet Russia. It is a curious fact that neither at the moment of the conclusion of this treaty, nor later, did any of our political personalities take exception to the wording of this document nor were they alarmed by its unmistakable significance.

Immediately after the conclusion of her pact of nonaggression with the Soviets, Poland concluded a railway and highway agreement with them. The agreement signed by Messrs. Titulescu and Litvinov followed almost verbally the Polish-Soviet text, with one remarkable difference. *In the Rumanian-Russian agreement the words "frontier," "custom office," "custom authorities," "frontier authorities," and any other words or phrases that would have confirmed, or implied, the existence of a frontier between Rumania and Soviet Russia were carefully avoided and replaced by circumlocutions that were a credit to the inventiveness of the two negotiators.*

The responsible factor in Rumania should have been alarmed not only by the fact that the Soviets had secured what had been until then denied to them, but also by the fact of the new material situation created by the resumption, without any explainable motive, of passenger traffic between the two countries, which had been wisely discontinued during the fifteen previous years.

Henri Prost, generally obtuse to our feelings and our worries, at least understood the significance of this development:

. . . Titulescu concluded with Litvinov, June 9, 1934, an agreement concerning the resuming of diplomatic relations between Rumania and Russia. The Russians pledged themselves to return the treasures which in 1916 had been sent to Moscow to avoid their capture by the Germans. They returned a standard meter of platinum . . . and also the bones of the Moldavian Prince Cantemir, buried in Russia two centuries before. They remained deaf to the other claims, especially those of the Rumanian National Bank, which has never again seen the 314 millions of leis, in bullion, which in 1916 formed its metallic covering. The railway bridge over the Dniester, between Tighina and Tiraspol, was rebuilt. The first train crossed it October 18, 1935, but scarce will be the passengers who will use this international railway. *The reunion of Bessarabia to Rumania not having been recognized by the Kremlin, the Rumanians ask themselves what this new agreement means for their country.*[3]

Mr. Prost did not need to worry about the prospective passengers on the newly opened railway, at least not about their "quality." The Tighina bridge was not completely reconstructed when a lonely but important pilgrim was carried over to the Russian side. He was Édouard Herriot, former and future Prime Minister of France, who was on his way to visit his friends in the Kremlin.

Mr. Herriot had once refused to shake hands with General Primo de Rivera, Spanish strong-man, under the pretext that his democratic feelings did not permit him such a friendly gesture toward a dictator—a dictator who, by the way, during all his administration did not shed a drop of his fellow-countrymen's blood. Those same democratic feelings did not prevent him from greeting the most repulsive of the Communist tyrants, the murderers of more than twenty million Christians.

I met Mr. Herriot in the autumn of 1934 at a reception in Riga nine days after he crossed the Rumanian-Russian frontier. He was enthusiastic about the reception he had received in Moscow. He told us with tears in his eyes—tears that might have been primed by the first-class vodka provided by our good Latvian hosts—that at a banquet offered by the Russian Military Command, after the customary exchange of speeches, all the officers rose as one man and threw at him all the flowers that adorned the table. *Ils m'ont couvert de fleurs! Ils m'ont couvert de fleurs!* ("They have covered me with flowers!") the heavy-set French statesman repeated over and over.

At my elbow, the French Military Attaché, Colonel A., whispered into my ear, "The bastard! We once tried to throw him into the Seine."

I did not fail to report Herriot's description of his meeting with Russia's military men to Mr. Titulescu, then our Minister of Foreign Affairs, and to show him how alarming those contacts might be for us if they were, as I believed, the prelude to a Franco-Russian military understanding.

[3] Prost, *op. cit.*, pp. 91–92. Italics added.

Before World War I the Rumanian representatives in the various European capitals had been recruited almost entirely from among the career diplomats. Men like Emil Ghyka, Grigore Ghyka, Dimitri Ghyka, Alexandru Lahovary, Ion Lahovary, Gheorghe Diamandy, Edgard Mavrocordatu, Gheorghe Cretzianu, Charles Mitilineu, Nicola Mişu, Antoine Bibescu, Derussi, and Filaliti were respected and admired by all their colleagues for their tact, their sagacity, the independence of their information, and the high level of their culture. They also enjoyed the full confidence of their King and their Government.

Two factors had modified, after World War I, this happy situation: The first was the big difference between the emoluments of the exterior and interior personnel of our foreign service. This had provoked a steady pressure from the political parties for the appointment of their own men to such comfortable positions. The second was the collusion between those political parties and the irresistible Mr. Titulescu, which almost always resulted in the placing of personnel loyal to him in the key posts of our foreign service structure. An atmosphere of almost terroristic uniformity and conformity settled, therefore, over the personnel of our legations and embassies. That is why in this critical period of our foreign policy there was, besides the writer, only one of our representatives abroad who chose to recognize and to denounce the danger of Mr. Titulescu's activities to Rumania's security. He was Victor Cadere, our Minister in Warsaw.

No sooner had Titulescu taken the Foreign Affairs portfolio in 1932 than he hastened to diminish and counteract the authority of my information, replacing me in Helsinki by one of his admirers. I still had Latvia and Estonia under my administration, but I had no doubt that this was a very provisional situation. It was, therefore, no surprise to me when I received word in the fall of 1935 that I was being transferred to Caracas, the capital of Venezuela.

This information was followed by telegraphed details about the travel expenses that were being put at my disposal—four thousand dollars, rather a big sum in those times. I have forgotten the exact amount of my emolument, but I remember that it was also in proportion to Titulescu's internationally well-known generosity.

My friend Cadere had been transferred from Warsaw to Rio de Janeiro in still more lavish circumstances. We both decided not to leave Europe. This was my telegram to Mr. Titulescu:

I THANK YOUR EXCELLENCY FOR THIS NEW PROOF OF CONFIDENCE STOP OUR RELATIONS WITH SOVIET RUSSIA ARE FOR US OF SPECIAL INTEREST AT THE PRESENT TIME STOP I PREFER THEREFORE TO PUT MY EXPERIENCE AND MY INFORMATION ON THE SUBJECT AT YOUR EXCELLENCY'S DISPOSAL STOP I ASK THEREFORE TO BE TRANSFERRED TO BUCHAREST AT OUR CENTRAL ADMINISTRATION STOP STURDZA

CHAPTER

VIII

The Murder in Marseilles and the Purloined Telegram

There is no better way to know the truth about certain controversial points in the history of Europe between the two World Wars than to take the opposite of Mr. Vladimir Potemkin's assertions in his book *History of Soviet Diplomacy*. And if Potemkin's assertions agree with those of Mme. Geneviève Tabouis,[1] you may be sure that you have hit it right.

King Alexander of Yugoslavia was killed on October 9, 1934, in Marseilles, by a Croat terrorist. Mr. Jean Barthou, the French Foreign Minister, fell under the same rain of bullets. For Mr. Potemkin and for Mme. Tabouis, the death of King Alexander was a simple accident; the intended victim had been Mr. Barthou, the untiring advocate of a military alliance between France and Soviet Russia. The crime had been therefore a "Fascist" crime, to use Mr. Potemkin's expression.

There had been two murders in Marseilles: a murder by *commission,* perpetrated by the Croat terrorist; and a murder by *omission,* for which the French authorities, and especially Albert Sarraut, the French Minister of the Interior, were entirely responsible.

The civilian and military official circles in Marseilles had taken all the proper measures of security for the protection of King Alexander's life. As a matter of fact, the measures they had decided upon were exactly those that had been taken a short time before for the reception of the Sultan of Morocco. At the very last moment, however, Sarraut ordered all these measures called off and replaced them with inadequate

[1] Mme. Tabouis belonged to the leftist group of French political writers. She was one of the League of Nations' "sirens," a great friend of Titulescu and of Litvinov. She is the author of *Ils l'ont appelée Cassandra* (New York: Éditions de la Maison Française, Inc., 1942).

64

ones. The motive invoked publicly by the French Minister was his desire not to impress unfavorably the Marseilles voters by too great a military display on the eve of a municipal election. In fact, the King's car was accompanied only by one officer on horseback; a few lonely police officers were posted at crossroads.

Mr. Sarraut publicly recognized his mistake and resigned immediately after the tragedy, stating, "A chief is always responsible."

We do not believe that this explanation is good enough, and we agree with the sentiment expressed in Paris by Queen Marie of Rumania, the mother-in-law of the murdered King, to an important French personality: "I am ashamed for France!"

Everybody knew, and Sarraut had to know better than anybody else, that King Alexander was the target for four terroristic organizations: the Croats, the Macedonians, the Hungarians, and the Communist terrorists in general. The temerity and the contempt of the fear of death of the Croat and the Macedonian conspirators were common knowledge. To call off in such circumstances all the security measures that had been decided upon *was simply to sentence the King of Yugoslavia to death.*

The consternation, the horror, were universal; they would have been still greater had it been known that the British and Rumanian Governments had offered to the French police the collaborations of some of their own agents who could even recognize personally some of the would-be murderers; but the French police declined their offer.

King Alexander had viewed with concern and disgust the course recently adopted by the foreign policy of Rumania and Czecho-Slovakia, Yugoslavia's partners in the Little Entente. The ostracism of the Soviets from European political life had been for the Yugoslav King not only a political necessity but also an inescapable moral obligation. He had refused to associate himself with the various steps in the process of "rapprochement" between Communist and non-Communist countries. Yugoslavia had abruptly abandoned the conference of the Little Entente in Zagreb in January 1934 when it was announced that Rumania intended to resume diplomatic relations with the Kremlin. The King's disgust rose to a rage when he realized that Titulescu and Beneš were after not only a better political and economic understanding with the Soviet Union, but were also striving for a new military alliance between France and Russia, with Rumania and Czecho-Slovakia as associates.

The purpose of King Alexander's visit to Paris was to declare, openly and firmly, Yugoslavia's opposition to any further steps in a political process which, in his opinion, would lead unavoidably to a new European war. He had already let it be known that a Franco-Soviet military alliance would free Yugoslavia of all of her contractual obligations toward France and the Little Entente, and would force her to look for security in another political system. At the moment of his assassination King Alexander was, therefore, the greatest obstacle to the Barthou-Titulescu-Beneš policy, the policy of the encirclement of Germany. The double murder in Marseilles was not, obviously, a "Fascist" or a "Nazi" murder, as Mr. Potemkin and Mme. Tabouis insistently suggested. King Alexander was the intended victim of both the murder by commission and the murder by omission.

The German reaction was immediate. Yugoslavia had never altered until then her attitude of hostile mistrust toward Soviet Russia; the connivance between Czecho-Slovak and Soviet officials, regarding policy, was common knowledge. Germany had to know, first, if King Alexander's murder was likely to bring about any change in Yugoslav foreign policy; and second, in what measure, exactly, Rumania had come over to the Czecho-Slovak side in her attitude toward Soviet Russia and Germany respectively.

I happened to be in Berlin the day after General Göring's return from Belgrade where he had attended King Alexander's funeral. At our Legation, Petrescu-Comnen, our Minister in Berlin, informed me that Göring had asked to see him the very day of Göring's return and had entrusted him with a very important message for our Government. Petrescu-Comnen showed me the telegram by which he was informing our Ministry of Foreign Affairs of the General's declarations and proposals.

Germany—Göring told him—had never, like Italy, encouraged Hungary's irredentism. She was not interested in Hungary, but was very much interested in Rumania because of the traditionally good relations that had prevailed between both countries before the last war, because of our natural riches and possibilities of development and because of our geographic and military situation. *Germany was prepared to guarantee Rumania's frontiers and integrity against any aggression.* Germany did not ask Rumania to change anything in her system of alliances. The only thing she asked was our pledge that, like our ally Poland, we would never permit the Soviet armies to pass across our territory.

Germany also offered, if we so wanted, to arm the Rumanian Army immediately, completely, at low cost, and with her best matériel.

Petrescu-Comnen asked General Göring if similar proposals had been made to our two partners in the Little Entente, especially to Czecho-Slovakia. Göring answered that all of Germany's friendly approaches had been unceremoniously spurned by Prague. With Yugoslavia a friendly understanding had been reached and continued to prevail.

Both Petrescu-Comnen and I realized without difficulty the importance for our country of General Göring's declarations and proposals.

I also saw in them excellent ammunition for the campaign I had decided to wage against Titulescu's pro-Soviet policy.

Back in Bucharest, after about a week, I asked my colleagues at the political department of our Ministry, Mişu Arion and Alexandru Cretzianu, the head and the assistant head of the department, what their opinion about Göring's message was. They had never heard of it, and had never seen Petrescu-Comnen's telegram. According to a new disposition, every telegram received passed directly from the cipher department to the hands of a bright young chap, Savel Rădulescu, whom Titulescu had brought with him to the Palais Sturdza. It was young Rădulescu who decided which of those messages was to be communicated to whom.

I went back several times to the political department, where I found my colleagues in the same state of ignorance and perplexity. Meanwhile, I had ascertained that neither the Secretary General of our Foreign Office, nor any member of the Government, had the slightest knowledge about Germany's proposals. When I realized that the unbelievable was true, that Titulescu intended to withhold this important piece of information until such time as he could find a way to make it useless for Rumania, I decided to act.

In fact, all that Germany was asking from us in exchange for their proposed guarantee was our promise to do that which, in any case, we should have been anxious to do: to defend our frontiers against any enemy. Her guarantee applied not only to our frontier with Hungary but also to our frontier with Soviet Russia, a guarantee we had not been able to secure contractually, in an undebatable way, from our allies of World War I. The only safeguard for those borders was our military and political arrangements with Poland. The German guarantee was, moreover, additional to all those, whatever their value, procured by our other international understandings. So there was no imaginable reason why Göring's offer should not have received at least fair consideration. I knew, however, too well, Titulescu's uncanny ingenuity, and I also knew there were many ways for an unscrupulous negotiator to bungle willfully, without much risk to himself even the arrangements that were most favorable for his own country.

I appealed to Gheorghe Brătianu, the chief of the Liberal Dissident Party and a distant kinsman—a man of action, courage, and patriotism (as he proved for the last time thirty years later when he preferred to die in a Communist prison rather than execute the wishes of the Red Government in Bucharest).

With an approximate reconstruction of Petrescu-Comnen's message before us, we pondered the best possible procedure. Brătianu asked for permission to declare publicly the information conveyed. I could not give this permission, because what was at stake had been the subject of a ciphered message; and besides I did not wish to betray Petrescu-Comnen's confidence. Moreover, it would have been imprudent to give Titulescu a premature opportunity at sabotage, which could have resulted in the German Government's playing its Hungarian instead of its Rumanian card.

We decided that Brătianu ought to go to Berlin, ask for an interview with Göring, and have Göring repeat his declarations and proposals. Brătianu did go to Berlin with one of his political friends, Ata Constantinescu, and was received by the General.

The reception by Göring was extremely cordial. "It is a happy country where the same family can count among its members three generations of statesmen," said the General, alluding to Brătianu's father and grandfather. "This does not happen today in Germany." Göring repeated to Brătianu the same proposals he had made to Petrescu-Comnen on October 22, 1934, stating once again that we were not asked to break any of our alliances and repeating Germany's offer to provide our army with complete and modern armament. All that Germany was asking from us in return was the pledge that Rumania—following her ally Poland's example—would never allow Soviet troops to pass over her territory without resisting, arms in hand . . . with, indeed, those excellent and abundant arms Germany was offering us.

Let us pause to observe that what happened—or did not happen—in the fall of 1934, and in the following months, between Rumania and Germany had a direct and decisive bearing on the events that led the world to the most recent fratricidal war between countries of Western Civilization. This World War, like the first one, was to leave only one victor on the political and historical fields: International Communism as embodied in Soviet Russia. At that time, and even after the first twenty-two months of the conflict forced on him by the Western Powers, Hitler wanted no other war than that for which he had reconstructed Germany's military power: the crusade against Soviet Russia, against the Communist monstrosity. What he feared—and what finally happened—was a new Franco-Russian alliance linking Communist Russia and the Western Powers militarily and politically, and bringing him against his will into a Western war in which Germany had nothing to win and perhaps everything to lose.

The idea of a Franco-Soviet military alliance, the alliance that eventually was to put the spark to the powder magazine, could not have been sold even to the leftist French legislators except for the promise of a practicable possibility of bringing Red troops into geographic contact with Germany without these troops having to fight their way across the territory of France's allies; such an attempt would have immediately brought Poland and the Baltic States onto Germany's side in the event of a European conflagration. Only Rumania could provide the pro-Soviet conspiracy with such a right-of-way; since this could not be done with the consent of the Rumanian people, it had to be arranged secretly and by stealth.

There was, indeed, a pro-Soviet international conspiracy that extended to the other side of the Atlantic. Its chief purpose at that special political moment was to divert upon the Western Powers the thunder with which Germany intended to strike Soviet Russia, in order to spare Communism's home base the first impact of Germany's smashing blows; to save, in other words, International Communism. Titulescu belonged to this international conspiracy and his henchmen followed blindly, and sometimes very cleverly, his instructions. Petrescu-Comnen, our Minister in Berlin, was one of them.

Unlike Mr. Petrescu-Comnen, I was unfortunately not able to preserve abroad even a part of my private records. I will appeal, therefore, to the appropriate passages I have found in his books, *I Responsabili* and *Preludi del Grande Dramma,* to establish the part that secret Rumanian policy played in the preparation of what Winston Churchill—one of Communism's rescuers—called "the needless war."

Petrescu-Comnen's records are all the more interesting because he was one of the principal tools of the Titulescu-Beneš strategy, a great admirer of King Carol, of Armand Călinescu and of Mr. Ostrowsky, the Soviet Minister in Bucharest, "who unfolded an excellent activity, helping in every way Mr. Titulescu's policy of reconciliation." Charity asks us to allow that Petrescu-Comnen perhaps actually believed that Soviet Russia would evacuate all of Rumania's territory and would not try to exercise any influence upon the political regime of the country if we permitted her troops to occupy it "momentarily," although I think that he was too intelligent for that. In any case, while in London with King Carol in 1938, according to his own memoirs, at no moment in his conversations with Neville Chamberlain and Lord Halifax did he ever mention even the existence of the specific danger to Rumania represented by Soviet Russia, and at no moment did he strive to obtain Great Britain's support for any eventuality other than that of German aggression. In Paris he adopted exactly the same attitude, thereby preparing the way for the sinister "guarantees" limited to our Western frontiers that struck the toll of Poland's and Rumania's independence. As Minister of Foreign Affairs he did everything in his power to embarrass our ally Poland in her relations with Germany. He was a member of the Government that managed Codreanu's assassination, and until his death he belonged to the host of the Legion's slanderers.

Here is the way Petrescu-Comnen reproduces in his memoirs the important statements made to him by General Göring on October 22, 1934, after lunch at the Rumanian Legation:

He started telling me that Germany wanted to establish sincere and friendly relations with Rumania and Yugoslavia and that no note of discord existed between Germany and these two countries. He did not make any allusion or reference to Czecho-Slovakia. To my question "What happened to your great friendship toward Hungary?" he answered, "Hungary does not interest us; we won't make again the error of pulling chestnuts out of the fire for others. Besides the numerous economic interests that connect us to Rumania and Yugoslavia, there is also the fact that you treat the German minorities very well." And in order to give more weight to his words, he told me that he had talked that day with the Führer, whom he told, incidentally, he was lunching with me, and that the Führer authorized him to talk as he had done.[2]

In this rendering of Petrescu-Comnen's report to Titulescu after the interview with Göring, five important elements that were present in the purloined telegram, and are still very vivid in my memory, are missing: 1. Göring had declared to our Envoy that Germany was prepared to guarantee all our frontiers against any aggression; 2. Göring had offered a complete and modern rearmament of our troops; 3. Göring had asked in exchange Rumania's pledge that she would oppose with all her forces any attempt of Soviet troops to cross her territory; 4. Göring had stressed the fact that we were not being asked to abandon any of our present alliances; 5. To a question concerning Germany's relations with Czecho-Slovakia, Göring had answered that Czecho-Slovakia was the first among the Little Entente countries to which Germany had addressed herself with friendly proposals, but that those overtures had always been disdainfully rejected by Beneš.

Petrescu-Comnen also had been completely acquainted with Göring's declarations to Gheorghe Brătianu, which were thoughtfully transmitted to him in detail. Petrescu-Comnen's lapse of memory is easy to explain. It was Titulescu's and his agents' policy to deny any importance and any sincerity to the German proposals, and to pretend that they represented only a clumsy attempt to dissociate us from Czecho-Slovakia. It was in this same way that the reiterated German proposals were treated by King Carol and all his Governments even after Titulescu's elimination from our political life. "Göring's overtures were considered with curiosity in Bucharest . . . they did not find the echo desired by the crafty German General," comments Petrescu-Comnen.

Nobody was asking us to part with Czecho-Slovakia, but to part with Beneš's and Titulescu's policy—which Germany had every reason to

[2] Petrescu-Comnen, *I Responsabili*, p. 233.

believe to be part of a policy of encirclement—and to give the proper assurances that we would not participate in that encirclement by permitting the Russian hordes to use Rumania as a base of operation. How justified were Germany's apprehensions is demonstrated by Joseph Paul-Boncour, former French Foreign Minister and Prime Minister, in his memoirs, quoted by Mr. Petrescu-Comnen in his *Preludi*:

> In his memoirs, Paul-Boncour, who was often a witness to the Russian-Rumanian negotiations, affirms that Titulescu and Litvinov had reached an agreement by which Rumania pledged herself to permit Russian troops and matériel to pass through her territory in case of a German attack against states that were bound by treaties of mutual assistance with Soviet Russia and with Rumania. Even King Carol, says the former Prime Minister, had been won to this idea of free passage for Soviet troops. In an audience at the Hotel Meurice in Paris, after an examination of this important question, the King told him: *"I promise you, Boncour, that I will conclude that agreement* [about the free passage of Russian troops]. *I understand very well its importance for the functioning of your alliance and therefore for us also. But give me time to accustom my people's mind to this idea, and in a certain measure my mind also."* [Italics added.]

Let us anticipate and observe that the first measure taken by Carol "to accustom his people's mind" to the idea of a Soviet military occupation was the assassination of Corneliu Codreanu a few days after Carol's conversation with Paul-Boncour, and the suppression, by murder and imprisonment, of the Legionary Movement's activities.

At that time—the fall of 1935—the sabotaging policy of Titulescu and his agents was to interpret certain German newspaper articles that were critical of Titulescu's pro-Soviet policy as insulting to Rumania and as proof of the insincerity of Hitler and Göring's friendly overtures. Those articles were taken as pretexts for provocative and even derisive interventions at the Auswärtige Amt (Foreign Ministry in Berlin).

> Titulescu then gave me [October 1935] the order to declare solemnly at the Auswärtige Amt [says Petrescu-Comnen] that this campaign [of denigration of his policy] was highly detrimental to Rumanian-German relations. Our geographic position forced us to take into consideration the Soviet reality. If the Soviets would declare themselves prepared to guarantee our territorial integrity together with that of our allies, we could consider a pact of friendship and *even of mutual assistance with them.* If Germany were prepared to guarantee not only our integrity but that of our allies, we could conclude a similar treaty with her.[3]

In other words, Petrescu-Comnen had been instructed to inform Germany that Rumania was prepared to sign a pact of mutual assistance with Russia, and to suggest the possibility of a similar pact with Ger-

[3] *Ibid.,* p. 236. Italics added.

many if Germany were prepared to guarantee Czecho-Slovakia's integrity. To realize the dimension of this act of provocation and of those that followed, we must remember the political atmosphere of the moment and the state of irritation and anxiety to which the whole of Germany, and certainly the German Foreign Minister also, had been brought by the signing of the Franco-Soviet and the Czecho-Soviet Pacts of military assistance. In Berlin nobody ignored the decisive part Titulescu had played in the preparation and the conclusion of those two diplomatic instruments. It is very likely that many also knew that the Franco-Soviet pact of mutual assistance had been entirely worded by Titulescu. As a riposte to this beginning of encirclement, Germany was preparing the reoccupation of the Rhineland, with all the risks this daring decision implied, and was awaiting only the ratification of the pact by the French Parliament to put her tank divisions in gear. Titulescu, who, with the signing of the Franco-Soviet and Czecho-Soviet pacts of mutual military assistance, had reached the apex of his career, without even waiting for Petrescu-Comnen's report about the result of his act of provocation, was organizing noisy press conferences at which he was boasting, in offending terms to Germany, about this peremptory act of sabotage with which his Envoy in Berlin had been entrusted.

Germany's interest in a Rumanian pledge to resist any Soviet incursion was so great that, despite all the rebukes she had already received, she renewed several times her insistences. On November 13, 1936, Petrescu-Comnen received a visit from Colonel Schunke, the German Military Attaché in Bucharest, who repeated the German offer of friendship and assistance and insisted again upon the fact that "Germany asks from Rumania one thing only: not to play the game of the Soviets, her intractable enemy. Germany does not ask Rumania to neglect any of her interests or abandon any of her alliances." At the same time an article in the *Völkischer Beobachter,* of obvious official origin and referring to Hungarian revisionism, renewed the assurances we had already received so often from Germany. "Fantastic revisionist exigencies," said this article, "are extremist impulses that do not, in the least, take into account the realities of life."

It was not due to Petrescu-Comnen's exertions, or to those of anybody at the Rumanian Foreign Office, that the occasion was given to Hitler himself to repeat the German offer, reiterating Germany's friendly dispositions toward Rumania, and specifying the only promise asked in exchange.

We had come to the conclusion with Gheorghe Brătianu that some new step should be taken to bring to the attention of the Rumanian public the fact that there were other possibilities for guaranteeing the integrity of our territory—against not only the theoretical danger of

Hungarian irredentist pretensions, but against also the real and even mortal danger of Soviet aggression—than those offered by the Little Entente or the Balkan Alliance. Accordingly, Gheorghe Brătianu again went to Berlin, this time to get an audience with Hitler, while I went once more to Paris to share my information with our friends in the French Parliament who were fighting against the ratification of the Franco-Soviet military alliance.

> Not only, said the Führer to Brătianu [as reported by Petrescu-Comnen] do we not wish Rumania's disintegration, but we believe that it is to our own interest that Rumania become as big and as strong as possible because she constitutes an important bulwark against danger from the East. In such circumstances, Germany will never encourage or approve Hungarian revisionism; I have let this be known to Admiral Horthy and to Kanya, who were advised to take example from Germany, which in the interest of peace and in order to preserve Europe from Bolshevism has given up many revendications—even that of Alsace-Lorraine.[4]

I think that for two reasons we are justified in asking our readers to follow further with patience the story of those repeated attempts of the German leaders to get Rumania's assurance that she would defend her own territory against a Soviet incursion: 1. The constant refusal of Rumania's responsible statesmen—King, Prime Minister, and Foreign Minister—to give this assurance was one of the principal factors in the shaping of the series of situations that led the world to the last conflagration, and is therefore not only of Rumanian but of universal interest; 2. The activities of those statesmen, which culminated in the disappearance of Rumania as an independent state and a free nation, show how easy it is for a clique of no more than a dozen persons, if they are the *wrong* persons in the *right* places, to bring a country—and perhaps a whole civilization—to its perdition by preventing the will-to-live of the majority from having an opportunity to manifest itself before the occurrence of the catastrophe.

A similar situation and the same dangers might present themselves today in other countries with less chance of being detected in time, the mechanisms of misinformation and of no information having been brought, meanwhile, to quasi-perfection.

Petrescu-Comnen tells us about another German attempt in December 1936 which was made under his administration of our Legation in Berlin, to convince Rumania's leadership of the necessity of defending Rumania's territory. Here is the account of his next-to-last interview with General Göring, as related by this representative-at-large of Rumanian interests. This interview, together with what preceded and what

[4] *Ibid.,* p. 250.

followed it, might be taken as a model of perfidious diplomatic sabotage of an historic opportunity:

> When we were left alone the General began with a résumé of the conversation the Führer and he had had with Gheorghe Brătianu. The version he gave me was entirely in accord with what I knew. Then he added the following with one comment that he was carrying out the Führer's instructions:
>
> "We would like to have the same relations with you that we have with Yugoslavia, with which we have reached 'eine ganz klare Abmachung' [a very clear understanding]. We do not ask anything else but the assurance that you won't enter into any combination (*sic*) against Germany. In exchange for such assurance we are prepared to give you a formal guarantee of state concerning your territorial integrity. We have no alliance with the Magyars. We offer you our friendship. If you reject it, do not wonder if we bind ourselves rather with the Hungarians and the Bulgarians. In case of a betterment of our relations we will offer you important economic advantages and we will help you to reinforce your military power. We will give you our best weapons, 'ganz vertraulich Waffen' [even the most secret]. . . .
>
> "We can only rejoice in your good relations with Poland, and I can assure you that I have always advised my friends in Warsaw (*sic*) to take care to keep and increase this friendship. . . . In what concerns the Little Entente, we have no objection to it, provided it adheres to its initial purpose of keeping the Hungarians warned. . . . In what concerns France, as long as her relations with Rumania are within the limits of the Geneva agreements, in my personal opinion they do not constitute any obstruction to our future relations." [5]

Petrescu-Comnen's objection to Göring, on the grounds that "he was astonished at the General's statements" was pure impudence, as those statements were the exact replica of what Göring had told the Rumanian Envoy a few months earlier, and were, besides, the very same thing Göring had told Gheorghe Brătianu. As for Petrescu-Comnen's declarations that he was "not prepared to take part in a political discussion" and that he had to "limit himself to certain precise questions of economic character," they were in such contradiction to all that is expected from the accredited envoy of a foreign country—whose obligation at least is to listen with polite attention to proposals of political character and to examine their extent and significance with the proposing party before referring them to his Government—that Göring ought to have considered them a coarse and premeditated rebuke.

> As a conclusion [says Petrescu-Comnen] the General told me that he had been ordered by the Führer to state that he, the Führer, was prepared to

[5] *Ibid.*, pp. 253–254. *Sic* in both cases was added by Petrescu-Comnen. *Sic* after "my friends in Warsaw" means that Petrescu-Comnen, knowing the sentiments entertained at that time in Bucharest toward our ally Poland, did not want to mention, without an accusing sneer, any allusion to friendly relations between Berlin and Warsaw.

renew personally and officially all those pledges and would be glad to receive me at my earliest convenience to confirm them personally.[6]

Our Envoy in Berlin took it upon himself never to answer this special and precise invitation from the chief of the German State—an invitation to which custom obliged him to respond, and permitted him to respond without further consultation with Bucharest. Instead of going to the highly authoritative source—Hitler—to fathom the sincerity and the reach of the German proposals, Petrescu-Comnen started a new campaign of harassment of the German Foreign Office because of certain articles in the German press—articles that he pretended contradicted the friendly proposals that he had squarely refused to consider.

In the face of what he pretended were those "astonishing" insistences of the German statesmen, Petrescu-Comnen felt obliged to go to Bucharest to get, personally, instructions from his superiors. He was extremely happy, he tells us, to receive from the King, from Prime Minister Tătărescu and from Minister of Foreign Affairs Victor Antonescu, instructions "substantially in accord with those I received from Nicolae Titulescu in 1935." Those instructions included, he tells us: 1. Fidelity to the League of Nations; 2. Fidelity to our allies; 3. The greatest possible improvement of our relations with Soviet Russia; 4. Development of our economic relations with Germany.

Regarding the second point alone, it is essential to observe that it refers, in fact, exclusively to Czecho-Slovakia, who by her participation in the new system of encirclement of Germany had lost her status and her usefulness as a member of the Little Entente—an alliance the purpose of which was to counteract Hungarian irredentist pretensions. At that very moment Beneš was wantonly provoking Germany and Italy by the huge armament matériel he was sending through France to Communist Spain, and by his telegrams of congratulations and sympathies to blood-thirsty Juan Negrín. The second point did not refer either to Yugoslavia or to Poland, both of which were also our allies. Indeed, the Bucharest Government, and Petrescu-Comnen himself, had openly manifested discontent, and even indignation, at the pact of friendship recently signed by Count Ciano and Mr. Stoidadinovici between Italy and Yugoslavia and Germany and Yugoslavia—two diplomatic instruments of obvious importance for our Balkan ally. We learn, on the other hand, in Petrescu-Comnen's *Preludi*, how he opposed, as Rumanian Foreign Minister, every effort of Colonel Beck, the Polish Foreign Minister, to find a stable understanding with the enemy.

An understanding with Germany would not only have been the best guarantee of survival history could have offered to heroically resurrected

[6] *Ibid*

Poland, but also the best guarantee for Rumania against the lethal danger represented by Soviet Russia's territorial ambitions and messianic aspirations. This danger was felt, by instinct or by wisdom, by twenty million Rumanians; but the dozen people who, with King Carol, held the responsibility of Rumania's foreign policy, along with two dozen servile henchmen like Petrescu-Comnen, decided or were forced under irresistible pressure to ignore this danger completely.

Petrescu-Comnen returned to Berlin, dauntlessly heartened by the encouragement and the instructions he had received in Rumania. Here is his narrative, concerning these instructions and the last interview he had with Göring before returning as Minister of Foreign Affairs to his doomed country:

> While I was still in Bucharest, Göring had asked several times about the date of my return, and urged our chargé d'affaires to tell me that he wanted to see me as promptly as possible. Abiding by the instructions I had received, I tried however, to delay the interview. But, pressed by the impetuous General, who wanted to talk with me "on behalf of the Führer," I went to his sumptuous lodging in the Leipzigerstrasse, March 20, 1937, *and I faced him with such declarations that we could today call them heroical.* Small Rumania surrounded by a world of enemies and of dubious friends had the courage to declare, without circumlocutions, that "Rumania wanted to stipulate first of all, that she had no intention of abandoning any of her present friendships or alliances." I declared also, as I had done before, that we did not intend to enter any arrangement that could bring us in conflict with Soviet Russia. That was the last interview I had with Göring. Later I was accused of not having had any understanding of the Führer's "generous" proposals.[7]

This heroic Parthian arrow did not terminate Petrescu-Comnen's participation in the work of sabotaging the essential interests of his country. The final torpedoing of any possibility of understanding between Germany and a Rumania still territorially and morally unmutilated was still to come. It fell to the Government in which Petrescu-Comnen was Minister of Foreign Affairs to condone both the assassination of Codreanu and the attempt to annihilate by murder, prison and barbarous oppression the only political formation that had foreseen the imminence, the enormity and the treachery of the events that eventually wiped free Rumania from the map of Europe.

It was the same treasonous indifference to specific Rumanian interests and specific Rumanian dangers, reinforced this time by the special financial interests of Carol and his camarilla, that made this ruling clique ignore totally another part of the German proposal: a quick and up-to-date rearmament of our troops. As a result, the Rumanian soldier

[7] *Ibid.*, p. 261. Italics added.

was forced to enter World War II, as he had entered World War I, with utterly incomplete and obsolete armament.

The year 1939 found our army in a state of complete unpreparedness. We had no armor, no modern anti-aircraft artillery; our artillery, all of it horse-driven, was composed of old Krupp guns of World War I and of guns that were captured from Bolshevik troops during the last months of that war. All of them were patched with a contraption that was supposed to bring their ballistics up to modern requirement. There was some heavy field artillery (also horse-driven), the clumsy Skoda matériel, which we were finally forced to accept. Our Air Force was neither in quantity nor quality a complement to our gallant and brilliant young airmen. Our infantry rifles and machine guns were of three different bores, and in that state of decrepitude known as "wild shooting." Meanwhile, in the period between King Carol's return and 1939, twenty-eight billion *lei* (about 140,000,000 dollars) had been spent from the budget for national defense.

Considering Rumania's political and strategic situation and the urgency of the menace at our eastern frontier, any wise and patriotic rearmament program should have provided for the hasty acquisition of heavy and semi-heavy material from some reliable foreign industry, and for the creation, in the central region of the country, of a complex of light weapons and ammunition factories. Instead, billions were spent in an insane attempt to create, in a fight with time, a national heavy-armament industry that would be able to produce tanks and artillery of all sizes. Factories were mounted and dismounted according to the interests of the King and his protégés. Billions were scattered and hoarded; but not a tank, not a heavy or light piece of artillery was produced, not even a machine gun or a rifle. Remaining permanent masters of the battlefields had thereby become an impossible task for our infantry, regardless of the gallantry of the soldier and the efficiency of his leader.

Göring's offer to rearm us completely and fittingly was not the first offer we had received of this nature: A previous Japanese suggestion had not even been considered. The same thing happened with Göring's proposal. We have also seen how one of our Governments declined in a moment of crisis the generous offer of King Alexander of Yugoslavia.

The same politicians, the same military authorities or advisers who had been accomplices, even if only by their silence, in the gigantic armament swindle that was one of the characteristics of Carol's reign, were compelled, when the hour of truth came with the Kremlin's ultimatum of June 1940, to admit along with the billionaire King that those twenty-eight billion *lei* had been spent in vain.

PART THREE

King Carol
the Murderer

At the prison we all entered one of the cells where Majors Dinulescu and Macoveanu demonstrated how we were to kill the Legionaries. Asking the chauffeur of our car to kneel, Major Dinulescu slipped from behind a bit of rope around the chauffeur's throat and showed us how easy it was to proceed that way.

After that we went into the prison courtyard and each of us received a Legionary in custody. I got one taller and stronger than the others; I learned afterwards that it was the Captain, Corneliu Codreanu.

Sergeant *SARBU*

Of the Gendarmerie

From testimony to the Investigation Committee of the Rumanian High Court

Our greatest national danger is in having deformed our national structure by creating that moral dwarf: the politician. The man who has nothing in common with our national pride and grandeur, the man who kills us and tries to dishonor us.

If that kind of man will go on leading our nation, it will succumb and Rumania will disappear.

Corneliu CODREANU

Pentru Legionari

It is not my life, which I have sacrificed long ago; it is the honor and the existence of this country that are at stake.

Corneliu CODREANU

To his judges

Titulescu and the Military Alliances with Soviet Russia

Two different political concepts existed among the victors of World War I: 1. That of a reconciliation between all the non-Communist countries before the greatest and most horrible menace ever faced by Europe; 2. That which considered the hostilities of World War I only interrupted, and asked for a political and military collaboration with Soviet Russia against Germany in a second World War that was supposed to be unavoidable. The ascent to power of Adolf Hitler and the National Socialist Party in 1933 provoked an acute crisis between the adherents of these two opposed ideas.

The partisans of these two concepts were grouped around two diplomatic instruments: 1. A four-power pact between France, Germany, Great Britain and Italy, proposed by Benito Mussolini and signed, but not ratified, by all the interested powers; 2. A projected pact of mutual military assistance between France, Czecho-Slovakia, and Soviet Russia. The four-power pact never came to life because it was not ratified by the French Parliament. It had been ratified, however, by the House of Commons of Great Britain.

There were indeed many independent and moderate elements in Great Britain ready to approve every process of rapprochement between Germany and her former adversaries. Prime Minister Ramsay MacDonald, Sir Samuel Hoare, Sir John Simon, Lord Hartwood, Lord Lothian, and Lord Rothermere were among them; also the Prince of Wales, who had organized the contacts between the British and former German combatants, and who later had to pay with the Crown for his candid statement to Mr. Stanley Baldwin: "As long as I am here, there will be no war."

Winston Churchill opposed with all his force the four-power pact.

His case deserves special mention. For years he had been the most eloquent and persuasive champion in the struggle against Communism, against the Nameless Beast, as he called it in his thundering book *The Aftermath,* from which we quote:

> An apparition different from everything that had been seen on earth until then, had taken the place of Russia. . . . We had before us a state without nation, an army without country, a religion without God. This government, which was born by revolution and nourished by terror . . . had declared that between it and society no good faith could exist in public and private relations, no understanding had to be respected. . . . That is how there was no more Russia but only an emptiness that persists in human affairs.

From the same work we extract the following interesting passages:

> It is the duty of the civilized world to reconquer Russia. The Soviets do not represent Russia; they represent an international concept entirely foreign and even hostile to what we call civilization. . . . *To win against Russia, militarily and morally, would be too heavy a task for the victors alone, and as we must do it, we will do it with Germany.* Germany knows Russia better than anybody else. . . . That will be for her the great opportunity. It will be this opportunity that will permit a proud and faithful nation to avoid defeat and humiliation. . . . She will pass thereby, almost without transition, from a cruel fight against us to cooperation with us. *Nothing is possible in Europe without Germany, everything is possible with her.* [Italics added.]

In schizophrenic contradiction to all his former, so strongly expressed convictions, Mr. Churchill, shortly after Hitler came to power, suddenly moved from the anti-Communist camp to become the irreconcilable enemy of that same Germany he once wanted to send against the Soviets in 1919–1922. We will find him about twenty years later asking forgiveness of Stalin, as he narrates it himself, for his former anti-Communist campaigns.

Anthony Eden followed with fanaticism the new policy of Mr. Churchill. His trip to Warsaw and Moscow in March 1935 had exactly the same scope as those of the defunct Jean Barthou: the organizing of Germany's encirclement. In Warsaw he had been given a rather cold reception by Marshal Pilsudski. The Marshal strongly advised him to leave Eastern Europe alone and to worry instead about the British Empire in general and about Jamaica in particular. From Moscow Anthony Eden returned to his country with pleasant reports only: "I have seen a people at work. . . ." He had not let himself see anything else. He also brought with him that celebrated declaration, which might easily be considered one of the most incredible statements of the century, "It would be absurd to believe that Russia has any aggressive intentions toward Poland."

In the French Parliament the partisans of a Franco-Czecho-Soviet alliance (members of the Radical Socialist, Socialist, and Communist parties) were encountering powerful and determined opposition that could have triumphed, perhaps, but for the big tactical error of Pierre Laval, the Prime Minister—an error which was to cost him his life.

After long resistance, Mr. Laval finally signed the Franco-Soviet treaty, May 2, 1935, counting upon his resourcefulness to turn up, at the last moment, a majority in the French Parliament that would refuse to ratify it. He was mistaken. By signing the treaty he had done all that was expected of him. He was promptly overthrown—with his British colleague Sir Samuel Hoare, when they tried to find a formula of conciliation between Italy and Ethiopia—by a joint and remarkable effort on the part of the philosophical and Fabian circles in France and Great Britain, roused in haste to action by Messrs. Herriot, Sarraut, and Blum in France, and by Lord Cecil and Mr. Eden in Great Britain.

The motives that animated the various opponents of the four-power pact and partisans of a Franco-Soviet alliance were of a different nature. There was among French people, of course, a traditional hatred of Germany. Such had been very likely the case of Jean Barthou, who had lost a son in World War I. The ineffable Vladimir Potemkin writes, in his *History of Soviet Diplomacy*: "Barthou, as every good Frenchman, hated the Germans." There had appeared, or reappeared, at that time a much more important and powerful factor, if less visible, in the worldwide political game: the Anonymous Powers—the malevolent jinns who midwifed the Bolshevik Revolution, who guided and protected its first steps, saved it several times from an impending death, condoned or covered all of its crimes and treachery—who had decided that the hammer and the sickle, and not the Cross, should be the symbol and the law of the world to come. The interests of those powers had very little to do with those of the nations concerned. Their intentions and their goals originated much farther back than the situations and events of that special epoch, and went far beyond them in their sweeping vision and all-embracing dreams. Those forces had been helped by the murders of General Štefánik, of Admiral Kolchak, of French President Doumer, of King Alexander of Yugoslavia, as they were to be helped later by the kidnapping—under the half-closed eyes of the French police—and the murder of General Kutiepov and General Miller. *They were helped more than anything else by President Roosevelt's letter to Kalinin and by the second Bullitt mission.*

From the other side of the Atlantic these powers were receiving the impetus that would eventually lead them over all hurdles and defeats to the final triumphs of Teheran, Yalta, Potsdam, and San Francisco. They had their devoted adherents and servants in non-Communist Europe, and the most opulently remunerated and easiest to identify by the flagrant contradiction between his activities and the interests of the country he represented was Nicolae Titulescu.

Again we open Vladimir Potemkin's book:

> Everybody knew that the representatives of the Little Entente had brought a certain contribution to the conclusion of the Franco-Soviet alliance [N.B. the pact of mutual military assistance between France, Czecho-Slovakia and Soviet Russia]. Mr. Beneš in Czecho-Slovakia and Mr. Titulescu in Rumania saw in this convention one of the most efficient guarantees of the security of their own countries. This was the motive for those two diplomats' *insistence on convincing the French government of the necessity of concluding very promptly its negotiations with the Soviet Government.* [Italics added.]

Potemkin does not exaggerate the energy and importance of the pressures of Titulescu and Beneš on the French Government to enter into an alliance that imperiled all the pacifying diplomatic arrangements concluded at that time between the former enemies. But those combined pressures would not have been enough to guarantee to the government a parliamentary majority for the ratification of such an instrument without the special and indispensable assistance that only Mr. Titulescu was able to procure.

I now ask my readers to glance at a map of Eastern Europe and to remember once more that Soviet Russia had no direct geographical contact with Germany. The treaty of mutual assistance would not have represented, therefore, any advantage for France unless some passage could be found and guaranteed for Soviet troops hastening to the rescue of France and Czecho-Slovakia in the event of an armed conflict with Germany. Poland and the Baltic states had taken an unmistakable stand concerning such an attempt by the Soviet Army: They would not permit it. They knew too well what to expect from the presence of "friendly" Communist divisions in their territory. *The only other possible passage was through Rumania.*

Public opinion in Rumania was as wary of contact with Russian troops as it was in Poland and in the Baltic states. But we did not even have the dubious safeguard of a pact of nonaggression; and besides there was the matter of Russian pretensions over one of our provinces. Nobody could believe that once Russia's job was finished in Central Europe, her troops would evacuate Rumania entirely. There was no doubt that Russia would keep Bessarabia, and the chances were that she would stay in Rumania as long as was necessary to make of it a sister Communist State.

Nobody knew better than Titulescu the Rumanian people's universal aversion toward and fear of its Communist neighbor; and nobody was better qualified to lead for four years between Bucharest and Paris this policy of dissimulation, subterfuge and lies. In Paris this policy permitted the partisans of the Franco-Soviet military alliance to assert on the basis of the most competent authority (the Minister of Foreign Affairs of Rumania) that Rumania would not object, should the moment ever come, to the passage of Soviet troops—although at present a certain amount of discretion had to be maintained concerning it. In Bucharest, this policy permitted the masked adherents, or unconscious helpers of the powers Titulescu was serving, to assert on the basis of the same competent authority that France did not need and did not ask us to take the risk of this passage, and that therefore the Franco-Soviet and Czecho-Soviet treaties did not endanger our borders and the integrity of our territory.

Says Mr. Prost:

> Titulescu will return to Rumania in November 1937 for a couple of days. . . . *Berated by the Iron Guard [the Legionary Movement], he will have the gall to declare that he had opposed in 1933 the dissolution of the Iron Guard and to add that he had made every effort in order to conclude with Germany and Italy pacts that would have put Rumania in the same relation with those two countries as with France and Great Britain. He will pretend also that he has never considered the passage of Soviet troops over Rumanian territory. He was given the lie with such abundance and precision that he hastily left Rumania.*[1]

The stubborn refusal of Titulescu even to consider Germany's proposals had no other explanation than his decision not to agree with the sole condition that was attached to those proposals: the pledge to fight Soviet troops if they ever tried to cross our borders. In fact, any serious scrutiny of Titulescu's policy in the matter of those proposals and of the Franco-Soviet and Czecho-Soviet agreements could not leave any doubt about his hidden thoughts and intentions, which were so detrimental to Rumania's interests. Not only did he exert himself to the utmost to help France come to the fatal decision of choosing the Soviets as her principal ally, but he himself wrote every word of the diplomatic instrument which brought this about; a generally little known fact. I do not know if it is true—as he himself boasted several times publicly—that the French Government paid him five hundred thousand francs, as a specialist in international law and lore for this job, but I think that this would not have been an exaggerated sum in payment for such a great service rendered thereby to the pro-Soviet crowd in the Quai

[1] *Destin de la Roumanie*, pp. 95–96. Italics added.

d'Orsay. Obviously Rumania would not oppose an international agreement that had been entirely drawn up by her Minister of Foreign Affairs.

The fight against Titulescu's machinations had to be waged on two fronts—in Bucharest and in Paris. I exerted myself assiduously in both places.

Since my recall from the Baltic States a sort of friendly embargo had been laid upon my person at the Palais Sturdza; I was not given any part in the daily activities of our Ministry. When I asked for some work to do, I was answered with a smile: "Don't they pay you your salary? Why do you complain?" Indeed they paid it to me very regularly, and in order to deserve it I had acquired the habit of remitting personally to Mr. Titulescu's cabinet a bimonthly report recording my views, my interpretations, my suggestions, my advice, and not infrequently my criticisms, about the international events of the preceding fortnight and our reaction to them. Besides, I made it almost a daily duty to try to make some of our political personalities share my misgivings and my fears.

For the Rumanian readers of this book I will mention, as only a part of the complete list, the following persons with whom I discussed (with some of them many times) Titulescu's policy and its dangers: King Carol, the chiefs of the political parties: Iuliu Maniu, Dinu Brătianu, General Averescu, Octavian Goga, Nicolae Iorga; the various Ministers of Foreign Affairs and other important personalities, Gheorghe Mironescu, Victor Antonescu, Constantin Argetoianu, Iuniam, Ion Mitilineu, Gigurtu, Marshal Presnan, and General Antonescu.

I employed the following arguments during those interviews:

1. The simple fact of Rumania's adhesion to the policy of Poland, Finland, and the Baltic States not to permit Soviet Russia to enter their territory would diminish considerably the danger of a new European war, in which Rumania had nothing to win and very much to lose.

2. If, despite all, this war should start and should find us on the same side as the Soviets, it would be a conflagration in which there would be no possible victory for Rumania. A victorious Germany would dismember us to the benefit of Hungary, Bulgaria and perhaps even Russia; a Soviet victory would mean our total disappearance as a national and political entity for an indefinite period in history.

3. In the most optimistic view, even if we could imagine that the victorious Soviet troops would abandon the rest of the country, they would certainly keep Bessarabia.

4. Titulescu's irruption in the Riga negotiations in order to permit the Soviets to maintain and proclaim their pretensions about Bessarabia, and the tricky wording he gave to the Rumanian-Soviet railway

agreement, were for me sufficient proof that in Mr. Titulescu's long-range policy this province (Bessarabia) had already been given up.

I found in the majority of our statesmen, and in King Carol also, a strange insensibility to what was without doubt the greatest danger to Rumania and what ought to have been their greatest worry: the Russian and the Communist menace. The sentimental attachments to our former allies and especially to France could have explained only in part, and only in certain cases, this strange aberration. There was in most of my interlocutors an unmistakable voluntary blindness, a stubborn sectarian docility to suggestions or injunctions of unknown origin that were stronger, it seemed, than their patriotism, which in all fairness I could not question.

Professor Iorga, upon whom I called at his country place in Valeni de Munte, seemed quite convinced by my protestations, and entrusting me with two articles that were strongly to the point and in perfect accord with my views, asked me to leave them in Bucharest at the office of his newspaper *Neamul Românesc*. When I went there, the chief columnist told me that Professor Iorga had meanwhile telephoned that he had changed his mind, and that the articles were not to be published.

Iuliu Maniu, the chief of the National Peasant Party, talked about the Roman empire that Mussolini could have reconstructed had he followed Maniu's advice, but showed a complete lack of comprehension, and even an alarming indifference, concerning the safety of our eastern frontier.

Dinu Brătianu, the chief of the Liberal Party, refused even to consider that there was a Soviet menace, talked only about the dangers that National Socialist Germany represented for the world, and almost showed me the door when I insisted.

General Antonescu, who later was to be the Prime Minister of the Government in which I was Minister of Foreign Affairs, simply cut me off with the question: "Are you also one of those persons who would use our weapons against those who gave them to us?" I asked him about which weapons was he talking; surely not about the Skoda artillery! This did not embarrass the General, who ended a long tirade with this memorable declaration: "Never against France!" I let him observe that we were not France's neighbor but Soviet Russia's, and that in France there were a lot of persons, among them two Marshals, Pétain and Weygand, who had energetically opposed an alliance with Russia. The General stuck to his guns.

Constantin Argetoianu felt that Titulescu's decision not to accept Germany's guarantees and to content himself with those of France and Czecho-Slovakia had very little importance. He, Argetoianu, would get those guarantees later, "And so we will have them both."

Regarding King Carol, suffice it to say that after a long account of my worries about the change in the course of Rumanian foreign policy, an account to which he seemed to listen with interest, he briskly asked me, "Why didn't you accept the Caracas appointment?"

Nicolae Iorga was killed at the hands of a Communist *agent provocateur,* a man named Boeru. Iuliu Maniu and Dinu Brătianu died in Communist prisons after long years of misery. General Antonescu fell under the bullets of a Communist firing squad. Argetoianu, the former member of about two dozen boards of directors of financial and industrial companies, died as a mendicant, of hunger and misery in the streets of Communist Bucharest. In fact, to the best of my knowledge almost all of my former interlocutors of those fateful days who were still alive at the time of the Communist invasion, spent long years, or died, in Communist jails or Communist concentration camps in Rumania or in Soviet Russia. Except, quite naturally, the two chief culprits, King Carol and Mr. Titulescu, who died in their permanent opulence and in an uneventful exile.

We had made several trips to Paris with Gheorghe Brătianu in order to help by our information the opponents to a new Franco-Soviet alliance. We made reiterated contacts with deputies, senators, ministers, prime ministers past and present, and with the press. Our purpose was to convince those political personalities, and through them and through the press French public opinion, that Titulescu was lying and deceiving them by assuring them that Rumania would permit without resistance Soviet armies to march over her territory. We wanted to let them know that opposition to such a possibility was unanimous in Rumania among civilian and military people alike, who saw in it a death sentence for their country.

The nationalist press, *L'Action Francaise, L'Ami du Peuple, Je Suis Partout, Gringoire,* which we supplied with ammunition, was leading a vigorous campaign against the pro-Soviet publicists, well-paid friends of Mr. Titulescu. Philippe Henriot—who later was to be assassinated by the "Resistance"—fought with eloquence and courage in the French Parliament on our side.

When the Franco-Soviet pact was nevertheless signed in May 1935, we applied ourselves with still greater energy in order to help our friends in the French Parliament prevent its ratification.

One day I gave to Philippe Henriot the verbatim text of a short speech by Mr. Titulescu to the Rumanian Senate, which I had heard two days before and which had not been reproduced in the Rumanian or foreign press. In this speech the Rumanian Foreign Minister reassured once more the Rumanian solons about the Franco-Soviet pact, solemnly declaring that the presence of Soviet troops in our territory had never been considered.

I was in the diplomatic tribune of the French Parliament when Henriot drew out of his briefcase the document I had given him the day before, and after a few introductory words started reading it. A team of Communist deputies, headed by Duclos, pounced upon him; a free-for-all fight ensued, and the President of the Chamber of Deputies—Herriot, if I remember correctly—solemnly put on his top hat, according to a time-honored tradition, and closed the session.

After the fall of the Laval Government in 1936, it was Albert Sarraut—long ago pardoned for the murder of King Alexander in Marseilles—who obtained the ratification of a pact that represented nothing less than Europe's death sentence. The vote was 362 to 136 with 100 abstentions—a hundred poor beggars who understood very well what this pact meant for their country and for the world, but who did not dare infringe upon the instructions received.

Prelude to War

When the new Franco-Soviet pact was finally ratified, Marshal Pétain declared to the press: "We won't be long in regretting it!"

The conclusion and the ratification of the Franco-Soviet military alliance was, indeed, an act of folly for France, whatever the advantages it presented for Soviet Russia's involved schemes, or those expected by Czecho-Slovakia. This alliance not only definitely ruled out any possibility of a peace-guaranteeing four-power pact between the former adversaries of World War I, but deprived France of the benefits of all the securities her diplomacy had accumulated in the last eighteen years—all of which were incompatible in letter, spirit and fact with the senseless new instrument. Those securities included the Versailles Treaty, the League of Nations Covenant, the Polish Alliance, the alliance with the countries of the Little Entente, the Franco-Britannic general staff agreement, the Kellogg-Briand Pact, the Locarno agreement and the Stressa agreement.

Marshal Pétain's pessimistic prediction was not long in coming true. Ten days after the ratification by the French Parliament, Baron Konstantin von Neurath, the German Minister of Foreign Affairs, convoked all the ambassadors of the countries that had been signatories of the Locarno Pact and informed them that Germany considered this pact had been transgressed by the Franco-Soviet alliance, and that consequently Germany had decided to reestablish her full sovereignty over the Rhineland. At the same time, Baron von Neurath declared that Germany was prepared to sign a pact of nonaggression with France and Belgium; to sign an air force convention with the Western Powers; to return to the League of Nations if it were in the first place admitted to dissociate the covenant terms and the stipulations of the Versailles Treaty. *It is worth remembering that, for reasons still unknown, those peace-assuring propositions were never accepted or even seriously considered by the opposite parties.*

On March 7, 1936, German troops reentered the demilitarized zone. Given the extreme mobility of modern troops, of tanks and motorized divisions, and given the part played by air forces in modern warfare, those few miles retaken by Germany did not represent any special menace to the defense of France. Nevertheless, this first manifestation of Germany's reconstructed military power provoked enormous emotion in France and in Europe. Albert Sarraut, the French Prime Minister, declared with resolution: "France will not negotiate with Strasbourg under the menace of Germany's artillery!" War seemed imminent. That it did not then break out was only due to Great Britain's refusal to admit that in the new circumstances created by the Franco-Soviet arrangement, the reoccupation of the Rhineland was a *casus foederis.*[1]

On July 13, 1934, at the height of the Barthou-Beneš-Titulescu anti-German activities, Sir John Simon warned Paris that Great Britain would not participate in any attempted encirclement of Germany. On April 26, 1935, the same Sir John Simon wired his Ambassador in Paris:

> It is necessary to explain to Mr. Laval that Great Britain is very uneasy about France concluding an agreement with Russia that is likely to force her [France] into a war against Germany in circumstances that are not allowed by Article Two of the Pact of Locarno.

The answer given to Ambassador Sir George R. Clerk in order to reassure him demonstrates how little the leading set at the Quai d'Orsay —Alexis Léger's set—understood the significance for the peace of Europe and of the world of the introduction of Soviet Russia—Lenin and Stalin's Russia—into the system of European alliances. Clerk reported:

> I was not able to see Mr. Laval, but I could talk with Mr. Léger [the Secretary General of the French Foreign Office]. He told me that Great Britain need not worry. The French Government stipulated, in signing the pact, the respect of all the dispositions of the League of Nations' covenant and of the Pact of Locarno.

Léger and Titulescu, the latter the redactor of the controversial instrument, did not understand, or pretended not to understand, that whatever the terms of an alliance with the Communist empire, this alliance represented a total upsetting of the contractual equilibrium, procured with such difficulty, between the non-Communist countries.

Stanley Baldwin and Anthony Eden explained to the British House of Commons, on March 8, 1936, that the reoccupation of the Rhineland

---

[1] *Casus foederis* specifies the exact circumstances in which allied powers are obliged to mutual military assistance.

did not represent an act of war in terms of the existing treaties—particularly since Germany had offered to conclude pacts of nonaggression with France and Belgium. Lord Astor, in the House of Lords, and Lord Lothian, in the House of Commons, took exception to the idea of a preventive war against Germany and interpreted the Franco-Soviet pact as an attempt to encircle Germany. Mr. Churchill, true to his new image, vituperated violently against the idea of signing pacts of nonaggression or air force arrangements with Germany, and declared: "The encirclement of a potential aggressor is no encirclement."

We appeal quite exceptionally to the prolific memory of Madame Geneviève Tabouis in order to show the alarm which the reoccupation of the Rhineland provoked in Paris and all of France.

> Paris was seized with panic. . . . Everybody wondered if war would break out. And this question was repeated many times during the three days that followed, three days which seemed years to us—days full of agony and doubts concerning the position our government would take toward Germany.

The French Cabinet assembled twice on March 7, the second time with the General Staff attending. Georges Mandel, Minister of Interior, asked for an immediate mobilization. But under the impression left by the visits of the British, the Italian, and the Belgian Ambassadors, France limited herself to a solemn protest and the decision to ask for an extraordinary session of the League of Nations Council, which had given its guarantee to the Locarno Pact.

The reaction of Rumania's Government to the possibility of a Franco-German war, and of Russia's troops trying to come to France's rescue in agreement with the new treaty, was of great significance for those who cared to appraise the effect it was bound to have on the coming events in Central and Eastern Europe.

In the middle of the night of March 8, 1936, I was awakened by my friend Miroslav Arciczewski, my former colleague in Riga and Reval, and now Poland's Envoy in Bucharest. Arciczewski had in his hands a copy of a document, procured I suppose by his military attaché, that alarmed him extremely and that he wanted to discuss with me.

It was an order from the Minister of Public Works, Richard Franasovici, to the director of the Rumanian railway system; its significance was manifestly of military character. The railway services in Moldavia, Bessarabia, and Bucovina were urgently ordered to accumulate all rolling transport stock at the Rumanian-Russian border. The Russian rail spread is broader than the Rumanian, and all organized traffic between the two countries required transshipment. This order meant simply that our railway system was being put at the disposal of the Soviet army. It took us, however, a while to understand the enormity of the treason and how its diabolical preparation had been hidden from Rumanian and Polish public opinion. If war had broken out then, Rumania would have been invaded, Bessarabia would have been handed over to Russia, and Poland, betrayed by her ally, would have seen her eastern defense unexpectedly outflanked by her enemy.

I spent the rest of the night considering the most efficient way to thwart this conspiracy against my country's most vital interests. For the polemical part, I decided to appeal again to Gheorghe Brătianu, a deputy in the Rumanian Parliament. But there was another side to it: force would very likely be required. I knew only one political group to which I could appeal in such circumstances for a decision that asked for as much independence and intrepidity as patriotism; this was the Legionary Movement, the young Iron Guard, led by the young Corneliu Codreanu. I had had, until then, no direct contact with it or with its leader, but I knew very well General Gheorghe Cantacuzene, second-in-command of the Movement and a legendary hero of many battles of World War I.

I went to see him early that morning before he had arisen. I showed him the incriminating text and explained the situation. If Soviet troops were to enter our territory with our consent, even if our cooperation limited itself at the beginning to a passive attitude, the unavoidable succession of events would quickly transform us to an active Kremlin ally. This would mean the end of our alliance with Poland, and would drag us into the hostilities against the Berlin-Rome Axis. If war, which seemed imminent, should start under such auspices for Rumania, it would end either with Rumania's disappearance into the capacious craw of her Communist neighbor (in the event of this neighbor's victory), or with her dismemberment into a runt country (in the event of an Axis victory). The very existence of Rumania was at stake! Contrary to the wishes of the King and the intentions of his Government, the passage of Russian troops had to be opposed with force. I knew of no organization that could take charge of this protective and imperative action other than the Legionary Movement.

Two hours after my visit the General returned it accompanied by Corneliu Codreanu. It was my first meeting with the young chief. Our relations, from then until his assassination at the order of King Carol, never belied the first impression he made upon me in that hour of peril. I had before me a hero in the legendary and the historical meaning of the word. He was wisdom and daring, dream and reality, vigor and handsomeness as of a demigod with evangelical simplicity and purity, and above all—from his serene forehead, from his ardent mien—a comforting breath of Rumania's soul, Rumania's past, and Rumania's soil.

Codreanu interpreted the situation as I did, as did General Canta-cuzene, and as Gheorghe Brătianu was to do that very afternoon before the Rumanian Parliament. Whatever the price, we decided the Soviets must not be permitted to enter our territory *as friends*. The first Soviet transport—according to Polish information a convoy of air force ground troops and technical matériel en route to Prague—was to be attacked and annihilated. The Legionary Movement would pursue the fight, whatever the circumstances. Codreanu assured me that disposition to that effect would be immediately taken; in fact, certain orders had already been given.

The same day, at lunch at the Swedish Legation, I met Franasovici. This is the short dialogue that ensued in French between us, in the presence of several foreign chiefs of missions.

FRANASOVICI: "Well, Messieurs les Diplomates, what interesting news can you give us?"

STURDZA: "*You* could give us the latest news, Mr. Minister. Tell us, for instance, exactly what you meant by the orders you gave last night to our railway services in Bessarabia, Moldavia, and Bucovina."

FRANASOVICI: "What orders?"

STURDZA: "The orders by which you put our railways at the disposal of the Soviet Command."

FRANASOVICI: "How can you, an official of our Foreign Office, spread such alarming stories? I did not give any orders!"

STURDZA (With his hand in his breast pocket) "Shall I show you the exact text?"

At this suggestion, Franasovici quickly took refuge among a group of the fair sex.

War did not break out that time because Great Britain did not want it, because the United States was not yet present, because Poland still followed Pilsudski's policy, and because the apparatus of the Anonymous Powers was not yet in a working state. But in Rumania the representatives of those Powers had taken good notice of the fact that the Legionary Movement—with its multitude, with its spirit of sacrifice and its contempt of the fear of death—stood firmly against their projects. Those powers understood that the execution of their projects required, first Codreanu's elimination and the extermination of the Movement.

All the Legionary manifestations that followed—Codreanu's messages to the King and to his Governments, the participation of the Legionary Movement in the Civil War in Spain, the fervent manifestations of admiration and respect that accompanied the funeral of those who had fallen there in this fight against Communism—strengthened the convictions and decisions of the Anonymous Powers.

King Carol II of Rumania, in 1933.

King Carol and his mistress, Magda Wolff, alias Elena Lupescu, in 1938.

King Carol, Magda Wolff, and her family. Old Wolff is at the extreme right.

Minister of Foreign Affairs Nicolae
Titulescu of Rumania; to his right,
Tewfik Rushtu Bey of Turkey.

Premier Léon Blum of France.

President Eduard Beneš of Czecho-Slovakia.

Count Pál Teleki, Prime Minister of Hungary.

King Alexander of Yugoslavia.

Neville Chamberlain and Adolf Hitler, in September 1938.

The principal conferees at the Munich Conference. Left to right: Neville Chamberlain, Edouard Daladier, Adolf Hitler, Benito Mussolini, and Count Galeazzo Ciano.

Europe on the eve of World War II.

Sir Nevile Henderson, British Ambassador to Germany.

Józef Beck, Polish Minister of Foreign Affairs; to his left, Józef Lipski, Polish Ambassador to Germany.

King Carol fired Titulescu in August 1936. This did not change the course of Rumania's foreign policy, however. King Carol took charge of it, and it must be recognized that he maneuvered it toward exactly the same goal, with the same constancy, the same daring, the same dexterity, but with still more dissimulation. Titulescu had been fired because he had tried to meddle in some negotiations with Vickers Arms Industry of England—a strictly royal hunting preserve—and because he showed too openly his hostility against Poland, a favorite of the Rumanian people. Three years of ruling had taught Carol that he could count upon the docility of almost all Rumanian political leaders, and that he could find half a dozen Foreign Ministers as ready as Titulescu to follow the policy, dictated from abroad by the Anonymous Powers of which he was himself an agent.

*   *   *   *

At no moment, from the conquest of the Russian empire by an international gang to the beginning of World War II, did the Anonymous Powers show more clearly their irresistible influence over men and governments than in the Spanish Civil War.

In 1936 Spain was nobody's enemy. She had no quarrel with France, none with Great Britain, and certainly none with the United States or with Czecho-Slovakia. By siding with the Communist gang (dubbed "Loyalist Forces" for the occasion), France was endangering three more of her frontiers—the Pyrenees, the Alps, and North Africa; Great Britain was prodding a conflict long since dormant, Gibraltar, and deeply offending the sentiments and interests of her oldest ally, Portugal; and the United States was gratuitously complicating one of the fundamental directives of its foreign policy—friendship with Latin America. What Czecho-Slovakia was risking was her very existence.

There was no national interest, and still less any moral reason, that could explain the fact that in Spain those Western Powers immediately took the side of the Communist terrorists. Nobody could have ignored the two years of murder and anarchy that preceded the assassination of Calvo Sotelo and the atrocities that followed the beginning of the Civil War. Newspapers and magazines reported daily, complete with pictures, the horrible massacres in Madrid—women and girls raped in public in the streets, then soaked with gasoline and cremated alive before the eyes of their manacled parents and husbands, and of reporters and diplomats; the nocturnal roundups; the systematic executions in such proportions that the tired firing squads threatened to strike if they were not granted two days of rest a week; the artistic treasures annihilated; the churches and cathedrals dynamited or transformed into brothels;

the priests, monks and nuns shot like flies (7,937 of them at the final count); the satanic and necromaniac orgies; the disinterred nuns lined along graveyard walls with the pipes of the profaners stuck between their teeth.

Let us remember also the financial and material subsidies sent to the Communist terrorists, the mendacious information from British bishops and duchesses, the formidable smile of Mrs. Eleanor Roosevelt when the murderers offered her a picture by Goya—cleansed, we hope, of the blood of its legitimate owners—as a token of gratitude for her moral and political support of the cause of Red Spain. Let us remember that the whole world represented at Geneva—the true prefiguration of the United Nations world—was engaged in a crusade for the executioners and against the victims, without even the excuse of a national interest.

In Paris on July 14, 1936, I had seen what a Communist triumph in Spain would mean for the world. French soldiers marched mournfully past Léon Blum, the Prime Minister, among the clenched fists of the crowds and the roars of "Les Soviets partout!" as the Prime Minister bawled to his partisans, "Today, anything is possible!" Yes, anything could have happened then in that part of the continent, and only General Franco's victory could prevent the establishment of the Franco-Spanish Communist-dominated empire predicted by Lenin. I decided therefore to offer my modest contribution to the efforts of the Nationalist troops in Spain.

After a hasty operation in Paris for a stomach ulcer, I went to Franco's headquarters where, I saw General Fidel Dávila, Chief of the General Staff, and was granted my enlistment. At the time I was to leave for the front, a violent relapse of my illness sent me to a military hospital, where I spent almost two months in complete immobility and where I was joined by my wife.

In Paris, before leaving for Spain, I had paid a visit to a distant kinswoman of ours, Queen Nathalie of Serbia. Her mother was the daughter of John-Alexander Sturdza, Reigning Prince of Moldavia. Hundreds of members of the Spanish aristocracy had already been murdered, and the Queen worried about the fate of her nieces, the señoritas de Pedroso y Sturdza. "If you meet them," she told me, "give them this little present." It was a nice box of sweets. When I asked the porter of the first hotel I tried in Burgos if he knew the señoritas de Pedroso cousins of mine several times removed whom I had never met before, he answered, "Here they are," and showed me two pretty young ladies, the only guests at that moment in the lobby of the hotel. It was a lucky break for me. Not only had I the opportunity of immediately delivering the message with which I had been entrusted, but it was thanks to Chiquita and Margarita de Pedroso that I found a private room in Burgos's over-crowded military hospitals. Their daily presence, together with that of my wife, who came running from Bucharest, soothed considerably the bitterness of my misadventure.

A short time after I left Spain for Italy—after receiving information from Rome that Count Galeazzo Ciano, Italian Minister of Foreign Af-fairs, would like to see me—General Cantacuzene and the group of Le-gionaries who fought in the Spanish Civil War reached Burgos. Those who had not been killed on the battlefields were all assassinated, with one exception, by King Carol after their return to Rumania.

In Rome, I saw Count Ciano, who made me realize the folly of Beneš's attitude (Beneš had jumped to the side of the Communist gang in Spain, with all of Czecho-Slovakia's industrial potential and political influence). Ciano told me, *Vous vous réveillerez un bon matin et vous apprendrez que la Tchécoslovaquie a volé en éclats* ("You will wake up one morning and find that Czecho-Slovakia has burst to pieces.") Poor Ciano! I could not have foreseen the circumstances of our next meeting, circumstances that—according to his posthumous memoirs—he considered no more pleasant than did I.

Back in Bucharest, I felt it necessary to acquaint King Carol with Ciano's warning, to which the King answered, "Czecho-Slovakia does not stand alone." I learned afterwards that only the vigilance of Luis Beneyto Spain's Consul General in Bucharest, and the energetic inter-vention of the Marquis de Nantouillet, Franco's Minister, prevented King Carol from sending to Red Spain, about one hundred fighter planes constructed for Rumania in Czecho-Slovakia's factories.

It was my friend Miroslav Arciczewski who drew my attention to cer-tain passages of a book published by Jan Sheba, Czecho-Slovakia's Min-ister to Bucharest, which were insulting to Rumania and highly alarming to Poland. This book, written in French and translated into Rumanian, had already been on the market for several months. Jan Sheba was a former gendarme, a noncommissioned officer who had been transformed into a diplomat by one of those "happy" social perturbations that fol-lowed each of the two World Wars.

Sheba's presence in Bucharest had already been signaled by an amaz-ing article in one of the capital's newspapers, in which, with no under-standable motive, he assailed with the rudest insults Queen Nathalie of Serbia, who was related to many of the Rumanian aristocracy and was, besides, an internationally venerated and beloved figure who consecrated to charity the last years of her unlucky life. Questioned, Sheba excused himself by explaining that he had confused Queen Nathalie with Queen Draga, her daughter-in-law, whose tragic death was known to everybody in Europe. This transformed his gratuitous insult of an elderly lady into the profanation of the memory of a dead and martyred one; but Mr. Sheba was forgiven in the name of Little Entente solidarity.[2]

In the incriminatory book, Sheba persisted in the same kind of offense —one of the biggest for a diplomat: that of meddling in the inner affairs of the country to which he was accredited. This time, however, he had blundered into an *affaire d'état* with a lack of diplomatic tact that not even his long membership in the gendarmerie could have explained.

Sheba viewed the Moscow-Bucharest-Prague Axis as a settled fact. Consequently, he was reproaching us for not having taken all the technical measures that would permit the quickest possible transport of the Soviet troops toward Czecho-Slovakia through Rumania. In comminatory terms Sheba asked the Rumanian Government to double its east-west railway system and to proceed with the building of highways (in the same direction) "with an Italo-Abyssinian rapidity."

Sheba's book did not provoke any reaction from our Foreign Office or from our Government despite the reiterated objections by the Polish Envoy and the growing indignation of our public opinion. This was all the more disquieting as it was insistently said that it was not Mr. Sheba, whose knowledge of French and whose literary talents were doubted by many, who had written this book. Deciding to get to the bottom of the mystery, I brought out and disseminated among deputies, senators, high officials and foreign and Rumanian diplomats, five hundred copies of a brochure I called "Czecho-Soviet Protectorate or Independent Rumanian Kingdom?" in which I showed the impropriety of Sheba's intervention in Rumania's affairs. I observed that in any country, and in our country at any time in the past, Sheba would have been asked to leave a long time ago; and I asked if the reason this had not happened already was not to be explained by the fact that his book had previously received the approbation of some of our responsible authorities.

---

[2] Alexander Obrenović, the last King of the Obrenović dynasty and the son of King Milan and of Queen Nathalie of Serbia, was murdered and hacked to pieces along with his wife, Queen Draga, by military conspirators led by the chief of the so-called Black Hand, Colonel Dragutin Dimitrijević-Apis. Despite the fact that there was no relationship between the British and the Serbian dynasties, Queen Victoria of Great Britain immediately broke off diplomatic relations with Serbia and they were not resumed until after her death. It is interesting to compare this attitude with the cordial reception granted at the Court of Saint James to the murderers of Czar Nicholas, a first cousin of King George V. Let us also remember that Lloyd George, as Prime Minister, forbade the General commanding the British troops in Vladivostok to take charge of the suitcase in which the tutor of the Czarevich had gathered the earthly remnants of the members of the Romanov family from the pit where they had been dumped by their Communist murderers. About Colonel Dimitrievič-Apis, we will add the interesting note that he was also the man behind the Serajevo assassinations. He ended his career in 1917 in Salonoki before a firing squad which stopped in their tracks other fanciful projects that were brewing in his inventive mind.

In the Parliament, Gheorghe Brătianu and Senator Orleanu also asked for an answer to this question. The indignation in certain circles was aroused to a vociferous pitch and Sheba was forced to leave Rumania, swearing without further explanation that he was not the real culprit.

The most important aspect of the Sheba incident was the effort made by members of our official circles in the Government, at the Palais Sturdza, in Parliament and in the Government's newpapers, to save Sheba and keep him in Bucharest.

Thanks to Sheba, more people in Rumania came to understand why the German proposals had been spurned, and what was behind the unprecedented terms of the railway convention, conceived and signed by Titulescu and Litvinov.

XI

Heroes, Scoundrels, and Fools

The return of the Legionaries who had fought in Spain, the transport of the mortal remains of those who had fallen there, and their funeral in Bucharest started a commotion in Rumania's population such as that country had perhaps never known. It was not only the peasants kneeling along the railway tracks over which passed the car bearing the caskets of Ion Moța and Vasile Marin from the frontier to Bucharest; it was the whole Rumanian nation that was bowing low in deep and silent communion before the sacrifice of the valiants. The Rumanians were living one of those unique moments in the history of any country, when the virtues of the nation, so often obscured by ambition, passion, enmity or indifference, reappear suddenly in all their imperishable vigor.

For that day, for that moment, all Rumanian thought, anxiety and sorrow massed around the Cross and the flag, which were then threatened more than they had ever been *by the enemy that was to overthrow them nine years later.* For that day, for that moment, the young man who stepped, statuesque and dreamy, at the head of the Legionary battalions, was not only their leader but the spiritual head of the hundreds of thousands of Rumanian men and women who saluted with bared heads or with lifted arms the passing hearse of the heroes and the columns of their comrades.

This was well understood by those who were peeping at those passing columns through their half-open curtains.

The Civil War in Spain represented an apex in the fight between the Anonymous Powers, mysterious inspirers of so many statesmen and governments of the bourgeois world, and those national powers that opposed in every country Communist and pro-Communist policies, whatever the name or the form they had adopted. It was therefore natural that the participation of the Legionary Movement in the Spanish hostilities, and

the manifestations of veneration and admiration with which the Rumanian nation surrounded the return of the dead and living combatants,
would determine the beginning of an acute crisis between the two personalities who represented those two rival forces more than any others in
Rumania: Corneliu Codreanu and King Carol.

I have never heard a shorter, more fitting description of Carol than
the one that was given me by his own mother, Queen Marie of Rumania.
I was paying my respects to the Queen in 1928 before leaving for the
United States, where I had been appointed Counselor to our Legation.
Her Majesty, alluding to the personal relations she knew I had maintained with her son—then an exile in France—despite the official inter-
diction to members of the Rumanian diplomatic corps, conceded with
indulgence that this relationship was understandable and even legitimate behavior: "Carol is young; it is quite natural that youth would
stick with him. *You want Carol as King? God help you the day you have
him!*"

Some of the traits of Carol's character will emerge from the facts contained in these pages. However, we will ask Mr. Prost, who could not be
accused of favoring the Legionary Movement, to give us some details
concerning the King's dominant vice, cupidity, which to my mind was
the source of all his other wickednesses and misdemeanours.

> The feeling against him [Carol] is motivated by his immorality, his
> knavery, and his cupidity. His ambition is such that he would stop at
> nothing.
> We have already mentioned his private life; he has never been forgiven
> his affair with Lupescu. We have talked about his businesses; everybody in
> Rumania knows his methods for acquiring wealth. . . .[1]
> The interests of the state will always be subordinated to his interests.
> . . . he will cautiously accumulate an immense fortune abroad for the day
> when he will again take the road to exile. . . .[2] He is the biggest share-
> holder in Rumanian companies. Those companies have taken the habit of
> offering gratuitously great bundles of shares. . . . He is the owner of one-
> third of the stocks of [Malaxa Industries]. . . . From information acquired
> from the national bank it seems that an armament order at a net cost of
> 182 million lei was billed to the state [by the Carol-Malaxa association]
> 1,600 millions. . . . To him alone the national bank yields its foreign stock.
> . . . Without paying a cent he became the owner of the greatest group of
> sugar refineries. . . . He will ask and get at a nominal price various great
> state owned agricultural exploitations. . . .
> These are only some of Carol's "businesses." . . . All these extortions
> are possible only in a country rich enough not to be very quickly ruined
> by them.[3]

[1] *Destin de la Roumanie,* p. 150.
[2] *Ibid.,* p. 51.
[3] *Ibid.,* pp. 99–100.

Who in Rumania was fighting against this immorality and corruption? Certainly none of the political parties and none of the political personalities who expected to benefit from the royal goodwill by governing and by participating in the general plunder. Even Iuliu Maniu, the chief of the National Peasant Party and a man of undisputed personal honesty, gave to his men the same high sign once given by Louis Adolphe Thiers, in France, to his partisans: "Enrichissez-vous!" Which they did, or tried to do at every opportunity, including contracts with foreign governments or foreign firms such as armament contracts with Skoda, highway building contracts with Sweden, and loan agreements with France or other countries. The Legionary Movement alone, as Mr. Prost is forced to recognize, challenged continuously and clamorously the corruption that under Carol had come to be a permanent form of government.

> *Besides those young guardsmen of more-or-less dubious origin* are all those who are following the Captain from pure idealism. There is, indeed, in the Iron Guard a revolt against political immorality. All the young Rumanians have listened to the accusations of prevarication that political parties are throwing at each other. They remember that many prosecutions had been opened, that many culprits had often been found in very high positions, and they remember also that no punishment has ever been imposed. They know that the King and his friends are setting an example of immorality and dishonesty. . . . *It is . . . a purification of the political morals that they beseech.* . . . No government has understood that the best way to fight the Iron Guard would be to comply honestly with its demands. . . . The majority of those who have governed [in Bucharest] have either tried to compromise with the Guard and use it against their political adversaries, or have tried to annihilate it with brutality; they have only increased its influence and power. Goga and Cuza are only the representatives of a purely reactionary party; they ignore more than their predecessors *the aspirations of the youth who see in the Legionary Movement the only political formation unsoiled by the vices of the other parties, the only one that is animated by an ideal.*[4]

Strange and miraculous is the power of truth, which springs out naked even from the mouth of a professional slanderer when he forgets for a moment the instructions he has received.

In November 1937, Carol, not being able to form with the existing Parliament a Government exactly to his heart's desire, entrusted Mr. Tătărescu, an offspring of the Liberal Party, and his liege man, with the formation of a new Government and with new Parliamentary elections. The Legionary Movement, the National Peasant Party of Mr. Maniu, and the Liberal Dissident Party of Gheorghe Brătianu took part in those elections on different lists but were united in a pact of mutual defense

[4] *Ibid.*, pp. 107–109. Italics added.

against the accustomed interference and terror from the Government's agents. The other political parties that participated in this campaign were the Liberal Party of Tătărescu and Dinu Brătianu and the National Christian Party of Goga and Cuza.

The Legionary Movement conducted its campaign according to the principles it had adopted from the beginning of its existence. It did not promise anything to the electoral masses except the cleaning from Rumania's domestic life of all the corruptions and impurities that had accumulated since the end of the war and the disappearance of the Conservative Party, and that had become the law of the country after the return of Carol. The Legionaries, on the contrary, reminded the voters of the sacrifices their country had the right to expect from them as Christians and Rumanians. They entered the villages in orderly formations, assembled before the local churches, knelt down and prayed, then rose and sang. The peasants looked with love and admiration at these young men who did not pester them with the bombastic speeches of the professional politicians but contented themselves with fervent prayers and songs of faith and heroism that everybody understood and approved.

Thanks to the control exercised by the three associated parties, the elections ended with a minimum of interference from the Government's side. The results were as follows:

The Liberal Party (Tătărescu, Dinu Brătianu)	152 seats
The National Peasant Party (Iuliu Maniu)	86 seats
The Legionary Movement (Corneliu Codreanu)	66 seats
The National Christian Party (Octavian Goga, Al Cuza)	39 seats
The Liberal Dissident Party (Gheorghe Brătianu)	16 seats

These elections did not give Mr. Tătărescu the forty percent majority of votes necessary to assure him, according to the existing electoral law, seventy percent of the seats in the Parliament, which would have permitted him to govern as Carol wanted him to do: without any significant opposition to the King's orders and whims. Therefore, with total contempt for the constitutional stipulations, Carol dissolved the Parliament even before its first assembly—an event unprecedented in Rumanian Parliamentary history or in the history of any parliamentary country.

Then, in a really clever move—a move aimed chiefly at the popularity of the Legionary Movement—Carol entrusted the formation of the new Government and the control of the new elections to Octavian Goga, the chief of the National Christian Party, which had gathered only 9.15 percent of the votes in the preceding elections. It was, moreover, a party of extremist rightist views, and was a declared adversary of the Legionary Movement. Carol's reasoning was easy to understand: By pitting two nationalist groups against each other in elections that were to be conducted in the most brutal manner by his henchmen, he would discredit the nationalist concept.

Carol's reliance on Octavian Goga—be it said in Goga's praise—was, however, not very great. Goga's political ambitions instilled in him some docility toward Carol's intentions, but Goga the poet, who had sung with such force, with such tenderness, with such melancholy, of Rumania's soul and soil, was a patriot; Carol could not exclude the possibility of energetic opposition from Goga the moment Goga realized that the country's destiny itself was at stake. With this in mind, Carol surrounded Goga with four men whose hostility toward the Legionary Movement had been sufficiently demonstrated. At the Ministry of the Interior of the new Government Carol placed Armand Călinescu, known for the atrocities committed by him under former Governments against the Movement. General Gavril Marinescu, the King's personal hatchet man, was made Undersecretary of State for Public Security. General Ion Antonescu, who had warned Codreanu in a previous meeting that he would not hesitate to machine-gun the Movement if the King were to order him to do so, became Minister of Defense. At the Foreign Office was Istrate Micescu, also one of the King's vassals, who had tried to persuade young Emilian, the recalcitrant chief of a small nationalist group, to do away with Codreanu.

From the first day of the new election campaign the wave of popularity that had grown continuously around the Legionary Movement had reached such proportions that it deeply alarmed the chiefs of the Movement themselves, who feared that this unmatched enthusiasm would provoke a recurrence of the persecutions. This is exactly what happened. To protect his Legionaries, Codreanu ordered them to cease any activity other than their simple passage in orderly formation through villages and towns, and to yield without resistance to the police and gendarmerie if the entrances to those villages and towns were obstructed by them. The wave of love and faith grew still higher around the Captain and his men.

News of the first casualties was brought to the headquarters of the Movement on the fourth day of the second election campaign, where my wife and I went to pay our respects to the dead and to try to comfort the grief-stricken parents. I had seen Goga the day before and he had impressed me as being under a great strain. From the tragic scene at headquarters I rushed, raging with indignation, to the Cantacuzene Palace, the seat of the Presidency. Jostling ushers and secretaries aside, I invaded the Cabinet chamber of the Prime Minister. I found Goga disheveled, red in the face, and profoundly discouraged. I asked him if he knew what was going on under his name and responsibility. He almost screamed at me, "Do you really believe that this is my doing?"

Calming down, he invited me to take a seat and asked me if I could manage a meeting between him and Codreanu. "It would be tragic and comic," he said, "if two nationalist movements could be maneuvered into destroying each other. We must come to an understanding." With that message I went back to Legionary headquarters. Without a moment's hesitation Codreanu agreed to the interview and put me in charge of the details. Back again at the Cantacuzene Palace I suggested to Goga our country seat, Tatarani, about forty miles from Bucharest, as the place for the meeting; I thought that it should be kept secret for a few days in order to arrange for the collaboration of the two movements, the Green and the Blue Shirts.

I do not know what prompted Goga to insist instead on the home of Mr. Gigurtu, his Minister of Commerce, in the center of Bucharest, as a place of rendezvous. I hope it was not any sentiment of mistrust toward me or toward the Movement. I knew, however—as the succession of events was to demonstrate—that the choice of such a conspicuous place was not very fortunate.

Next day at a quarter of five I left headquarters with Codreanu. At Gigurtu's home we met Goga; he silently shook hands with Codreanu and they went into the next room. With Gigurtu I smoked cigarette after cigarette for more than an hour. Gigurtu seemed to share my impatience and my hopes. When finally the door opened for Codreanu and Goga, we did not need any explanation; their handshake was long and friendly.

On the way back to headquarters Codreanu interrupted the silence with the answer to the question I had not ventured to ask: "Yes, we did come to an understanding." They had done it all the more easily as Codreanu did not want his to be the majority group in the next Parliament. It was a situation he shunned for the moment; and he was prepared to help Goga with his influence in as many electoral districts as necessary.

Home, I found my friend Arciczewski, who was happy to hear the news. "Have you thought of everything?" he asked me. "Even of something like the 'March on Rome'?" Yes, I had, but I had not done anything about it.

Next day at about eleven I was at Goga's prepared to sell him the idea of a "March on Rome." But as I greeted him with "Mr. Prime Minister," he answered sadly, "I am no longer Prime Minister."

He had been called to the Palace early in the morning and the following dialogue ensued between the King and him:

CAROL: "My dear Goga, your conflict with the Legionary Movement has gone so far that, to my great regret, I must have your resignation."

GOGA: "Sire, yesterday I came to a full understanding with Codreanu."

CAROL: "You came to an understanding with him? Did you? Bad, very bad, Goga. I really must ask you for your resignation."

Goga was furious and understood only then how he had been fooled. I told him, "You have not resigned yet. You are still Prime Minister. Stay where you are. With the Green and the Blue Shirts united you have the whole nation behind you."

"That is easy to say," he answered. "You don't know, but I do, that I am surrounded by traitors." I did not ask him the names of those traitors because I knew them already.[5]

I have often admonished myself for my lack of wakefulness and action in those critical days; my excuse was my health. Concerned about what had happened to me in Spain, I decided on a fourth and radical operation that at that time, only Dr. Finsterer, the famous Austrian surgeon, could perform. When I took my leave from Codreanu, he, reading in my eyes what he believed to be some anxiety for my probable durability, put his hands on my shoulders and said, "Don't worry, I know! You will soon be back healthy and strong. This will be your last operation." The Captain's prediction has been born out by fact, in any case for the last thirty years. But the anxiety he detected in me was not for my life; it was for his.

I was with Goga in Vienna when German troops entered the city to the delirious enthusiasm of ninety percent of its population. "If I had known that they could come so quickly," said Goga, "I would not have let myself be dismissed so easily." If the two nationalist chiefs had come

[5] In their book, *The European Right*, written with the obvious purpose of discrediting any past, present, or future associated efforts to stop the conquering Communist advance, Messrs. Hans Rogger and Eugen Weber, professors of history at the University of California, offer their readers—among other more important distortions of facts and pure inventions—a totally erroneous story of this last-hour understanding between Codreanu and Goga:

> Intervention from various quarters—including the Germans, who were heavily backing Goga, and from General Antonescu, then a minister in Goga's cabinet— led to negotiations between Codreanu and Goga, as a result of which, on February 8, 1938, Codreanu announced that his party would abandon further electoral activity. It would run but, henceforth, keep out of the campaign [p. 551].

There was absolutely no other intervention between Goga and Codreanu and no other negotiations, than those I mentioned here, which we kept as secret as possible. In the Goga-Călinescu Cabinet, General Antonescu was on the Călinescu, not the Goga, side. Goga did not specify, but there was no doubt in my mind that he included Antonescu among the traitors who surrounded him. It is not true that Codreanu announced the abandoning of further electoral activities "as a consequence of his understanding with Goga." On the contrary, this understanding provided for *de facto* collaboration between Codreanu's and Goga's partisans during the rest of the electoral campaign— collaboration that Carol and Călinescu could not have tolerated, nor Antonescu desired.

to a full understanding sooner, I do not think we would have needed the help of any German divisions to bring back honesty and national pride to our domestic and foreign policies.

I saw Goga once more before his death; it was on his return from a short trip to Bessarabia. He looked very ill.

"How do you feel, Mr. President?" I asked.

"I feel sick, very sick," he replied. "But how stupid of me to take lodging in the same house where they said my brother was poisoned."

XII

From Palm Sunday to Crucifixion

The beginning of the year 1938 had seen in Rumania the apotheosis of the Legionary Movement. Says Mr. Prost: "In the beginning of 1938, Codreanu's Movement is more powerful than it has ever been. One has the impression that not only the members of this Movement but all the [Rumanian] youth followed the Captain." [1]

The whole web of lies that had been spun around the Movement by envious or corrupt politicians, and by the press and publicity media at the beck and call of the Anonymous Forces, had totally dissolved before the eyes of the Rumanian people.

The end of 1938 was to see Codreanu's two trials before Carol's kangaroo courts, his assassination, and his tortured body being buried stealthily at night under tons of cement. It was also to see all of the Legionary chiefs in prison, where they finally became the victims of the massacre in which hundreds of Legionaries were murdered without even the pretense of a trial.

The reason for this new tragedy in the life of the Movement was the same as for the preceding ones. The Captain had to be "suppressed," to use the expression preferred by Prost, and the Movement had to be exterminated because it fearlessly blocked the execution of the fundamental design of the powers of darkness. Indeed, the moment those powers had chosen for the outbreak of the conflict in which our Christian Civilization was to perish was close at hand; and the part assigned to Rumania required the previous smothering of any possible resistance there.

The countries of Western Civilization were not divided at that time between a group that wanted this fratricidal conflict and one that did not want it. The clash between the two forces occurred within each of those countries. In France, in Great Britain, and in the United States

[1] *Destin de la Roumanie,* p. 107.

there were many political personalities and groups which considered peaceful coexistence with Germany to be a historical necessity and which understood that the time had come for rectifying the nefarious errors committed at Versailles.

It was the so-called pacific groups which fiercely opposed any concession whatever to Germany, although they knew too well that the bisection of this great nation by the Danzig Corridor, and the presence of three and a half million Germans under an oppressive foreign rule at the very frontier of Germany, were situations that needed reexamination.

The position of those anti-German groups, rightly dubbed the "pyromaniac firemen," had been seriously weakened by the energetic initiative taken by the Central European powers and by Italy's adhesion to the anti-Comintern pact. The Japanese armies were advancing victoriously in Manchuria and had begun the occupation of western China. The truly loyalist forces in Spain—we mean of course General Franco's troops—were slowly but irresistibly beating back the revolutionary troops and the international brigades. Mussolini's Italy had occupied Ethiopia almost without resistance. Germany, after the reoccupation of the Rhineland, had finally realized the *Anschluss* without losing Italy's friendship. Her relations with Poland were friendlier than they had ever been.

On the other hand, the anti-German and pro-Soviet forces were organizing themselves in every country and organizing their cooperation between countries and between continents. *Those forces received important assistance—assistance that would finally be decisive in the fight between the powers of chaos and the advocates of a dynamic understanding between non-Communist powers—by the active cooperation of Roosevelt's United States with Stalin's Russia, inaugurated by Mr. Bullitt and developed into a real and fertile friendship through Mr. Davies's "Mission to Moscow."*

Any careful observer of Rumania's foreign policy would have realized that the covert activity of the various Governments that rose and fell in Bucharest according to the caprices of the King tended to place us in the same camp as Soviet Russia in the event of a European conflict. These Governments sentenced us, in other words, to certain national death, regardless of the fortune of our arms: victory or defeat.

On November 30, 1937, Codreanu made the following public declaration: "I am against the policy of the great Western democracies. I am against the Little Entente and the Balkan Alliance. I have not the slightest confidence in the League of Nations. I am with the countries of the National Revolution. Forty-eight hours after the victory of the Legionary Movement, Rumania will be allied to Rome and Berlin, thus entering the line of its historical world-mission—the defense of the Cross, of

Christian Culture and Civilization." Several times during the beginning of 1938 he confronted the King and his Ministers, through his declarations to the press, with the insistent question: "Did they or did they not intend to allow Russian troops to pass over our territory in case of a new European war?"

Codreanu's only answer from King Carol and from the powers that controlled Carol was PRISON and DEATH. But eight years later, in 1946, in an address to the Peace Conference in Paris, the representatives of those who had finally provided for the establishment of Communist rule in Rumania, Grigore Gafencu, Constantin Vișoianu and Niculescu-Buzești, revealed what would have been the correct answer to Codreanu's question: *"At that time (1938–1939) Rumania was on the way to joining a regional organization in connection with a system of security including France and Soviet Russia."* Not one word about our ally Poland, whose betrayal had already started.

The parallelism between international events and the unfolding of the persecutions against the Legionary Movement became more obvious in 1938.

On February 20, Hitler, in a speech that was understood by everybody, openly announced his intentions concerning Austria and expressed his position on the Sudeten problem with equal clarity. In Rumania on February 21, the King had proclaimed the newly "granted" Constitution, which suppressed the irremovability of the magistracy, the most prominent feature of which was a series of dispositions unmistakably directed against the Legionary Movement and against its Chief. These features established the "legal" machinery for all the new iniquities Carol and his gang had long before planned. In Great Britain the conflict between the party of peace (at that time still led by Mr. Neville Chamberlain himself) and the party of war (led in open politics by Mr. Churchill—who already had established his contacts with President Roosevelt—and backed by Lord Cecil through his powerful sectarian agitation) had gone so far that Anthony Eden had resigned February 20, 1938, declaring that dissension existed between him and the Prime Minister "not only concerning the methods but also the respective point of views." Ten days later, Carol illegally dissolved the Parliament, in which the Legionary Movement, with sixty-six seats, would have been the third most powerful party, and called to power Patriarch Miron Cristea, head of the Rumanian Orthodox Church, who formed the Government to which Carol entrusted the annihilation of the Legionary Movement.

On February 24 a "referendum" took place surrounded by old and new terrorist apparatuses put at the disposition of the Cristea Government; Carol and his Ministers wanted to give an appearance of legality to the imposed Constitution. As in every other state administration, the employees of the Ministry of Foreign Affairs were ordered to assemble and to present themselves *in corpore* at the polls.

When the Department of Protocol delivered this order to me, I answered rather rudely; so the next day, when I was summoned by Mr. Tătărescu, the new Minister of Foreign Affairs, I prepared the answer I would have given him if he had reprimanded me about my absence during the lamentable procession. I could have spared myself that trouble. Tătărescu received me almost with effusiveness. He told me that the new regime wanted to employ young blood, and that consequently he had thought of me for an assignment abroad. Would our Legation in Santiago de Chile appeal to me? I thanked him for the attractive proposal, but told him frankly that a post in Europe would be more to my convenience. I suggested Copenhagen: he took good note of it and I was sent there after a few weeks by his successor Petrescu-Comnen.

The only members of the Goga Government who were kept in the Cristea Cabinet were three declared enemies of the Legionary Movement: Armand Călinescu, Minister of the Interior; General Ion Antonescu, Minister of National Defense; and General Gavril Marinescu, the most brutal and venal of Carol's cutthroats. Both Călinescu and Antonescu were well-known partisans of Titulescu's foreign policy, which was the same as that of King Carol. Călinescu had specialized in former Governments as persecutor and torturer of Legionaries.

After the *Anschluss,* the process of transforming Rumania into a police state was completed. Political parties were suppressed and royal decrees were given the force of law. One of these decrees enumerated a whole series of new crimes, among which was the singing and playing of music when such songs and music could be interpreted politically. This of course was aimed at the Legionary songs, so popular in villages and cities all across the country. The stage was being prepared for the enforcing of the punishment to which the Anonymous Forces had sentenced the Rumanian youth. Having humiliated and abased all the political parties and all the state institutions through corruption and intrigue, Carol then chose the head of the Rumanian Orthodox Church for the enacting of the most shameful page of his shameless reign—the assassination of Codreanu.

Codreanu felt that he had no right to expose his hundreds of thousands of young partisans to this new ordeal—new prisons, new tortures, new assassinations. In a moving directive he ordered the general demobilization of the Movement and the end of any Legionary activities. Everyone, students and professionals, was implored to strive to be among the first in his studies or trade. Fearing that even this pacific measure would not protect his partisans against new violence, he ordered them not to resist whatever iniquity or brutality might befall them. At the same time, he announced his decision to leave Rumania for a couple of years for Italy, where he would employ his time writing the second volume of the history of the Movement.

One will never find any mention of these facts in the books and publications of the scoundrels, Rumanian or foreign, who even today—under whose orders?—try to justify somehow the assassination of the Captain and of the hundreds of Legionaries who followed him to martyrdom.

At first, the Cristea Government granted the Captain the passport he had solicited. On second thought—or very likely upon new orders received from those powers represented in Rumania by Carol—Codreanu's passport to Italy was confiscated at the last moment. Codreanu was caught in the royal trap, the foreordained victim of the frame-up and of the assassination for which the new Rumanian judiciary apparatus had already been established.

Codreanu could still have left Rumania. At the insistence of several of us he had finally accepted the idea of a carefully prepared flight. A clever change of appearance and of clothes would throw anyone following him off the trail. The rendezvous was to be that night at the home of one of my sisters. My wife was to take him from there by car to Tescani, the country place of my aunt, Alice Rosetti; from there one of her two grandsons, experienced pilots, would have flown him to Poland and safety. Arciczewski had assured me of the good disposition of his Government. Everything was prepared; men and women were at their posts of action. The Captain did not come to the appointed meeting that night nor on the following nights when the same arrangements were kept ready by his friends.

Several explanations have been given for this sudden change in Codreanu's plans. Knowing the Captain as I knew him, I think that this is the most valid one: When his passport was taken from him, Codreanu realized that, contrary to what he had hoped, the fight and dangers were still on; in such circumstances, leaving the country and his partisans would have seemed to him an act of desertion impossible for him to commit.

Visiting Codreanu a few days after the night arranged for his escape, I urged him once more to leave and mentioned that the Polish Government had promised us every assistance in case he chose to pass through Poland or even to establish himself there. Codreanu answered me somewhat abruptly: "I don't like suggestions!" I left very disappointed but not offended. Still a little shaky from my recent operation, I went straight to bed. Half an hour later, Codreanu, believing perhaps that he had been somewhat discourteous, was at my bedside. We had a lengthy and earnest talk; and I felt once again that soothing calmness that emanated from him.

The handshake at his departure was the last we ever exchanged.

"The audacity of some and the cowardice of all," said Costa de Beauregard when trying to explain the years of terror of the French Revolution. Many were those who through their cowardice contributed to the creation of the situation that permitted the two mock trials of Codreanu, his imprisonment and his assassination. There are three persons, however, who bear the responsibility for those crimes in the most direct way and consequently for all those that stained Rumania until the end of Carol's regime: Carol, Armand Călinescu, and Professor Nicolae Iorga.

For those who know the facts, the most repulsive of the trio was Iorga, formerly the hero of Rumanian youth and the symbol of its nationalism. I say the most repulsive because he was the last person from whom our young people would have expected the cruel and dastardly blows they received at his hands. Everybody had learned what could be expected from the insatiably rapacious Carol and from Călinescu, and what were generally their incentives; the cynical and fundamental cruelty of their characters and their subservience to the powers to which they owed, and from which they expected, everything. Trying to find the motive that caused Iorga to send Codreanu to his death, and to pursue Codreanu even into his tragic grave with hatred and slander, there seems to be only one: envy. "Who is this young man," he asked in an article in his newspaper, "who is saluted like a Roman emperor by the youth of this country, who have forgotten their old teachers?"

Iorga, the genius, could not understand that there was room enough for him and for Codreanu in the hearts of our young people.

The international situation became more and more menacing. Hitler had reiterated his claims and complaints concerning the three and a half million Sudetens. German troops were concentrated at the Czecho-Slovak borders. War was imminent. At any moment the Rumanian nation would be faced with the *fait accompli* of the presence of Soviet troops on her territory. Therefore, the Captain and the Movement had to be utterly destroyed.

It was Nicolae Iorga who supplied Carol and Călinescu with the pretext for a short but immediate imprisonment of Codreanu, pending the necessary preparations for the monstrous framing that brought the longer incarceration—prelude to Codreanu's assassination.

A few years before, in an editorial in his newspaper, Iorga had suggested that Codreanu wage war against the cornering of almost every market by the Jews, by organizing and developing his own national trade. That is exactly what Codreanu did; and in 1938 "Comertul Legionar" was a flourishing organization with branches in every big city. But Iorga now vociferously asked through his newspaper, *Neamul Românesc*, that every Legionary shop be closed by the authorities. Codreanu answered in a personal letter accusing Iorga of "intellectual dishonesty." A few days before, Iorga had donned the blue frock coat of the newly appointed royal counselors. He took advantage of this circumstance to ask, and get, an indictment of Codreanu for offense to a high official.

The judicial system in Rumania had always been an upstanding and independent institution. Rumanian magistrates, from the lowest to the highest, were irremovable, sheltered from any governmental or other pressures; a corrupt judge or a false judgment was unthinkable. Carol had changed all that by suppressing the irremovability of the magistracy, by appointing his own men to low and high courts, by creating a new and uniformed magistracy who were entirely submissive to his orders and to whom were presented all cases implying opposition to or disapproval of his regime, as well as any case relating to the Legionary Movement.

It was in one of those special courts that the case of Codreanu's "insults" to Professor Iorga was heard. The Captain was hastily sentenced to six months' imprisonment. A few weeks later, another of those courts framed the so-called Legionary conspiracy, for which Codreanu and all the Legionary leaders were indicted—a never-to-be-forgotten example of a perfect judiciary crime. No witnesses for the defense were permitted to appear after the first one, who proved too embarrassing for the court. Shotguns collected from a few Legionary gamekeepers and rangers were considered sufficient as exhibits. There were no known fraudulent methods and devices that were not used. All that was to be expected. There was, however, a new and frightening aspect to Codreanu's second trial! More than one hundred motions for appeal or for annulment invoked by the Legionaries' lawyers were rejected by the highest courts, which also bowed before Carol's orders and special methods of subordination. Codreanu and his companions were then sentenced to long terms of prison from which they emerged only for their assassinations—this time without even a pretense at justice.

A stupor prevailed throughout the country; party newspapers and party leaders kept silence in their shame. Some manifestation of disapproval came only from Iuliu Maniu, the leader of the National Peasant Party, who, while the trial was going on, had the courage to go to the bench of the defense and shake Codreanu's hand. *Professor Iorga alone pretended to believe in the righteousness of the verdict and was hysterically jubilant in his newspaper.*

With this conviction, the international significance of which I understood perfectly, I realized there was no longer any possible compatibility between Rumania's interests and Carol's activities. I realized that the national cause was defended in those critical moments by one political group only: the Legionary Movement. I decided, therefore, to consider myself as liberated from any bond of loyalty toward the felonious King, whom up to the last moment I had expected to return to duty and patriotism. But with the full approval of my wife and my son, I decided to keep continuous contact with the Movement, I decided to consult it regarding the way I could help in its efforts to survive and in its fight to save Rumania as a political and national entity. I further decided to put all of my experience, my contacts, and my information in matters of foreign policy at its disposal.

Bitter experiences had taught the Movement to organize in such a way that it was never left without a leader. The command passed as in a military organization from the general to the last corporal, if he should happen to be the last leader alive. A few days after Codreanu's second trial, when I was informed by Petrescu-Comnen of my appointment as Rumanian Envoy to Copenhagen, I consulted with the new leaders of the Movement about accepting or declining this offer. They urged me to accept it because of the liberty of movement and contacts it would afford me.

Contrary to the time-honored ceremonial practice of the diplomatic corps, I left Bucharest without presenting myself to the King. I stopped in Berlin, where I wanted to get first-hand information about Germany's immediate intentions concerning Czecho-Slovakia, and to secure, if possible, an audience with Hitler without the intervention of our Legation. In the Reichskanzlei I found only Captain Weidemann, Hitler's personal secretary. He offered to arrange an interview with the Führer, who was then in Berchtesgaden. However, I could not accept this offer as I knew that my trip there could not have been kept secret. I had to content myself with Weidemann's solemn promise that he would convey to his chief our great anxiety: Codreanu's life was in danger, and this danger would increase with the intensity of the international crisis.

CHAPTER

XIII

Visit to London and Codreanu's Assassination— The Two Grynszpans

Between September 12 and October 1, 1938, international events were piling up with unmatched velocity. Hitler's speech at Nürnberg was followed by Lord Londonderry and Lord Runciman's[1] mission to Germany and Czecho-Slovakia, by the third meeting of Chamberlain and Hitler, by the signing of the Munich Pact—the most intelligent diplomatic instrument conceived in Europe since the defunct Locarno Pact in 1925—and by the entrance of German troops into the Sudetenland. In Great Britain, parallel to that long series of events, a violent quarrel was raging in the Government, in Parliament, and in the press between Mr. Beneš's partisans and those who did not understand why seven million Czechs should have the right to rule and even misrule over three and a half million Germans.[2]

Mr. Duff Cooper, Lord of the Admiralty, had noisily resigned, follow-

[1] Lord Runciman was sent to Prague by Chamberlain as a special envoy to induce Beneš to a yielding attitude towards Germany's demands. Runciman backed those demands entirely and came back with a report entirely favorable to Germany.

[2] Georges Bonnet was French Foreign Minister at the time of the Munich conference. In his book *Defense de la Paix* (page 319) he answers the accusation that the Munich agreements were an unhappy compromise. We quote: "To how many new Munichs have they (the Western Powers) been forced to subscribe since 1944! We must make, however, this distinction: At Munich the Sudeten population by a massive vote expressed their will to be united to Germany. Today millions of families have been torn away from their countries. . . . They were not consulted about their fate. Various nations have disappeared; others have kept only their names. Where is the respect of the right of self-determination? What has happened to the sonorous stipulations of the Atlantic Charter? After having a glimpse at the present map of Europe, who could dare criticize the Munich agreements in the name of the 'great principles,' violated a hundred times since . . . ! We were hoping that once the war was won we could have got rid of falsehood; but this has not happened. It is to the law of falsehood that the world has succumbed today."

ing Mr. Eden's example. Powerful political and social groups in Europe, backed very stealthily but efficiently by President Roosevelt's attitude and policies and by the North American press, had risen in arms and decided to resort to any means to thwart the impulse toward peace given at Munich to European events.

The anti-Munich activities were gravely handicapped by the fact that the Munich arrangement had been received with almost delirious enthusiasm by the French and the British people. Seldom had the secret powers of revolution and war been in a more alarming situation. The panic was on when it was announced that a Franco-German pact of friendship, similar to that which had been concluded between Germany and Great Britain, was to be signed in Paris by Herr Ribbentrop himself. This was the moment chosen by the powers of darkness for sending Herschel Grynszpan, a Jewish refugee from Poland, to the German Embassy in Paris on November 7 to kill young Counselor Ernst vom Rath.

Here are the comments of Anatole de Monzie, a politician of leftist persuasion and former lawyer of the Soviet Embassy in Paris, concerning Rath's assassination:

> November 7, 1938: a young Polish Israelite, Grynszpan, has mortally wounded the Counselor to the German Embassy. Since the Franco-German Pact has just been signed, the coincidence of this agreement and of this crime prompts one to believe that there is a connection of cause and effect between the diplomatic action and the crime. We could perhaps eliminate the hypothesis of a political complicity. . . . But as a result of this crime, all of that which seems to be the prelude to a Franco-German rapprochement is again called in question. The young Jewish murderer will be defended, one will fight for his defense and gather money to help this defense. . . . The French workers' susceptibility will increase the danger, danger for us, danger for the Jews *because it associates the activities of the Jewish proletariat with the bellicose activities of Jewish capitalism.* [Italics added.]

Mr. de Monzie was right in his predictions, but it was not the French but the North American "sensitivity" that manifested itself thunderingly. The United States press went immediately to work extolling the action of the "young hero." Public meetings were organized from New York to San Francisco in defense of Grynszpan and his crime. The *New York Times* announced triumphantly that thirty thousand dollars already had been put at Grynszpan's disposition. President Roosevelt, with the uncanny precision of the pyromaniac, chose this moment for recalling Ambassador Hugh Wilson from Berlin. The German Government in turn recalled its Ambassador to Washington, Hans Diekhoff.

The murder did not have the grave consequences expected by those who had planned it. The German Government hastened to demonstrate that it did not consider France in any way implicated. Herr Ribbentrop, who had signed the Franco-German arrangement, generously distributed medals and praise to the doctors and nurses who had assisted Rath, and to the French veterans who had offered their blood for the necessary transfusions.

The Anonymous Forces had, however, another "Grynszpan" in reserve in Rumania.

The first visit of Carol to Great Britain had resulted in a total fiasco. As a king and as a relative, he had been automatically invited to King George's funeral on January 29, 1936. He left Rumania accompanied by a whole battalion of infantrymen which he wanted to parade in London at the obsequies. At Calais he was informed that his troop was not wanted and that he had to wait in France for the day that had been assigned for his reception on British soil. In London there were other disagreements and humiliations. Queen Mary refused to receive him. The newspapers had a good laugh about his frustrated "invasion of England" and about a strange character who paraded around in Rumanian national garb and who seemed especially attached to Carol, following him even at the funeral rites. The press described him as Carol's "masseur." The only bright point in all the unhappy voyage was the hasty collection by the Rumanian National Bank of all dollars, pounds, and Swiss francs that could be found on the Bucharest market, which were then delivered into the King's custody as traveling expenses for his military expedition.

London's attitude toward Carol changed suddenly. Ten days after Rath's assassination, Carol, *persona grata* again, received a special and urgent invitation from the British Government. After a short stay in London and a diabolically calculated visit to Hitler, he was back in Bucharest on November 28. That same night he had a long conference with Armand Călinescu and General Marinescu. Within thirty-six hours, on the night of Saint Andrew—the night of the vampires, in Rumanian folklore—Codreanu was assassinated in the woods of Țâncăbeşti by Carol's executioners.

An explosion of cheers shook the international press at the news of the Captain's murder. The *Times* in London and the *Times* in New York both came out with the same comment: "Well done!" Ward Price, the well-known British publicist, visiting Carol a short time after the murder, had this to say about him: "I was impressed by the firm and determined attitude of a man we in Great Britain had considered not a very serious character." The Minister of Great Britain in Prague felt compelled to pay a special visit to our Minister, Radu Crutzescu. "It was a great act of courage," the British Minister told Crutzescu, referring to the murder of the Captain.

As Codreanu's death is always related by French, British and German books and publications—with the complicity of some Rumanians, still more despicable than the foreign impostors—in a misleading way, calculated to attenuate Carol's infamy or even to obliterate it completely, we cannot end this chapter without telling it as it happened and as we lived it.

I was home from Copenhagen on a short leave; I had just left my wife and son downstairs listening to light music on the radio and gone to my room for some rest when my son, white-faced and scarcely able to talk between the sobs that choked him, shouted to me: "They have murdered the Captain!" Between a waltz and a jazz piece the radio had announced that Codreanu and thirteen of his companions had been shot to death in an escape attempt while being moved from one prison to another. Immediately after this announcement the light music started again. Ten months later, when Călinescu, Codreanu's murderer, was executed by nine Legionaries, the young men, before giving themselves up to the police, got hold of the radio station and, interrupting the light music for a minute, announced to the nation: "The Captain has been avenged!"

Here follows the description of Codreanu's murder as given in November 1940 to the investigation committee of the Rumanian High Court of Cassation, by one of the executioners:

We left that night [November 29 to November 30] in two police busses. The gendarmes, Majors Dinulescu and Macoveanu, were with us. In Ramnic we alighted at the Gendarmerie barracks where Majors Dinulescu and Macoveanu made contact with Major Rosianu, commander of the local gendarmerie.

At the prison we all entered one of the cells where Majors Dinulescu and Macoveanu demonstrated how we were to kill the Legionaries. Asking the chauffeur of our car to kneel, the major slipped from behind a bit of rope around the chauffeur's throat and showed us how easy it was to proceed that way.

After that we went into the prison courtyard and each of us received a Legionary in custody. I got one taller and stronger than the others; I learned afterwards that it was the Captain, Corneliu Codreanu.

We put them in the two police cars. There we attached their hands to the rear bench and their feet to the lower part of the front seat in such a way that they could not move one way or the other. Ten of them were bound in the first car and four of them in the second.

I was in the first bus with the ten, seated behind the Captain; a gendarme was seated behind each Legionary. In our hands we had the ropes. Major Dinulescu was in my car, Major Macoveanu in the other. There was complete silence, as neither we nor the Legionaries were allowed to talk.

When we reached the Tâncăbești woods, Major Dinulescu, with whom we had agreed about a signal, turned his electric lamp on and off three times. It was the moment for the execution. But I don't know why none of us moved. Then Major Dinulescu stopped the car and went to the other car.

In the other car Major Macoveanu had been obeyed, and the four Legionaries had already been strangled.

The Captain, turning slightly toward me, whispered: "Comrade, permit me to talk to my comrades." But in the same moment, even before he had finished his sentence, Major Dinulescu appeared with his revolver in his hand and growled between his teeth: "Execute!"

Then the gendarmes threw their ropes. . . .

We proceeded with lowered curtains to Jilava. We reached it at seven o'clock. There we were received by Colonel Gherovici, the legal medic, Lieutenant Colonel Ionescu and others. . . .

The grave was already prepared. The corpses of the Legionaries were then shot several times in the back to substantiate the story of an evasion attempt, and thrown in the prepared grave. Some weeks later the same gendarmes were called to Jilava, and after opening the grave, we threw over the corpses fifteen gallons of vitriol. We were asked to sign a declaration confirming the story that the Legionaries had been shot while trying to escape. . . .

Later I was summoned by Colonel Gherovici who told me: "You are mighty strong; you could have done away with three of them." Then he made me sign a receipt for 20,000 *leis* as medical help. I told him that I was not ill. "Keep your mouth shut," he told me. "If you don't, I will stop it with mud." And he showed me a Mauser pistol that was on his table.

We can easily imagine Carol and his mistress anxiously awaiting on this Saint Andrew's night the news of the Captain's death—news that Armand Călinescu or Gavril Marinescu no doubt took to them personally.

The assassination of Rath in Paris did not provoke the war as expected by the anti-Munich conspiracy; they had far better results with the assassination in Tâncăbești. It was Codreanu's murder that prompted Hitler to a radical tactical change in his foreign policy—a change loaded with the most fateful consequences not only for Germany but for the entire world of Western Civilization.

XIV

Codreanu's Suppression and Hitler's Policy

The British historian H. R. Trevor-Roper, from Oxford University, an official investigator of the documents captured from the National Socialist Government, has commented as follows on Hitler's sudden change of attitude in 1939 toward Soviet Russia:

> It has been said that Hitler's real war was against the West; that he decided against Russia only in order to break the blockade imposed upon Germany by the West; that the war against Russia was in fact an irrelevant, perhaps even an unwelcome tactical necessity in that most serious struggle against the West. . . .
> I do not believe that Hitler's real struggle was against the West.
> In *Mein Kampf,* and again in his last book on foreign policy, which he wrote in 1925, Hitler expressed his dream of a British alliance that would neutralize French opposition and make possible the German conquest of the East. *This war that broke out in 1939 was declared by Britain. Hitler would have done anything to avoid this* tedious diversion in his rear. . . . The war in the West in 1939 was, as far as Hitler was concerned, an unwanted war.
> How different was Hitler's attitude towards Russia! There was a period of agreement of course, 1939–1941, but it was a reluctant and treacherous agreement, and it was with a cry of relief that Hitler finally jettisoned this irksome expedient *"contrary to my whole past, my ideas and my previous obligations."* [Italics added.]

We postulate that no reader of *Mein Kampf,* no observer of Hitler's behavior, character, and policy, could in good faith be of another opinion than that of Professor Trevor-Roper. Everybody was aware of the following:

1. That Hitler had passionately sought Great Britain's friendship, offering even to defend the British Empire if ever it were in danger;

2. That he had declared in *Mein Kampf* that only idiots or traitors

could seriously contemplate Germany's reconquest of her western frontiers of before World War I;

3. That all his dreams and all his ambitions were directed toward the East, where he was convinced Germany would find her destiny;

4. That he had never thought of the possibility of a war with France, unless that country, blind to her own interests, were to oppose his action against Soviet Russia—the goal of all his preparations, his thoughts, and his whole life.

When in July 1940, Carol, who had just yielded without a fight Bessarabia and eastern Bucovina to the Soviets, sent Prime Minister Gigurtu and Minister of Foreign Affairs Manoïlescu—who was my predecessor at the Palais Sturdza and who told me the whole incident—to Salzburg with the mission of trying to win Hitler's favor, the two Rumanian pilgrims tried to convince the Führer that Carol's Rumania had adopted almost the same political and social ideals as Hitler's Germany. Hitler, after listening attentively, replied that an ideal was a beautiful thing in the life of a country, of a movement, and of a man; and as an example he gave them in minute detail the history of the Legionary Movement, ending with the assassination of Codreanu and with the following words: "What I will never forgive your King is that it is he who forced me to change my policy toward Soviet Russia."

Hitler did not exaggerate. In the plan of encirclement, immobilization, and finally destruction of Germany, Rumania was assigned a decisive part. Cooperation between the Soviet army and those of France and Czecho-Slovakia could not even have been imagined without Rumania's consent. Armed Rumanian resistance would have immediately brought the Polish armies into action, Soviet aggression being the fundamental *casus foederis* of the Polish-Rumanian alliance. Yugoslavia would have entered the fray on the side of Central Europe's defense, and Hungary, pushed by Germany, would no doubt have come in also. Rumania's willingness alone could have given real political or military value to a Soviet promise of intervention.

Hitler knew very well that in Rumania all the political factions except one had abandoned to the King all power and initiative in matters of international policy. Carol's *coup d'état* had evidently had international implications. It was upon the plea of France and Great Britain that the Goga Government had been dismissed; the only ministers from the Goga Cabinet who had been kept in the Government of Miron Cristea were those who had openly professed their fidelity to the alliances of World War I: Armand Cálinescu, General Ion Antonescu, and General Gavril Marinescu. Hitler also knew that only one important political group, the Legionary Movement, young, dynamic, prepared for any sacrifice, was opposing and defying Carol on the question of Rumania's relations with Soviet Russia. He also knew that in an open declaration, written shortly before his incarceration, Codreanu had warned the King that Rumania's youth would oppose any Soviet attempt to cross our frontiers.

The fact that Carol had Codreanu murdered hours after Carol's return from London, where he had undoubtedly been summoned in order to receive the directives of the powers to which he was subjected by his cupidity and his ambition, could have only one significance: *The anti-Munich faction had won, Great Britain was clearing for action, and Rumania was going along with Germany's enemies.*

Due to the gravity of the situation and the urgency of the menace, urgency that was clearly demonstrated by Codreanu's hasty assassination, Hitler made two speedy decisions: The first was of military character, the occupation of Czecho-Slovakia, which put his motorized divisions within twenty-four hours of Rumania's oilfields and within thirty of the Danube delta. The second was a bold political decision meant to explode the Franco-Czecho-Soviet alliance—he would negotiate an understanding and an economic arrangement with Soviet Russia.

Immediately after the assassination of Codreanu and his comrades, Carol and his men started the hunt for Legionaries and especially for the leaders who were still at liberty. The High Command of the Movement, along with all but one of the Legionaries who had participated in the Spanish Civil War were already incarcerated in the various prisons of Jilava, Dofteana, Ramnic, Mercurea, etc., where they were soon to be the victims of a huge mass execution. A group of Legionaries had been instructed to leave the country, as soon as they could, for Germany; and here again it was the Polish Government that helped the organization during the exodus. The members of the new Legionary staff had found a refuge in the non-Legionary homes of good Rumanians prepared to risk the severe penalties prescribed by the new regulations for such infractions.

It was to such a house that my son led me in order to meet Gheorghe Pavelescu, the son of General Pavelescu, who had been left as leader of the Bucharest sector. Gheorghe Pavelescu, who was killed in prison a few months later, wanted to ask me just one question: "How do we answer the murder of Codreanu?" If I had known then what I was to learn a few days later, namely the decision Hitler had been about to make when he was informed of Codreanu's murder, I would not have hesitated, perhaps, in giving Pavelescu the answer I already had in mind. I did not do it because of Christian scruples and patriotic uncertainties. *I do not know, even now, if provoking war in the East when Germany and Poland were still on the same side of the fence—a war that broke out anyway only three years later—would have saved my country from Com-*

munist tyranny and the world of Christian Civilization from the abyss toward which it is now rolling.

En route to my diplomatic post in Copenhagen I stopped in Warsaw and Berlin. In Warsaw, my friend Arciczewski, then Undersecretary at the Polish Foreign Office, assured me again of the good intentions of his Government toward the Legionaries who, abandoning Rumania, were passing through Polish territory, and offered me his house as a refuge in case I had already decided to take a similar course. But this was not what my friends had asked me to do. Arciczewski informed me of his Government's decision to renew *prematurely* its pact of nonaggression with Soviet Russia. The wise Arciczewski did not seem any more pleased than I by this decision, which Germany might consider as the next thing to an act of provocation, and which would not bring Poland any greater guarantee concerning Soviet intentions.

In Berlin it was again Captain Weidemann whom I found at the Reichskanzlei. He told me of Hitler's indignation and wrath upon learning of Codreanu's murder. He added that Hitler had for a few days seriously entertained the idea of sending his divisions through Hungary toward Rumania but finally contented himself with recalling Herr Fabricius, his Minister in Bucharest. I learned later that it was his Generals who dissuaded the Führer. In the book *Hitler's Testament,* in which his conversations with Martin Bormann in the last days of the war are recorded with an obvious authenticity, Hitler, talking of those moments, expressed his regret at not having then started the war in the East, when his relations with Poland were still what they had been in the last years of Pilsudski's life. We believe that Hitler was right, not the Generals, and that neither France nor Great Britain would have dared to ask from their people the sacrifice of a new and unwanted war without the defense of Poland as a pretext.

Once this moment of wrath passed, Hitler decided to continue adopting toward Carol and his Ministers an attitude of pretended ignorance of their real intentions, designs, hopes and machinations, and to draw from this attitude all the economic benefits offered by Rumania's enormous resources. Indeed a few days before Carol's departure for London, Hitler had sent him an economic mission to make purchases of as much as possible of Rumania's produce, such as oil and grain, together with a routine telegram of congratulations for Carol's birthday.

Twenty days after Codreanu's assassination, Grigore Gafencu was appointed Minister of Foreign Affairs; his administration of Rumania's international interests turned out to be more nefarious than any that had preceded it since the departure of Titulescu. It corresponded with a long and stupid attempt to fool Germany about Carol's intentions. Sir Reginald Hoare, the British Minister in Bucharest, told me himself during my short passage at the Rumanian Foreign Office that it was with Gafencu's and the King's consent and help that British, French and American agents and specialists were preparing for the destruction of Rumania's oilfields and oil industry, and the obstruction of the Iron Gates passage on the lower Danube. German Intelligence was of course aware of all this schemery and its smallest details, as was to be proved even before Gafencu's resignation when the German newspapers published the names of all those specialists and agents. Meanwhile Carol and his advisers deluded themselves into thinking that they were successfully masking their surreptitious activities and were fooling the German Government by the establishment of the so-called *Frontul Renasterei Nationale,* the FRN, in August 1939 on the model of the National Socialist and the Fascist movements. They even dolled up the chiefs of the former political parties, who were taught the Roman salute, in the new winter (blue) and summer (white) uniforms, and forcibly enlisted Rumanian young people into the *Straja Tării,* an imitation of National Socialist and Fascist Youth Organizations.

"Carol," says Mr. Prost, "applied himself to the regimentation of Rumanian young people in order to awake in their souls a love of their country." Such an affirmation coming from someone who had spent twenty years of his life in Rumania is a brazen effrontery and an act of discourtesy towards his readers. It was not the Rumanian young people who needed a lesson in patriotism. And it was not Carol (who had the blood of these young people still on his hands, who was deeply absorbed at that moment with the confiscation and appropriation of the big industrial Auschnitz fortune and other lootings, and who a few weeks later gave up with no fight two Rumanian provinces to the Soviets) who could give the Rumanian youth such a lesson.

Carol's purposes were many. Besides deceiving Berlin and Rome, he was also trying to deceive the Rumanian youth with the illusion of an idealistic organization similar to that of the Legionary Movement, hoping to make them forget what they had suffered at his hands. Carol failed on both counts. Berlin and Rome were not fooled. Concerning the Rumanian youth, let us hear from Mr. Prost:

> It was frivolous to hope that the *Straja Tării* could victoriously supplant the Legionary Movement. The Legionaries were convinced that they belonged to an élite. Their organization, semi-secret, did not accept everybody. *The donning of the green shirt was preceded by a religious initiation.* They had the feeling of being summoned to a great fight for glory and profit. The *Straja Tării* did not offer anything similar to the schoolboys who were forced to enlist.[1]

[1] *Destin de la Roumanie,* p. 124.

Mr. Prost is a bookkeeper by profession, and such is his turn of mind that it is very difficult for him to understand why the Legionaries would have risked and suffered unflinchingly all that they risked and suffered, if there was not also a little "profit" implied, besides that other thing he calls "glory."

Miron Cristea, the Patriarch, who as Prime Minister covered with his canonicals all of Carol's abuses, usurpations, and crimes, died in March 1939. His successor was Armand Călinescu. Along with the independence of Slovakia, Bohemia, and the Memelland's occupation by Germany, March and April brought Franco's uninterrupted victories in Spain, Italy's cynical invasion of Albania, the signing of an Italian ten-year military alliance, and the adhesion of Hungary to the anti-Communist pact. The Government in Bucharest had lost much of its confidence. Indeed, it was in a state of panic that the Crown Council on March 17, 1939, proclaimed its decision to defend the country's frontiers wherever they might be attacked—a more than superfluous announcement if such had really been the intention of Carol and his Government.

The rehearsal for a general mobilization, which was ordered a short time after, resulted in a total fiasco; all the deficiencies and shortcomings of the Rumanian army appeared suddenly for everyone to see and to draw their own conclusions—and they did.

The Phony Guarantees

The measures of "political security" taken by the Călinescu-Gafencu Government were still more disastrous for Rumania than the military insecurity in which Carol's corrupt administration had left her.

I am talking about the phony guarantees that this Government asked for and got from Great Britain and France. I say "phony," since those guarantees, given also to Poland, did not cover the eastern frontier of the two countries. This was certainly known to our diplomats, and to our King, for it is impossible to believe that our special negotiators and our accredited Ministers would have been so stupid as to fail to ask about the geographic compass of those guarantees, and especially whether they included Bessarabia and Bucovina. It is to be remembered that it was the same King, the same group of politicians and diplomats, who had refused the German guarantee for those frontiers with the promise of armaments thrown into the bargain.

Titulescu's policy was thereby perpetuated by Călinescu—a policy that was, in our opinion, not only wrong but treasonable, because:

1. The danger for Rumania and for Europe was not Germany but Soviet Russia.

2. Against this danger we could not count upon the assistance of those powers that had saved the Bolshevik Revolution; that had done everything in their power to save the regime of Béla Kun in Hungary and a Communist regime in Spain; that delivered Kolchak, Kutiepov and Miller to the Soviets; that had helped Soviet Russia build her military establishment; that had requested and received a military alliance with Soviet Russia; and that had introduced Russia into the League of Nations in Germany's place.

3. The Little Entente and the Balkan alliance did not represent any guarantee for Rumania. Czecho-Slovakia was, on the contrary, a heavy

handicap to us, all the more so since Prague did not miss any opportunity to provoke its powerful neighbor. We did not need Czecho-Slovakia to defend us against Hungary, nor did we need Turkey or Greece to defend us against Bulgaria.

4. The Hungarian revendications represented a danger to Rumania only if they were backed by Germany. The refusal in 1934 to accept Germany's guarantees of our frontiers with Hungary and with Soviet Russia had been a crime against Rumania's security.

5. There was only one power in the world that could have defended us, and defended Europe, against the Soviet and Communist menace, and this was Germany, restored to her prewar political and military status. We recommend that those who think we are wrong take a look at a political map of today's Europe, of Asia, Africa, Oceania, and not overlook Cuba, where the Soviets are building a powerful garrison and stockpiling assorted armaments under the very nose of the United States.

6. The argument of our fidelity to our old alliances was not sincere, or was not seriously examined. The war toward which Europe and the world were shoved by forces friendly to the Soviets and hostile to the Germans was not the war of France or Great Britain. Large political groups and important personalities in those two countries were also opposed to this war, the war for the collapse of the British and the French empires, for the end of those two countries as great international powers, and for a short North American pseudo hegemony.

7. This pseudo hegemony was inevitably destined also to collapse under the pressure and infiltration of European and Asiatic Communism and with the collapse of Japan and Germany, *the only two real barriers against this pressure and this infiltration.*

8. Fidelity toward our former allies should have prompted us to use all our influence to make them understand the danger and pitfalls of the course they had chosen. This was all the more true with regard to Poland, as directly exposed as Rumania to the Soviet danger, and toward whom we had not only the right but the duty to consult and advise. We had cowardly abandoned this right and duty when our Ambassador, Mr. Franasovici, was ordered to leave Warsaw at the most dangerous moment of the German-Polish crisis.[1]

The Ribbentrop-Molotov understanding was signed August 23, 1939. It was, on both sides, a tactical move, *une ruse de guerre.* Both sides knew it, and the Western Powers knew it also. The Western Powers knew that the Soviets would be on their side before the end of the war.

---

[1] I have it from a most authoritative source that no political directive whatever was sent from Bucharest to our Embassy in Warsaw, and no political information or suggestion was sent from our Embassy in Warsaw to Bucharest from the end of August 15, 1939, until the end of the hostilities in Poland and the evacuation of the Polish Government to Bucharest. In Bucharest there was complete and absolute indifference to the fate of our unhappy ally.

That was why they did not declare war on Soviet Russia as they did on Germany when Russia invaded Poland and the Baltic States, and that was why they did not guarantee the eastern borders of Poland and Rumania.

The Ribbentrop-Molotov understanding, which authorized the occupation of Bessarabia by the Soviets, was invoked after the fact as an excuse for our anti-German attitude. For Hitler, who knew that his troops would soon expel the Soviet armies not only from Bessarabia but from the whole of the Ukraine, a momentary Soviet domination in this province did not have great importance; for the population of Bessarabia and Bucovina, however, this temporary domination represented the greatest tragedy those embattled territories had known in their history. *The responsibility for this tragedy belongs entirely to King Carol and to all those who controlled our foreign policy between 1931 and 1940.*

Germany had offered to guarantee all our frontiers, including those adjacent to Soviet Russia, and to arm us thoroughly—an obviously sincere proposition as it coincided entirely with Germany's interest. We had scornfully refused even to consider it. There was a last attempt on Hitler's part to secure at least the neutrality of Rumania in the impending conflict and perhaps even the collaboration of this country of twenty million inhabitants and of important material resources. In April 1939, four months before the signing of the Ribbentrop-Molotov arrangement, he invited Mr. Grigore Gafencu, our Foreign Minister, to visit Berlin.

Mr. Gafencu left for Berlin with the firm determination to concentrate his efforts on a program of action absolutely contrary to Hitler's hopes, and with the childish illusion that he could conceal his anti-German activities under the masquerade of the uniform of the FRN, the pseudo nationalist party that Carol's police had rapidly organized in Rumania. In Berlin Mr. Gafencu was warned courteously but firmly of the dangers for his country of further commitments with Germany's prospective adversaries—as, for instance, any formal "guarantee" asked by or accepted from those adversaries. From Berlin Mr. Gafencu went to Paris and London, where of course, he changed back into his mufti. If the German Government did not learn immediately what was negotiated there, it was informed thoroughly a few weeks later when it discovered, and followed step by step, the proceedings and preparation of the demolition team expertly directed by one Vanger—a man of several citizenships—at the oilfields in Ploeşti and of the obstructing team at the Iron Gates.[2]

[2] The reader, no doubt, remembers the way Germany's insistent proposals to guarantee our frontiers and to rearm our forces had been constantly spurned by Carol and his Governments. Grigore Gafencu, who was then Rumania's Minister of Foreign Af-

The German Government learned immediately—as I did through Signor Giuseppe Sapuppo and Herr Cecil von Renthe-Fink, my Italian and German colleagues in Copenhagen—of the foolish attempt of Mr. Gafencu in Rome of convincing Mussolini and Count Ciano that Italy's interest was on the side of the Western Powers, and of selling them the idea of a Latin axis with France and Rumania.

Count Ciano's answer, as reported to me later by Alexandru Duiliu Zamfirescu, our Minister in Rome, was very much to the point: "Listen carefully to what I tell you. Give up the idea of securing guarantees from France and Great Britain, which in any case have no value for you, and nothing will happen to Rumania. But you can not even imagine how badly you will end up if you persist in your attempts in that direction."

Mr. Gafencu went back to Bucharest convinced that he had fooled the Führer. Carol shared Gafencu's optimism and answered those who tried to show him the perils of his double-dealings: "Germany is very pleased with me." Hitler had decided to oppose Carol's play with the same duplicity, but soon was to hit back with all his brutality. It was a great mistake—a mistake for which Germany paid very dearly—to punish Carol by maiming Rumania territorially, and therefore militarily and morally; for Rumania was Hitler's only possible important ally on the Eastern Front. But it was treasonous for Carol and his Ministers to prod Hitler into committing this error.

Such was the state of material, political and moral unpreparedness; of decay of willpower; of childish and felonious scheming in which

---

fairs, tells us in his book, *The Last Days of Europe,* of the last efforts of Hitler and Göring to secure from Rumania the promise that she would oppose any attempt of Soviet troops to cross her territory. Hitler had invited Gafencu to Berlin in April 1939 in still another attempt to avoid the necessity of a repugnant but unavoidable arrangement with Soviet Russia; an arrangement whose first victims would be Poland, Finland, the Baltic States, and Rumania. On April 18 Göring told Gafencu: *"If Rumania is our friend, we wish her to be great and powerful. If she joins the policy of encirclement, we will abandon her to the covetousness of her neighbors."* Hitler told him the next day, after a long exhortation: *"As long as I can count upon Rumania's friendship, I will never lend a hand to any vindication directed against her territory."* Gafencu's answer to those last warnings, after visits to Paris and London, was to hasten back to Rumania and prepare the sabotaging of some of Germany's most important military and economic interests in the East.

There was still another attempt from Germany's side, on the very eve of the signing of the Ribbentrop-Molotov Agreement. On or about August 12, 1939 Fabricius, the German Envoy in Bucharest, phoned Gheorghe Brătianu that he had been instructed by Marshal Göring to ask him earnestly to try once more to convince King Carol and his Government of the necessity to give Germany, without delay, the guarantee that the Red Army would not be allowed to cross Rumanian territory. *In the absence of such a guarantee, added Göring, there would occur a change in Germany's foreign policy very detrimental to Rumania's interests. The warning was transmitted; Carol and his ministers refused to pay any attention to it.*

Rumania was about to face a storm from which only the stronghearted and the brave could hope to come out alive.

I did not have any illusion concerning the ability of our political leaders to confront the intricacies and dangers of the times we were facing. The news I was receiving from Rumania and the information I had received in Copenhagen from my colleagues from the two opposed camps did not give me any reason for giving up my pessimism. Reasons for hope I found only on my short visit to Berlin with the Legionaries who had been instructed to gather there. They were planning, and preparing materially as well as they could, an answer to treason and a last attempt to save all that could still be saved of the fortunes of a country for which each of them would have gladly given his life. It was there that I met Horia Sima for the first time, the young man of penetrating eyes, of orderly thoughts, of the broad and steady vision of a real states-man, who was to be the leader of this last attempt.[3]

Mrs. Codreanu, the widow of the murdered Captain, and Father Borcea, the Chaplain of the group of Legionaries who had fought in Spain, were, under other names, the standing guests of the Rumanian Legation in Copenhagen. Father Borcea was the only Spanish fighter who had escaped Carol's massacres. Mrs. Codreanu told us the strange story of a postcard she had received from Cairo, signed with the nickname by which she called her husband and with his handwriting perfectly reproduced, in which she was told not to worry. This reminded me of a mysterious message I had received a few days after Codreanu's assassination, purported to have been written in the Dofteana prison by a Legionary. This message stated that Codreanu and his companions had been safely brought to the prison, and asked us not to take any false steps.

Creating confusion about whether or not a murder had been committed seems to be a tactic of a certain kind of political assassination. A striking example of this ritual was the famous case of the false Anastasia; and because I had a firsthand opportunity in Copenhagen to form an unshakable opinion about this case, I mention it here.

*　　*　　*　　*

Throughout our stay in Copenhagen my wife, my son, and I were honored by the friendship of a saint: Grand Duchess Olga, sister of the murdered Czar and, therefore, the aunt of Grand Duchess Anastasia.

---

[3] Horia Sima was thirty at the time, and a professor of literature. He had been head of the Legionary organization in Banat province, but had taken refuge in Berlin after the assassination of Codreanu. He became leader of the group in Berlin by sheer force of personality. In May 1940, Sima returned to Rumania, clandestinely, in order to prepare for the overthrow of King Carol.

Grand Duchess Olga would have given her last penny to anyone in need of it; she had in money and material goods the naïveté and the disinterest of the grande dame she was by birth and by nature. On her little farm in Knuts Minde she worked like a hired hand—milking her cows, feeding her pigs, manuring her field. No invitation was needed to Knuts Minde; it was home for every Russian refugee who happened to pass by, and of course for her old friends, who were attracted by her warmth, her intelligence and her interesting presence.

Grand Duchess Olga was in Copenhagen with her mother, the old Czarina, when rumors spread suddenly that a person who pretended to be Grand Duchess Anastasia had reached Germany. Ardently eager to know the truth, Grand Duchess Olga rushed to Berlin and an interview with that person was quickly arranged by the Danish Legation. Grand Duchess Olga received the unknown girl in her hotel room. The person she saw bore absolutely no physical resemblance to Grand Duchess Anastasia, nor did she know any facts going back to Anastasia's childhood that would have established her identity. Not only did she not speak German, French and English, which Anastasia had spoken fairly well or fluently; she did not speak Russian, but only Ukrainian.

Grand Duchess Olga, always prepared to find the most indulgent interpretation for her fellow humans' behavior, did not exclude the possibility that the false Anastasia might be a psychotic case, convinced of the truth of what she pretended. Grand Duchess Olga treated the girl accordingly, received her twice, fed, and helped her.

Grand Duchess Olga and her mother did not give any more importance to the Anastasia case. People who have known these two ladies and who know of the interview of Grand Duchess Olga with the false Anastasia could not continue to propagate this imposture without accusing two ladies who were Charity itself of being able to abandon to material misery and mental torture the very person they would have been called to help by every law of nature and every Christian feeling.

* * * *

On August 24, the day the alarmed world was informed of the Ribbentrop-Molotov Agreement, several of the Ministers accredited to Copenhagen were lunching with us at the Rumanian Legation. The British and Polish Ministers were exchanging words of encouragement. "They believe, perhaps, that something has changed!" the popular Sir Patrick Ramsay was saying. "Nothing has changed!" answered Minister Stargewski, his heart aching with anxiety for his beloved country.

"How long do you think we could resist if Germany attacked us?" the Polish Minister suddenly asked me. I answered: "Two months if you had to deal only with the Germans. You could not resist at all if you had to face a German attack and a Russian menace."

The fact is that a lot had changed for the worst, for Poland, Europe and for the world, *Germany included,* with the German-Soviet pact of nonaggression and of friendship. It was the duty of every government, every statesman, every diplomat, who pretended to be a friend of Poland to point out to her leaders the dangers of the new situation, and to prompt them to a radical change in their recently adopted intransigent attitude. I almost had an altercation with the newly appointed United States Minister in Copenhagen—a gentleman whose name I have forgotten, but who was formerly United States Minister in Sofia— because of my pessimistic prognosis concerning Poland's fate if she persisted in the policy that London, Paris and Washington were advising her to follow.[4] If our Ambassador in Warsaw, instead of leaving at the critical moment, had expressed the same pessimism, with all the authority of our Government behind him, and he had insistently advised our allies accordingly, he could have perhaps succeeded in countering the pressure of the Western Powers.

The betrayal of Poland had already started.

* * * *

Fishing for the powerful tuna in Skagerrak off Snekesten was the way we used to quiet impatience and worries, where we could forget about reporting, ciphering, deciphering and the febrile reading of newspapers. That was where the afternoon of September 1, 1939, found me, hooked to one of those giant fishes, which was leading our boat in large zigzags all over the waters of the strait. Suddenly three slim and majestic Dorniers with the Iron Cross emblem passed westward bound in arrow formation low over our heads. Another angler was sailing our way. It was Prince Axel of Denmark, who shouted from his boat to us: "War! It is war!"

I cut loose from my tireless tuna and hastened toward shore.

[4] When taking leave of me, the new United States Minister's predecessor, Alvin M. Owsley, my congenial American colleague, told me with conviction: "Our hour will come, and after that you will look in vain for Germany on the map of Europe."

XVI

The First Betrayal of Poland

It was a strange story that Józef Lipski, Poland's Ambassador in Berlin, told us on his way through Copenhagen after the rupture of diplomatic relations between Poland and Germany. This story has been completely confirmed through the publication of official documents by the two opposed parties.

"Have you seen Ribbentrop yet? Don't you know that he has been waiting for you since the day before yesterday, and that this evening is the deadline he mentioned for the beginning of the negotiations with Poland?" This is how Robert Coulondre, the French Ambassador, briskly addressed Mr. Lipski on August 31, 1939, mentioning that he had received this information by chance from British Embassy circles. Lipski answered that he had seen Sir Nevile Henderson, the British Ambassador, the same day at two o'clock in the morning, *and that this diplomat had not mentioned Ribbentrop's wishes and the deadline attached to them.* Lipski, realizing the gravity of this unexplained negligence of the British Ambassador, immediately asked for an interview with the German Foreign Minister, which was granted without delay.

From Nevile Henderson's *Final Report* (No. 55) it becomes clear that not only did the British Ambassador not warn Lipski that he was expected up until twelve midnight (the meeting with Lipski and Henderson was at two a.m., August 31), but Henderson advised Lipski against seeing Ribbentrop at all: "I saw, however, the Polish Ambassador at two o'clock a.m. I gave him a brief account, studiously moderate, of my conversation with Herr v. Ribbentrop . . . [and] suggested that he recommend to his Government an interview between Marshals Śmigly-Rydz and Göring. *I felt obliged to add that I could not conceive the success of any negotiations if they were conducted by Herr v. Ribbentrop.*" Although Coulondre, the French Ambassador, at least had the honesty to inform Lipski that he was expected by Ribbentrop before midnight, he does not seem to have been very eager either that such a meeting should bring an understanding between the two interlocutors. For, according to Lipski (Polish White Book, Document No. 109), Coulondre advised him to get in contact with Ribbentrop *only after twelve o'clock*. Advice that Lipski wisely disregarded.

Ambassador Lipski was received at the Wilhelmstrasse with all the honors due an envoy extraordinary. A company of honor presented arms, the Polish national anthem was sung, and Ribbentrop greeted him with the effusion of an old friend, exclaiming happily, "At last, we can negotiate!" This oversight of the British Ambassador, which was to have historical consequences, had not given Lipski the time or the opportunity to explain the situation to his Government; so he had to tell Ribbentrop that he was not provided with the necessary special mandate. Deeply shocked, Ribbentrop told Lipski that he would communicate this fact to Hitler. Thus ended the interview that could have spared Europe and the world the disaster of a war between non-Communist powers.

It may strike the reader as highly irregular that Ribbentrop should send his invitations to Lipski through the British Ambassador, rather than directly to Lipski. However, this latter course was impossible.

On August 4, 1939, Poland issued an ultimatum, which was based on a false rumor, to Germany, to which Germany replied with a most vehement answer. This followed a speech which had been delivered by Józef Beck, the Polish Foreign Minister, to the Polish Parliament on May 5, 1939. In this speech Beck had taken the initiative to break off any direct negotiations with Germany. Therefore, as both Ribbentrop and Baron Weizsäcker, German Undersecretary of State, told Sir Nevile Henderson, "a German initiative was unthinkable" (British Blue Book No. 75). Furthermore, one must not forget that as early as May 1939, Lipski had been ordered not to accept, orally or in writing, even as an agent of transmission, any German proposals, much less discuss them. Nevertheless, Ribbentrop did take the final initiative, and although it would have been unthinkable for him to contact Lipski directly, Ribbentrop had every reason to believe that his repeated invitations, of August 26 and of August 28, would be transmitted to Lipski by the British Ambassador.

However, as mentioned already, even if Ribbentrop had followed the regular procedures, it would have availed him nothing. From a telegram of Lord Halifax to Sir Nevile Henderson (British Blue Book, Document No. 82, August 30, 1939): "Could you not suggest to the German Government to adopt the normal procedure, to notify the Polish Ambassador when the conditions have been drawn up, and hand them over to him to be transmitted to Warsaw?" From Sir Howard Kennard, British Ambassador in

Warsaw, to Lord Halifax (British Blue Book Document No. 96, August 31, 1939): "I have asked Mr. Beck what attitude the Polish Ambassador [in Berlin] would adopt if Herr von Ribbentrop, the person who had received him, would hand over to him the German propositions. *Mr. Beck told me that Mr. Lipski would not be authorized to accept such a document.*" [Italics added].

The reader might ask why Hitler did not wait longer before invading Poland. Actually, he had carried on friendly, courteous, insistent negotiations and proposals from February 1938 right until the very end. These were brutally interrupted by Beck's speech of May 5, 1939. A speech which Beck was forced to deliver, against his will, by Śmigly-Rydz, Marshal of Poland, and by President Ignacy Mościcki. After this, further negotiations were impossible. But for the actual situation in Germany, let us quote from Sir Nevile Henderson's *Final Report*: "It was the opinion of the military advisers that counted more than anything else with Hitler. I have always been of the opinion that it was those advisers who convinced him to establish a protectorate in Bohemia. It was the same advisers that told Hitler that any new delay would be fatal and that the bad season in Poland might upset all their plans for a rapid campaign [which was vital because of the possibility of England and France invading Germany in the West]. The Army fought with him about this even during the week of August 25 to September 1." [1]

The truth is that not only did Sir Nevile Henderson take the responsibility of concealing from his Polish colleague the message with which he had been entrusted by Ribbentrop, but that Sir Howard Kennard, the British Ambassador in Warsaw, had received, along with the news of this message, instructions not to communicate it to the Polish Government.

The anti-Munich faction had triumphed at Downing Street, and Neville Chamberlain, defeated, was nothing more than a tool in its hands. This is how Jörgen Bast, a gentleman of anti-German persuasion, and correspondent for the *Berlingske Tidende*, commented on the situation:

> When he left [for Munich], Mr. Chamberlain had seen all his cabinet accompanying him to the airport and wishing him good luck on his mission. At his return nearly all the British people welcomed him. Thousands upon thousands of people lined the way from Huston to Buckingham Palace, where the King and Queen received him warmly.
>
> The King asked him to appear at the balcony with the Queen and Mrs. Chamberlain. New ovations accompanied him to Downing Street, where from a window on the second floor the tired statesman shouted to the crowd: "My dear friends [I bring] peace with honor. I believe it is peace for our time!"

[1] From the official British translation in French.

Such was Mr. Chamberlain's hope that day. He was soon to feel, however, the thorns concealed among the roses of Munich. The same day, Lord Admiral Duff Cooper resigned because he could not accept the Munich agreement, and this was only the beginning of a fierce struggle. Stranger still: the same Prime Minister who had shouted his conviction that peace was guaranteed for one generation declared thirteen days later in the House of Commons that the consequences of Munich for Great Britain could not be anything else than "Arming! Arming! Arming!"

Let us remember that Chamberlain's bellicose speech of October 13, 1938, and his speeches of January 23 and 28, 1939, were delivered before the occupation of Czecho-Slovakia by the Germans.

In my book written in 1943, *La Bête sans Nom,* I explored, with a profusion of documentation, the question of the responsibility concerning World War II, a war that started over the defense of Danzig and of the Polish Corridor. I did not know then that my conclusions were to be tragically confirmed by the surrender into Soviet hands of the whole of Poland along with nine other European countries.

My conclusions were as follows:

1. The Corridor and Danzig had been only pretexts. Poland had been knowingly pushed—by the phony guarantees of Great Britain and France, by the most unrealizable promises, and by the most deceptive tricks—into a war from which the responsible cliques in London, Washington, and Paris knew very well she could not emerge alive and free.

2. The British Government, which had suddenly taken the direction of those opposed to the Munich settlement, had been backed throughout all of its activities, by the Washington Government or, more accurately, by the dark and grim coterie surrounding the incapacitated President; a coterie firmly determined not to lose what was perhaps its last opportunity to provoke war against Germany and to save, thereby, Soviet Russia and Communism from almost certain annihilation.

3. The British Government and its Ambassadors in Berlin and Warsaw—obviously under instructions—had done everything possible to encourage Poland not to accept the moderate German proposal of October 24, 1938, and to ignore completely the very acceptable conditions offered by Ribbentrop in the last phase of the dispute.

"Poland had started toward war when Beck received the encouragement of London, which seemed to imply also the support of Paris," reported Anatole de Monzie, Minister in the French War Cabinet, in his book *Ci-Devant.* Serious warning had not failed, however, to reach Poland's Government. In his report of March 29, 1939, Juliusz Lukasievici, Polish Ambassador to Paris, wrote:

It is childish, naïve and at the same time disloyal on the part of Great Britain to ask a country that is in Poland's situation to jeopardize its relations with a neighbor as powerful as Germany, and to throw the world into the catastrophe of a war, just to satisfy the inner political necessity of Mr. Neville Chamberlain.

The November 28, 1938, report of Count Jerzy Potocki, the Polish Ambassador in Washington, was no less alarming:

> Ambassador [William C.] Bullitt told me that only a war could stop Germany's expansion in Europe. As I asked him how he imagined this future war would evolve. He answered that, first of all, the United States, France and Great Britain ought to arm massively. Only then, the situation being ripe, should the decisive step be taken. I asked him how the conflict could be provoked, as Germany very likely would never attack France or Great Britain. I could not see the connecting point in this combination. . . . Bullitt answered that it was the wish of the democratic countries that Germany should eventually get into a conflict in the east.

It is strange that the Polish Government did not grasp the purpose of the maneuver, to which Lukasievici alluded and which was so precisely described by Mr. Bullitt; and that, instead, it fell into the trap of the promise of unconditional military assistance offered by Great Britain (in her own name and in the name of France) at the very moment when Germany was offering Poland an arrangement that was the only true guarantee of Poland's national survival.

Here is how on March 31, 1939, before the British Parliament, Neville Chamberlain formulated this promise of unconditional assistance, equivalent to an undated British declaration of war on Germany, entrusted to Poland, to be produced the moment Poland chose to produce it.

> As this House knows, certain consultations with other governments are presently taking place. To make the position of the Government of His Majesty [King George VI] perfectly clear before the end of those consultations, I must immediately inform this House that if any action were to endanger Polish independence, and if the Polish Government were to think it of vital interest to resist with its national forces, His Majesty's Government would consider itself immediately obliged to come to the assistance of the Polish Government with all the means at its disposal. I may add that the French Government has authorized me to affirm clearly that its attitude is identical with ours in this matter.

On July 10 of this same year, 1939, when an armed conflict between Germany and Poland seemed an imminent possibility, Mr. Chamberlain, in order to deny the tragic responsibility taken by Great Britain, found it necessary to make some subtle distinctions concerning the order of events:

> When the German Government made certain offers to Poland in March 1939, offers which were accompanied by a press campaign, the Polish Gov-

ernment realized that it might very soon find itself confronted by an attempt at a military solution that Poland would have to oppose by all means at its disposal. . . . On March 25, it took certain military dispositions and on the 28th it sent its answer to Berlin. I ask the Parliament to take good notice of those two days. It has been openly asserted in Germany that it was the British guarantee that had encouraged the Polish Government to undertake the mentioned action. I must point out that our guarantee was given only on March 31.

This attempt at misrepresentation must have cost Mr. Chamberlain, an honest gentleman by nature, almost as much mortification as his final imposture the day Britain declared war on Germany. As official Polish documents reveal, on March 21 Sir Howard Kennard proposed to Poland a military alliance with France, Great Britain, and Soviet Russia. On March 20 Lord Halifax had informed the House of Lords that the British Government "has hastened to consult in an intimate and practical way with other governments that were interested in the present problem." It would be absurd to think that Poland was not among the consulted governments.

The interval from March 28 to March 31 in no way substantiated the alibi Mr. Chamberlain was trying to establish. Everybody knew Great Britain's general attitude towards Germany in that hour; everybody knew the negotiations in which she was engaged in Paris, in Moscow and, most especially, in Warsaw; and nobody could believe that the uninterrupted conversations between the British and Polish Governments had not touched on the question of British military assistance—even if Lord Halifax's declarations and Polish documents had not given the lie to the British Prime Minister.

We must point to another and still more important error in Mr. Chamberlain's speech of July 10, 1939. The German proposal to Poland of March 1939 *was not the first.* There was a standing proposal offered to the Polish Government on October 24, 1938, in Berchtesgaden, by Herr Ribbentrop to Mr. Lipski. Its terms were as follows:

1. The free state of Danzig was to return to the German Reich.

2. An extraterritorial highway and railway line with several tracks was to be constructed through the Polish Corridor.

3. In the Danzig territory Poland was to have an extraterritorial highway and railway line and a free port.

4. Poland was to receive a guarantee for the distribution of her goods in the Danzig territory.

5. The two nations were to recognize and guarantee each other's frontiers and respective territories.

6. The German-Polish treaty was to be prolonged from ten to twenty years.

7. The two countries were to add a consultative clause to the treaty.

Today anyone can assess the responsibility assumed by those who encouraged Warsaw to refuse even to discuss this proposal, a proposal open to Poland for more than a year. Was the German proposal, which was read by Herr Ribbentrop to Sir Nevile Henderson on the evening of August 30, 1939, much more severe? Sir Nevile himself has given us the answer in his *Final Report*: The terms "are in general not too unreasonable." [2]

Actually, the new German proposal was perfectly equitable, or in any case worthy of consideration. Why should Sir Nevile have intentionally concealed from his Polish colleague the fact that the German Foreign Minister was awaiting him in order to discuss them, and that the deadline for those discussions had been extended *for a second time* by twenty-four hours?

These were the new German conditions:

1. Danzig was to be German.

2. Gdynia was to be Polish.

3. An international administration was to be established for one year in the Corridor.

4. A plebiscite under the control of this administration was to be established at the end of the year.

5. An extraterritorial highway one kilometer wide was to be placed at the disposition of Germany should the Corridor become Polish.

6. An extraterritorial highway one kilometer wide was to run toward Gdynia should the Corridor become German.

7. Privileges and special rights were to be established in Danzig and Gdynia on the basis of reciprocity.

8. Both ports were to be demilitarized.

9. Germany was to accept the principle of exchange of populations.

[2] Besides his *Final Report,* Sir Nevile Henderson also published his memoirs. The Foreign Office immediately stopped their distribution. Why? Concerning Hitler's final proposals to Poland, which would have been handed by Herr Ribbentrop to Mr. Lipski on the evening of the thirty-first at 6:15 p.m. had Lipski's government not forbidden him to accept any such document, here are the comments of Pierre and Renée Gosset, authors of *Hitler,* a classic in anti-Hitler literature (page 170 of the Spanish edition): "Nevertheless, he [Henderson] understood enough to realize that it was a proposition of extreme moderation based on a plebiscite. . . . This was an offer that no Western statesman could have rejected in good faith." It has been objected that Ribbentrop did not permit Henderson to take the written proposals with him. This is a futile point, for the full text of those moderate proposals was sent by Göring to Sir Nevile next morning. Henderson could have immediately passed them to the Polish Ambassador— if such had been the spirit of London's instructions. Furthermore, the British Government had almost twenty-four hours in which to exercise the necessary pressure on the Polish Government. Contrary to Pierre and Renée Gosset's affirmation, nothing was done in that direction; and, as we know, after his last interview with Ribbentrop, Sir Nevile Henderson met his Polish colleague but did not communicate to him the fact that Ribbentrop was expecting him.

10. Should there be an agreement, there was to be a general demobilization.

At no moment did Herr Ribbentrop specify that these conditions were not negotiable.[3]

It is interesting to recall what had been said about Germany's disection, under the Treaty of Versailles, June 1919, by those who were now prepared to throw the world into another catastrophe for Danzig and the Corridor.

On November 29, 1919, Winston Churchill insistently requested from the House of Commons:

> . . . the satisfaction of the legitimate revendications of the defeated, especially concerning the Corridor and Danzig. Failing which, contrary to our wishes and our interests, we could be led into a war to correct the errors and satisfy the revendications that disrupt Europe today.

British Prime Minister Lloyd George wrote in 1919 in a memorandum for the conference of Versailles:

> Peace can be assured only if motives of exasperation, continually exalting feelings of justice and honor, were to exist no more. . . . That is why I am firmly opposed to the submission—unless it is absolutely necessary—of Germans to foreign domination. The proposition of the Polish committee to put 2,000,000 Germans under the laws of a people of another religion, a people that have proved through history their ineptitude for governing is, in my opinion, liable to provoke a new war.

In January 1936 before the British Parliament, Sir Austen Chamberlain, a declared enemy of all things German, expressed his conviction that:

> Great Britain would not move a finger to defend the Corridor, a region in which none of its interests were at stake.

In June 1932 in the House of Lords, Lord Noel-Buxton had drawn the attention of his colleagues to the treatment inflicted on the German population in Poland:

[3] We quote Ambassador Lipski's report to his Government from the Polish White Book:

August 31, 1939   Received: 10 o'clock p.m.

I have been received by Herr v. Ribbentrop at 6:30 p.m. I followed the instructions I had received. Herr v. Ribbentrop has asked me *if I was empowered to negotiate* [*de conduire des négociations*], I answered that I was not. He asked me if I had been informed that, upon London's suggestions, the German Government had declared *that it was ready to negotiate directly with a representative of the Polish Government.* I answered that I had no direct information on the subject. Concluding Herr v. Ribbentrop told me that he believed that I was authorised to negotiate. He will communicate my visit to the Chancellor. [Italics added.]

LIPSKI

> Lord D'Abernon has recently described Danzig and the Corridor as the powder keg of Europe. . . . The gravity of the situation proceeds principally from the way the German population is treated by the Poles. . . . The question of the German population in Poland is a question very urgent and serious. Since the annexation, more than 1,000,000 Germans have left the Corridor because the conditions of living were intolerable for them.

These were the circumstances that prompted Chancellor Gustav Stresemann and all the German Chancellors before Hitler to refuse any concession or declaration that could have been interpreted as an acknowledgment of the stipulation of the Versailles Treaty concerning Poland, the Corridor and Danzig. The leader of integral nationalism in Germany was the first German statesman who admitted publicly and formally the "Polish fact" as an irrevocable contingency, and the first who proposed an arrangement, a generous arrangement, for the open problems between Berlin and Warsaw.

Poor Chamberlain! The same powers that had made him abandon, after a resistance of only a few days and without any visible reason, the pacific, patriotic, and humane consideration approved unanimously by the British people, brought this scrupulously honest statesman to the radio broadcast of September 4, 1939, in which every assertion was false and in which he tried to explain to the British people why he was engaging the British Empire in a frightening and incalculable adventure.

> The so-called German proposals were made to the Polish Ambassador Thursday the thirty-first in the evening, two hours before the German Government announced that they had been refused. Far from having been refused, there had been no time to consider them. . . . The Polish representative was told to come at a fixed moment to sign a document that he had not even seen. This was not negotiating, but dictating! No government conscious of its dignity and of its power could have submitted to such methods. Negotiations in conditions of equality could have had quite different results.

Friendly negotiations between Germany and Poland could have started in 1938 over the first formal German proposals, had Poland so desired.

On August 29, 1939 Sir Nevile Henderson received from Hitler and reported to London the assurance that Germany was ready to negotiate with Poland under the conditions suggested by Great Britain herself: that security be given to Poland relative to her vital interests, and that the final agreement be internationally guaranteed. The acceptance by Hitler of these two conditions was never communicated to Mr. Lipski by Sir Nevile Henderson. Germany waited for a Polish negotiator—who could have been the Polish Ambassador in Berlin—until August 31 at twelve o'clock. The time limit for negotiation had even been prolonged, at Britain's suggestion, for twenty-four hours. However, Sir Nevile Henderson had taken it upon himself to keep his Polish colleague in total ignorance of the situation during the entire forty-eight hours.

A general idea of the German proposition had been given to the British Ambassador during his interview with Hitler and had been communicated to London on August 29 in the evening. The detailed conditions were read to Sir Nevile the night of August 30 at twelve o'clock and were transmitted to London immediately.

Of even greater importance is the fact that Sir Howard Kennard had informed his Government—in time to permit wiser advice to be given to the Polish Government—*that Mr. Lipski had received an order not to accept any document from the hands of Herr Ribbentrop, should the German Foreign Minister try to acquaint Lipski with the proposed German conditions for a settlement.*

The German Government, far from having insisted that those conditions be signed without even being read, had assured Mr. Chamberlain on August 29, via Hitler himself, and as reported by Sir Nevile Henderson, that the negotiations would take place as between equals. We maintain that these assurances were never communicated to Ambassador Lipski or to the Polish Government.

There are also some interesting omissions in the British official publications. We read in the Foreign Office Blue Book:

> [Dr. Carl] Burckhardt, High Commissioner of the League of Nations in Danzig, accepted Hitler's invitation to visit Hitler in Berchtesgaden. Therefore, Mr. Burckhardt had a private conversation with Hitler on August 11 during which one may suppose that the question of Danzig was discussed in relation to the general situation in Europe.

This information omits the most important part of the interview—the part that concerns the British Government and the pacifying ways in which it could have intervened in the German-Polish situation, especially in the Danzig question.

I met Mr. Burckhardt in the home of our mutual friend Mr. Helmer Rosting, the former's predecessor in Danzig. Burckhardt told us that Hitler, who knew that Burckhardt had the confidence of the British Government, had asked him to use his influence to persuade Chamberlain to send him someone with whom he, the Führer, could talk directly and openly. Hitler suggested General Ironside, with whom he could have talked in German.

From Berchtesgaden Burckhardt went to London, where he had the opportunity to transmit Hitler's request to Neville Chamberlain. The Prime Minister rejected it immediately, arguing that Sir Nevile Henderson was the British Ambassador in Berlin. It is true that Mr. Chamberlain was not obligated to comply with Hitler's demand; but the problems at stake were of such importance, and the desire of the head of the German state was expressed so insistently, that it is difficult to understand how Chamberlain could have passed up this opportunity to discover exactly what were Hitler's intentions, and to come, perhaps, to a settlement with him. Chamberlain's rebuttal was even less understandable in view of the fact that this same General Ironside was sent to Moscow a short time later, where Great Britain also had an Ambassador. The General's mission was to negotiate a military alliance with the Soviets, directed, of course, against Germany.

CHAPTER

XVII

Danger of Peace—Massacre of the Legionaries

Great Britain's firm decision to fight Germany was to reveal itself twice more in the first days of September 1939.

Only hours after the outbreak of hostilities between Germany and Poland, Mussolini, renewing his efforts for peace, proposed to all the interested powers an immediate suspension of hostilities and the immediate convocation of a conference between the great powers, in which Poland would also participate. Mussolini's proposals were, without any delay, accepted by all governments concerned except Great Britain.[1]

Mussolini had asked for the *possible*—a suspension of hostilities, and the stopping of marching armies. As a matter of fact, German troops were twenty miles deep into Polish territory, and Polish troops had crossed in various places the frontiers of East Prussia. British inventiveness was not, however, at a loss; it found very quickly the *impossible* thing to ask in order to frustrate Il Duce's pacifying attempt. The British Government demanded that German troops be withdrawn to German territory before it would accept Mussolini's proposal and start negotiations.

[1] "The French Government and other foreign governments were the recipients yesterday of an Italian proposition tending to secure a settlement of the present European difficulties. After deliberation, the French Government has given a positive answer." (Information of the Havas Agency, September 1, 1939.)

The positive answer given by Georges Bonnet, the French Foreign Minister, was accompanied by the following commentaries (French Yellow Book, piece number 327): "It is the opinion of the French Government that such a conference must not limit itself to partial and provisory solutions—to limited and immediate problems. It should evoke all problems of a general character and reach a general appeasement that would permit the urgent and firm reestablishment of a durable peace." Adds Mr. Bonnet in his *Défense de la Paix*: "We should have proposed, therefore, a broader Munich and transformed it into a general conference of all interested powers: the United States, the USSR, Poland, and the Balkan States included." How different would have been the history of the world if Great Britain had joined France in accepting Mussolini's proposal.

London asked Daladier to cancel France's former consent, and Daladier, the "captive chief," as de Monzie called him—yielded to London's injunctions. We quote from Mr. de Monzie's *Ci-Devant*:

> September 3, Bonnet [the French Foreign Minister] told the cabinet of London's insistence on an immediate ultimatum. When leaving the council I urged Bonnet not to take any heed of the British *non possumus*. To demand *the withdrawal of the German troops was an indefensible pretension*. [Italics added.] [2]

Of the position of Daladier, the captive of the hidden powers, and of Paul Reynaud, their principal representative in the French Cabinet, Mr. de Monzie gives the following memorable information:

> Paul Reynaud is back from London, where he participated in the Supreme Council meetings. He has operated alone, he has negotiated alone, and he has pledged France not to negotiate a separate peace. I found Daladier in his office at Rue Saint Dominique totally prostrated, disheartened. He told me: *"He* [Reynaud] *has consented to everything they wanted—everything that I did not want. Monzie, I am terrified when I think of what such a man can do to our country!"* [Italics added.]

Daladier was the Prime Minister. Who empowered Reynaud to decide the fate of France?

But another opportunity was opened to Poland—an opportunity that has not been mentioned, to date, to my knowledge, by any modern historian or by any commentator. That opportunity was lost to the heroic and betrayed country—again because of British promises, pressures, and threats. I am referring to Göring's speech a few days before the invasion of Soviet Russia's troops into Polish territory.

I had been informed by the German Minister in Copenhagen, Herr Renthe-Fink, of the genesis of this important manifestation. Göring had always had a special sympathy for Poland; he had always considered her as Germany's probable ally in a war against Soviet Russia. He had seen with sadness and disapproval the beginning of the hostilities, and had insistently asked the Führer to permit him to try a last attempt at conciliation. Hitler gave his consent and approved the text of Göring's speech, the significance of which was unmistakable. More than that, Hitler backed it openly by his demonstration of deference and admiration at Pilsudski's grave.

I was so convinced at that moment that a surprise opportunity for an arrangement between Germany and Poland, spoiled by Great

---

[2] Bonnet, the French Foreign Minister, and Daladier, the French Prime Minister, did not want war; neither did France. Paul Reynaud wanted it. On the French side he is principally responsible for the catastrophe into which his country and Europe were wantonly precipitated in September 1939.

Britain on the diplomatic field, could be found on the battlefields before the imminent invasion of Poland by the Soviets, that I wired our Minister of Foreign Affairs, asking his authorization to come to Bucharest for forty-eight hours. The authorization was refused and I had to content myself with a telegram trying to explain the new situation created by Göring's speech, and suggesting that Poland be advised to suspend *de facto* her hostilities on the Western Front and concentrate all her forces against the impending Soviet aggression.

I still believe that Germany, which at no time was bound by any obligation of mutual assistance to Soviet Russia, would have considered favorably, from the position gained in the Corridor and Danzig, this suggested new turn in the military and the political situation. Poland would have outlived thereby the lunatic behavior of President Ignacy Mościcki and Marshal Śmigly-Rydz, and Rumania would have been given an opportunity to honor her obligations to Poland, defending with all her strength the sector assigned to her in the fight against the common enemy.

President Mościcki during his trip through Bucharest, after Poland's defeat, was asked by a high Rumanian prelate why he had again thrust aside the hand extended by Germany. He answered that his Government had considered very seriously the advisability of acting upon Göring's suggestions, but that it was prevented from doing so by British military and diplomatic representatives, who were backed by their American colleagues. A prompt forcing of the Scandinavian straits by a British armada and a landing, somewhere on Polish or East Prussian territory, of French and British troops was promised. A few months later I heard exactly the same tale from another Polish authority.

My suggestion for a Polish-German settlement received a completely indifferent reception in Bucharest, which was hardly surprising since they completely contradicted the intentions and the hopes of the three personalities who were at that moment handling Rumania's foreign policy: King Carol, Prime Minister Armand Călinescu, and Minister of Foreign Affairs Grigore Gafencu. At no moment had these three personalities given up hope for new circumstances that would permit them to take part in the fight not only as allies of Great Britain and France, but also, conforming with the Barthou-Titulescu-Beneš plan, as allies of Soviet Russia. Armand Călinescu, the most fanatic pro-Westerner of the three, pleaded earnestly for an immediate declaration of war on Germany.

Without asking for any further authorization, I went to Berlin for a few days in order to benefit from the information and impressions of Radu Crutzescu, our Minister there, who was more in harmony than I with our Government's policy. According to Mr. Crutzescu's information,

Hitler was deeply impressed by the losses suffered by the gallant Polish Army, which was fighting with cavalry regiments against his tanks and his bombers. Mr. Crutzescu did not think there would be any alteration in the policy of waiting, adopted by our Government, as long as war in the West continued to be what it was: troops guarding, with arms stacked, their frontiers. My telegram, therefore, could have held no interest for our Government. Crutzescu himself did not accord any great importance to Göring's speech or to Hitler's demonstrations before Pilsudski's grave.

I was in the office of Edvard Munch, the Danish Foreign Minister a few days after my return from Berlin when a secretary brought him some papers he had probably perused already. He delicately extricated one of them and, pointing to it, informed me to my great astonishment that Rumanian Prime Minister Armand Călinescu had been shot by a group of Legionaries. What had happened, I learned later, was that a horsedriven carrige had stopped Călinescu's auto at a crossroads and that nine young men had killed him. The nine Legionaries seized the radio station for a few minutes, announced that Codreanu had been avenged, and gave themselves up at the next police precinct. They were immediately executed at the spot where Călinescu had fallen.

As I could not help muttering something about the numbers of Legionaries, men and women, Călinescu had himself assassinated, Munch very calmly retorted: "Well, maybe; anyhow, please transmit our condolences to your Government." Rather torn between the total contempt I had for the murdered man and the traditional obligation to transmit to my Government condolences of the legation and the Rumanian colony, I took my clue from Mr. Munch and wired as follows to our Foreign Minister: "Munch, the Minister of Foreign Affairs, has asked me to transmit his and his Government's condolences for the amazing murder of the prime minister." I learned later that the word "amazing" (*grozav*) had received contradictory interpretations among the young people at the cipher department.

I went to bed that night greatly worried by the probable consequences of Călinescu's execution, all the more so because my wife and my son were at that time in Bucharest exposed to all the iniquities of which Carol and his men were capable. The news next day was more horrifying than anything I could have imagined. Mr. Prost, following the formula adopted by almost all the Western commentators, concerning the slaughter which followed Călinescu's death—when they care to mention it—speaks vaguely of two or three Legionaries executed in each "province." This misleading information is all the more disgraceful since Mr. Prost had lived in Rumania for twenty years, and had had no doubt many opportunities to see the almost two hundred crosses in the Predeal cemetery that marked the tombs of a few of the murdered Legionaries.

In every county seat, in every town, and in every prison, following Carol's orders, more than four hundred young Rumanians were killed, sometimes in the most barbaric ways. Some of them were thrown alive into crematoriums; young Eleanora Bagdad was taken from her hospital bed while convalescing from a long illness; Professor Ionică escaped execution once when, gravely wounded, he hid under the corpses of his fellow victims. He was caught later and finally executed. The bodies of those murdered were left for days at the crossroads as in the times of Genghis Khan. In Bucharest the Royal Counselors were asked to march in their absurd uniforms past the corpses of the nine Legionaries who had avenged their Captain and so many of their comrades. Some of those dignitaries, like Argetoianu, who was promoted to Prime Minister, even let themselves be photographed during this performance.

All of the Legionaries who had been with Codreanu in the Rimnic prison, including all but one of the former fighters in Spain, were massacred in the prison yard. Two brothers of Codreanu were murdered also. The slaughter of the flower of the Rumanian youth was trusted to army colonels whom Carol had appointed country prefects. Argetoianu, who replaced General Argeșanu (the head executioner, appointed immediately after Călinescu's murder) as Prime Minister, announced to the nation and to the world that he would "eradicate even the seeds of the Legionary Movement."

Meanwhile the international press had only words of approbation for Carol and for his murders. The London *Times* dedicated a whole lead to the praise of General Argeșanu, "a dapper little cavalry general."

I found it necessary to communicate by telegram to the Government in Bucharest my feelings regarding what was going on in Rumania, and also to inform it of the indignation of all of my colleagues without exception, and of every decent person, official or private, with whom I was in contact. It was by telegraph also that Argetoianu, our Prime Minister, informed me I was dismissed.

Together with my telegram to the Government, I sent a series of letters to our principal political leaders, trying to show them that they shared the responsibility of Carol and his executioners by not protesting against all of those atrocities and by not trying to stop them. I received only one answer. It was from Professor Iorga, who informed me that "in such circumstances it was unavoidable that some innocents also had to pay for the culprits."

CHAPTER
XVIII

The Panicky Tyrant

The pages of glory written by our soldiers, during World War II, on their victorious march to the Don, the Volga, and the Caucasus were preceded and followed by two of the most disgraceful and unhappy chapters of Rumanian history: the reign of Carol II, and the short reign of Michael, the legatee of his father's sins.

There were ruthless rulers in the history of Moldavia and Walachia, the two Rumanian principalities. But Ştefan the Great, Vlad the Impaler, Ion the Implacable, and Ştefan Lăpuşneanu were as merciless and as fearless with the enemies of their country as with the rebellious boyards at home. We forgive the cruelty of Vlad the Impaler and the fits of passion of Ştefan the Great because, without their harshness, our country would have been long ago blotted off the map of Europe by some foreign invaders.

Carol, oppressor and murderer, corrupt to the bone, usurped all the powers of the State not in order better to defend it in its hour of need, but in order better to satisfy his avidity and gratify his lust. The man who had murdered without justice, without pity, and without reason hundreds of young Rumanians because they kept up the fight against treason and corruption, stripped himself, in a panic, of all of his authority, of all of his legally and illegally acquired prerogatives, when the hour of danger and decision was upon him and his country. He dropped all of his responsibilities upon those whom he had transformed from statesmen and military chiefs into servants; and he even tried to hide himself behind the Legionary Movement, which was prepared to accept all responsibility during this frightful situation but was not prepared to accept just a fragment of it.

After turning over my responsibilities to Alexandru Duiliu Zamfirescu, my successor in Copenhagen, I divided my time the following months

150

between the Danish capital and Berlin. In Berlin, along with the group of Legionaries who lived there, we watched, powerless, Carol's policy of simulation and subterfuge, a policy that we felt certain was leading Rumania toward dismemberment and perhaps disappearance.

In February 1940 the last Balkan conference ended with our Foreign Minister's attempt to convince Mussolini to take the lead in a league of neutrals. This was a senseless renewal of Mr. Gafencu's attempt of April 1939 to attract Il Duce into the camp of Germany's enemy, two diplomatic errors that could be explained only by a total ignorance of the relations that had existed for years between Germany and Italy. Our economic agreement with Germany, which for a time had been correctly carried out by our authorities, was again sabotaged by them. We had exact information concerning the activity of the agents of the Western Powers in our country, and concerning the participation of our authorities, military and civilian, in certain projects of military and economic sabotage that would gravely imperil the position of Germany, in case of war with Soviet Russia. As Mr. Prost seems especially well informed about those projects, we will quote him once more:

> The Rumanian authorities do not reject the German demand . . . but they examine them with a carelessness that is a way of defense. The negotiations are indefinitely prolonged. Once an agreement is concluded, the same evasions interfere with their execution.
> There stops the Rumanian resistance. If some oil-carrying convoys are prevented from passing through the borders, if barges loaded with cement try to enter the Iron Gate channel, so prone to sabotage, it is not Rumanians who are in charge.[1]

No real Rumanian was in charge indeed; only the King and his Government, who, deaf to the interests of their country, and with the cooperation of British, French, and American technicians, were preparing the blocking of the Danube and the wrecking of our oil production, both of which were indispensable to Germany's military program, especially in the event of a war with Soviet Russia.

Things started to change in Bucharest only after Hitler's blitzkrieg in Norway, which preceded by twenty-four hours the landing of the troops that France and Great Britain had been preparing since January 14, 1940.

From then until the end of the German campaign in France, every new success of the German Army was marked by an attempt on Carol's part to convince Hitler of his good intentions and of his good behavior. Those attempts did not change Germany's decision concerning the integrity of our country. Hitler's final decision had already been made

[1] *Destin de la Roumanie,* p. 141.

—after Gafencu's visits to Berlin, Rome, and the Western capitals, when, against the earnest advice of the German and Italian Governments, Rumania asked and accepted Western guarantees *limited to our western borders,* guarantees which placed us directly on the French-British side of the barricade. Only a complete and radical change of leadership in Bucharest, a change to leaders of daring and unmitigated patriotism who had kept their eyes open to our eastern frontiers and to Soviet Russia's intentions, could perhaps have changed the course of events that deprived Rumania of four provinces.

In Berlin I succeeded in establishing more or less clandestine contacts with our Military Attaché, Colonel Vorobchievici, contacts of which the Colonel's superiors would, very probably, not have approved. Toward the middle of May 1940, the Colonel informed me that at the German General Staff headquarters his attention had been drawn to important movements of Soviet troops at our eastern borders, movements that could have only one significance. The German officers were surprised by the fact that Rumania had taken no steps to confront this obvious menace. Colonel Vorobchievici understood that the German General Staff would have liked to have us take such measures as promptly as possible.

It could be argued today that the attitude of the German military was in contradiction to the secret part of the Ribbentrop-Molotov Agreement relating to the occupation of Bessarabia by Soviet troops. Events have shown, however, and every informed person knew, that this agreement was only a transitory formula and that the war would not end with German and Russian troops in the same camp. The occupation of Finland after an exhausting war was nothing but a prelude to the future hostilities between Russia and Germany. The same thing could have been said of the occupation by the Soviets of Rumania's eastern provinces. It was therefore quite natural for the German Generals, from a strictly military point of view, to want the Soviet armies to be met in Bessarabia with at least as stubborn a resistance as in Finland, from an army four times as numerous. That this was indeed what the German military wanted was later confirmed to me by two German military authorities.

Moreover, it is my conviction that had fighting broken out between Rumania and Soviet Russia before June 1941 the Germans would have been forced to back our resistance—despite the German Government's intention to choose, if possible, the moment of the outbreak of war in the east—as they could not have permitted the Soviets either to approach nearer our oil fields or to seize the Danube delta. Those of my readers who have the patience to follow these memoirs through the next chapters will see that it was this conviction of mine that caused the only serious political divergence of opinion between General Antonescu and myself during the few months I was Minister of Foreign Affairs in his Cabinet. In any case, Germany could not have failed to help us defend the Carpathian passes and the strategic Nămoloasa-Galați line of fortifications, which covered the oil-fields, Bucharest, and the Danube.

Colonel Vorobchievici immediately referred to Bucharest the information and warnings he had received. Those warnings were repeated by his German comrades some days later; and the Colonel, seeing that his previous report had not been taken seriously enough by his chiefs, left for Bucharest in order to inform them verbally. Neither at our General Staff nor at our Foreign Office did he find anyone interested in the serious piece of news he was bringing. At the Foreign Office, incensed by Gafencu's attitude, Vorobchievici asked to be relieved of his responsibilities as Military Attaché. Gafencu answered him, smiling: "Colonel, you are an alarmist."

Colonel Vorobchievici's contacts in the German General Staff were not mistaken. On June 26, 1940, our Minister in Moscow, Gheorghe Davidescu, was summoned to the Soviet Foreign Office and presented with an ultimatum, to the Rumanian Government, demanding the beginning of the evacuation within forty-eight hours not only of Bessarabia but also of a part of Bucovina, a province over which neither Czarist nor Soviet Russia had ever had any pretention.

Gafencu had unexpectedly, but very conveniently, resigned his office as Foreign Minister a few weeks before the presentation of the Soviet ultimatum. When King Carol was told about it, he took two series of steps calculated to throw upon others the responsibility for making a decision:

1. He urgently convoked the Envoys of Germany and Italy, the two countries against which he had conspired for years, and asked them whether they would advise him to defend Rumania's territory and sovereignty. We can imagine the contempt the Envoys must have felt for this move of the panicking, deflated tyrant. A King who asks his adversaries' permission to defend his country has obviously already decided not to defend it. It was perhaps at that moment that Berlin irrevocably decided that Hungary's friendship had more value than Rumania's. Germany had her own program concerning Soviet Russia, and Italy was finding in Carol's capitulation a wonderful opportunity for her client nations, Hungary, and Bulgaria. Therefore, Carol received the answer he was expecting: he was advised to evacuate and comply.

2. He convoked a Crown Council, which was attended by some of those generals who a few months earlier, during a royal visit to Bessarabia, proclaimed him the most powerful King alive, and by that sorry flock of politicians who were active or passive accomplices of his plun-

ders and his atrocities. Without any hesitation or shame, Carol, giving up all the power legally his, as King and Commander-in-Chief of the Army, and all the power he had usurped at the price of so much Rumanian blood, meekly asked those present if they believed that Rumania was sufficiently prepared to resist the Soviet invasion. Carol knew the answer better than anyone else; among his usurpations was the royal monopoly over all armament contracts with foreign and national companies.

But even the state of quasi-disarmament in which the Rumanian Army had been abandoned did not justify the order he gave the same day, to evacuate without resistance the two provinces claimed by the Kremlin, and to abandon 3,500,000 Rumanians to their tragic fate. Had Rumania fought, it would not have been the first time that Rumanian soldiers had been expected to use outdated and insufficient weapons. They had done it before and were prepared to do it again if they had been ordered to do so.

There was no obligation for Carol to follow the cowardly advice of his cowardly advisers. If he had wanted to fight, he could have found statesmen, generals, and colonels other than those he had used for imprisoning and butchering the most gallant among the Rumanian fighters. His well-known lack of personal courage was also no excuse for handing over Rumanians and Rumanian territory to the cruelest of enemies. The day had passed when a king was expected to appear on the battlefields, and, besides, an airplane would always have been at his disposal.

The explanation of Carol's behavior in July 1940 must be sought elsewhere.

Many have misinterpreted Titulescu's firing by Carol. At no moment was Titulescu's foreign policy abandoned until Carol's expulsion by the Legionary Movement. In some manner it was continued even during the National Legionary Government in the form of the intrigues that provoked the schism between General Antonescu and his Legionary Ministers, and later in the clandestine relations maintained with the enemy by Antonescu's new collaborators. *King Michael applied it in full force when he handed over Marshal Antonescu and his country to the Communists and when he accepted from the hands of Marshal Tolbukhin the Order of Victory.*

The cardinal purpose of this foreign policy had always been that in the event of a new European conflict, Rumania must end up in the same camp as Soviet Russia. Not even the most stupid Rumanian statesman could have believed that in the event of such a collaboration, a victorious war could have ended with Bessarabia still a Rumanian province. The sacrifice of this half of Moldavia had been foreseen and admitted by Titulescu ever since his intervention in the Riga negotiations and the drawing up of the Rumanian-Russian railway treaty. This sacrifice was also admitted by those who were ready in 1936 to put our railways and our highways at the service of the Russian High Command, and by those who solicited and accepted the Franco-British guarantees, *knowing that they did not include our eastern borders.*

The Western chancelleries, who during the first years of the war never lost their contacts with the Kremlin, knew very well the inevitability of an armed conflict between Germany and Russia. For them, and for their friends in Bucharest, the part that Rumania was to play in case of such a sudden change in the military and political situation was decided in advance. Therefore, the sooner a solution could be found to the question of Bessarabia—the only serious obstacle, it was thought, to Rumanian-Russian military collaboration—the better for everybody. The easiest solution was evidently the occupation of Bessarabia by Soviet troops.

After the Russian ultimatum the idea of military collaboration with the Soviets was still alive among those factors in Bucharest responsible for this fiasco. Let us go back, for a moment, to the "alarmist" intervention of Colonel Vorobchievici, and to the indifference with which it was received by Gafencu. And let us consider the following dates: 1. Toward the end of May 1940 information about Soviet concentration of troops at our eastern borders reached our Government. 2. On June 1, 1940, Gafencu resigned unexpectedly after eighteen months of activity. 3. On June 26, 1940, his successor received the Soviet ultimatum. 4. On July 27, Gafencu was appointed Rumanian Minister to Moscow, an appointment that would not have been possible, even with a minimum amount of decency, if he had been the Foreign Minister who had received the ultimatum.

Two other facts also have to be taken into account: 1. At the moment in 1941 when our troops started to reconquer Bessarabia, Carol, who was then in exile in Mexico, hastened to inform the Russian Ambassador, with whom he enjoyed most friendly relations, that he disapproved of this Rumanian initiative. 2. *In the memorandum presented by Gafencu, to the Paris conference in 1946, a memorandum that was supposed to enumerate all the losses suffered by Rumania and all her revendications, Bessarabia and Bucovina were not even mentioned.*[2]

Mr. Prost explains that the sending of Gafencu to Moscow was supposed to coax the Soviets. It is true that the Soviets could only have been pleased by the appointment of Gafencu, the most fervent advocate

---

[2] Gafencu had no official standing at the time. He did not represent the Communist Government in Bucharest which was then the official party. Together with Messrs. Vişoianu and Niculescu-Buzeşti, also former Foreign Ministers and the organizers of Rumania's capitulation under King Michael, Gafencu pretended to represent the real interests of Rumania before the Paris Conference.

of resuming diplomatic relations with the Kremlin, and the most friendly guest and host of the Soviet envoys in Bucharest. But was this the moment to attempt any coaxing of the Kremlin bandits? Gafencu had not been sent to Moscow by King Carol in order to obtain the restitution of the lost provinces; he was sent there in order to prepare the Rumanian-Soviet military alliance that was finally achieved by King Michael and the spiritual heirs of Titulescu who surrounded and still surround him.

XIX

The Arbitration of Vienna and the Legionary Movement

Among the thousands of Legionaries arrested after Călinescu's murder was my son Elie-Vlad. As Carol's mercenaries entered our home, Elie-Vlad, after jumping through a rear window, passed under their noses in full military garb without being recognized. Kurt, the Danish chauffeur, took his muftis to him at the Swedish Legation, where old friends of ours hid him for a while and helped him plan his escape. He had no luck, however, and was caught when trying to cross the Hungarian frontier on his way toward Budapest, where his grandmother was expecting him with Kurt and the Chrysler, en route for Copenhagen.

He spent eight months in Carol's prisons. When after two months my wife was finally allowed to visit him, she found that his feet were in such a state from the bastinado, the standard treatment applied to Legionaries, that he was scarcely able to walk. My wife told me later that when, thanks to a tip of 100,000 *lei*, she could send him some clean underwear, the old set they gave her was stained with the blood of the tortures to which he had been submitted. My wife received the customary visit from a delegate of the murder syndicate, Marinescu-Moruzov, to which she had to pay 3,000,000 *lei* ($30,000) for the promise, for whatever it was worth, that our son's life would be spared.

A few days before being confined herself to house arrest, under which my wife spent three months, she went to see, among other foreign envoys, Herr Fabricius, the German Minister, to ask him to try and stop the atrocities that were defiling the country. Herr Fabricius replied very calmly: "You exaggerate, my dear lady, you exaggerate."

Later, I was deeply distressed when I saw my mother-in-law arrive alone from Budapest, where I knew she had been expecting my son. My worries were not quieted by the news she brought with her. My anxiety for my son and my wife did not end until a few months later when, after the rape of Bessarabia, Carol, knowing that further mutilations were in store for his country, tried to "pass the buck," or at least a part of it, to the Legionary Movement, offering it an "understanding" and liberating the imprisoned Legionaries. Until then, the only direct news I had received from Elie-Vlad were a few words written on the torn page of a book that he had succeeded in smuggling past the prison's gates: "Dear Father, if I have to meet the Snub-Nosed [death], which might happen at any moment, you may be sure that I will confront her with the impassibility I owe to the name I bear."

My first reaction to the news of the unexpected truce between the Movement and its enemies was that of great relief. For the moment at least, it meant the end of the menace hovering over the heads of so many Legionaries, my son among them. But I did not get an explanation of the decision taken by the Movement's leadership in Bucharest until I took another trip to Berlin, where I was fully informed by my friends.

Horia Sima, one of them, had smuggled himself back into Rumania, and by general consent had taken the lead in the Movement's activities. After many vicissitudes he was discovered and arrested. Had this happened a few months earlier, he would have been shot immediately. But in that summer of 1940, after the German victories and the rape of Bessarabia, a great fear had already entered the vitals of Carol and of his men. So when a group of friends of the Movement observed to a certain General Bengliu, one of Carol's chief stooges, that the time had come for less simple measures than a bullet in the neck, Sima was liberated and a few days later brought to the palace with some of the principal Legionary leaders in Bucharest.

Carol assured them immediately that his foreign policy was now perfectly in agreement with the views of the Movement and asked them to participate in the formation of a new government. Sima's answer to Carol was, in substance, as follows: Carol could organize his own police force and take all the precautions he felt necessary for his personal safety; but only a Legionary Government could assure Rumania of the respect due to an independent country firmly determined to defend itself to the end against any aggression. Carol, who could not by nature believe anybody's sincerity, dodged this proposal and offered the Movement some secondary responsibilities and freedom of the press. Horia Sima and his friends reflected long and deeply; the decision they made sprang from only one motive, the country's welfare.

The loss of Bessarabia had left Rumania crushed with grief at the spectacle of the suffering of the inhabitants, whose mass abductions and mass executions had begun already, Soviet fashion. But there was also the anxiety of the menace of other dismemberments. The storm was

Corneliu Codreanu.

Headquarters of the Legionary Movement, Casa Verde, built by the Legionaries.

The Legionary squad, photographed just before its departure to fight in Spain. In the middle, a Legionary priest who fought as an ordinary soldier in the Spanish Civil War.

General Prince George Cantacuzene, Rumanian hero of World War I and right arm of Codreanu.

Ion I. Moța, second highest personality in the Legionary Movement.

Bucharest: The funeral of the Legionaries who fell in Spain. (Right and below.)

Legionaries killed and thrown in the streets during the huge massacre of September 22, 1939. Note the orderly attendance and, behind the lines of police, the silent crowd.

Horia Sima, Codreanu's successor as head of the Legionary Movement.

Bucharest, the day of the proclamation of the National Legionary Government.

The burial of Corneliu Codreanu.

Ceremonies when Antonescu joined the Legionary Movement.

Ion Antonescu, Adolf Hitler, Paul Schmidt, and the author.

The author, seated center, in Bulgaria with Legionary comrades.

roaring on all our borders. Two other neighbors were lusting after our badly defended territories. The Italian press, in articles whose inspiration was easy to identify, was openly asking for new transfers of Rumanian soil to Hungary and Bulgaria. The final decision belonged, however, to Berlin. The Legionary Movement, which had not yet realized the incapacity of the German leaders to recognize and evaluate the spiritual, moral and material forces in any people other than their own, had reason to believe that a new Government composed of members of the Movement would have some weight in Berlin regarding Germany's decision to refuse or to accept Italy's suggestion. Trying, therefore, to efface from their memory all recollections of the mass murders, mass tortures, and mass imprisonments of which they had been the victims, the Legionaries accepted Carol's offer to participate in the formation of a new Government, but with one condition: his promise that not an acre of Rumanian soil would be yielded from then on without a fight.

The Movement firmly decided not to permit Carol to go back on his word. That is why Horia Sima, on seeing that there were neither signs of a change of attitude among the members of the Cabinet he had consented to join, nor any military preparations to cope with the new threats, briskly resigned on August 8 from a Government in which he had spent only a few days.

There was no dearth of ominous signs for the Rumanian people. After the visit of Count Pál Teleki and István Csáky, the Hungarian Prime Minister and Minister of Foreign Affairs, respectively, the Bulgarian Prime Minister had also been received by Hitler. The German press relished in the publication of a complete list, by first and second name, of the foreign agents who were busy in Rumania with various projects of military sabotage. This press had a good laugh when our Prime Minister, Gigurtu, and our Minister of Foreign Affairs, Manoïlescu, announced the withdrawal of Rumania from the League of Nations, whose existence at that time had been forgotten by everybody. Nobody in Rumania doubted that the country was again on the eve of a grave decision; but nowhere except in the Legionary Movement did one observe a determination to face the decisive moment with the fortitude of those who are prepared to fight, impossible though victory might seem. The Movement decided, therefore, that Carol had to go.

Only those who have been continuously mistaken or misinformed about the nature of the relations between the Movement and the German Government could have wondered at the fact that all during this period, and even at the moment of Carol's overthrow by the Legionaries, Germany had continuously backed Carol and not the Movement. For the well informed, there had been only two incidences of real collaboration between the Movement and the Germans: The time the German

Government put its system of transportation at the disposal of the Legionary Movement for the transfer to Rumania of those killed in Spain; and the time, nine years later during the last months of the war, when Hitler and Ribbentrop asked the Movement's leaders, those in German concentration camps and those who were free, if they were prepared to raise again the flag that King Michael and his advisers had hurriedly hurled away.

The true intentions of Carol and his ministers had never escaped Hitler. He was finding, however, in the very duplicity of their attitude an element of debility that permitted him to secure all the raw material Rumania could offer him. The feelings of the Führer towards Carol and his emasculated Government can be understood. What cannot be understood, and what was one of the imponderables that brought the ruin of the Germans, was and is the arbitration of Vienna, by which the German and Italian arbiters, Herr Ribbentrop and Count Ciano, tore away another part of Rumania, almost half of Transylvania, and gave it to Hungary. Hitler, yielding to Mussolini's and Ciano's pressures, was maiming materially and morally the country that would be his only serious ally in the war against Soviet Russia, the only war he really wanted.

After my dismissal, I had kept very friendly relations and continuous contacts with my German and Italian colleagues. I had expressed several times to them my amazement at the sympathies their governments seemed to entertain toward Carol. They answered with the same arguments that were used by the German and Italian representatives in Bucharest when advising the Legionary leaders. Carol's departure could provoke chaos. We had better, therefore, come to an understanding with him. It was not difficult to see that the real explanation for Rome's and Berlin's objections to an overthrow of Carol by the Movement was their conviction that Carol would accept, without resorting to arms, the new sacrifices that the Central Powers were about to ask from Rumania.

In a rather animated discussion with Giuseppe Sapuppo, the Italian Envoy, I reiterated my conviction that only Carol's departure could restore decency, order, and tranquility to Rumania and assure the respect of our frontiers; I communicated to him at the same time my intention to return immediately to Bucharest. The next day, when I sent my passport to the German Legation, this document was returned to me with a very courteous note that at that time the Legation was not able to grant me the visa, which they had, until then, so often given me. I will add immediately that my friend Sapuppo confessed later to me that it was his intervention that had provoked this temporary embargo.

The result of the Vienna Arbitration was phoned to me by one of the counsellors of the German Legation. In my indignation I shouted at him, "With that, you have lost the war!" I did not know that at about the same moment Count Miklós Banfy, the former Minister of Foreign Affairs of Hungary, was telling our Chargé d'Affaires in Budapest, Dan Geblescu: "This arbitration means the end of our two countries." Count Banfy's reasoning was very likely identical with mine. The new configuration given in Vienna to the Rumanian-Hungarian boundaries, the new loss of population inflicted on Rumania with the corresponding loss of recruiting material, and more than anything else the cruel and thoughtless blow delivered to Rumania's national pride and the legitimate wrath and hate it provoked, could only result in a dangerous diminution of our country's value as a natural bulwark against Soviet ambitions, which were as dangerous for Rumania as for Hungary, and, in the final analysis, for Germany.[1]

I was informed the same day that the German Legation was expecting my passport. In Berlin where I met my wife, who was no longer under house arrest, I had a remarkable encounter, the importance of which I grasped only a few months later, on an official visit to the Reich's capital.

I personally came in contact with the Canaris conspiracy in the first days of September 1940. It started, however, in the very first hours of the Second World War and its consequences are still molding modern history. With the treatment inflicted on the Russian population by the German forces and Italy's foolish expedition against Greece, it had been one of the three principal factors that saved the Communist world from utter destruction at the hands of the German Army.

As mentioned earlier, the international situation had brought me several times from Copenhagen to Berlin, where as a free agent I hoped to be able to establish with the German Government some useful contacts for my country. I had found every door closed to me. I was rather astonished, therefore, when I received the visit of a certain Captain Müller who informed me that Admiral Wilhelm Canaris wanted to see me at my earliest convenience.

Admiral Canaris was the head of the Abwehr-Dienst, the intelligence service of the Wehrmacht, and one of the less accessible men in Ger-

[1] Count Pál Teleki, the Hungarian Prime Minister, was a better European than Ribbentrop or Ciano. In March 1940 he declared to the latter: "I will do nothing against Rumania, as I do not want to be responsible, even indirectly, for having opened the gates of Europe to Soviet Russia. Nobody would forgive me for that, not even Germany." It would not be fair to censure Count Teleki for having accepted, a few months later, that half of Transylvania which Ciano and Ribbentrop offered him on a silver tray at Vienna, for meanwhile Carol's Rumania had proved to be a very poor watcher at the gates of Europe. But Teleki's statement to Ciano perhaps explains the Hungarian Prime Minister's suicide at the moment of the invasion of Yugoslavia, when Hungary was asked to participate, at least by permitting German troops to cross her territory, in this military operation provoked by Italy's absurd pretensions upon Croatia and large Balkan territories. It seems that with a remarkable sagacity Teleki had foreseen that the unfortunate Balkan expedition would bring the triumph of Communism in Eastern Europe.

many. The proposed interview was of special interest to me as I had not solicited it, and I was told that Canaris had recently met some important Rumanian personality. "You will soon be back in Rumania," the Admiral told me. "You will very likely be given an important office. For the sake of our common interests, I ask you to promise that you will do your best to protect Moruzov's life and liberty."

That was, indeed, the last topic I would have imagined the Admiral wanted to discuss with me. Moruzov had been one of Carol's chief executioners in the still recent massacre. A former Soviet official who migrated to Rumania in 1919, Moruzov was employed by the Rumanian state police, first as a simple informer, then in more important functions. King Carol, to everyone's astonishment, had suddenly appointed him chief of our army's intelligence service, a post corresponding to Canaris' post in Germany.

I reminded the Admiral of the part Moruzov had played in the recent massacres, and also of his dubious origin. I informed him that some time ago one of Moruzov's chiefs had singled him out to me as a probable double agent. The Admiral was adamant and insisted with such vehemence that I finally asked him why he was attributing such importance to Moruzov's welfare. "Because," he told me, "it is through Moruzov that we have the best information concerning Soviet Russia's military preparations."

Before leaving Berlin, we again received a visit from Captain Müller, bearer once more of his chief's insistences. We asked him to lunch, and the conversation that ensued left my wife and me perplexed.

Captain Müller informed us that Great Britain had never been and would never be defeated. He added: "What I am about to tell you, coming from a Prussian officer, might perhaps be considered as an act of high treason. Pay attention however. Don't, under any circumstances, take the responsibility, as Minister of Foreign Affairs for your country, of pushing it into a war where you will have Great Britain as an adversary. You will be crushed; Great Britain is always victorious."

I must confess that at that time I did not attach too great an importance to Müller's statements. I attributed them to the commendable desire of an intelligence agent to probe the political beliefs of Rumania's next Minister of Foreign Affairs; and I answered him accordingly. My wife thought otherwise. She had a much less favorable, and even an ominous, interpretation of Müller's indiscretions, which showed again the genuineness of a woman's intuition. I had not the faintest idea that I had been in contact with the greatest spy ring and traitors known to the military history of any country.

When the news reached Bucharest that Carol's delegates in Vienna meekly accepted another intolerable mutilation of our territory, a wave of horror and of indignation swept the country. It was the Legionary Movement that took the lead in the following rebellion, for which it had been preparing itself since Sima's resignation from the ephemeral appeasement Cabinet. The general mobilization of the Movement was ordered. It was to the shouts of "Not an acre more!" and "Fight or go!" and with posters bearing the same slogans, that thousands of Legionaries came out into the streets and that the Royal Palace, against which a few symbolic warning shots were fired, was besieged. When Carol asked General Coroama, the Commander of the Bucharest Army Corps, if he was prepared to order the troops to fire against the rioters, the General answered in the negative.

The well-organized movement spread all over the country. In Constanta and Brasov several Legionaries were wounded or killed in the encounters with the army and the state police. The Legionary insurrection proved uncontrollable, and Carol had to leave in haste with his mistress (the latter, the greatest nuisance our country has ever known) and with a last and not unimportant piece of booty: paintings by masters that his granduncle, King Carol I, had donated to the nation.

The enemies of the Legionary Movement did not fail to spread, by commission and omission, an incredibly distorted version of what happened in Bucharest and in Rumania in those first days of September 1940. They fabricated a supposed collaboration between the Movement and German authorities, with Carol's expulsion as a common purpose. Somewhat contradictorily, they tried to diminish or deny the part played by the Movement in this eviction, attributing it principally to General Antonescu's activity.

The truth is that far from helping the Movement in its violent reaction to the Vienna Arbitration, the German authorities in Berlin and the German representative in Bucharest urged the Legionary leaders, until the last moment, to reach an understanding with Carol, of whose servility they were by then assured. *Infiltrieren nicht sturtzen* ("Infiltrate, don't overthrow.") was what we heard continuously until the moment Carol, in another panic, packed off again for more restful shores. What the slanderers want to consign to oblivion is the fact that the Legionary Movement, so often accused of being a regional office of National Socialism, *had been the only Rumanian political group to ask that the Vienna Arbitration be resisted with all our armed forces; which meant war not only with Hungary, but also with Germany.*

It was this same recommendation of conciliation that the leaders of the Movement received from General Antonescu, until the General understood that the Movement, around which the whole country, military and civilians, had gathered, would never countenance his personal ambitions as long as he continued to advocate a hybrid solution for this final crisis. Without the support of the Movement, Antonescu had no way of forcing Carol to give up part of his royal authority. Antonescu had no support in the army, where he was cordially and unanimously detested under the nickname *Cainele Rosu* ("the Red Dog"). His popularity in the country was nil at best. What was perfectly true, however, was that the General had taken very clever advantage of the situation.

I saw Herr Ribbentrop before leaving for Bucharest, where Horia Sima had urgently summoned me. Present at the interview from the German side was State Secretary Wilhelm Keppler. I was accompanied by the Legionary, Victor Vojen.

After the usual preliminaries, the following dialogue took place between the German Foreign Minister and this writer.

RIBBENTROP: "I was informed that your Movement intended to resist, with arms in hand, the Vienna Arbitration. If this is true, I can only attribute it to the youth of your organization."

STURDZA: "I am glad, Mr. Minister, to be able to dispel your doubts. I can assure you that if the Legionary Movement had had the decision to make, the Rumanian Army would have opposed with all its force both invasions, that of Bessarabia and that of Transylvania. I can assure you also that if we should be the Government of tomorrow, no further violation of our frontiers will be permitted without armed resistance. This corresponds I believe with Germany's interest, since in Vienna you guaranteed the inviolability of the territory you left us."

I had further opportunities to meet Herr Ribbentrop, and he always impressed me as a dreamer, a dreamer of Germanic dreams, a patriot who lived, as I am sure he died, with his pensive gaze still on the unattainable vision.

PART FOUR

Antonescu,
the Insane Leader

Marshal Antonescu was an historical calamity. In the final analysis he caused Rumania as much evil as did Carol. He created the climate in which the conspiracy of August 23, 1944, was born and prospered. He allowed contacts to be established between irresponsible persons and organizations and the enemy, in the absurd hope that the country's independence could be saved that way. He allowed himself to be surrounded by people in the service of the adversary, and he gave them access to the most confidential state affairs and to the management of military operations.

By his lack of reaction to the activities of the enemy agents he favored defeatism, he weakened the inner resistance of the State, disorganized its institutions, and permitted thereby the carrying out of the coup d'état of August 23.

By removing the Legionaries from his Government and keeping them in prison until the outbreak of the catastrophe, he sabotaged the last possible means of saving his country.

Finally, he was himself the victim of the political system he had created. He was devoured by the sharks he had gathered around himself.

Horia SIMA

Cazul Iorga-Madgearu

Nobody tried to help him. Not even his personal guard. The only persons who would have assisted him in the hour of need, the Legionaries, were in prison, had been sent to the front in special extermination battalions, or were biting their nails in German concentration camps.

As Commander-in-Chief of our fighting forces, nobody had the right to rebel against him. It was a sacred and elementary duty for every citizen after the beginning of war not to have other preoccupations than what was happening at the front, putting off any personal dispute. The man who had declared war had all of its historical responsibility, and he alone was entitled to decide when and how this war ought to end.

Raging in our misery, we did not undertake any action that could have harmed the conduct of the military operations. In what concerns the war he was leading in the East, we were in complete accord with the Marshal, despite the fact that his political titles were not quite in order.

We considered the war he was leading like an historical necessity and as an integral part of our doctrine. And we condemn without any qualification those who from the positions where they have succeeded to creep, substituted their authority for that of the Marshal.

Horia SIMA

Cazul Iorga-Madgearu

CHAPTER

XX

A Tortured Man

We have often been asked why we chose Antonescu as Prime Minister. The answer is that we did not choose him; we accepted him as the most expedient and, after all, apparently unobjectionable solution to the crisis provoked by Carol's departure.

Carol, before being forced to leave, had delegated the greatest part of his constitutional prerogatives to Antonescu. Thanks to the General's maneuvering ability, he was able to avail himself of the state of panic into which the Legionary insurrection had thrown the King, and to wring from him this delegation of power. In other words, Antonescu's loot was a clear case of the chestnuts pulled out of the fire.

It had always been the intention of the Movement to put a General at the head of the first Legionary Government. We would not, very likely, have chosen Antonescu, but on the other hand we had no categorical objection to him. We knew that he had been a partisan of Titulescu's foreign policy, but we attributed it principally to his ingeniousness in such matters. We knew that he had never been a friend of the Movement, but we decided to accept his present declaration of friendship. It happened also that the German Government and its representatives in Bucharest had come to consider him a safe bet, including in their trust a certain Mihai Antonescu, said to be perhaps a distant relative of the General's and in any case one of the latter's intimate collaborators, who four years earlier had published a book which supported Titulescu's policy and in which he urged "the promptest possible annihilation of National Socialist Germany"! But we knew that General Antonescu was a man of indisputable personal correctitude as opposed as the Movement to the corruption and immorality of Carol's era. We decided therefore to be completely satisfied with his solemn promises, oral and writ-

167

ten, of loyal collaboration with the Movement in both foreign and domestic policy.

I have often thought of writing a book, a product that would be entitled *Heroes and Scoundrels I Have Known*. Antonescu would be the most difficult case to classify. The following three incidences will show how difficult it was for those who knew him to decide what sort of person he really was.

We were attending a Cabinet Council. The General had asked for some expense reductions that were, I thought, not quite in agreement with what ought to have been our attitude toward the Rumanian victims of past and present Hungarian injustices in Transylvania. Antonescu, red in the face, interrupted me, shouting, "Why life annuities for them? What life annuity do I receive for that bullet in my head?" At the end of the meeting I told General Pantazi, the Minister of National Defense, that I had not known General Antonescu had been a war casualty. "War casualty my eye!" answered the General. "He fell on his head at a horse show in Brașov." General Antonescu, one of the most blatant liars I have ever known, nevertheless did not lie in such circumstances. He really believed he had been gravely wounded in imaginary circumstances rather than in a simple riding accident for the former was more in accord with the figure he wanted to establish in the history of his country.

On the day after a Legionary manifestation that ended in loud acclamations for his person, the General sent his tanks and battalions in a surprise attack against the Movement all over the country and arrested as many of his Ministers as he could lay his hands on. He had no other motive for this *coup d'état* than his firm intention not to share with Codreanu's Movement, and with Codreanu's memory the glory of a victory on the Russian battlefield, which he believed to be near at hand. By his new attacks he threw the country into the agony of new disturbances on the eve of a fateful war.

Sold by his King to his direst enemies, the Soviets, abandoned by all those with whom he had surrounded himself after his onslaught against the Legionaries who would not have abandoned him even in the last moment of a lost war, Antonescu stands erect and disdainful, facing a firing squad of foreign riffraff rigged out in Rumanian uniforms. No Rumanian soldiers had been found for this business. The General shouts with a loud voice, "Straight to the heart, vermin! It is a Rumanian heart!"

After so many years of becalming wrath and cooling indignation, I believe that justice asks that this be the memory we keep of the betrayed General. Yes, this heart was indeed a Rumanian heart.

General Antonescu was a tortured man, tortured by the well-known symptoms of the illness of which he was a victim; tortured by a boundless ambition and ego, signs of a growing paranoia; tortured, more than anything else, by his irrational jealousy of Codreanu, a man Antonescu saw as blocking his way to personal glory and fame, a man against whom no intrigues, no breaking of promises, no *coup d'état* and certainly no assassination could be of any avail. He never understood that the words with which the Legionaries greeted one another and with which they insisted on addressing him, "Long live the Legion and the Captain," were the best guarantee of the Movement's fidelity to his own person.

After Carol's departure, the first problem that the Movement and the General had to discuss was that of the Crown; they came to an understanding quite easily. Both the Movement and the General believing that it would not be fair to ask the son to pay for the sins of the father, decided to recognize Michael as King, *de jure* and *de facto*. They even asked the new King to sanction the written agreement that determined the conditions of the collaboration between the General and the Movement.

I had an interesting experience when I presented myself for the first time to the General as his Minister of Foreign Affairs. The reader will recall, perhaps, my first meeting with Antonescu, which was in my brother's house. It was at the height of my fight against Titulescu's policy. Of the persons I tried to convince of its undesirability, Dinu Brătianu, the chief of the Liberal Party, and General Antonescu, both future victims of Communist terror, were those who rejected my arguments with the most vehemence. The General had cut short our discussion with a peremptory "Never against France!" forgetting that Soviet Russia, not France, was our neighbor and our enemy. I was rather surprised, therefore, when the General did not give any sign of being aware that we had already met. I was even more surprised when he delivered for my benefit a lecture against what he called "the romantic policy," the very policy he had so fervently supported four or five years earlier.

A few days later, I received a reprimand from the General when, at a diplomatic reception, after warmly shaking hands with the Dutch Envoy, I had a longer talk with him in order to thank him for his help during my son's attempt to leave the country. That was, the General told me, what he meant by a "romantic policy." What could the German Envoy, who was also present at the ceremony, think of such a demonstration of friendship toward the minister of a country that was occupied by German troops?

A series of quarrels followed between the General and this writer, each provoked by the General and, with occasional intermissions of more gracious relations, each more serious than the former. The General, who for years had been Military Attaché in London and could not, therefore, have been totally ignorant of diplomatic lore and manners, had taken to ordering me to go to various legations to tell or ask this or that of the respective envoys. I never did, of course, but rather I asked the foreign envoys, as had always and everywhere been the custom, to come and see me, or I arranged things by phone when it was feasible. "Why didn't you go to the airport to receive Herr von Papen?" the General asked me once during a Cabinet Council. I explained to him that it was not for me to do that, and that Herr Papen had quite correctly paid me a visit. "You did not go," growled the General, "because you are a dirty boyard." I decided to take it as a compliment in disguise.

For reasons of economy, Antonescu had decided to lower the status of our embassies to that of legations. I objected that this degradation of our diplomatic representation abroad, just after having been robbed of four provinces, might give the impression that we had admitted the perpetuity of those spoliations and of the corresponding diminution of our country's political importance, an attitude that I knew contradicted the position the General had always maintained. I tried also to oppose the suppression of our Legation in Helsinki, explaining that the position of our two countries toward Soviet Russia had been, and very likely would soon be again, exactly the same. In both cases the General held to his original decision. I had the uncanny feeling that Antonescu opposed my suggestions not because of any lack of merit but because they came from me.

General Antonescu's attitude toward me, his Minister of Foreign Affairs, seems perhaps too personal a thing to deserve so much attention. However, along with a similar attitude toward his Minister of Interior, General Petrovicescu, it was an early indication of Antonescu's hidden intentions, intentions he had held from the moment he signed the written contract with Horia Sima. General Petrovicescu and I, the former in the field of internal security and intelligence, the latter in that of foreign information and activity, represented the first two stumbling blocks in the way of Antonescu's morbid ambitions, the fulfillment of which required the previous destruction of the Legionary Movement.

For the execution of his project the General had in Herr Fabricius, the German Envoy, a most efficient helper. I had had an unpleasant experience with the German Envoy at the time of the funeral of the Legionaries who had fallen in Spain. Instead of answering with proper dignity, as did his Spanish and Polish colleagues, the reproaches of our Minister of Foreign Affairs concerning his presence at the religious ceremony that terminated the Legionary demonstration, Herr Fabricius preferred to hide behind me, pretending that I had invited him officially to attend, which was a total fabrication.

There were other experiences concerning Herr Fabricius's behavior that brought him especially to my attention: there was his attitude of complete indifference concerning Carol's treatment of the Legion and his friendly relations with our enemies. The "Egeria" of the German Legation was an intimate friend of Madame Lupescu's. Nevertheless, when the German Envoy came to me, almost in tears, complaining that his position as German Minister was endangered because Horia Sima, the Vice President of the National Legionary Government, had not yet received him, I helped to arrange the desired and indispensable interview. But I could not help availing myself of this opportunity to remind him that he had continuously opposed the Movement in its fight against Carol. Herr Fabricius referred to orders received, and with a frankness for which I am still grateful, he added, "This way, at least, nobody can pretend that you ousted your King and came to power with foreign help."

The Vice President received Herr Fabricius, and great was his mistake and mine. The departure of the German Minister at that moment would not have had any important consequences. His recall a few months later, however, started the series of events that brought the final break between the General and ourselves; and his intrigues up to his last moment in Bucharest helped considerably to make it impossible to repair later this separation.

Between the General and his Minister of Foreign Affairs there had been only one serious divergence of opinion concerning questions of a political character. This difference of opinion was born of our different reactions to the Vienna Arbitration.

The General's response was of a purely oratorical nature. Quite rightfully, and with an impressive eloquence, he availed himself of every opportunity to blast against that unfortunate piece of political imbecility, disastrous for every party concerned, Hungary included. I was of the opinion that those very justified condemnations did not take advantage of what the Vienna Arbitration offered to us as maneuvering possibilities. There was an important part of the Vienna text of which we could try to make use: This was the guarantee of our frontiers, by Germany, as they existed after the rape of Bessarabia and Bucovina and after the Vienna Arbitration.

This guarantee had not been given by Germany just to please us; it protected vital German interests. The occupation of Bessarabia by the Soviets before the time stipulated in the Ribbentrop-Molotov Agreement, and the rape of a part of Bucovina, which had not been foreseen by the German Foreign Minister, were more than enough to provoke alarm among the German military circles and within the party. Germany could not permit the Soviets to get one step nearer our oil producing provinces, or to control the Danube by getting hold of the three branches of the delta.

It has always been my opinion that Germany ought to have started her war against Soviet Russia one year earlier, giving up any idea of an offensive operation in the west. A Western offensive could have had only one justification: the prelude to an invasion of Great Britain. Concerning the matter of a two-front war, the occupation of France and the garrisoning of the Atlantic walls deprived Germany of more divisions than would have been necessary to defend the Siegfried Line against a France that manifestly did not want to start a real fight.

From our point of view, in any case, World War II did not present any interest other than that of the inevitability of a conflict between National Socialist Germany and Communist Russia. Indeed, unless a German-Soviet war ended with a German victory, Rumania's fate, as subsequent events have demonstrated, could only be that of being the fourth European country, after Estonia, Latvia, and Lithuania, to be entirely swallowed by the Communist flood.

It was my conviction, therefore, that after the Vienna Arbitration our policy should have been to try to bring about, as soon as possible, a German-Soviet armed conflict by taking advantage of the guarantee this arbitration had given us. Enough opportunities were offered by the behavior of the Russian troops at our new frontiers. The Soviet's pretension when they presented their ultimatum, went no further south than the line of mid-current of the northern branch of the Danube delta, the Kiliya branch. This moderation was, probably, to be attributed to their desire not to provoke too early a German reaction. Nevertheless, since the first days of the National Legionary Government, Soviet troops had been making continuous incursions on the fluvial islands close to our shores, and sometimes onto those shores themselves. There were, for us, two possible reactions: We could consider those incursions as simple frontier incidents, or we could consider them as real acts of aggression, answering them with the means, and in the form, corresponding to such a situation.

We could have created, therefore, a state of war that would have eventually involved German forces. And this was what I favored.[1] The General and Fabricius were of quite a different opinion, and I must admit that they both had excellent reasons for that. As a military man, Antonescu was taking into account, first of all, the state of unpreparedness in which the Carol regime had left our army, and Fabricius could only defend the procrastinating program adopted by his Government.

One night, however, instead of limiting themselves to the customary harassment, the Soviets, after intense artillery bombardment, attacked in battalion force and occupied a large part of Rumanian territory,

---

[1] To snatch a morsel of Rumania's territory had become quite a habit with her neighbors. I thought it imperative—quite independently of other considerations—to give warning without delay that those times were over.

killing or capturing the soldiers at our outposts. General Antonescu was ill, confined to his bed at Predeal, a mountain resort in the Carpathians. The chief of our General Staff, who arrived in the early morning with two other Generals, consulted me about the kind of answer I thought we should give the Soviets. I asked them if they had at hand the necessary artillery and the necessary troops. At their affirmative answer I expressed my astonishment that that piece of Rumanian real estate was not already back in our hands.

The army had been deeply shocked and humiliated at being ordered to abandon without a fight first our eastern provinces and then Transylvania; therefore, the Generals left the Foreign Ministry exulting at the authorization they had received from the Foreign Minister himself to get even, if in a small way, with their abhorred neighbors. Things would have followed as they and I would have liked if by ill-luck they had not met, on their way out of my office, a certain General Șteflea, an Antonescu crony who later was the first to betray him in his hour of need. Șteflea immediately phoned the alarming news to Antonescu, at Predeal. Antonescu ordered our troops to leave the Soviets where they were and scolded me by phone for the initiative I had permitted myself to take. Fabricius came to see me and insisted on the necessity of keeping things nice and peaceful at our eastern borders, alluding vaguely to certain negotiations then taking place.

The Soviets kept their booty, and the German-Russian war started only nine months later. But I still keep asking myself what would have happened if it had broken out in the fall of 1940, before the nonsensical Italian campaign against Greece, which forced Hitler to send over the Danube more than forty divisions that ought to have been used on the Eastern Front, and before Antonescu's *coup d'état* against the Legion left him, in the long run, at the mercy of his enemies.

The sending in 1940 of about three German tank units to Rumania was requested by us. Those units, and the accompanying military agreement, were the best guarantee we could have against new Soviet attempts. If Germany had sent us four or five divisions instead, we would have felt still safer. There never was a German occupation of Rumania, as there never was a British occupation of France. The Little Entente, the Balkan Alliance, the French Alliance, had fallen, as Codreanu had foreseen, like houses of cards at the first puff of the hurricane. Against the perils of the hour, and against those of the approaching war in the east, our only ally was Germany. German troops were in Rumania as allied forces against a common enemy—until the moment that the irresponsible Michael, and the fearmongers and recreants who controlled him, joined forces with the enemy.

It was not the fault of the Rumanian people, and still less that of the Legionary Movement, that Rumania did not accept Germany's offer four years earlier, when friendly relations between Germany and Poland would have permitted the constitution of the only possible concentration of forces able to defeat Communist Russia without her friends in the west daring to come to her rescue.

Bloodshed in Transylvania,
Visit to Rome—The Two Forums

Besides the menace at our eastern borders, we had as a major worry the brutality with which Hungarian authorities were thrusting their domination upon the Rumanian population in the territories granted them by the Vienna Arbitration. Although there was no comparison between the behavior of those authorities and the evils, the process of uprooting and annihilation to which the people of Bessarabia and Bucovina were submitted by the Soviets, we could not let this matter pass without protesting to those who had guaranteed a fair execution of the Vienna decisions.

The arable land that had been distributed by Rumanian agrarian reform throughout the country, Transylvania included, to all our peasants without distinction of national origin (Rumanians, Hungarians, Germans) was taken away by Hungarian authorities from the Rumanians who had tilled it for more than twenty years and who considered it their legitimate property. This, and other vexations, had provoked bloody incidents. We already knew of several Rumanians killed and wounded when the news came of a village in which almost the whole male population had been massacred by Hungarian soldiers.

It was easy this time to convince the General of the proper procedure to follow. Along with a guarantee of our existing frontier, Berlin and Rome guaranteed in the Vienna Arbitration the humane treatment of those Rumanians who were under Hungarian administration. In two almost identical letters to Herr Ribbentrop and Count Ciano, after describing as accurately as possible the violence and persecution to which Rumanians were submitted, I urged the formation of a German-Italian commission to check the veracity of my information, to make proper remonstrances to Budapest, to stop further atrocities, and to force Budapest to indemnify the victims. In order to prevent too long a delay in getting the answers, I dispatched Manoïlescu, my predecessor at the Foreign Office, with the letter to Ciano, and Valer Pop, a former Undersecretary of State, with the one to Ribbentrop. The required members of the commission—Minister Roggieri for the Italian Government, Minister Altenburg for the German Government—were not long in presenting themselves at my office.

It was decided that they would also visit the part of Transylvania that was still in our possession so that they could see how we were treating our minorities. I took care of all of the necessary arrangements for their journey. They had to be accompanied by both Rumanian and Hungarian officials. Mr. Alexandru Randa, who headed the Rumanian group, followed scrupulously the instructions he received: to limit himself to the geographical and material indications necessary for the investigation, but to avoid any aggravating comments concerning the investigated lawlessnesses and, still more, any tirade concerning the injustice of the Vienna Arbitration. I was of the opinion that this was too important and solemn a subject to allow an opportunity for an incident, and wanted to avoid any verbal, or other, conflicts between the accompanying Rumanian and Hungarian officials.

The day before they left Bucharest for their tour of inspection, I invited the German and Italian delegates to the Ministry, and before them and their travel companions, I pointed once more on the map to the places where violence had occurred and Rumanian blood had been shed. I described as accurately as I could the nature of the information we had received concerning those excesses. At the end of this first part of the meeting, Minister Altenburg, whom I was later to meet again in most tragic circumstances for our two countries, addressed me with the following words: "Although this is not a part of our mission, we would like to have your opinion concerning the way in which you believe the Rumanian-Hungarian problem could be solved with both sides sufficiently satisfied so that this solution might be considered as final."

I was prepared for such a turn in our discussions, and with an ethnographical map by the famous German geographer Justus Perth before us, it was not difficult to demonstrate that the desired solution was not, in any case, that which had been found in Vienna. The new ethnographical distribution represented such an injustice for the Rumanian element that there was no reason to hope that the inner popular pressure and the outer political pressure we were able and determined to maintain would ease up at any moment in the years to come. On the other hand the configuration of the new borders made the defense of the territory given to Hungary an absolutely impossible proposition from a military point of view.

As for Herr Altenburg's question concerning the frontiers we were prepared to accept, I answered that they could not be very different from those the two countries had before the Vienna Arbitration. We could not consider changes other than small local rectifications, made on the basis of strict reciprocity and taking into account the ethnic character of the villages involved.

Both Herr Altenburg and Signor Roggieri left me with the impression that they were considering their mission with open and impartial minds. Minister Altenburg, before leaving for Berlin, sent me a message through Alexandru Randa and complimented me on the exactness of the information I had given him, saying, "Not a corpse less or more than you told us." We were not astonished therefore when about a week after the end of the Altenburg-Roggieri investigation, we received from our Envoy in Berlin, Constantin Grecianu, the news that the report of the commission was entirely favorable to our position.

But the Altenburg-Roggieri mission was about to end otherwise. Both the Rumanian and the Hungarian officials who accompanied the foreign investigators maintained gentlemenly relations and a dignified attitude during the whole trip. But in the Oradea Mare station, at the Rumanian-Hungarian frontier, Mrs. Goga, the wife of the former Prime Minister, appeared in flowing black veils and crepe. Obstinately barring the way of the two delegates, she delivered a thundering and accusing harangue and did exactly what I had instructed my people *not to do,* namely, another speech *à la* Antonescu upon the injustice of the Vienna Arbitration. All the efforts of Randa were needed after that to prevent the two infuriated delegates from immediately abandoning their mission.

When I referred the result of the investigation to the Cabinet Council I could not help mentioning this incident and the unpleasant consequences it might have provoked. I learned that it was Antonescu who had sent Mrs. Goga, one of the Movement's staunchest enemies and a great favorite of General and Madame Antonescu, on her oratorical mission. The General provisionally scored a point, however, when, alluding to the good news Grecianu had sent us, he observed that if the investigation were to end favorably for us, it would not be because of the way I had prepared it, but because our grievances were so well grounded.

Meanwhile the General and I had received an invitation from the Italian Government. Before leaving for Rome we had the full official text of the final Altenburg-Roggieri report. It was quite different from the one that our Minister in Berlin had perused at the Wilhelmstrasse. I congratulated myself for not having tried to deprive the General of the small revenge he had taken on me at my mention of the Goga incident to the Cabinet Council.

It is said that when, after the occupation of Austria in 1936, which occurred without the expected Mussolini opposition, Hitler wired him, "Duce, I will never forget that!" Mussolini, vigorously striking his desk, exploded, "Christo la Madonna, neither will I!"

If this is not true, it is nevertheless to the point. Mussolini's conduct since then seemed indeed to have been always determined by the fixed idea of never letting Hitler outpoint him at the game of force. It was this political incentive that caused him to commit his first major mistake with his disgraceful, ridiculous and sterile aggression against a France that was already defeated. He thereby abandoned, despite Hitler's exhortations, his policy of non-belligerency, which would have guaranteed him the position of a pacifier or even of an arbiter among the embattled powers.

We have it from the most authoritative sources that it was this same desire to "keep up with" the Führer, who had "occupied" Rumania, that influenced Il Duce, again against Hitler's advice, to try to occupy Greece, a fantastic and disastrous decision that, with the treatment of the Russian population by German forces and Canaris' treason, was one of the three principal factors in Germany's defeat and in Communism's victory.

From Count Ciano's diary:

October 8, 1940

A telephone call from Il Duce, requesting that we take action in Rumania to elicit a request for Italian troops. He is very angry because only German forces are present in the Rumanian oil regions. The step is delicate and difficult, but I imagine that Ghigi will carry it through all right.

From October 12, 1940

But above all he [Il Duce] is indignant at the German occupation [sic] of Rumania. . . . "Hitler always favors me with a *fait accompli*. This time I am going to pay him back in his own coin. He will find out from the papers that I have occupied Greece." [1]

Ghigi, the Italian Envoy in Bucharest, could not carry it through because we did not want any "occupation" troops in our territory. As for the Italian surprise attack against Greece, it turned into a victorious surprise counterattack. The Italian troops were saved only by a massive German intervention, which had a fatal effect on Germany's general strategy for the war in eastern Europe.

[1] Count Galeazzo Ciano, *The Ciano Diaries, 1939–1943*, Hugh Gibson, ed. (Garden City, New York, Doubleday & Company, Inc., 1946), pp. 299, 300.

Our visit in Rome from November 13 to November 17, 1940, coincided not only with the first debacle of this inglorious expedition, but also with the destruction by the RAF of the battleship *Cavour,* the glory and pride of the Italian Navy. I did not know whether it was our mutual indignation over the change, under Italian inspiration, of the text of the Altenburg-Roggieri report, or the circumstance that the General was removed from the influence of his evil genius Mihai Antonescu and was surrounded only by Legionaries, but the fact is that our personal relations had never been warmer than during our trip to Rome. It was, comparatively, a pleasant journey, interrupted only by two incidents in which I was not directly involved, but so characteristic of the General's mentality that I cannot help but record them.

The official of the protocol department of the Italian Foreign Office who boarded our train in Florence handed us the written program of our reception in the Rome railway station and informed us that the General and I would both have to detrain from the General's car. The General insisted that each detrain from his own private car. Protocol convinced him finally that it would have been difficult for Mussolini and Ciano to run from one car to another in order to greet us both with the same cordiality. An identical scene, with the General's same objections, was repeated at our departure.

In Rome we were surrounded by every attention and courtesy; but the defeat of the Italian forces in Epirus, the wrecking of the *Cavour,* our feelings toward the part played by Italy at Vienna, and the information we had received that it was Ciano who provoked the change in the conclusion of the Altenburg-Roggieri report, explained sufficiently the somewhat strained atmosphere that surrounded our short stay in Italy's capital. This tension manifested itself acutely the day after our arrival at the meeting between Mussolini, the General, Ciano and the writer.

I had already made one blunder that day. I was seated at lunch on Mussolini's left; at his right was King Victor Emmanuel, and further right, General Antonescu. Mussolini asked me in a friendly way what I had done that morning. I answered that I had spent about two hours in the Forum. "What forum?" he asked, frowning. "There is more than one forum." I had forgotten that there was also a Forum Mussolini, of which Il Duce was particularly proud.

The conversation between us then moved to the military situation. I admired the serenity and the characteristic assurance of a man who deserved companions other than the dubious personalities who stood between him and his gallant and faithful Black Shirts. The battleship *Cavour* would promptly be refloated; it was a matter of three months. In the Balkans Italy would conquer. ("It is certain, since we can pit four divisions to every Greek division.") Concerning the air fight over London, Mussolini confided: "It is not like this that Great Britain will be defeated." He did not say more, but it was obvious that what he would have advised was a serious German attempt to occupy the territory of Italy's principal enemy.

Later, we found Mussolini at his headquarters in the Palazzo Venetia between two piles of newspapers, one at his feet, the other on his desk almost hiding him. General Antonescu, first in a calm manner but with growing violence, broached the subject of the altered report, enumerating once more Hungarian misdeeds. Suddenly Count Ciano interrupted, observing, "Yes, we must admit that the Hungarians have sometimes had a tough hand." This infuriated Antonescu, who, rising from his chair, declared, "We will show them what a tough hand is! If these atrocities don't stop there will be a general massacre of Hungarians in Rumania." [2]

He calmed down presently, and with a lucidity and a forcefulness of which he was often capable, demonstrated again to our host the enormous injustice that had been committed at Vienna. With the original Hungarian map in front of him—the only map used by the arbiters—he pointed out the falsifications committed by the learned and subtle geographer Count Teleki, the Hungarian Premier. The large mountain region, sparsely inhabited but inhabited nonetheless by Rumanians, was marked by large white patches. The difference between the Rumanian and Hungarian population was not indicated by two strikingly different colors such as blue and red, but by two shades of red. Mussolini, his eyes on the map, seemed very interested, but not so Ciano, who was quite likely as well informed on the subject as was the Hungarian Premier. "And do you think," said General Antonescu, "that such crazy boundaries could stand?" Ciano answered, "Not only have we recognized them, we have guaranteed them." "Guarantee or no guarantee, we will break them. I guarantee that!" concluded the General.

Between Ciano and this writer the following exchange occurred, without the General interrupting me, as was his custom.

STURDZA: "You even tried to deprive us of our industrial regions."

CIANO: "That is not true; we have never had that intention."

STURDZA: "You meant, I suppose, to punish Carol and his clique, but it is we, who fought the King, whom you stabbed in the back. It is

---

[2] The story of an untoward interruption by this writer of General Antonescu's declarations to Mussolini and Ciano, told by the General to Herr Fabricius and reported by Herr Andreas Hillgruber in his book *Hitler, König Carol und Marschall Antonescu*, was totally invented by Antonescu, whose imagination knew no limits when circumstances required such an effort. Antonescu was trying to produce an excuse for his attitude toward me while we were in Berlin; the implication was that he was afraid of being interrupted by me again during his presentation to Hitler.

against a Legionary Rumania that you have struck. You will perhaps be the first to regret it when you have to face your real enemy."

CIANO: "Our real enemy?"

STURDZA: "Soviet Russia, of course."

CIANO: "We are not at war with the Soviets."

I did not know that Ciano and Mussolini were engaged at that time in a process of rapprochement with the Kremlin. I quote from Ciano's *Diaries* the following observation made in September 1940: "Mussolini speaks of our relations with Russia and believes that the moment has come to take further steps to better them. I agree." On November 28 he noted: "One thing is sure, and that is that for many months Germany has been supplying arms to the Finns. I did not neglect to find a way of informing the Russians of this."

An indifference and a lack of vision in such questions of universal interest as the Communist danger are astonishing traits of the Mussolini-Ciano policy. It shows how wrong are those who equate all nationalist movements. No comparison can be drawn between the foreign policy of the Legionary Movement, which did not include any idea of conquest or oppression, and that of Fascist Italy, which was based entirely upon considerations of prestige, fame, power, and aggrandizement.

Despite Ciano's unaccountable animosity toward Rumania and the Legionary Movement, I had great admiration for his brilliant intelligence and personal courage and even sometimes for his politics when, for instance, he concurred with Mussolini in sending Italian divisions to Spain.[3] We had understood each other very well four years before, at our first meeting; and I was deeply shocked by his unjust death.[4]

*   *   *   *

There are two courts in Rome, and after an audience with King Victor Emmanuel we went to pay our respects to His Holiness, Pope Pius XII. Conforming to protocol, which considered General Antonescu as

[3] I did not approve, of course, of his brutal, senseless attack against harmless and proud Albania, and still less of the day he deliberately chose for this onslaught, the very day the Queen of Albania, the beautiful and valiant Geraldine Appony, was expected to be confined. He explains in his diaries that on this day he was sure the royal family could not run to the mountains to organize the resistance.

[4] Ciano's execution by his father-in-law was in no way justified. Mussolini was much more responsible than Ciano for the quandary in which Italy had been brought. Ciano was against the sordid aggression against France. He would have kept Italy in the position of non-belligerency which would have finally made her umpire in the contest. The attack against Greece was also Mussolini's idea, although Ciano finally concurred. Concerning fidelity to their German ally, Mussolini sinned as much as his son-in-law. Even after his fantastic rescue by Skorzeny, which he owed entirely to Hitler's faithfulness to his friends (the German *Treue*) Mussolini still schemed against Hitler and kept contacts with the enemy.

head of state, the General was first received alone. I was introduced a few minutes later, whereupon His Holiness told me abruptly, "We appreciated very much the talents and the qualities of Petrescu-Comnen, your former envoy; we regret very much his departure." I assured His Holiness that the person I had chosen to replace Petrescu-Comnen would give him at least the same satisfaction. I asked him to understand that it would have been very difficult for us to keep as our representative at the Vatican a man who had been a member of the Government that had tolerated the strangling of Corneliu Codreanu. When I said the word "strangling" I could not help but make a corresponding gesture, and His Holiness recoiled, I am sure, in surprise and horror.

CHAPTER

XXII

Visit to Berlin—Four Are Three

It has been said that no nation knows better than Germany how to organize its forces, and none uses them less wisely. There is no reference here to the handling of armies; the last World War demonstrated once more that few military leaders have ever surpassed the German Generals whose skill and imagination were only overcome by the endless masses of men, sometimes in the proportion of five to one, and of matériel that the Allies were able to throw into the battle. We are talking to the lack of a certain ultra-strategic and even ultra-political feeling, of an instinct for the possible and the impossible, of an ability to guess the most hidden reaction in the enemy's mind, of an exact knowledge of the eventual worth of even the most modest among friends.

Into this category must be placed, I believe, the attempt in the fall of 1940 to shore up a quadripartite association between Germany, Italy, Japan, and Soviet Russia. Before we left for Rome, Herr Fabricius had informed me of certain negotiations between Berlin and Moscow concerning a pact of friendship and mutual assistance between Berlin, Rome, Tokyo, and Moscow. A few days after our return, at a reception at the German Legation, the German Envoy told me that Molotov was in Berlin and that a conclusion of the negotiations could be expected soon. I could not hide my anxiety. I had understood the necessity of the Ribbentrop-Molotov Agreement of 1939—to pull the carpet from under the feet of the French and British delegates who were then in Moscow negotiating an East-West coalition; but I could not understand the necessity, at this moment, of tightening political and military bonds that were in opposition to what I believed to be Hitler's ultimate intentions. We had paid for the Ribbentrop-Molotov pact with Bessarabia and a part of Bucovina; what would be the price for us of this new understanding between National Socialist Germany and Communist Russia?

Events have proven that my worries were unfounded. Hitler, as it turned out, preferred to give up his plans rather than permit another violation by the Soviets of our territory and of our sovereignty. What were Hitler's plans, in fact? Herr Fabricius explained them with an optimism that was also felt, no doubt, by his superiors. The idea was, he told me, to convince Great Britain, by means of an alliance that covered two continents from the Pacific to the Atlantic, that the war had already come to an end. Hitler intended to avail himself of this new situation by calling again on Great Britain with new proposals of peace and friendship.

Berlin's optimism was, in my opinion, faulty in two ways: it ignored the uncanny perspicacity of Soviet leadership and their limitless intelligence sources; and it ignored the nature of the forces that had thrown Great Britain into a war that was not hers.

The Kremlin had no reason for wanting an end to German-British hostilities; it had every reason for wanting them continued and increased; the Soviets knew very well that it was only his fear of a war on two fronts that had prevented Hitler from starting a march toward the East, which was the dream of his life. The interest and purposes of those who were then controlling the destiny of the British Empire had nothing to do with the interests of Great Britain; they had already knowingly sacrificed the empire the moment they involved it in World War II.

Things did not proceed as smoothly as Hitler and Ribbentrop had hoped. Molotov, after exhausting every possible pretext to avoid accepting Ribbentrop's invitation for a meeting, even going so far as to exhibit a medical certificate, demanded such conditions as prerequisites to his subscribing to any agreement that they obviously could not have been accepted. He was therefore able to leave Berlin without any further commitment toward the three former members of the anti-Comintern.

Molotov's conditions referred to the recognition of a certain sphere of influence for the Soviets that would have included Rumania and the Danube delta, Bulgaria, and the Dardanelles. Molotov's evasiveness was easy to anticipate, and the double error of Germany's leaders cost them one year of possible military operations, lost between the hope of winning Great Britain's friendship and that of fooling the Soviets over the real purpose of Germany's redoubtable military establishment.

Along with the news of Molotov's successful evasion, we received the information that the four-power pact was instead to be a three-power pact between Germany, Italy, and Japan. We also learned that Count Teleki and Count Csáky were in Berlin and that they had adhered to the new instrument. We were invited to do the same.

The text of the pact in which we were asked to participate was communicated to us before our departure for Berlin. To my great astonishment, it seemed to be identical with that described to me by Herr Fabricius when Germany still had hopes of seducing the Soviets into subscribing to it. Therefore, the text did not foresee, and could not have foreseen, the reciprocal obligation of the three partners in the event of a war with Soviet Russia. It unavoidably implied, on the other hand, Germany and Italy's obligations in case of a war between Japan and the United States.

Such a war would represent grave consequences for us if Germany, our only protector against the Soviet menace, were involved. The only war, the only victory that concerned us, was against the Soviets. Providing the same agreement for those two so different situations seemed to me to be an error of which we might eventually be the victims.

As we traveled from Vienna to Berlin, I imparted my reflections and my worries to General Antonescu, and suggested that he ask Hitler and Ribbentrop, with a measured insistence, that before our adhesion to the agreement an "additional protocol" be signed, secretly if necessary, that would establish symmetrical positions and obligations for the three signatory powers in case of *both* possible conflicts: war with the Soviet Union, and war with the United States. The advantage represented by the tripartite pact for Japan was so great that there was ample reason to think that Japan would have accepted this change if sufficient persuasion had been applied. The General did not acquiesce.

Except for his demonstration before Hitler of the ineptitude and the danger of what had been done in Vienna, the General's activities in Berlin had been absorbed by preparations for the coup against his own government and the Legionary Movement. Antonescu had had this coup in his tormented mind from the first hours of our collaboration, from the moment he ordered General Coroama—the general who had declared that he would never order his troops to fire against the Legionaries—from his Bucharest command to a command in the north of the country. It was of supreme importance to Antonescu that the German authorities be won over to his plans, or at least that they be prepared to acquiesce to the *fait accompli*.

From our first moment in Berlin I realized that something was going on between the General and his German interlocutors that the General did not want me to know about. This "something" could not have anything to do with the most confidential item of our Berlin agenda, the discussions about the probability and even imminence of hostilities with Soviet Russia, as I had always been present at those discussions.

After our first meeting with Ribbentrop, General Antonescu managed two interviews with him *tête-à-tête,* an unusual procedure, about which he gave me no notice and no account. Each time I met Ribbentrop, he asked me, "Why do we not meet more often?" He once gave me an interesting inkling about what was going on between the General and himself during those conversations in which he would have liked me, it seems, to be present, when he told me in a very serious tone, with sincere concern in his voice, "Don't ever get in a conflict with the army. Your Movement would be annihilated." Surprised, I explained that love and respect for our armed forces were a law and a tradition in the Legionary Movement, and that a general, General Cantacuzene, a paragon of honor and gallantry, had been the right arm of Corneliu Codreanu. By choosing General Antonescu as leader of the new regime we had once again given proof of this love and respect.

What happened during our audience with Hitler went even beyond what I would have expected from Antonescu's uninhibited scheming and left no doubt in my mind about the nature of his activities behind my back. At our arrival at the Reichskanzelei, Antonescu was invited into Hitler's office first—a normal procedure if one accepted the fiction that the General was somewhat of a chief of state (this idea was accepted at the Vatican but not at the Quirinal). When after about half an hour of waiting I was also invited into Hitler's office, I found to my great astonishment that Ribbentrop was there. What had been said among those three was divulged to me next day at lunch at the Reichskanzelei when Hitler suddenly turned to me and said, "You do not know General Antonescu. You could not find a greater patriot to defend Rumania's interests." Rather irritated by this second unjustified attempt to put the Movement in a reprehensible position toward Antonescu, I answered the Führer briskly, "If we had not realized this, we would not have chosen him as our leader." I added, "Our sacrifices have been great, as Your Excellency knows." In a calmer tone Hitler told me that he knew all about it.

That same morning I had informed General Antonescu in a violent outburst that I would not have any more contact with him in Berlin, that he was not to count on me for our adherence to the Tripartite Pact, and that I would not leave Berlin with him. The reason for this last decision will be explained in the next chapter. Antonescu protested, arguing that the ceremony of our departure had been communicated to us by the protocol department and that my presence was obligatory. I explained that I had already arranged things with the Wilhelmstrasse: after the official leave-taking, our train was to stop at a suburban station where I would get out.

Another proof of Antonescu's intrigues came before our departure, when I received a visit from the chief of the protocol department, a Pomeranian who was six feet nine inches tall and who, somewhat embarrassed, tried to explain why there was to be no customary exchange of decorations this time. I understood very well. The National Socialist regime had distributed many ribbons and decorations to members of Carol's administration who were later accused of murder and who were now in prison; Antonescu's intrigues had left the German authorities with the impression that the same deplorable situation could again develop with another group of bearers of German decorations.

CHAPTER
XXIII

Treason by Misinformation—Past and Present

The reader will remember my interviews in Berlin with Admiral Canaris and with his subordinate Captain Müller. It was not until three months later that I got a clearer understanding—although perhaps not clear enough—of the real meaning of Canaris's and Müller's insistences concerning Moruzov's welfare and Great Britain's invincibility.

The stage is Berlin again, during our state visit with Antonescu. This time we were at the headquarters of Feldmarschall Wilhelm Keitel. Four persons are seated around a table upon which a map of Eastern Europe is spread: Feldmarschall Keitel; General Antonescu, Rumanian Prime Minister; this writer, Rumanian Foreign Minister; and Dr. Paul Schmidt, the unnecessary but inevitable interpreter. We are discussing the military situation in connection with the possibility of an armed conflict with Soviet Russia and in connection with the cooperation of our armies in such an eventuality.

Needless to say it is the Feldmarschall and the General who are controlling the discussion, and I am awaiting with impatient curiosity their well-informed opinions about the comparative importance of the forces that would be engaged in such a conflict. It is with the greatest amazement that I listen to the following:

ANTONESCU (Tracing his forefinger across the map): "From the Baltic to the Black Sea, a mere line of defense. Behind it, a military territory absolutely empty."

KEITEL (With conviction): *Es stimmt!* ("Perfectly true!")

I had good reason to be deeply shocked by such an incredible underestimate of Russia's military possibilities. I ventured therefore certain observations, courteously listened to by the Feldmarschall, but rudely interrupted by Antonescu.

Back in my rooms at the sumptuous residence that had been reserved for the General and me, I tried to find an explanation for the strange and identical delusion of the two men who, by their profession and positions of high responsibility, ought to have been better informed than anyone else about Soviet Russia's military preparedness. Recollections were suddenly brought to my mind: Canaris, Moruzov, Müller!

There was no doubt for me that without knowing it both Keitel and Antonescu had drawn their information from the same source, and that this source was very likely an intentionally misleading one. Moruzov was, after all, nothing but a Communist agent. Canaris of course was more difficult to explain; but neither is it easy to explain the activities of the Fabian Socialists in Great Britain, for instance, nor the activities of the anti-anti-Communists, who have penetrated the defense and security organizations in so many countries of the Western World.

The relations between General Antonescu and this writer, already tense, were reaching the breaking point in Berlin. To take him into my confidence in such circumstances would only have provoked useless and, perhaps, even dangerous complications for me. That is why I decided, despite the General's opposition, to remain in Berlin a few days after his departure. I wanted to see Ribbentrop alone and tell him the whole story, the mistaken optimism of the two military men included, and let him draw his own conclusions.

Ribbentrop failed to appear for the scheduled appointment. I had a very short interview at the Wilhelmstrasse with Baron von Weizsäcker, one of the Undersecretaries of State. When I arrived in Bucharest I was almost immediately forced to resign, and I soon witnessed the *coup d'état,* by which Antonescu, under the protection of German tanks and howitzers, overthrew his own Government. For six months I was one of Antonescu's prisoners in this scuffle. I never had the opportunity therefore to warn any of the German authorities about the eccentric activities of their highest intelligence agency.

At the Nürnberg trials General Franz Halder, one of the state witnesses and a prominent member of the Canaris conspiracy, which worked from the very first day of the war for the defeat of its own country, explained what the policy of this organization had been:

1. To represent Great Britain to Hitler and to the German Command as secretly, but formidably, prepared to repulse an invasion at a time when there were only eight anti-aircraft batteries for the defense of London.

2. To represent Soviet Russia, on the contrary, as unable to defend herself for more than a few weeks.

General Halder also explained how Canaris had sent Captain Müller to investigate a report that a member of the German Embassy in Rome was in contact with enemy agents, and how of course Müller came back with a misleading report. At this Göring rose and cried, *Aber dass war gemeiner Verrat!* ("But this was vulgar treason!") Mr. Jackson, the United States Prosecutor, retorted: "As it was against Hitler, the General can only be congratulated."

Why were not Himmler and his security department able to discover the treasonable activities of Canaris and his group? The question is still unanswered. Were there two enemy infiltrations, a pro-Western one in the Defense Service and a pro-Communist one in the Security Department? There are many reasons for not excluding this possibility.

At the last reception at the Reichskanzelei, Hitler, commenting on the possibility of discovering new oil fields in Rumania, said to me, "I understand the hesitations of your experts when they have to choose the place for new borings; I am like that when I have to decide where to begin new military operations." Was Hitler still hesitating at the last moment between war in the east and an invasion of Great Britain? What would have happened if I had uncovered the secret of the German Defense Service? Would this knowledge and disclosure have been enough to bring about the abandonment of the theory of the "mere line of defense," and an earnest preparation of the German Army for a victorious winter campaign in Russia?

I would not venture an answer, but after reading jovial Baron Weizsäcker's memoirs, I warmly congratulated myself for having resisted the temptation to tell him during that short interview at the Wilhelmstrasse what was on my mind. The Baron himself belonged to this strange my-country-to-be-defeated underground; and I wonder what would have been my chances of returning safely to Rumania if Canaris's dedicated and expeditious services had been warned of my suspicions and my intentions.

Keitel, Jodl, and other German generals who kept to the end their oath of fidelity to their country and to their Commander-in-Chief have been criticized for having consented to operations contrary to sane military doctrine. Those criticisms are unjust; the operations entrusted to them and their comrades were carried out with unsurpassed brilliancy and professional competence. It was treason—the same treason that lurks and operates today in the Western camp—that threw the German Command into the pitfall of an unexpected winter campaign without adequate preparation! It was Hitler's hypnotic vision of a German-British association for the defense of Western Civilization that deprived this command of the only real benefit of their victory in France: the possibility of conquering Great Britain. It was the Führer's hesitation between the two new offensives that gave Mussolini an opportunity to undertake the disastrous campaign against Greece, which deprived the German generals of forty divisions that would have permitted them to conclude victoriously their march on Moscow before the first flakes of snow.

When Keitel and Jodl were murdered in Nürnberg as a punishment for their patriotism and their fidelity, their ashes were thrown into a dustbin—as *Time* magazine reported with relish—by a French general, carried by him and three other generals, representing the four victorious armies, to a mountain inn, and thrown into the privy. We wonder if with Keitel, Jodl, and the other generals who were hanged or imprisoned, we did not lose the only kind of men who would have been able to stop the next unavoidable Communist avalanche.

Misinformation is today, as at Canaris's time, serving the purposes of Communist interests. As an object lesson in treasonable information, the Canaris case applies faultlessly to the present precarious situation of the Western World, encircled, and penetrated by the Communist assault. The Free World is dying of a lie, of the most unforgivable sin according to our Christian creed: the sin against the spirit—to know the truth but to ignore it; to know the creeping, deadly universal advance of the Nameless Beast, and to deny its existence. If we try to discover through the past half century of dire experiences what has been the principal auxiliary of Communism's triumph, we will find it in treacherously organized misinformation, directed and coordinated from some mysterious headquarters through many hidden or notorious channels, the principal visible vehicle of which is the so-called free press. That so many United States politicians accepted so easily the felonious advice of American pro-Mao Tse-tung agents, losing China thereby to the free world, was chiefly to be attributed to the enormous volume of propaganda ground out by newspapers and magazines in order to present Mao and his gang as a group of honest patriots and agrarian reformers.

It was also organized press misinformation that bamboozled those politicians into accepting the substitution of Communist or Communist-leaning leaders in many Central and South American countries for the pro-American statesmen who had been in charge.

When the time came for the destruction of United States Senator Joseph R. McCarthy it was not the American press alone but the free press all over the world that got down to work in an unrelenting campaign of slander and misinformation the like of which had never been seen before, in a successful effort to silence a man who courageously exposed the conspiracy.

We could continue these illustrations *ad nauseam*.

The universal coverage, the parallelism, the visible discipline of the campaigns of lies, slander and *silence,* do not leave any doubt about the existence of a central directing factor. Therefore today there are many important facts which simply cannot be brought to the knowledge of the public at large. On the other hand, all the organs of the fourth estate participate as an unanimous chorus, or with unanimous silence, in the directed conspiracy of misinformation and concealment.

Every retreat of the Western World before the Communist advance, every gratuitous concession to the exigencies of the Beast, have been preceded by long periods, sometimes years, of treacherous misinformation. Never have these nefarious activities been more brazenly at work than at the present moment. This is understandable, because Western public opinion has to be prepared to witness, without realizing it and without protesting, the early destruction of the only weapon that can guarantee a Western victory in the event of a conflict between West and East: the potential power of explosion and resistance of the millions of slaves behind the Iron and Bamboo Curtains. I could quote one of the most brilliant generals of the United States, a man well-versed in world military and political affairs, who bluntly wrote me that he agreed that it is only this power of explosion that can make up for the ominous numerical inferiority of the NATO powers.

It was, therefore, easy to understand how earnestly and diligently the misinformation machinery has applied itself to help the Western Powers rid themselves of their responsibilities toward the countries they handed over to the Communist Moloch at Teheran, at Yalta, and at Potsdam. Here, briefly, was the process, as disclosed by the activities of the free press and of the special advisers attached today to nearly every government and to nearly every statesman in a post of command:

The machinery of deception has succeeded first in creating the impression of a growing softening of East-West tension; this in a period when Communist insolence, Communist audacity, and Communist hostility have been increasing in both international dealings and in subversive activities around the world. Then, the imposture of what was called National Communism was put over on the gullible public, the *New York Times* being the standard bearer of this successful campaign. Then came the masquerade of a decisive split between Soviet Russia and Red China, which had as a logical consequence the necessity of giving the Kremlin five million tons of wheat and whatever else it might need, thus transforming it into a quasi-ally of the powers from which the enslaved nations had once expected their liberation. What followed was the combined deceptive campaign about alleged fundamental changes in the lives of the enslaved peoples (a rapid policy of liberalization was supposed to be taking place), and about how the satellite governments were gallantly defying the Kremlin's tyranny.

This last paroxysm of misinformation was directly connected to the new negotiations with the Bucharest Government announced by United States Secretary of State Dean Rusk "in order to see how economic and other relations could be improved and extended between Rumania and the United States." Selling the Rumanian Government industrial equipment, according to Rusk and Ambassador-at-Large W. Averell Harriman would help Rumania liberate herself from the Soviet yoke. Was it in order to help Soviet Russia liberate herself from the Rumanian yoke, in this new fight between giants, that the United States Government "sold" five million tons of wheat to the Soviet Government?

Another of Dean Rusk's arguments—a part of the National Communism hoax—goes like this: "What we shall ask of a Communist country is not what is its particular system of government, but what is its attitude toward its neighbors." Did the United States Government consider the attitude of Soviet Russia toward her neighbors, Estonia, Latvia, Lithuania, Poland, Hungary, Rumania, Czecho-Slovakia and Bulgaria, before extending to the Soviet Government economic and industrial help so generous in quality and quantity that former Eisenhower aide Harold Stassen once refused to communicate its particulars to the United States Senate, saying that it was too confidential a piece of information?

Some reporters are perhaps misinformed, but others are misinforming their readers. How could anybody who has passed even a few days in the captive countries believe that the murderous scoundrels who form the so-called governments would really dare break with Russia? They know that only the presence or the proximity of Soviet bayonets saves them from being hacked to pieces by their own people. How could anybody suggest that the captive peoples prefer the new order of things knowing, as even the Hearst press has recognized, that if leaving their country were not strictly forbidden ninety percent of those peoples would already be on the Western side of the Iron Curtain?

If I will dwell specially on Rumania, it is only because I can talk about it more knowingly. But the reader may be sure that our plight is not in any way different from that of the other enslaved countries, and that the discouraging effect of this new chapter in organized misinformation is the same on all the peoples in Communist-dominated territories.

From the contribution of the Hearst press to the perpetuation of Communist tyranny in Rumania and in other enslaved countries we pick the two following contradictory statements:

> Freedoms praised by the West, freedom of the ballot and the right to criticize openly those in authority, are nonexistent. Armed guards and police dogs roam their borders, reinforcing a lace-work of barbed wire. *The proletarian paradise still requires naked force to keep the inhabitants safely immured.*

And then, two columns of double-talking, highly paid journalese further on:

> There is every possibility that the people in East Europe prefer the new order of things, for all the oppression, to the ancient regime of their forefathers.

In Rumania the last repartition of the land, 1919–1920, had put ninety-two percent of the tillable land and pastures into the hands of the peasants, who formed eighty percent of the population. For this last and biggest redistribution of Rumania's agricultural domain, the former owners were paid only one-third of one percent of the real value. *No mention of this important fact will be found in Hearst or Scripps-Howard press reports.* This was to be expected, for who would believe that the Rumanian peasantry preferred "the new way of doing things" when all that they had was taken away from them.

A more realistic account of conditions in the captive countries comes from a correspondent of the *Neue Züricher Zeitung* traveling in Rumania in July 1965, who observed with amazement that wherever he saw peasants working in the fields they were working like a gang of convicts under the watchful eyes of rural policemen.

As for the workers in industry, for which twenty percent of the peasantry was forcibly transported to the cities, it is enough to look at the pictures in the illustrated reports of American magazines to see in their faces the unmistakable ravages of hunger and misery. An American lady who had known prewar Rumania and visited it again in the summer of 1965 wrote to my wife: "Those who have not seen the terrible conditions of life there cannot imagine them."

The "free press" loudly rejoiced upon learning that about two thousand political prisoners had been liberated from the Communist prisons in Rumania. Many of these human wrecks had spent twenty years of their life there. What did the same press say or do for the defense of those prisoners while they were rotting in their endless captivity? Why did that press not mention those tens of thousands of captives still incarcerated in Rumanian or in Russian slave labor camps? What life is like in the Communist jails in Rumania the gentlemen of the press could have found out by simply reading Leonard Krishner's best seller, *Prisoner of Red Justice.*

We know what life is like in Rumania. We know it by the contact we still manage to have with our dear ones—those who have not been liquidated or who did not die in captivity. "For the past fifteen years I have been living in a basement which has never seen a ray of sunlight," writes one of our correspondents. Subnutrition, sordid lodgings, and slave work; this is the truth regarding the Hearst "paradise."

In such conditions you may easily imagine how disastrous is the impact on the morale of our people, on their hopes and dreams of liberation, of such statements as those of President Johnson, another obvious victim of the conspiracy of misinformation when, in an appeal for peace addressed to the Kremlin gang, he tells them: "On both sides [of the Iron Curtain], people are now more prosperous than they have ever been in the past."

Recently, one of my American correspondents expressed the fear that "the dangerous nonsense published by the Hearst press could result in the discouragement of our allies behind the Iron Curtain." Indeed it has. It seems to be the aim of the mendacious campaign to which the Hearst press, the Scripps-Howard press, the *New York Times,* and many newspapers and magazines in the United States, and in almost every country, contribute so brilliantly.

CHAPTER
XXIV

More About Truth and Directed Information

As a part of his keynote address in New York on June 19, 1966, for the National Conference on Peace, Dr. John C. Bennett, President of the Union Theological Seminary, deplored American obsession with Communism:

> Communism is cruel in its early stage. But after the revolutionary period it does become in many ways constructive. The United States should not assume the responsibility of taking any measure to prevent a nation in Asia from becoming Communist.

The theme submitted by Dr. Bennett and, strange to understand, by so many clerical personalities of every faith and denomination, has been for years a favorite with the international press. Communism, so goes this theme, has passed the revolutionary stage; it has slowly emerged from its turbulent youth into an honest, peaceful, constructive, and beneficial regime. Accepted and appreciated by the populations under its rule; it has assumed different characteristics in the different Communist countries, emancipated itself from Moscow, and ceased to be a menace to the rest of the world.

Rumania was recently chosen by the international opinion-building conspiracy as the best illustration for the propagation of this utterly false theme. Bucharest has suddenly been bombarded with swarms of reporters from every free country and from every controlled and controllable newspaper—even from Spain, which learned the hard way what a Communist regime represents, and even from the most Conservative of the Spanish papers.

The methods used by these zealous pilgrims are not always the same. A pretense of believing in potemkin villages is the most innocent one; but recourse to downright fabrication is an accepted technique also.

American, German, French, and Spanish newspapers barefacedly affirmed, for instance, that under the Communist regime something has been done for the first time in Rumania for the Rumanian peasant, although every informed person must know—and reporters and chief editors are generally well-informed persons—that the so-called "capitalist regime" had put into the hands of Rumania's peasantry ninety-two percent of its agricultural land and that the Communist regime came along and confiscated all of it. A typical attempt at similar misrepresentation was offered by Madrid's *Arriba* in an article of July 26, 1966, by Cristobal Paez:

> There are unmistakable signs of the existing evolution inside this society [Communist Rumania and others] that after twenty years of new political experience it is about to pursue, without too much risk, some autochthonous formulas inspired by a democratic socialism. It would be improbable that those nations would follow a regressive direction, because it is very doubtful that Rumanians, Yugoslavs and Bulgarians have suffered more under the present [Communist] socio-economic order than under the oligarchic capitalist order of yore.

The Reverend Richard Wurmbrand is no paid reporter, and he has no vested interest in an economic agreement with the Bucharest Government. His credentials are only his obvious sincerity and the fact that he spent twenty years in Communist Rumania—most of them in prison. It is to his testimony that we will turn to help our readers discover whether the Communist Government has changed in Rumania, or whether things there are now the same as they were during the early years of the regime. Perhaps we shall also discover that all the uproar about Rumania's return to a "democratic" way of life is due not only to some powerful industrial interests but also to the fact that—as Alfons Dalma points out in the *Deutsche Wochen Zeitung*—the Bucharest Government has been assigned a special mission by the Kremlin of confusion and disruption complementing de Gaulle's too erratic performances. Choosing Nicolae Ceaucescu, among other Communist stooges, to play "grandmother" wolf to NATO's Little Red Riding Hood (to use an *Arriba* metaphor) was for Moscow a natural thing to do, Rumania being the most controllable of all the subjugated countries due to its unique geographic position and its lack of any direct contact with the free world.

Here, then, are some of Reverend Wurmbrand's declarations before the United States Senate Internal Security Subcommittee, and some private institutions:

Before the United States Senate:
Such talk from people of the cloth is incomprehensible. Dr. Bennett had to know better than that. Those clergymen say we must help the Communists. Where were they when so many Christians needed their help?

New York Times, September 4, 1966:

A Rumanian evangelical minister stripped to the waist during the Senate hearing today to show eighteen scars he said had been inflicted by Communist torturers. "My body represents Rumania, my country," he said, "which has been tortured to the point that it can no longer weep."

Glendale News Press:

As he told his story in Washington's modernistic Saint Matthew's Lutheran church, parishioners wept. When he told details of his imprisonment to Senators and Congressmen, faces turned white.

Detroit News, July 5, 1966:

He told the Senate Internal Security Subcommittee of fourteen years imprisonment in Rumania prisons. . . . His captors attempted to force him to inform on persons who took part in clandestine religious meetings, and used knives, clubs and other weapons in their efforts.

Minneapolis Tribune, August 5, 1966:

"I have eighteen holes in my body put there by Communists. I was beaten with nylon whips made in America and transported from prison to prison in American cars. I do not ask Americans to help me; I ask them to stop aiding our oppressors." In fourteen years in prison the Pastor Wurmbrand and some four hundred other Christians "were fed sometimes a slice of bread a week. Often prisoners had to eat excrement and drink urine. I still cannot look at an American breakfast without feeling it is too big, too wonderful. . . . I am terrified." During the period of Christian oppression, Dr. Wurmbrand said, the Americans gave more and more to the Rumanian government and did nothing about the condition of the Christians in Rumania.

Human Events:

"It was only during the period when the Rumanian Communist government was intent on getting American aid dollars that they interrupted their demands for money in exchange for freeing anti-Communist prisoners," said Pastor Wurmbrand. "Now again, no one can get out of jail or leave the country without paying money, sometimes as much as $25,000." In the United States for the first time, this extraordinary man, whose faith burns with the same bright flame as Saint Paul's, is a convert from Judaism.

San Mateo Times:

"When I was in Philadelphia I attended an anti-Vietnam war rally and heard a man actually praising the Communists. I asked him how he knew about Communism and then I showed him my back. They would not let me talk. Someone cut the microphone wires." Wurmbrand described one particular grisly episode that involved a friend of his, a Catholic priest. "They tortured him until he went mad. They made him say the Mass over his own excrement. He did not know what he was doing. It was terrible."

New York Times, September 5, 1966:

Mr. Wurmbrand said the Rumanian Orthodox church [more correctly the pseudo-Rumanian Orthodox Church] has sent agents to the United States to conspire against an estimated total of 300,000 Rumanians living here.

South Bend Tribune, May 19, 1966:

He [Pastor Wurmbrand] arrived here Tuesday as a guest of Clarence E. Manion, head of the Manion Forum, an organization of conservative political thought. "Drugs were sometimes used [said the pastor] to induce confession. . . . A more subtle method of gaining testimony was to force a victim to swallow three or four teaspoons of salt an hour without water. . . ."

Florida Times-Union, May 7, 1966:

Wurmbrand quoted the prison commandant in Bucharest as addressing the prisoners in this fashion: "You fools! You expect the Americans to come some day and release you. They are coming now to do business with us! If you beg Americans to help you, they ignore you. If you insult them, they help you."

Before the United States Senate:

I have seen Communist guards single out a young Catholic priest and demand he denounce God in front of his fellow prisoners. The priest refused and they dragged him away. We never saw him again. But in his face we had seen God and our faith grew that much stronger. I lived with the saints and martyrs of the twentieth century. . . . I saw a Catholic priest die boasting that the Pope would never shake hands with a Communist. I am glad he does not know it happened.

As Reverend Wurmbrand told his story, says an eyewitness, Senators' and Congressmen's faces turned white and bystanders wept. We wonder how many of those who heard him are still obsessed by what they had been told, and how many of the Senators and Congressmen who know now what they should have known years ago have made a decision to dedicate themselves to a constant effort to help the oppressed nations in their yearning for liberty and finally in their fight for it, rather than continue to help their oppressors establish more firmly and more safely their abhorred domination.

Reverend Wurmbrand, this "convert from Judaism whose faith burns with the same bright flame as Saint Paul's," this gallant defender of the throttled and the persecuted, this brother of all captives of the Nameless Beast, preaches, we are afraid, in the desert. The clamor of his denunciation will soon be smothered by the deafening and bewildering vociferations of the "free press"; unctuous bishops will continue to pour forth their insidious pro-Communist balderdash; hypocritical or opportunistic politicians will still recommend financial and economic help to Communist governments; tyrants and torturers will continue to be the guests and the hosts of presidents, kings, and popes.

XXV

Another Night in Jilava

Jilava is the dampest, ugliest group of casemates in the old line of fortifications that surround Bucharest. From the very beginning of the anti-Legionary terror, Jilava was the most used and the most sinister of the prisons into which Rumanian young people were thrown without a trial, were tortured and killed. It was to Jilava's back yard that the garotted corpses of Codreanu and his companions were taken, bullet-riddled to simulate an escape attempt, and buried in a common grave. It was in Jilava also that a selected group of the murderers of Codreanu (and of more than four hundred Legionaries) had been incarcerated under a Legionary guard, doubling the military garrison.

The listing of the group of murderers who were to be brought before the Rumanian courts was determined by Prime Minister Antonescu and by Vice President Horia Sima, who was also Commandant of the Legionary Movement.

After the fall of Carol [says Horia Sima] the Legionaries could have been left to take their revenge. Although during the anti-Legionary terror—when so many friends and comrades were strangled, shot in their prisons, or burned alive—I often swore to be equally merciless on the day of our victory, the idea of such a bloodbath profoundly repulsed me. I simply couldn't go through with it, and I could read the same sentiment in the eyes of all those who surrounded me in those moments. There was first of all the Christian foundation of our Movement. Also we felt that it would have been degrading the greatness of our sacrifice if we were to indulge in an act of vengeance. We are not a blood thirsty people; killing for a Rumanian is a difficult thing. . . . Carol's regime was not a Rumanian regime. The assassination of the Captain and of his followers was the result of a concerted international plan, the control of which was not inside Rumania. The Iron Guard [the Legionaries] represented an obstacle to the Communization of Rumania and of Eastern Europe, and this obstacle had to be removed. Carol, Călinescu and all their stooges belonged to a conspiracy of European origin. . . .

We therefore chose justice, chose the legal way. Huge demonstrations, songs of victory, acclamations, yes . . . but all in perfect order. No Legionary lifted a finger against any of his enemies. The greatest victory we won was over ourselves. It was the victory of Light and Spirit. Just out of prison, with our physical and spiritual wounds still fresh, with the distressing vacuum left around us by so many victimized comrades, we did not choose to take justice into our hands.

The drawing up of the list of culprits was not an easy thing. If all those who had contributed to the murders of our comrades had been arrested without some sort of discrimination, they would have numbered about one thousand individuals. . . . Nobody would have been surprised if all those who had filled the many appointments of Carol had been considered as responsible. Legally speaking, the members of a government are responsible for governmental decisions even if they have not personally taken part in their execution. But in [Carol's] Government there were two categories of bureaucrats; those few who had been among the most ruthless enemies of the Movement, who were prepared to embrace any criminal activity; and those, much more numerous, who were simply covering up those activities with their names and their prestige in exchange for the advantages of their ministerial status. . . . The Carol regime, like every dictatorship, had an inner structure. This network of assassins had ramifications in the judicial system, the army, the police—in fact in every state apparatus. It represented what was then called the "state permanency"; it was in fact Carol's NKVD, which depended directly on him and reported only to the Royal Palace. This group did not consist of more than about one hundred persons.

We limited responsibility for crimes to this group (in fact to only a part of this group of notorious criminals). . . . General Antonescu was astonished at our restraint. He wanted many more arrests; he wanted to include in the projected trials purely political cases, which we refused to do. I refer here to the General's attitude before November 1940. After that it changed completely. My part at the beginning had been to try to moderate Antonescu's personal vendettas. . . . We limited ourselves to the principal criminals, but separated them into three categories: 1. The Generals and Colonels under whose control, as county prefects or province Governors, four hundred of the most prominent Legionaries had been executed. Those Generals and Colonels were not molested in any way but were sent back to their posts in the army. 2. The gendarmerie officers, police officers and agents who had limited themselves to the execution of orders received without committing any special cruelty or demonstrating any excess of zeal. They received only an administrative penalty; they were dismissed. 3. The group of notorious assassins who had been principally responsible, whatever their origin—army, police, gendarmerie, civil or military justice, etc. They were arrested and were brought before the courts.

I repeat that this conception of limiting to the minimum the list of alleged culprits was exclusively ours. [*Cazul Iorga-Madgearu* (*The Iorga-Madgearu Case*) by Horia Sima.]

It was this group of sixty-four individuals who were detained in Jilava. The Movement, its leaders, the victims of so much slander and silence, were impatiently awaiting the beginning of the trials. Rather than for the satisfaction of revenge, they were waiting for the day of truth to arrive, when all of the injustices, the cruelties, and the humiliations to which they had been subjected, all that they had had to endure in their flesh and their spirit, would be revealed.

It was left to Mihai Antonescu, the Minister of Justice, to determine the nature of the proceedings and the date of the appearance in court of the accused men. After two months no progress had been made in the inquiry except for the publication of the interrogation relating to the murder of the Captain. The two principal culprits were of course beyond the reach of justice, Călinescu being dead and Carol being in Portugal. There was on the part of the Minister of Justice an open and willful bungling of the judicial procedure and continuous and unexplainable postponements of the trial's opening. Before leaving for Berlin, I had warned him about the grave consequences of his continuous procrastination, unpleasant for everybody concerned. "You would not like," I told him, "to see one morning sixty-four corpses before the stairs of your Ministry, lined up like wild boars after a hunt."

Mihai Antonescu's motivations were easy to understand. Formerly an active partisan of Titulescu's politics and, consequently, a declared enemy of the Movement, he had many friends among the Jilava prisoners and, quite likely, sympathies for all of them. But, more important than this, the continuation of the tense situation created by his inaction was opening new areas for his intrigues between the General and the Legionary members of the Government. Those who knew the aversion of Horia Sima and of his Legionary colleagues for any sort of bloodshed, knew also that if the trial of the Jilava prisoners had finally taken place, the number of those who would have paid with their lives for the crimes they had committed would have been only a small part of those who had been arrested—in fact probably only three or four.

I was still in Berlin when my wife phoned me the distressing and shocking news of the mass execution of the Jilava prisoners by a group of Legionaries. My wife informed me also of the consternation and exasperation of Horia Sima and of my other Legionary colleagues in the Government at this act of violence which was contrary to the principles, the intentions, and the most fundamental interests of the Movement. Their anger was so much greater because two men against whom no charges had been brought, Professor Iorga and Virgil Madgearu, a former Minister of Iuliu Maniu's party, had also been assassinated. This, they realized, could only be the work of instigators, enemies of the Movement. Those two murders were indeed scientifically calculated to do as much harm as possible to the Legion: they provoked the indignation of European opinion, Professor Iorga having been a universally admired historian, and they might have caused Iuliu Maniu, chief of the National Peasant Party, the only important politician who had shown any sympathy for the Captain and the Movement, to turn against us.

The infamous Nürnberg court established the following judicial precedences: 1. That of collective guilt and collective punishment. 2. That of the responsibility of a subordinate in executing the orders of his superior. 3. In the case of Julius Streicher and others, that of the responsibility—to the limit even of capital punishment—of those who were convicted of having helped, by their books or articles, to create an atmosphere propitious to crime.

If the Legionary Movement had followed the Nürnberg road, it could have arraigned before its tribunals not only whole governments, but whole political parties; and among the dozens of publicists, newspapermen and columnists who could have been indicted for their constant, mendacious, and perverted activities in helping the murderers by their pen and prestige, the most conspicuous would have been Nicolae Iorga. Without his complicity neither Carol nor Călinescu would have dared suppress Codreanu.

It was not only the removal of Codreanu from Rumania's political life that Iorga had wanted; it was his death. It was Iorga who provided the Palace camarilla with the pretext for the arrest and condemnation of Codreanu at the very moment Codreanu was about to leave for Italy and had ordered the demobilization of his followers, ordered them back to their studies and work, and requested that they accept passively any injustices and acts of violence; and it was Iorga who, with Carol and Călinescu, contrived the necessary measures to prevent the victim from escaping the claws of his kidnappers. It was Iorga again, alone among the heads of political parties or important politicians, who helped actively to promote the false idea of a Legionary conspiracy, a lie that eventually brought the Captain to the cell from which there was no way out but to his grave in Jilava.

However, besides those few misguided fools led by Traian Boeru, an *agent provocateur*, every Legionary from the ranks to the highest command was shocked and revolted at Iorga's assassination, and realized that Iorga dead hurt them more than Iorga alive could have ever done in any imaginable circumstances.

When passing judgment on the acts of violence of individual members of the Legionary Movement—acts justified, if violence is ever justified, as a result of inhuman provocations—we must not forget that those provocations had always been premeditated, organized, ordered and executed by the official organs of the regime: the King, members of the Government, and their higher and lower officials. The Legionaries' acts of violence had always, without exception, been perpetrated without the knowledge of and contrary to the intentions of the Legionary leaders. Also, we must observe that each time the command of the Legion was disorganized or destroyed by incarcerations and murders, the Movement was obliged to produce new leaders, who needed a certain time to make themselves known and to establish their authority. Such a situation existed after the incarceration of the Captain and of his principal lieutenants, and as a result of the general slaughter that followed Călinescu's execution.

Exactly what happened on the night of November 26 to November 27, 1940? Mr. Prost, to whom we always like to refer, says only this in his aforementioned book about Codreanu's assassination: "During the night of November 29 to November 30 [1938], Codreanu was *suppressed.* . . ." [1] He is much more loquacious when he talks about that other night in Jilava, when Codreanu's murderers paid for their crimes:

> In order to exculpate themselves, the murderers pretended that on the night of November 26 to 27 [1940], they were in the graveyard of Jilava exhuming the bodies of Codreanu and the other Legionaries, who had been executed on November 30, 1938, in preparation for the solemn funeral that was to take place on the second anniversary of their death. When they saw the corpses they were struck by a sacred wrath that made them turn upon those who had tortured their [Captain].[2]

When Mr. Prost tells so great a part of the truth he has to put it in the hypothetical mode in order not to weaken his theme. What Mr. Prost pretends not to believe is exactly what happened, or more exactly, a part of what happened.

General Antonescu had appointed as president of the commission of inquiry into Carol's atrocities a member of the Court of Cassation, the same court that had rejected each and all of the more than one hundred appeals brought forward by Codreanu's lawyers. General Antonescu did not allow any representative of the Movement to take part in the investigation, although such participation would have been perfectly legal in an investigatory commission.

As long as the General, for motives better known to himself, was more implacable than the leaders of the Movement about the punishment of Carol's stooges, the commission showed a certain amount of activity. In the first weeks of November, however, the General suddenly changed his whole attitude, and the commission, which followed rigorously the instructions of the Minister of Justice, slowed down its activities almost to a full stop; later it transformed itself into a medical commission, demanding the transfer to a sanatorium of the major culprits. Asked by

---

[1] *Destin de la Roumanie*, p. 122. Italics added.
[2] *Ibid.*, p. 156.

Horia Sima how much longer the inquiry commission would need to make ready its report, Mihai Antonescu answered that it needed at least seven or eight months more. Sima tried vainly to convince General Antonescu that such a delay would be interpreted by the Legionaries as an effort to save Carol's butchers.

It was under such circumstances that, in preparation for the solemn funeral that was decided for the second anniversary of the Captain's assassination, a group of Legionaries were ordered to exhume the bodies of Codreanu and his companions. They found them hidden under several tons of concrete, corroded by the vitriol that had been poured on them, the ropes still twisted about their throats, with fettered feet and arms. The Captain's body was recognized by its size and by a little crucifix Codreanu always wore around his neck. But the sight of those lamentable and cherished remains would not have been enough to provoke the state of "sacred wrath" mentioned by Mr. Prost, had not two well-calculated acts of provocation occurred.

"Nothing would have happened in Jilava," says Horia Sima, "if to the former provocation two others much more dangerous had not occurred during the exhuming itself." That which brought their spirits near the point of explosion was the sacrilegious intervention of Eugeniu Bŭnescu, member of the Court of Cassation and president of the inquiry commission, who appeared suddenly during the exhuming and found it necessary to shout to the toiling Legionaries: "Have you not ended yet this sinister comedy!" But the explosion proper was provoked by General Antonescu's order, which reached the prison at this very inappropriate moment, that the Legionary guard be dismissed and replaced by the military garrison.

> The General took this step [says Horia Sima] in a question that directly concerned the Movement, without consulting me. The order had been transmitted to the military authorities that shared with the Legionaries the garrisoning of Jilava. I learned about this order the next day, when the arrested people were no longer alive. But among the Legionaries who were busy with the exhumation the revolting news spread like lightning during the very night the order was transmitted. The perturbation was general. People looked at one another with dismay and did not know what to believe. "The General has betrayed us," they argued. "We have had several indications already. The removing of the Legionary guard is the final proof." Lashed into fury at those thoughts, they left shovels and spades and ran to pay their debt to their Captain's memory. . . . The punishment of the Jilava criminals was not a premeditated action. Legionaries who in normal circumstances would not have been capable of the slightest act of brutality took part in it.

Mr. Prost covered his face, mentioning that one of the executioners was only twenty-two years old. He never mentioned the age and sex of the hundreds of massacred Legionaries. The "free press" and the commentators of our time still express their horror when referring to the execution of the sixty-four murderers; but they expressed no indignation when the Captain and four hundred Rumanian young people were butchered like cattle and thrown into common graves.

Responsible for the mass execution at Jilava were General Antonescu and his alter ego, Mihai Antonescu. My comrades in the National Legionary Government, younger and therefore more generous than I, continued to believe for a long time in the General's sincerity toward the Movement; almost from the beginning I was convinced that his only sincerity was toward his own morbid ambitions. I call them morbid because Antonescu had in his hands enough to satisfy the most ambitious leader of men: a population of content and active peasantry that owned more than ninety percent of Rumania's arable land; disciplined and gallant soldiers; a youth eager to redeem the shame and the errors of the past regime; a nonexistent opposition; and, to defend him against conspirators and traitors, all the moral, spiritual and physical power of the Iron Guard, of the Legionaries.

This ought to have satisfied him if his ambitions had been identical with those of his mutilated and threatened country. But this was not the case, as was shown when the General, on the eve of an imminent war, deprived his country of the enthusiasm, the valor and the steadfastness of the most faithful of its sons. He did this solely because he did not want to share a page of glory, which he believed easy to write, with the shadow of Corneliu Codreanu.

CHAPTER
XXVI

How We Parted

At the end of November 1940, upon returning from our conference in Berlin, I found General Antonescu in a somber mood, pretending to believe in the possibility of a Legionary conspiracy and even in a projected attempt against his life. Everyone admitted into his presence, except the members of the Government, was thoroughly searched for hidden weapons by his aide-de-camp, Colonel Elefterescu. The acute crisis between him and the Movement, provoked by the Jilava tragedy, had, however, already subsided. In fact, I believe that the General and Mihai Antonescu were much less distressed by what had happened than the Legionary members of the Government. They no longer had to worry about the trial of the accused men, which would have confronted them with important political and personal difficulties. As for Mihai Antonescu, his principal mission at the Justice Department —saving those men—no longer necessary, he was able to concentrate upon securing the appointment of his dreams: that of Minister of Foreign Affairs. In the strategy of their long-planned coup against their own Government, the capture of the Foreign Office and of the Ministry of the Interior were for the Antonescus two important preliminary steps.

My intention had always been to keep my office until the moment I was able to summon the Soviet Envoy and present him with an ultimatum for his Government to evacuate the stolen provinces within twenty-four hours, after which I would have joyfully yielded my armchair to anybody who wanted it, and gone to join my regiment. My experiences in Berlin and a confidential message I had received from Herr Fabricius to the effect that "the Cossacks will very soon regret the day they brought their horses to water in the Danube" reinforced my decision to stick it out and not to break with Antonescu, no matter what the provocation, until the long-awaited moment.

The trouble was that for the same reason—the knowledge that war between Germany and Russia was close at hand—General Antonescu decided desperately to break with the Movement at whatever price. This was a rather knotty undertaking that called for some preparatory operations, the first being to win the control of our contact with Berlin. This led to outbursts of verbal aggression of increasing impropriety against his Minister of Foreign Affairs. These outbursts greatly amused bystanders and I generally shrugged my shoulders at them.

The final crisis between the General and me was provoked—as I learned later—by the recall of Fabricius and the substitution of a prominent member of the National Socialist Party, Baron Manfred von Killinger. The General was convinced that Fabricius's recall was the result of some intrigues of mine, and that that was the purpose of my extra three days in Berlin. He was absolutely wrong.[1]

The General's annoyance was understandable. Fabricius had given him complete cooperation in his intrigues between Berlin and the Legionary command. In the appointment of a militant member of the National Socialist Party, the General saw the danger of better relations between the German Legation and this Command, a fact that would have ruined his most cherished plan: to break with the Movement without antagonizing Berlin. Antonescu's alarm was superfluous for two reasons: Fabricius left Bucharest only after causing the Movement the greatest possible harm; Killinger, as German Envoy, was to be still more obtuse with regard to Rumanian circumstances and to the importance of the Movement in case of a conflict with Soviet Russia. During all of his activities in Bucharest, Baron Killinger was our greatest enemy, until that night in September 1944 when he blew out his brains, accompanied in his suicide by the poor girl who was his private secretary.

At the news that Fabricius was leaving, the General really got to work. I received unexpectedly from him a severe note on the margin of an old report of the Ministry of the Interior, relating to a rather unimportant incident between Rumanian and Hungarian customs authorities. "Did my Minister of Foreign Affairs inform me about it? No, he did not!" read the note. I replied that the report was long overdue, that the incident had already been settled, and that it occurred while we were in Berlin and Mihai Antonescu was my interimary. The General did not

---

[1] According to Herr Andreas Hillgruber, Antonescu told Fabricius that I had boasted to him of having provoked, while in Berlin, Fabricius' recall. The truth is that at no moment did I busy myself while in Berlin, or at any time, with the question of Germany's representation in Bucharest, and that I had nothing to do with Killinger's appointment. It was another item in Antonescu's collection of fabrications, the purpose of this one obviously being to feed the hostile feelings of Herr Fabricius toward the Legionary Movement. Antonescu relied on these hostile feelings to help him in Berlin in his campaign of intrigue and slander against the Movement.

relent; the report came back to me with another comment: "Did my Minister of Foreign Affairs try to find out if Mr. Mihai Antonescu had informed me about the incident? No, he did not!"

I was used to such proceedings, and generally they amused me. But to my great astonishment there was another marginal note on the same report, absolutely irrelevant to its content. In red ink and underlined it read, *"What does my Minister of Foreign Affairs intend to do—provoke a war with Russia?"* A few days later, and with apparent concern, the General told our Envoy in Rome, Victor Vojen, "With his brutal ways Sturdza was about to throw me into a war with Russia."

With blue pencil under the red-penciled question, I wrote, "Of course I would like to have a war with Russia" and sent the document back to the General. But even today I do not know for the life of me what prompted General Antonescu to challenge me about Rumania's relations with Moscow on the occasion of such an unrelated episode. Two months had passed since the border incident at the Rumanian-Russian frontier and nothing had occurred since then that could explain the General's dramatic outburst, unless he had completely and suddenly lost his mind.

I remembered, however, a visit of the Soviet Envoy two days before Antonescu's unaccountable outburst. The interview went off exactly as had five or six others with that same individual. The Envoy always came accompanied by a secretary. Without shaking hands I always asked them very courteously to sit down. The Russian Envoy would then extract from his pocket a document, read it in Russian, punctuating his reading by jabbing his finger at the paper. After that, his secretary would read a French version of the same document. The whole procedure was, of course, unusual and even somehow impertinent. In order to indicate my displeasure, all during the Russian reading I would busy myself ostensibly with some papers on my desk. At the end of the French reading, I would ask the secretary if his boss had anything more to say. The answer was generally negative and my guest would depart with no more handshakes than at their arrival, leaving behind them the French text. The answer was communicated to them after consultation with the generals who were our delegates at the Rumanian-Russian commission of Tighina and who were in charge of the solution of the various questions left unsolved after the departure of Rumanian troops.

Nothing out of the ordinary had happened during the last interview except, perhaps, that I shortened it because of the accumulated matters on my desk. If the Russian Envoy had decided to complain about the way I treated him, and if this had motivated Antonescu's intemperate outbreak, it meant that once again the General had broken the promise he had given me not to receive foreign envoys in my absence. Realizing that this time Antonescu was prepared for any extremity, I decided to steal a march on him and send him that same night a formal letter asking him to choose between my resignation and his promise to let me administer my department from then on without unnecessary interference.

My only further contact with Antonescu was when his aide-de-camp, Colonel Elefterescu, at the usual time of the yearly distribution of distinctions, phoned me on behalf of his chief to learn my preferences. I asked Elefterescu to thank the General, but to tell him that I did not know where to hang the hardware I already had.

As I have mentioned, Fabricius did not leave Bucharest before playing his last and meanest trick—a trick that could not even have been tried if I had still been Minister of Foreign Affairs.

Fabricius had been ordered to transmit to Prime Minister Antonescu and to Vice President Horia Sima, the Commandant of the Legionary Movement, Hitler's invitation to visit him in Berchtesgaden. If such a meeting had taken place, it would have been very difficult for the General to continue his intrigues against the Movement, with the Führer and Herr Ribbentrop, and very easy for Horia Sima to thwart them.

Fabricius' duty called for him to inform the Vice President, personally, of Hitler's invitation. He did not do this, but preferred to entrust Mihai Antonescu with the message. *Mihai Antonescu falsified it.* Horia Sima was informed that, thanks to the insistence of the General and Mihai Antonescu, he, Sima, had also been invited to accompany the General on his visit. Sima, who had not forgotten what had happened to me in Berlin in the Führer's anteroom, excused himself, and the meeting which would have forestalled General Antonescu's coup against the Movement did not take place.

CHAPTER
XXVII

Antonescu's *Putsch*

It is, perhaps, because of the stability in the political life of the two big English-speaking countries that there is no appropriate word in that language for a violent attempt against the established order. Between the French *coup d'état* and the German *Putsch* we have chosen the latter for the title of this chapter, since without the assistance of the astute Fabricius and of the opaque General Hansen, commander of the German troops in Rumania, Antonescu could not have carried out his long-premeditated assault against the Iron Guard and his own Government.

This history of the Legionary Movement offers problems that even Mme. Denise Basdevant, one of the most specialized slanderers of the Movement, has not been able to solve in her book *Terres Roumaines conte Vents et Marées (Rumanian Cliffs against Wind and Tide)*, the worthy counterpart of Prost's *Destin de la Roumanie*. She expresses deep perplexity when talking about what she calls the "Legionary Rebellion": "It seems to me difficult to understand that the Legionaries, who already had the power in their hands, would have prepared a *Putsch* in order to get it." We can easily help Mme. Basdevant with this puzzle. In January 1941 there was no Legionary *Putsch*, but a *Putsch* of General Antonescu against his own Government in order to take by force that bit of authority that had been assigned to the Legionary Movement by the written arrangement between him and Horia Sima—an arrangement that had been ratified by the King and was the fundamental charter of the National Legionary Government.

At what moment did Antonescu decide to violate this charter and all the solemn verbal assurances he so often gave the Movement's leaders? Personally, I am convinced that it was at the very moment of the signing of the agreement. The General's pledge was accompanied by an important mental reservation, which of course could not have been perceived by Horia Sima and his companions. According to the written agreement, the Movement in its organic entirety, with its Commander and its hierarchy, subordinated itself to the General in exchange for the promise that its hierarchy and its entirety would be strictly respected. The General had never been satisfied with this arrangement; he wanted to take the direction of the Movement not only from Horia Sima's hands, but most especially from the hands of Corneliu Codreanu, dead and nonexistent for him but forever alive for the Iron Guard and forever its standard bearer.

The Legionary greeting, even after the Captain's assassination, had always been and still is *Traiască Legiunea și Căpitanul,* which means "Long live the Legion and the Captain." Antonescu could not understand it and wanted it to be changed to "Long live the Legion and the General." The Movement's leadership would have perhaps agreed to it, but they knew that such a change would have provoked a real revolution among the ranks. It was perhaps unjust to ask an egomaniac such as the General to understand this immovable fidelity for a deceased chief, and still more difficult to convince him that this fidelity was the best guarantee of the Movement's faithfullness to him.

Antonescu had conceived the sharing of the power that the Legionary insurrection had forced Carol to relinquish only with the unexpressed hope of snatching, sometime and somehow, the command of the Movement from the hands of its accepted leaders. Signs of this mental reservation had been visible from the first contact between Antonescu and us. In fact, it was obvious from the moment he had sent General Coroama to a far removed command because Coroama had declared to Carol that he would never shoot at Legionaries. In the same vein, only a few days after the constitution of his National Legionary Government, complaining about the alleged intransigence of the Movement's leaders, toward the delegation of a certain women's organization, he expounded: "But, be sure that I will never be another Kerensky!" Indeed, those words, when applied to his Legionary collaborators, represented the General's intentions very accurately.

Two conditions were to be fulfilled before he could consider himself able to carry out those intentions: the securing of the army's cooperation, and Berlin's consent. He took care of the first by certain appropriate changes in the corps and divisions command and by canceling with a stroke of the pen all the debts of officers, of every grade, contracted at their special bank of credit, one of the two State institutions functioning for all the State officials, civilian and military. The salaries of State employees in Rumania were so shamefully low that canceling all existing indebtedness would have been considered by many an act of justice. Canceling only those of the military men was quite a different thing.

Antonescu's maneuvering to win over Hitler to the idea of liquidating the Iron Guard started while we were in Berlin. Hitler and Ribbentrop had felt it necessary to mention something about it to me; but the General's activities were substantially cramped in Berlin by the presence of so many Legionaries. Hitler's final consent was won in Berchtesgaden, where thanks to the Fabricius-Antonescu maneuvers nobody was around to challenge the General's deceitful accusations. When Hitler informed him of his final decision to attack Soviet Russia and of the date he had chosen for the start of this new military operation, Antonescu objected on the ground that he could not guarantee Rumania's full cooperation until he had taken radical measures against "the revolutionary spirit of the Legionary Movement." What all the arguments were that the General employed to convince Hitler we cannot know; but the Ghyka and Groza episodes, which will be related later, are proofs that in such circumstances Antonescu did not hesitate at any imposture or even at crime.

Indeed, it was a crime against his country's most sacred interests, to assert to Hitler—contrary to all that he knew of the spirit of sacrifice and patriotism of the Iron Guard—that the behavior of the Legionaries in case of war could have jeopardized Rumania's contribution to the common effort. Antonescu knew very well that this was a lie, that in the event of a war with Soviet Russia he would have seen the Legionaries, the majority of his Ministers included, in the first row of the battle, and models of discipline, endurance, and courage. The General lied to Hitler on that fateful day with the same imperturbability with which I had heard him lie in many minor circumstances. Antonescu's behavior in Berchtesgaden proved once more that his patriotism was a subordinate aspect of his ambition, rather than his ambition a subordinate aspect of his patriotism. The country had a chance with him only when both passions could be satisfied simultaneously.

This distinction explains General Antonescu's "collaborating" with the Movement while trying to annihilate it, and it explains why, during the victorious part of the war in Russia, he uselessly immolated 70,000 Rumanians in a frontal attack against Odessa: the Germans in their communiqué had wisely taken the precaution of stressing that the battle of Odessa was strictly Antonescu's battle. Odessa would have fallen in any case through regular maneuvers, just as Hango was falling in Finland at the same time and under identical circumstances. It was this same vacuum in the General's soul that did not permit him to find the spiritual wings to lift him above the first reverses, but forced him to abandon into the hands of political cretins, weaklings, and traitors the authority that could still have been his.

Back from Berchtesgaden in January 1941, the General, assured of Hitler's approval of his intended *Putsch,* got rid of his Minister of the Interior, General Petrovicescu, a hero of World War I. Petrovicescu was a hard-working soldier whose only fault had been that seven years previously he, as State's Attorney, had presented an honest case to the military court before which Codreanu had been arraigned. For the operation against Petrovicescu a handy pretext presented itself with the assassination of a German officer in the streets of Bucharest by a drunken or deranged Greek citizen. This permitted Antonescu to accuse his Minister of the Interior of negligence. How it happened that this assassination occurred at just the right moment only Eugeniu Christescu might have known. Christescu—a few years later a staunch pillar of the Communist Rumanian Government—was the head of the General's personal security service, which was independent of the state's security service, the latter then headed by Alexandru Ghyka, a friend and distant relative of this writer, who was dismissed along with General Petrovicescu.

Antonescu's dismissal of Petrovicescu, Ghyka, and this writer was an open violation of the agreement that had brought him to power. The agreement stipulated that these three Ministries belonged to the Legionary Movement. There followed a convocation of all the district prefects in Bucharest, a measure that, along with other ominous signs, greatly alarmed the Legionary ranks. No one had forgotten that under Carol the replacement of civilian prefects with military ones had been a preliminary to the great slaughter, and everybody had the impression that some new foul play was afoot. The general restlessness manifested itself in a big Legionary demonstration, which was carried on in an orderly way, proclaiming anew the fidelity of the Movement to the General but voicing also the Legionaries' anxieties.

The Legionaries did not have to wait long to see how well-founded were their worries. The night of the demonstration, January 20–21, the General ordered the army to take control of all the district prefectures and police headquarters. Throughout the whole country the Legionaries, who had not received any orders either from the administrative authorities or from the Movement's hierarchy, resisted the *Putsch* and refused to evacuate their legally occupied stations. They resisted because that was the natural reaction of a heroic and disciplined organization; they resisted because everybody understood that this was the beginning of new persecutions, imprisonments, and assassinations.

In Iași, the capital of Moldavia, where my son was the local Legionary leader and where General Coroama commanded an army corps, order and tranquility were assured by the collaboration of the army and the Movement. The same situation existed in most of the country. If Antonescu had warned his Vice President and the other Legionary members in his Government of his intentions, violence could have been avoided.

This was not, however, what the General wanted. He hoped to demonstrate to the Germans that the Legionary Movement was a disorderly and dangerous faction. Consequently in Bucharest and Ploești, which were directly under the General's control, Legionary blood was immediately shed. In Bucharest two tanks appeared before the police headquarters and immediately opened fire, killing two Legionaries. The Legionary guard seized the tanks, caught their crews, officers and men, and sent them away unharmed. They then set the two tanks in position, so as to defend the police headquarters from further attacks. In less than an hour all the Legionary-occupied positions in the capital were in a state of siege. The Legionaries barricaded themselves in those State institutions that they occupied legally and that no authorized person had ordered them to abandon.

I joined my comrades at the district prefecture, where my wife and other ladies brought the necessary provisions for a siege of unknown duration. Now and then I went to chat with my comrades at the police headquarters, another Legionary stronghold, in front of which reposed the two captured tanks, manned by sleepy Legionaries. From the tower of the telephone building, the highest building in Bucharest, where the General had wrongly placed a couple of machine guns that ought to have been fired from the basement, the tanks were fired at without appreciable success. The Legionary-controlled tanks did not answer. Moreover, during the three days of the Movement's resistance no Rumanian soldier was killed or wounded. The Legionaries always fired over their heads. The massacre of civilians and Legionaries occurred afterwards, when disarmed citizens were victims, once more, of foul play and betrayal.

During the night of January 22–23 we received a perplexing call from the Legionary "nest" known as Ion-Vodă. Two trucks loaded with what appeared to be prisoners and their guards, had passed before the Ion-Vodă position. The Legionaries tried to stop them, but they were fired on and the trucks broke through. They asked Ion Popa, the Prefect who was taking the call, what his orders were. The orders were to follow, to investigate and to arrest. Half an hour later we were informed that in a field not far from the city limits about sixty corpses were found, all of them from the Jewish suburbs of Bucharest. With them were a few wounded men. What were the orders? The orders, transmitted and executed immediately, were to transport the wounded men at once to the nearest hospital and to stop at any price all other trucks passing the same way.

We do not know to this day for sure who the culprits were. In his book *Un Chapitre d'Histoire Roumaine* this is what General Chirnoagă tells about this cowardly massacre:

> The Legionaries were immediately blamed for it; but one never knew who the real culprits were. The Government that replaced the National Legionary Government, and the Jewish Bucharest Community, applied themselves to careful investigations, but nothing came of them. This is almost certain proof that the Legionary Movement was not implicated, otherwise the culprits would have been quickly discovered. So, in the end it was more desirable to leave uncertainty and suspicion alive.

It is useless to remember that the number of victims was quickly multiplied by ten, then once more by ten, and reached eight thousand in some postwar reports, which included the story—also used five years before against Franco's troops in Badajoz—of human flesh sold at butcher shops.[1]

We can easily imagine who were the criminals. Paid provocateurs had infiltrated our ranks from the moment of the Legionary victory to the time, *perhaps too late,* that we stopped new enlistments. We also know who was directing their activities: those shadowy individuals who served with the same diligence the Carol and Antonescu Governments and finally the Communist regime, to which they had probably always belonged. Three hundred unarmed civilians and Legionaries (a figure given by Antonescu's information service) were mowed down in the streets of Bucharest by the General's machine guns after the cease-fire agreement, when everybody had reason to think that peace had been re-established in the capital. No one mentions those three hundred innocent victims of Antonescu's madness, but the corpses of the sixty unfortunate Jews—a figure that, as we mentioned, has gradually reached that of eight thousand under the pen of some enthusiastic anti-Legionary "historians"—are and will continue to be paraded in every almanac for centuries to come.

---

[1] It is interesting to note that such accusations came, after all, from the side of those who not only allowed the slaughtered corpses of Mussolini and the young girl who shared his fate to be hanged by the feet like pork in a butcher shop—and this time there is a widely published photograph that vouches for the authenticity of the fact—but made the executioner a member for life of the Italian Senate.

CHAPTER

XXVIII

Fooled Again

The second night of Antonescu's *Putsch* I was visiting at the police headquarters when a German officer presented himself with a message for Horia Sima from General Hansen, the commanding officer of the German military mission. With this officer and with Dr. Victor Biriş, another Legionary, we left immediately for Sima's hideout. General Hansen's message read: "Important events are in preparation in this part of Europe which ask for order and tranquility in Rumania. The Führer appeals to the patriotism of the Legionary Movement and asks that the disorders be stopped. General Antonescu has promised that there will be no measures taken against any Legionary if the Movement's resistance ceases immediately."

Horia Sima, fearing with very good reason new treachery, asked that the German Chargé d'Affaires, Dr. Hermann Neubacher, be present to confirm both the message and the promise. Fabricius, his mission accomplished, had left Bucharest to the tune of machine gun and artillery music; Manfred von Killinger, the new Envoy, had not yet presented his credentials; this left Neubacher provisionally in charge. Neubacher appeared promptly, confirmed Hitler's appeal and Antonescu's promises backed by Hitler's assurances. Sima pointed out to him that it had not been the Movement but Antonescu who started the fighting; Sima was ready to order the end of the Legionary resistance, but for the sake of his followers' security he could not ask them to put down their weapons before having reached a written and precise arrangement with the General. *This arrangement should also cover the attitude of the German troops,* as it was more or less an ultimatum that General Hansen had sent Sima.

Neubacher and Minister Vasile Iasinschi, chosen for his firmness and his talent as a negotiator, went to see the General. They came back with the conditions of the cease-fire scribbled on a piece of paper. The conditions were agreed upon by both parties, and the attitude of German troops present in the capital was guaranteed by the German representative. The Legionary Movement pledged itself to cease all resistance by eleven o'clock that morning, a delay necessary for transmitting the orders to the rest of the country. The General pledged himself not to take any measures against the Movement and not to prosecute or molest any of its members for the recent happenings. As Sima mentioned the possibility of ordering the Movement out of any political activity, Neubacher protested: "We need you, especially in the present circumstances." We were even informed that in the discussion with the General various government formations with Legionary collaboration had been considered.

Without losing a minute, all the necessary measures were taken to inform the provinces of the cease-fire. In Bucharest it was this writer and Biriş who made the rounds of all the Legionary positions and saw to it that they were evacuated without delay. Complete evacuation was fulfilled in Bucharest before eight o'clock, three hours in advance of the agreed time.

This done, tired and hungry, I went home for a bath, breakfast, and some rest. I did not get the rest—at least not immediately. About nine o'clock we had a visit from Alexandru Randa accompanied by one of the secretaries of the German Legation, whose name I have forgotten. We were commenting about the recent deplorable events when suddenly we heard new machine-gun bedlam coming from the direction of the telephone building. Leaving my guests I hastened into the Calea Victoriei and arrived in front of the Royal Palace in time to see two German motorized howitzers arriving at full speed and preparing for action. Rumanian troops were barring the street. I asked a young officer exactly what was the trouble and received this reply: "What could it be but General Antonescu shooting at Legionaries again!"

I could not understand the situation. In the direction toward which Antonescu's machine guns were firing, from the telephone building eastward along the Calea Victoriei, there had been no other center of resistance than the district prefecture and the police headquarters, the evacuation of which I had myself overseen. To increase my perplexity another machine gun suddenly started shooting at the other extremity of the Calea Victoriei, from the direction of the Presidential Palace, Antonescu's residence. I reached the central office of our organization, where I found half a dozen comrades as dumbfounded as I. We could not understand at whom Antonescu was shooting.

Among the crowd I saw in the street, a typical crowd of loafers and bystanders, there may have been some Legionaries, but so few that I was not able to identify any. It was this harmless public that would pay, with more than three hundred killed and about a thousand wounded, for Antonescu's last stratagem to demonstrate to Hitler that despite all his efforts no arrangement had been possible with the Iron Guard.

I found my German guest still at my home and reminded him of the Führer's and General Hansen's pledge concerning the attitude of the German troops. I expressed my amazement at the participation of those troops in this unbelievable act of betrayal. "In the end you will lose all your friends!" I told him. With irony and sadness he answered: *Wir brauchen keine Freunde, wir haben Panzerdivisionen* ("We need no friends; we have the Panzer divisions").

The Iron Guard had been fooled once more; but this time the Movement was neither the only nor the principal victim. Few have realized that it was the Antonescu *Putsch* and the ease with which National Socialist Germany had once more, as she had in Slovakia and Hungary, allowed and even helped the suppression of a Nationalist Movement (the only type of movement that guaranteed a fight to the last man in the event of a war with Soviet Russia) that had deprived Prince Paul and his Nationalist Government in Yugoslavia of their prestige and authority, and had permitted the triumph of the Simović-Donovan-Tartaruga foreign conspiracy.[1] It was the Simović conspiracy and the necessity of preventing an Italian disaster that provoked the otherwise absolutely unexpected conflict between Germany and Yugoslavia and finally forced Germany to send more than forty divisions and her crack parachute troops across the Danube and as far as Crete—divisions and troops that would very likely have secured the fall of Moscow before the beginning of winter, as Hitler fully expected.

It seemed very important, not only for us but for the country, to inform the new German Envoy of the Movement's sincere desire to main-

---

[1] In March 1941, Yugoslavia under the regency of Prince Paul, and with Draža Svetcović as Prime Minister, also adhered to the Tripartite Pact (Germany-Italy-Japan) as Hungary, Rumania, and Slovakia had done. The Yugoslav statesmen did it, principally, in order to safeguard their country, threatened by Italy's unjustifiable ambitions and intrigues concerning Croatia. Two days after the signing of the Tripartite Pact a military conspiracy, led by a certain Colonel Dušan Simović, overthrew the Svetcović Government, drove Prince Paul out of the country and replaced him by the child-King Peter, whom Roosevelt—in an appropriate broadcast—proclaimed to be the future Peter the Great. The conspiracy had been engineered by foreign agents under the clever direction of, then Major Donovan, an American citizen in the service of the British. Crowds joined the conspiracy instigated by Communist agents. Colonel Simović (who promoted himself to General) has disappeared from further Yugoslav history, as has Marshal Śmigly-Rydz disappeared from the history of Poland, after having thrown his country into an irretrievable disaster. King Peter of Yugoslavia has been seen lately at festivities masquerading in his royal mantle and crown. This is what we find in *Who Was Who in the United States* about William Joseph Donovan: ". . . advanced to the rank of Colonel, wounded three times, unofficial observer for Great Britain's Secretary of Navy July–August 1940, and South-East Europe, December 1940–May 1941."

tain order and unity among the Rumanian people at the price of whatever sacrifice from our side on the eve of the important events that were about to come. Therefore Alexandru Randa, who had already made contact with Killinger, arranged a meeting for me with Fabricius's successor that same afternoon at the Italian Legation. I spent the hours prior to the meeting in a friend's home to avoid a possible premature arrest, which would have prevented me from keeping this rendezvous. Imprudently, however, I decided to pay a short visit to my sister's. Hardly were we seated for our afternoon tea when the house was overrun by a dozen plainclothes detectives commanded by an army captain who declared me under arrest. We invited him to join us at the table, an invitation he declined, but he very courteously allowed us to continue the meal.

I was entrusted to two mamelukes, one of whom I recognized without too much surprise as the detective who had been assigned for my personal protection when I took possession of my office and whom I had immediately dismissed for reasons of principle and because of his homicidal countenance.

I was taken to the Malmaison military prison, where I was placed in a cell about seven by five feet in size with two bunks, one above the other. Exhausted by three active days and two sleepless nights, I immediately lay down, faced the wall, and fell into a deep slumber. About three o'clock in the morning I was awakened by somebody shaking my shoulder. Another inmate, I thought, and grumbled some protest. This did not seem to satisfy the newcomer, who kept on shaking me. Completely awake now, I realized that the "intruder" was my wife. Her totally unmotivated arrest was in perfect accord with Antonescu's innate vulgarity. He had my wife imprisoned for five months in a military prison where there were only males as guards and inmates. I must immediately add that everybody, from the prison commandant to the last soldier, behaved with such courtesy and good breeding that my wife was probably much better off there than she would have been in a women's prison.

There is one possible excuse for Antonescu's unusual behavior: I believe that in the weeks that preceded and followed the beginning of the war in Russia he passed through a severe mental crisis bordering on actual insanity. This explains to some extent the imprisoning of thousands of persons without any detectable motive, the shooting and killing of hundreds of innocent passersby, the shelling of factory gates instead of asking the gatekeepers to open them, the murdering of one more brother of Corneliu Codreanu, the machine-gunning of the attendants at this brother's funeral ceremony, and so on. I believe also that the siege and conquest of Odessa in the manner in which this operation was carried out under the General's supervision was a direct result of Antonescu's paranoia.

The next day the prison started to fill up with former and present Ministers and high officials of the National Legionary Government, among whom were General Petrovicescu, the former Minister of Interior; and Alexandru Ghyka, Chief of State Security. I spent about six months in prison, which is nothing compared to the ordeal of some of my comrades who were moved from Antonescu's cells to those of King Michael and then to those of the Communist regime, where many died and where hundreds of others, like Alexandru Ghyka, still remain at the very moment I am writing these lines. I hope that none of my readers will ever have the same experience. But just in case, let me give some friendly advice: if you are ever incarcerated, consider that it will last forever and adjust yourself mentally to such an eventuality. Falling into a state of claustrophobia and expecting at any second a miracle that will open the door of your cell or the gates of your prison will quickly finish you physically and mentally and will not hasten by an instant the moment of your liberation.

This philosophy was so much the easier to apply as our guardians, all of them military people and not political stooges, behaved with the instinctive humanity and intelligent generosity that is characteristic of those of our people who are direct products of Rumanian villages and Rumanian soil, and who have not been degraded by contact with corrupt and denationalized authorities and politicians. Thanks to the prison personnel, our contacts with the outside world were never completely severed, and we had news from comrades and kin in other prisons. Through them we heard that our son was alive, but that he had been pursued, found, and arrested. From his cell in Jilava, as he told us afterwards, he heard the defiant songs of six of his comrades who were executed in the prison yard.

At night, when the civilian police who guarded the prison walls during the day had left the premises, our doors were unlocked for our nightly get-togethers, the chief attraction of which was the humorous rhymed journal read aloud by our beloved poet Radu Gyr. Sometimes we laughed so loud that the night officer, a constant bystander, had to warn us to quiet down lest the outer guards would think we were rioting. The poems that Radu Gyr read to us were not always on the comic side. Some of us, those whose children had been submitted to so many ordeals and torments, had tears in our eyes when we heard for the first time "You have robbed us of our youth!"—an immortal slap in the face for all the torturers, kings or knaves, of a heroic and unlucky generation.

The newspapers informed us daily about the deceitful and insanely persistent maneuvers by which the General tried to accredit his version of the latest events and discredit the Legionary Movement, in the eyes of the Germans, as a possible partner in a war against Soviet Russia. All this took place during circumstances in which all his efforts should have been to bring about a concurrence of feeling and action among the Rumanian people. With consternation we read in the German papers a communication of Ribbentrop to the press to the effect that Groza, one of the Legionary leaders, had recently paid a visit to Moscow. There was a Groza among the Legionary leaders who was at that very moment a refugee in Germany, but everybody knew, and certainly Baron Killinger knew, that the Groza who had paid a visit to Moscow was not our Groza but a former Minister in a National Peasant Government, the same individual whom Vyshinsky forced King Michael to accept four years later as the first Communist Prime Minister of Rumania.[2]

At the time of Ribbentrop's declaration, Killinger announced to the German minority in Transylvania that "the Legionary Movement had committed suicide and therefore did not exist any more." I had been able to keep in written contact with Killinger all during my six months in the military prison; so I tried to make him understand that suicide implied initiative and death of the subject, and that we were still alive and had not taken any initiative in the last events. Little did I know, and Killinger very likely still less, that suicide would be the way he would choose to expiate his part of the responsibility for the fraud whose victims were not only the Iron Guard but also Rumania and his own country.

After about six months of imprisonment we were finally taken before one of those routine kangaroo courts. A somewhat refined procedure had been developed by first bringing to trial thousands of Legionaries from the ranks and sentencing them for a rebellion that had never occurred. Our cases, since we were their chiefs, could not, therefore, promise any surprises, and except for the obvious similarity to proceedings in Carol's courts, did not present any interest.

For the record, however, here are some of the facts:

Among other charges we were accused of having clandestinely introduced twenty-five submachine guns from Germany. I asked the State's Attorney, Colonel Pion, if those twenty-five submachine guns were identical

---

[2] Among the biggest impostures of the Antonescu team was that of a list of alleged Legionary misdeeds, published in *Pe Margina Prapastei,* a book that appeared when we all were in Antonescu's prisons or muzzled in Germany. Hans Rogger and Eugen Weber chose this book as the main source of information for their own book, *The European Right.* The phoniness of the whole list was demonstrated by the fact that among the thousands of cases that were brought against the Legionaries after Antonescu's *Putsch, none concerned those alleged misdeeds.* Indeed, none could have been substantiated by the State's Attorney any better than was the false accusation relating to the clandestine introduction of submachine guns, or the accusation of "high treason" brought against Alexandru Ghyka.

General Ion Antonescu, de facto Chief of State of Rumania during World War II.

King Michael I of Rumania.

Martin Bormann.

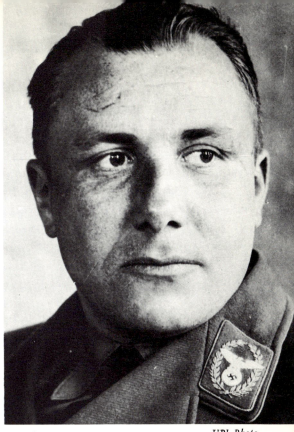

Reichsführer Heinrich Himmler.

Yalta — gravediggers and morticians: Winston Churchill, Franklin Roosevelt, Joseph Stalin. Back row, left to right: Lord Leathers, Anthony Eden, Edward Stettinius, Alexander Cadogan, Vyacheslav Molotov, and Averell Harriman.

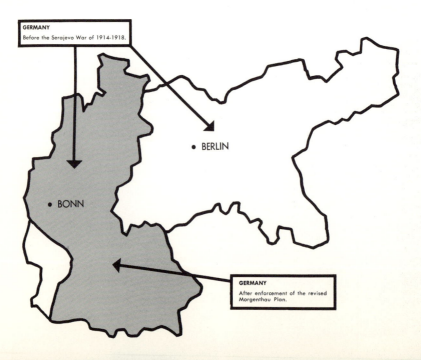

GERMANY
Before the Serajevo War of 1914-1918.

• BERLIN

• BONN

GERMANY
After enforcement of the revised Morgenthau Plan.

Nürnberg. Left to right, front row: Reichsmarschall Hermann Göring, Foreign Minister Joachim von Ribbentrop, Generalfeldmarschall Wilhelm Keitel, and Alfred Rosenberg. Back row: Grossadmiral Karl Dönitz, Admiral Erich Raeder, Baldur Schirach, Fritz Sauckel, and Generaloberst Alfred Jodl. Rudolf Hess, who usually sat next to Göring, is absent.

Reichsmarschall Hermann Göring in his cell at Nürnberg.

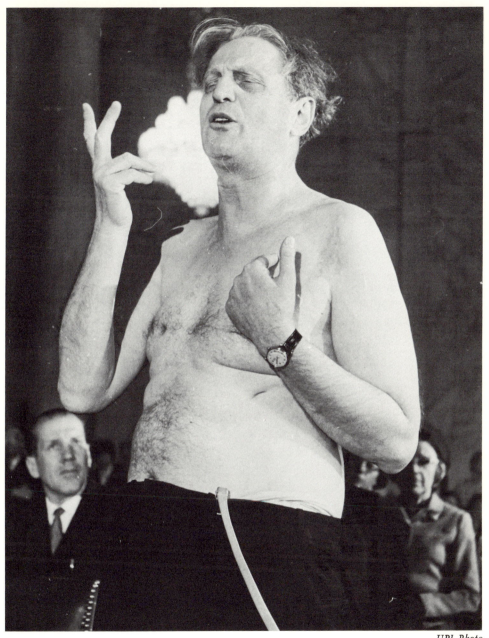

Rev. Richard Wurmbrand, stripped to the waist before a Senate Judiciary subcommittee, shows the scars he received in a Communist Rumanian prison.

The Monastery of Voroneţ, built by Stefan the Great.

to those that Mme. Antonescu, General Antonescu's wife, had distributed with her own hands at a public ceremony to twenty-five Legionaries who formed her husband's personal guard. The Colonel answered affirmatively. I asked him if it were not true that neither those weapons nor those twenty-five Legionaries had played any part in the recent events. The Colonel answered affirmatively again. When I asked how, in such circumstances, it could be pretended that those weapons had been clandestinely introduced into the country, I was reminded that we were there to answer, not to ask questions.

One of the accused, an Undersecretary of State at the Ministry of Public Works, was indicted for having bought one gallon of aviation fuel; the absurd claim was made that this fuel could only have been purchased with pyromaniacal intentions.

But the most shameful case of all was that of Alexandru Ghyka, Chief of State Security. Codreanu had once reproduced in a public declaration from the columns of various newspapers an order to the local gendarmerie forbidding the Legionaries access to voting places. On this basis he had been accused of high treason and sentenced accordingly. As Chief of State Security Alexandru Ghyka, descendant of a long line of reigning princes of Moldavia and Walachia, had, among other responsibilities, the problem of security for the German officers, members of the German military mission, a rather important part of his duty as was demonstrated by the assassination of a German officer on the streets of Bucharest. He had, consequently, dispatched instructions to all the country's prefects to keep him informed about the presence of German military personnel in their territory. Ghyka would have been derelict in his duties if he had not taken that or similar precautions. Using with imperturbable cynicism the very same trick that Carol had used to secure Codreanu's condemnation, Antonescu asked that on the grounds of Ghyka's orders to the prefects, Ghyka be found guilty of high treason.

If Ghyka had indeed collected such information in order to communicate it to an enemy, this enemy could have been only the Soviets. Here again, as in the Groza case, Antonescu was evidently trying to convince the Germans that there were guilty relations between the Movement and the Kremlin. This was insane, for no one who knew the facts could believe it either of Ghyka or the Movement.

On closing his case against us, Colonel Pion, the Attorney for the State and the only more or less honorable figure among the gorillas Antonescu had chosen for this pet case of his, expressed himself as follows: "Concerning the accusation of high treason against Alexandru Ghyka, it is impossible for me to support it; I know too well his patriotism and that of the Movement to which he belongs."

Ghyka's lawyers thanked the State's Attorney for this outburst of unexpected sincerity and did not worry further about this stupid attempt of the insane General.

The court's decision was read to us in our cells: *Ghyka had been found guilty of high treason and sentenced to twenty-five years at hard labor.*

Ghyka is still in prison as these lines are written. After Antonescu's fall, none of the successive governments included Ghyka and his Legionary cellmates in the lists of political prisoners who were to be liberated —lists that included all the available Communists and traitors.

From Carol's cells to Antonescu's; from Antonescu's to Michael's; from Michael's to the Communists'. What was the common infamous factor among all these regimes? Is it possible that all of them were clandestinely and conspiratorially based on a Communist substratum? *And if this is the case, would it not be worthwhile for every patriotic individual or organization in every country to look around with worried and insistent attention?*

CHAPTER
XXIX

Too Late, Gentlemen!

I was sentenced to five years in jail for participating in the so-called Legionary Rebellion. From the Malmaison prison I was taken to Jilava, where I parted from my wife, who had been discharged, and where I found my son, who had been sentenced to seven years at hard labor. From Jilava we were sent after a few days with a whole trainload of political and criminal convicts to the Lugoj prison in Transylvania. To the warden of that new jail, whose name I have regretfully forgotten, I dedicate here a few grateful thoughts. He did everything he could to indicate the admiration and affection he had for the Movement. I was moved from a small cell to a spacious room where my comrades could gather daily, and where those who were natives from that province supplied me with many of the victuals they received from their families: homemade bread, ham, sausages, cheeses.

We asked for and received permission to arise an hour earlier than the regulation time to attend Mass in the prison chapel, served by one of our clerical comrades. Before leaving we always sang the hymn, cherished by Legionaries, "God Abide with Us." In other prisons the singing of this hymn was considered and treated as the beginning of a rebellion. Often we saw some of the non-political prisoners furtively join our group, kneeling and singing with us. One of them, Filip, a peasant from the Moldavian highlands who had been assigned to me by the thoughtful warden as an orderly, was a man of no ordinary appearance and bearing and had an intelligent and noble nature. I had long talks with him; he had killed someone fifteen years previously in some obscure circumstances, but he could have given lessons in patience, truth, and Christian behavior to many of the leaders of the Carol and Antonescu era.

It was in the Lugoj prison that we received the news we had been awaiting with such impatience: Rumania's general mobilization and declaration of war against Soviet Russia. On behalf and in the name of all my comrades I immediately sent the following telegram to Antonescu: "All the Legionaries of the Lugoj prison await the orders of the Commander-in-Chief. God bless our armies." During the twenty-four hours that passed before we received the General's answer we were convinced it would be the one we wanted. We knew that thousands of imprisoned Legionaries had sent identical messages, and our optimism was based on the assumption that Antonescu would be more than willing to form special battalions with the hated Legionaries and send them into the hottest center of the fracas, which would have been all right with us.

However, we were mistaken. Antonescu's answer to our telegram was one that only a maniac could have composed: "Too late, gentlemen!" Antonescu's plans concerning the war and the Legionaries were already formed: they were to be sent much later into battle in disciplinary battalions along with felons and other criminals.

Two weeks later, at the German Legation in Sofia, Bulgaria, I was informed that Hitler had insistently asked that the Legionaries be liberated and sent to the front, and that Antonescu had promised to take steps to that effect. Here again we could witness not only another of Antonescu's tricks, but also the complacency with which German authorities in Bucharest and Berlin let themselves be fooled. The "liberation" that followed Hitler's demand and that freed me was so limited that of the more than two hundred Legionary inmates in Lugoj only two were permitted to leave with me. Also, measures were immediately taken to prevent all of the liberated ones from reaching the battle lines. At no moment did Antonescu abandon the fixed idea that had dominated his activity throughout this decisive period: to separate completely the Legionary Movement, Codreanu's Movement, from the war of reconquest, which must be his war alone.

Only those Legionaries who had been sentenced to terms of five years or less were freed. There were about twenty of them in all among the thousands who filled the prisons. Some of the conditions of our liberation were written in the corresponding decree; others I discovered only after my return to Bucharest. We had to present ourselves in person each week at the nearest police precinct; we were allowed no political or press activity and no contact with foreign persons under the penalty of being sent back to prison for the rest of our term or more.

My last order of mobilization as a Reserve Captain, which I had received two years before, had assigned me to my old World War I unit, the First Artillery Group of the First Cavalry Division. I decided to conform to this order just as if it had been the recent order of mobilization received by all other reserve officers. I donned my uniform and presented myself to the garrison command office. By chance I found there Captain Tomiță, whom I had known as a youth in Târgu-Ocna, town of my childhood. He told me that none of the liberated Legionaries had been or would be, mobilized, and that my being caught in uniform might expose me to arrest, which meant of course being sent back to prison.

Knowing from past experience how easy it was for unit commanders in the combat zone to arrange their order of battle as they pleased, I asked Tomiță if for the sake of old times he could not make just one mistake and give me a waybill to where my division was supposed to be and let me arrange the rest with my chiefs there. After pondering for a while, Tomiță told me that it would be too risky for him and strongly advised me to change to muftis as promptly as possible.

That evening we went with my wife to see Mrs. Ionică, the widow of Professor Ionică, who had been executed during Carol's regime. While we were there some police rabble invaded her home and searched it, pretending that flashes of light, which could have been meant to direct enemy aircraft, had been seen coming from the roof of her house. Having carried out their mission of intimidation and persecution, they left as suddenly as they had come. Some German officers who also were guests of Mrs. Ionică expressed very aptly the general feeling: "Die Schweine!"

My decision was made very quickly: I would leave the country before the first weekly appointment with the police. I would do my best to reach Finland, to which I had been Rumanian Envoy for many years. I felt sure that Marshal Mannerheim, an old acquaintance, would consent to my enlistment in the Finnish Army.

During the last days of the so-called rebellion, before my arrest, the Germans had offered to get me safely out of Rumania. I had declined with thanks, since, at that time, I preferred to stay in Rumania even as a prisoner. I could still have availed myself of this offer in those new circumstances, but I did not do so because of what I had heard about the way those comrades of mine who were in Germany were treated. I preferred not to owe my escape to anybody; I bought it.

A magic moonlit night, shared with my wife from the balcony of our home, was the last I spent in Rumania. I departed, leaving in one of Antonescu's prisons my son, whom I would meet again years later, under circumstances that proved once again that life is often more unpredictable than fiction.

From Bucharest to Giurgiu on the Danube I traveled in the trunk of a small car. When I complained to the professional who was helping me escape that the trunk was too small, he assured me that a few days previously two fugitives of almost my size had traveled together in the same trunk in full comfort.

With my head on a cushion I slept until I was awakened by the noise of our crossing the pontoon bridge that our engineers had thrown over the Danube for the German Armies. I had crossed this river twenty-eight years before, during the Balkan War, also on a pontoon bridge. But it was under much more dignified circumstances: I was on my beautiful black stallion Hades, with my artillery regiment.

In Rusciuc, Bulgaria, on the other side, I found Gheorghe Caraiani waiting for me. He was the youngest of the Legionaries and had been sent by my comrades who were already in Sofia. The sun was setting; through the light evening mist that drifted along the river we threw a last longing look toward our beloved country, which neither he nor I have seen again.

PART FIVE

Michael:
The Puppet King

*A few days ago Maniu told Le Rougetel, my Brit-
ish colleague, that if the British Government wished
that Rumania cast her lot with the Soviets rather
than with the Anglo-Saxon powers, in case a decision
becomes necessary, he would quite understand the
position but he would be grateful to receive an indication to that effect. . . .*

*Last evening with me Maniu developed more fully
the same thought. He said* if he had known the Soviets were to be given a free hand in application of
armistice terms he would not have advised the King
to sign the armistice. He argued that his pressure and
the Rumanian action which resulted from it had actually advanced the Focsani-Galatz line, which might
have been held a long time, to the very gates of
Budapest.

*. . . He was convinced at that time that the demo-
cratic powers would preserve an independent and
sovereign Rumania. Everything today however indicated that this was not the intention of those powers.
On the contrary it appeared that Soviet Russia was
deliberately planning to communize Rumania while
the democratic powers silently watched. . . .*

*With considerable emotion Maniu asked if America
and Great Britain wished Rumania to become a part
of the Soviet Union. "If so, please advise me accordingly for this can be arranged and even today*

late as it is I can arrange it to the better advantage to Rumania than can the Rumanian Communists." [*Roman added.*]

Burton Y. BERRY

Foreign Relations of the United States Diplomatic Papers, 1944, Volume IV. Europe. *Page 279. The American Representative in Rumania (Berry) to the Secretary of State. Bucharest, December 9, 1944—7 p.m.*

You will be present at the conference [Yalta]. You should trust us. Great Britain has entered this conflict to defend your independence; I can assure you that I will never forsake your country. . . . I know that Germany and Russia have destroyed your best elements, particularly your intellectual class. I sympathize most deeply with your suffering. But remain confident; we will not forsake you, and Poland will be saved.

Winston CHURCHILL

To General Anders before the campaign in Italy, when the cooperation of the Polish divisions was essential, as reported in General Anders' memoirs.

We have never guaranteed Poland's eastern borders. We possess now sufficient troops ourselves, and we do not need your cooperation any more. You may withdraw your divisions; we will do without them.

Winston CHURCHILL

After Anzio and Yalta, as reported in General Anders' memoirs.

You can have them. But let us not disclose this understanding before the next Presidential election in the United States. We have in the United States millions of Poles, Lithuanians, Estonians, etc. . . . and as a practical man I would not like to lose their votes.

Franklin D. ROOSEVELT

To Stalin at Teheran in December 1943, as revealed in U.S. State Department publications.

Falsehood, the Scoundrels' Weapon

Neither murder, torture, nor imprisonment, but slander and falsehood were the ugliest of the weapons used against the Legionary Movement. Against violence and injustice the Legionaries pitted their fortitude, and they never lost faith in final Divine justice. But what could they do to oppose the calumnies and impostures that were propagated by practically all newspapers and magazines, almanacs, calendars, encyclopedias, dictionaries, and "history" books—in fact by nearly all the mass media of communications.

The methods used by the slanderers of the Legion were, and are generally based on the principle of reversal—in other words, the repetition of the Big Lie, which has proved to be the most effective weapon with the gullible public. The following are some examples of the slanderous charges used to discredit the Movement.

The Movement is a terrorist organization. It is the Movement that has been, without interruption from its foundation and up to now, the victim of the most cruel terror by all successive Rumanian Governments, from the most "conservative" to the Communist Government of today with its special concentration camps for the extermination of Legionaries, described by Leonard Krishner in his book *Prisoner of Red Justice.*

The Movement has been a permanent menace to the State. Among all the political groups and parties that aspired only to power and its material benefits, the Movement was the only defender of the State against corruption, usurpation, treason, and finally against the surrender of the State itself to Communist domination.

The Movement is an enemy of legality. The Movement's history is that of a long fight for legality. It never asked for more than the benefit of its legal and natural rights, benefits that were denied to it by every Rumanian Government without exception.

The Movement's activities were controlled by foreign influences. The history of the Movement is, actually, that of a long, arduous and perilous fight against anti-national influences. It never looked for endorsement in Paris, London, Moscow, Rome, or Berlin. It was not at any time prepared to open the country to Soviet forces simply because that was what Eduard Beneš, Léon Blum, the leftist French politicians and the international mafia were demanding. It was the Legion's adversaries who carried out Blum's and the mafia's orders to annihilate by terror, imprisonment, and murder those of our youth who reacted against corruption and treason. And finally, the Legionary Movement was the only political group in Rumania to urge that the Vienna Arbitration be resisted with arms in hand. This meant war not only against Hungary but also against Germany and Italy. The Legionary Movement was never guilty of yielding whole provinces to Rumania's neighbors without a fight.

We will not stoop to refute the insinuations made regarding the personal correctitude of the Legionary leaders, but we will show how far the professional dishonesty of certain publicists could go when writing about the Legion. I relate two characteristic episodes with which I have been directly acquainted.

Jérome Tharaud, one of the authors of the famous book *Quand Israel Est Roi,* which described the Béla Kun terror in Hungary, spent a few days in Bucharest in 1937, not to gather authentic information for a book that could have been called *When Esther Is Queen* or *When Poppaea Rules,* but to give some unwarranted authority to the book he had been asked to write about Corneliu Codreanu, *L'Envoye de L'Archange.* The book's timely first edition came out a few days before Codreanu's assassination as a precursory exculpation of this dastardly crime.

Between one appointment and one lunch at the Royal Palace, Tharaud solicited and was granted an interview with Codreanu. I was in Codreanu's anteroom with a dozen other persons at the time of Tharaud's visit. At one moment the Captain opened the door of his office and looked out at the people present. In a calm and low voice he asked one of the Legionaries to fetch chairs for two ladies who were there standing, and closed the door. Now, here is how Mr. Tharaud describes this incident, without explaining where and how he learned the Rumanian language. "Codreanu violently opened the door and shouted to his Legionaries: 'Don't make so much noise, or I'll kick you out of this room!'" And Tharaud adds sanctimoniously: "The words and intonation were probably learned from his patron Adolf Hitler."

If the readers of *L'Envoye de L'Archange* had been informed of this fraud they would have understood immediately that the author was prepared to go to any limit in order to deliver the exact goods he was asked to deliver: the moral assassination of the Captain before his murder in Tâncăbești.

A. L. Easterman is another writer who paid a visit to Bucharest that same year. He also lunched at the Royal Palace with the notorious couple, Carol and Lupescu, and also solicited an interview with Codreanu, who granted it without any hesitation. Mr. Easterman is a Jew, and this bit of information was among the routine biographical notes about him that I gave to Codreanu for his information prior to the interview. The conversation with the Captain lasted quite a while; Princess Despina Cantacuzene, sister of General Cantacuzene, served, if I am not mistaken, as interpreter. Mainly because of the ethnic origin of his visitor, the Captain took special pains in welcoming him. Codreanu even presented Easterman with a picture of himself with the following inscription: "To Mr. Easterman, a loyal adversary."

The Captain had once again been too big-hearted in his attitude toward the people he met. This adversary was not, after all, as loyal as he seemed. How different would have been the image of the Captain if Easterman had written a truthful account in his book *King Carol, Hitler and Lupescu* of the friendly way Codreanu received him, a declared political adversary.

Here is how Mr. Easterman told the story: No one in Bucharest, except for a few friends of his, knew he was a Jew. When he told those friends he intended to interview Codreanu, they insisted that he give up this dangerous plan. "This man has already killed many Jews," they said. "If he discovers that you are a Jew, you are a dead duck." Easterman, with professional intrepidity, decided it would be better to risk his life than to give up the opportunity of talking with the leader of a "terrorist, secret" organization. Two uniformed Legionaries, armed to the teeth, arrived in Codreanu's car at Easterman's hotel to take him to the interview. At every moment during his ride, during the interview, and during the return trip to the hotel, where his friends were awaiting him breathlessly, he expected to be recognized and liquidated.

The truth is that Codreanu had always proclaimed that violence against Jews was a stupid mistake. He would have immediately expelled from the Movement any fool who had so much as broken a window in a Jewish-owned shop. The Legionaries sent to escort Mr. Easterman, the courtesy with which he was surrounded, the photograph with the friendly inscription—all were manifestations of Codreanu's courteous and chivalrous nature, a nature his deceitful guest was incapable of understanding.

It is a pity that Easterman's book is out of print today since it disclosed for the first time "the real story" of Mme. Lupescu's parentage without any consideration for Papa Lupescu's most delicate feelings. Mr. Easterman was the first to "discover" that Élèna was not the daughter of the honest Jewish pharmacist Lupescu, but was the illegitimate daughter of King Carol I, her lover's great-uncle. This made her somewhat of an aunt of Carol II, a fact that gave her no small claim to the Rumanian Crown. Mr. Easterman's book is "suggested reading" by Messrs. Hans Rogger and Eugen Weber in their book, *The European Right*.

Who were, who are, the slanderers of the Legionary Movement? They are to be found, first of all, among the agents of the international mafia, which controls almost all the communication media and means of information. This is the same group of criminals that established Bolshevism in Russia and handed over to the Communist empire eleven European countries and all of China with more than a third of the world's population and half of its land area.

They are to be found also among those perverted educators who have gotten hold of so many significant professorships in the universities of the West and have taken upon themselves the task of brainwashing a deceived generation.

They are to be found, too, in every country among those conspirators whom United States Senator Joseph R. McCarthy tried to smoke out of positions in the U.S. Administration.

Aside from the three or four hundred members of the Rumanian Communist Party, the majority of whom were of foreign origin, the Rumanian enemies of the Movement generally fall into three categories: 1. Those politicians who followed in peacetime the policy of Titulescu because they were thus able to guarantee their own political and material status. 2. "Bourgeois" groups connected with the different political parties that did not realize in time it was the Legionary Movement that offered them the best defense against the attacks of international Communism. They witnessed without protesting the persecution of the Rumanian youth by Carol and his stooges, thus confirming the well-known fact that it is sometimes easier to forgive those who have sinned against you than those against whom you have sinned. 3. The fiercest Rumanian enemies of the Movement were those who, constantly conspiring with the enemy during Rumania's war in the East, finally delivered their country into his hands—those whom the United States and all other Western governments recognize today as the only authorized defenders of the enslaved and tortured Rumanian people.

Sifting through the pile of accumulated slander, the last always worse than the one preceding it, we come to two characters, James Dugan and Carroll Stewart, who decided to go all out. They sprinkled their book

Tidal Wave,[1] which otherwise would have been a matter-of-fact account of a U.S. Air Force raid over Rumanian territory, with an incredible collection of lies directed against not only the Legionary Movement but also against Rumania in general. For any Rumanian the book is an object of amusement rather than bitterness. But *Tidal Wave* was a best seller in the United States because it recounted the remarkable exploits of U.S. airmen. As a result, hundreds of thousands of Americans were forced to swallow, along with the truthful details of the raid, the lies that are liberally sprinkled throughout the rest of the book.

Let us examine a few samples from the dozens that could be gathered.

"Marshal Antonescu [explain the two maligners] won his fame in 1919 when he was the head of a gang that specialized in the looting of stores, hospitals and private homes in Bucharest." In truth, Marshal Antonescu was a distinguished career officer, and until 1919 had been the head of the Operation Department of the Rumanian General Staff. After that he had been Military Attaché in London, Commander of a division, Commander of an army corps, Minister of Defense, Prime Minister, and Commander-in-Chief of the Rumanian Army.

In June 1940, we are informed, "Antonescu's terrorists" captured all the allied engineers working at the oil fields and threw them into the "torture rooms of the Iron Guard." Actually, by June 1940, the Iron Guard, its leaders having been assassinated by King Carol and its members having been imprisoned or exiled, no longer existed as a political group. As for General Antonescu, he was a prisoner of the same King Carol in the Monastery of Bistritsa.

Referring to a conversation between American Sergeant Robert Locky and Princess Caradgea, the authors say: "Antonescu's Fascists would have closed their eyes to her anti-Soviet ideas; but if she had been involved in an evasion attempt [of American prisoners], the Iron Guard would have undoubtedly tried to hang her." [2] In the summer of 1944, when this interview took place, the Iron Guard was no longer in control of Rumania's Government. For three and a half years its members had been in Marshal Antonescu's prisons, in German concentration camps, or at the front.

Marshal Antonescu kindly paid a visit to the wounded American airmen in their hospital. Here is the jesters' account: "The Marshal entered the hospital surrounded by a crowd of unknown people who were dressed in long leather mantles, looked like assassins, and bore machine guns under their arms."

---

[1] This book was also published as *Ploesti: Great Ground-Air Battle, 1 August, 1943* (New York, Random House, 1964).

[2] Why would the Iron Guard have to forgive Princess Caradgea for her "anti-Soviet ideas"? The Iron Guard was anti-Soviet by definition; she would have had to be forgiven only if she had had pro-Soviet ideas, which we assume was not the case.

To crown the collection we quote these last words put in the mouth of one of the American airmen: "Tomorrow morning we will be out of this country of SOB's."

In a much too courteous letter directed to those extraordinary authors, General Chirnoagă, of the Rumanian Army, asked them to divulge the source of their fantastic information. He received no answer. We cannot believe that the source could be Princess Caradgea; and we would be very sorry if it were Sergeant Robert Locky or any of his comrades, for no prisoners of war have ever been treated with more solicitude, better cared for, or more pampered than the American airmen who were brought down on Rumanian soil.

We ask any honest American citizen: Are such methods commendable? How could their victims—individuals, groups, or nations—defend themselves against such slander, since there is no tribunal of honor before which the slanderers would have to substantiate their allegations.

Again special mention is due the learned and painful exertions of Hans Rogger and Eugen Weber, professors of history at the University of California, in *The European Right* in which the Legionary Movement is only one of the political groups laboriously studied by various contributors, with the obvious general purpose of discrediting any organized effort toward the reconciliation of classes and the concentration of mutual energies, the common denominators of all the "Rightist" movements and of any fight against Communist infiltration or conquest.

We could not help but admire, though not approve, the diversified ways of keeping the mind of the absorbed reader from the fundamental substratum of all this hocus-pocus—the master question that has never been examined in *The European Right: Had any other political formation in Rumania really ever tried to fight the Communists?* We recognize also the unity of intent and of method through almost six hundred pages written by ten different authors; but we must deeply regret that those methods, judging by the chapter concerning Rumania and the Legionary Movement, include a wild assumption of facts that have never occurred, and the untruthfulness of which would easily have been demonstrated if sources of information other than those hostile to the Movement had been studied. This was the case, for instance, with the so-called "partial list of Legionary exploits committed before the final rising of January 1941 and exclusive of the Jilava murders," published by Antonescu in his account of those days. This list is as fraudulent as "the Legionary plan to murder their political enemies on New Year's Eve, so that Rumania could enter the New Year purified of the leprosy of the past." Those pieces of "information" mentioned by the learned professors are nothing more than a fantastic product of what Antonescu himself called his "polemic talents," the Ghyka and Groza affairs being cases in point to prove that these talents stopped at nothing.

But we have another quarrel, a more subtle one, with Professor Weber. We quote him:

> The legionaries reminded one . . . of the fundamentalist mentality described by Alan F. Westin in his essay on the John Birch Society. . . . Both assume the existence of total conspiracies and total solutions, both "refuse to believe in the integrity and patriotism of those who lead the dominant social groups"; both "reject the political system [and] lash out at 'politicians,' the major parties and the give and take of political compromise"; both despise existing recipes for solving current problems and favor "drastic panaceas requiring major social change"; both *advocate direct action, even to the point of calculated violence.*[3]

We have not "assumed" the existence of "total conspiracies"; we have been forced to ascertain the undeniable existence of that conspiracy which has already handed over to Communist imperialism one-third of the population of the world, including our nation and our country. We do not lash out at all the politicians, or at every political party as such, but at those that have brought the world to its present situation. We do not know exactly what Messrs. Weber and Rogger mean by the "give and take of political compromise"; but if they mean, on the inner political field, this symbiosis between supposedly opposed political groups, which helps solidify public opinion in the illusion that the country's interests are always served by a watchful opposition; or on the international field, the "meeting at the middle of the road" with a Communist establishment that has never budged one inch from its fundamental position, then certainly we do not believe in this "give and take of political compromise."

Finding, however, a similarity between the Legionary Movement and The John Birch Society because "both advocate direct action, even to the point of calculated violence," is unjust for The John Birch Society and by the same token for the Legionary Movement. The former, as Professor Weber knows very well, has never advocated direct action and violence; and if the latter was unable to limit itself to the calm ways of The John Birch Society, it is only because the most brutal direct action and the most cruel violence was used against it.

There is however a point of similarity that Messrs. Weber and Westin have failed to detect in their attempt to hit two birds with one stone. Both The John Birch Society and the Legionary Movement are the targets of a similar bombardment of slanders and impostures emanating from the same quarter and for the same motives. We are, each in our

[3] Weber, in "Romania," *The European Right,* pp. 570–571. Italics added.

sphere of action, among the genuine and unwavering opponents of Communism, whatever its masks, and the adversaries of all those who consciously or unconsciously, guiltily or stupidly, purposefully or by opportunism, openly or stealthfully, for minor motives of immediate financial gain or for long-range motives of political and ideological nature, sincerely or by pure mischief, lend a hand to Communist advance, infiltration, and corruption.

Roving in Foreign Parts

I had to spend several weeks in Sofia, Bulgaria, a friendly but noncombatant country, waiting for Ribbentrop's authorization to cross Germany, without which I would have risked being interned or in some other way immobilized—as Marshal Antonescu would have liked me to be. Authorization was finally granted with the single condition that I should not try to contact those of my comrades who were already in Germany.

On my way to Vienna we had to change trains at the bridge over the Drava, which had just been blown up by Yugoslav Partisans. This unhappy country had already entered, weeks before, the insane war that had been engineered by foreign agents and that, after wonders of heroism and endurance, would lead Mihailovich and his gallant Chetniks to Tito's slaughterhouses, which were also those of Churchill and Roosevelt.

In Berlin, by pure chance, I ran into Constantin Stoicănescu, one of my comrades. Without breaking my promise I was able to learn therefore that Horia Sima, who had left Rumania sometime after me, was already in Berlin, and that he and about four hundred Legionaries who had taken refuge in Germany had been assigned forced domicile. All of them had asked to enlist separately or as a body in the German Army and to be sent to the Eastern Front. On Antonescu's insistence, no doubt, this satisfaction had been denied to them exactly as to their comrades in the Rumanian prisons. Stoicănescu suggested that I try to convince the Helsinki Government to accept the idea of the formation of a Rumanian Legion in the Finnish Army. I knew that Marshal Carl von Mannerheim, who had fought in World War I on the Rumanian Front and had been saved from capture, as he told me himself, by a Rumanian cavalry patrol, had great admiration for the Rumanian soldier and sympathy for our country. The chances were not small, therefore, that this suggestion would have been accepted if I had had the opportunity to make it.

On August 7, 1941, I was in Copenhagen, the guest of my friend Giuseppe Sapuppo, the Italian Envoy, while awaiting the answer of the Finnish Government concerning my personal request for enlistment. The consent came, along with the welcome of a country where I had been Rumania's Envoy for several years. I was making final preparations for the winter campaign, already near at hand in those nordic regions, when I was informed that, on afterthought, the Finnish Government, thanking me for the sympathy I had shown for Finland, had found that it was impossible for it to make use of my services because I did not speak Finnish.

What had happened was that Radio Helsinki had announced my enlistment prematurely. Antonescu intervened immediately in Berlin, Berlin intervened in Helsinki, and Helsinki had to change its mind.

The Finnish project having been exploded, thanks to the mad Marshal's intrigues, I tried to thwart at least some of his future schemes. In a letter to Ribbentrop I told the whole story of the so-called Legionary rebellion and explained the gross deceptions of which he had been the victim, especially with regard to the Groza and Ghyka cases. I did not, of course, expect any immediate reaction or even an answer, but hoped to warn him of other attempts at mystification.

Sometime later, in two letters (one to Hitler, the other to Ribbentrop) I again took up the question of the formation of a Rumanian Legion on the German Eastern Front. For a long while I received no answers to those letters nor to all my warnings about the uncertainty of the Rumanian situation as long as Rumanian affairs were exclusively in the hands of enemies of the Legionary Movement. When the answer finally came, in tragic circumstances I will relate later, it recognized all the accuracy of my predictions and adopted my suggestions concerning the participation of the Iron Guard in the defense of Eastern and Central Europe against the Communist menace; but it was too late then for anything but a last and desperate effort.

From August 1941 to September 1944 the political situation in Rumania and in Europe immobilized me in Denmark where, a short time before, my wife, my son, and I had spent the last happy days of our lives. Denmark is a hospitable country, intended to live through uninterrupted peace with an eternal smile on her face, where the memory of a greater past left no bitterness but only a legitimate pride, and where the quickness of the mind is like a sudden ray of sun amidst the heavy fogs of a Scandinavian autumn. Shakespearean phantoms still wander in romantic Denmark, Ophelia still floats dolefully over lonely lakes among the water lilies, and Hamlet still dreams in Elsinore. In the park of Holsteinsborg, under the lofty ivy-covered oak, Hans Christian Andersen still tells his enchanted tales to the children of his friends.

Foreign occupation and a fratricidal war have induced in this people, whose public life and personal relations were those of a big family, strong currents of hate and disintegration for which its soul was not prepared. The friendly welcome that greeted me and other refugees of both camps even in the most acute period of turmoil was proof, however, of the measure of sanity and decency that still remained.

Three personalities, it seems to me, dominated those troubled times: King Christian X, Prime Minister Thorvald Stauning and Foreign Minister Scavenius. Stauning and Scavenius were of quite different social and political backgrounds, but both were of equal prudence and both conducted themselves faultlessly throughout a period when no one knew what the next day would bring. An atmosphere of moderation and justice disappeared when Stauning died. Lamentable incidents that many Danes would like to forget would not have happened if King Christian and Stauning had been alive at the time of the violent denoument.

Holsteinsborg, the elegiac castle of Count Bent Holstein, where at night one was lulled to sleep by the rhythmic complaint of the Kattegat waves, and where we had frequently gathered for the fall drives in the rich pheasant covers, has often been a tonic to my nostalgia and my worries. Another friendly home was that of Helmer Rosting, former High Commissioner of the League of Nations in Danzig, where he succeeded in preventing during a dangerous situation a conflict between Germany and Poland. Captain Schallburg, a great friend of my son and a frequent guest at the Rumanian Legation, was at the time of my return to Denmark, on the Eastern Front as Commander of the heroic Denmark Legion. Each of these three friends of mine, Count Holstein, Helmer Rosting and Captain Schallburg, enlightened intelligences, generous hearts, and ardent patriots, died victims of the same drama— a drama so much greater for them or for those who loved them that they passed away without having been understood by their compatriots.

During this period of inactivity I made use of the help of friendly diplomats, and of my personal experiences, to gather from lucrative private and official materials, information on the origins of World War II and its attendant responsibilities. I published the result of my research in a book entitled *La Bête sans Nom—Enquete sur les Responsabilités* (*The Nameless Beast—An Inquiry into the Responsibilities*). The sum of my conclusions was that those who provoked the last conflict could not have been ignorant of the fact that a German defeat meant the victory only of international Communism. This could not have been interpreted as an attack on Germany's interest; on the other hand I did not at any moment attack Antonescu or even allude to the difficulties we had with him. I was therefore rather startled when the German censor to whom I had to submit my typescript informed me that Ribbentrop asked me not to publish the book in order not to irritate Marshal Antonescu with whom, he let me know, they already had had enough difficulties because of the Legion. The simple appearance of a book of mine with German authorization, I was told, would be enough to send the Marshal into a tantrum again. So I had to publish my work under a transparent pseudonym. As an act of routine courtesy I also asked for the authorization of the Danish Foreign Office, which was functioning at that time without a titular head under the direction of the chiefs of the various sections. *The authorization was reluctantly granted by an official who warned me of the personal risks I was taking in case of a victory of the Soviet-Western coalition.* I believed that such kind thoughtfulness concerning my personal welfare deserved more than a mere verbal acknowledgement. Therefore, home again, I renewed my thanks by letter, assuring my interlocutor that "whatever those risks might be, they were much smaller than those which were taken on the Eastern Front by millions of youth fighting for the defense of a world to which Denmark also belonged."

The fear of the Germans, of irritating Marshal Antonescu, manifested itself anew in much more unpleasant circumstances for the Movement than that of the censure of my book.

We were still far from the Italian betrayal and still farther from the betrayal of which Rumania was to be a victim. However, the special sensitiveness we had been able to acquire during so many years of struggle with the occult powers, and our instinctive familiarity with Rumanian contingencies, gave us as early as the last months of 1942 the certitude that contacts with the enemy had been established by certain groups of the old Rumanian political cliques. We thought also that it was almost impossible that Antonescu would not have known something about this.

Dr. Werner Best, the German High Commissioner, and other German interlocutors to whom I was expressing our suspicions, identifying themselves not unnaturally with the feeling of the Rumanian people, all answered with the same argument: "How could you imagine that somebody in Rumania would wish a Soviet victory? This would mean the end of your country!" None of them could have imagined how foreign to the Rumanian soul and the Rumanian feelings were our political cliques, abased and corrupted by the methods of the Carol-Lupescu regime.

In his forced residence in the Berlin suburbs, Horia Sima, in more direct contact with the country, discovered still more reasons for alarm. His conviction was much stronger than mine regarding the imperviousness of the German Government to any information that would have questioned the authority of Marshal Antonescu or the fidelity and good faith of those who surrounded him.

Sima decided consequently to leave Germany clandestinely and to go to Rome where he hoped to find in Il Duce or in his son-in-law, Count Ciano, more attentive listeners to his warnings.

When in December 1942 it was announced in the German newspapers that Horia Sima had disappeared, Antonescu, furious, asked immediately that all the Legionaries in Germany be sent back to Rumania. Hitler gave an ultimatum: Sima had to return to Germany without any delay; failing that, all the Legionaries in Germany would be delivered to Antonescu. Count Ciano, who had apparently no special interest in letting his father-in-law hear anything about "contacts with the enemy," under the pretext of leading Sima to an interview with Il Duce had him arrested by the Italian police, delivered to the Gestapo and sent back by plane to Germany.

During that same period I was shown at the German High Commissariat in Copenhagen, in an official weekly news bulletin, the information that Marshal Antonescu had let Hitler know that he would be obliged to withdraw a part of his troops from Russia to maintain order in the country if the head of the Legionary Movement and all the Legionaries in Germany were not immediately arrested and sent to concentration camps—again the same lack of responsibility, the same imposture, the same fixed idea, even in an already very critical military situation.

Horia Sima and the approximately four hundred Legionaries present in Germany were immediately deprived of the relative liberty they had enjoyed until then, and were interned in the Buchenwald and Dachau concentration camps, to suffer new persecutions in new prisons from which they would emerge two years later when the betrayal they had foreseen and announced had indeed taken place.

CHAPTER

XXXII

The Betrayed Army

The history of this betrayal is written in few but adequate words in the memorandum presented at the Paris peace conference in 1946 by Messrs. Vişoianu and Gafencu on behalf of the group of Rumanian politicians who had undertaken the direction of Rumanian affairs after the fall of Marshal Antonescu. Vişoianu and Gafencu reminded the representatives of the Western Powers and the Soviets that this group itself had "asked that a powerful Russian offensive break through the Rumanian Front" in order to enable them to be done with the Antonescu regime and with any further Rumanian resistance. Gafencu is dead, but Vişoianu is quite alive and has been chosen as head of the Rumanian National Committee to represent the interests of twenty million Rumanians who have been reduced to slavery, thanks to the offensive Vişoianu and his clique once clamored for.

Mme. Basdevant, who collected all her documentation in the Vişoianu-Gafencu circles, completes this information:

Not only have the political parties organized an active propaganda in order to liberate their country from the Nazi yoke, but they have participated, according to their means, in the democracies' fight. By 1940, Maniu [Chief of the National Peasant Party] had set up an organization for collecting and transmitting information to the allied governments.

General Chirnoagă, a gallant and faithful soldier, thus manifests his indignation in his book *Un Chapitre d'Histoire Roumaine:*

So! While the Rumanian armies were fighting the Soviets for the salvation of the Rumanian people, Iuliu Maniu and other political leaders were collecting information concerning our fighting capacities and the military operations in preparation, and were transmitting them to the Western Powers, which transmitted them to the Soviets.

The leaders of the old political parties, which at no moment had ceased to exist and to operate openly or secretly, had not declared themselves in agreement with the reoccupation of Bessarabia and Bucovina, because otherwise they would have lost all that was left of their popularity. But their political horizons and their instinct for national self-preservation did not extend further than that. Even if they had denied it, they were much more sensitive to French and British circumstances than to Rumanian ones. In fact, they were also the slaves of those dark forces that had thrown France and Great Britain into a war that was not theirs and that would deprive them forever of their rank and station among the great and independent nations of the world.

Besides the politicians, there were some Generals who had likewise been broken by Carol, enough to make a working proposition of the politicians' conspiracy. There was General Şteflea, for instance, the man who did not want us to drive the Soviet troops from that stolen bit of territory, and who, at Antonescu's trial by a Communist court, boasted of having, as Chief of the General Staff, betrayed the Marshal's confidence by continuously sabotaging the sending of materials and troops to the Eastern Front. There was General Racoviţă, Commander of the Operational Forces, who concocted with the politicians the faked armistice that sent half of the Rumanian Front troops to Siberia's concentration camps.

The defeatists and traitors, civilians or military, those who have not atoned for their sins (as did Iuliu Maniu and Dinu Brătianu by death in a Communist prison) invoked two extenuating circumstances: 1. Antonescu ought not to have sent our troops further than the Dniester, the old Rumanian borders; 2. The country had to be saved from National Socialist occupation and from National Socialist tyranny.

The idea of halting the advance of Rumanian troops at the Dniester could have been hatched only in brains deprived of any political or military vision and experience. Who could have guaranteed not only our further possession of the two Eastern provinces but also our very existence in case of a Soviet victory? Certainly not Mr. Roosevelt and Sir Winston Churchill, who did not hesitate to sacrifice their allies Poland and Yugoslavia in order to comply with the insolent demands of their friend Stalin. Even if the only motive of our Iliad in the Russian Steppes had been the obligation to defeat completely and at whatever price such an implacable enemy as Soviet Russia, it would have been fully justified. For centuries, however, the inescapable destiny of the Rumanian people had been to defend against the assault of the heathens those embattled borderlands of Christian Europe; and I must emphasize, by the way, that Marshal Antonescu had a deep consciousness of this ultra-Rumanian dimension to Rumania's destiny. I believe that in circumstances other than those he had created by his senseless aggression against the Legionary Movement, he would have preferred to fight to the last man with the Legion at his side rather than consent to a capitulation which might have meant "Finis Daciae" for a hundred years and more.

The astronomical lies to which the advocates of the "National Socialist tyranny" argument are forced to resort when trying to exculpate themselves are the best proofs of their falseness. This tyranny had to be based on force, upon the number of German troops that were "occupying" Rumania. Gafencu tells us that in December 1940 the Germans had 500,000 men in our country. Mme. Basdevant goes a little further and talks of about 1,000,000 men. The truth is that until the end of February 1941 there were never more than 60,000 German soldiers in Rumania. Those troops had been requested by us as a guarantee against the permanent danger of further Russian aggression. When the first three divisions were sent, we would have been very glad if there had been more; I know, I was then the Foreign Minister of my country. When the troops destined to the Balkan Front began to come, they passed through directly to Bulgaria without stopping in Rumania. When in April and June 1941 the Second German Army formed in Moldavia for the campaign in Russia, its effectives never went beyond 250,000 men. Furthermore, it never was an occupation army but an allied army, which was temporarily stationed on Rumanian soil and with which our soldiers fought shoulder to shoulder against the common enemy. All these facts were perfectly known to Mr. Gafencu and Mme. Basdevant.[1]

Great Britain declared war on Finland, Rumania and Bulgaria on December 7, 1941; but it was Mihai Antonescu, as Rumanian Minister of Foreign Affairs, who declared war on the United States, a foolish move which demonstrated his total servility to the suggestions of the Wilhelmstrasse. Foolish because he was taking the initiative in a conflict that could bring us only trouble. Superfluous because Finland, who fought as a German ally in the same conditions as we, did not commit the same mistake.

It was Mihai Antonescu, however, who at the moment in which the situation on the Russian front seemed to take a turn for the worse for Germany, tried without delay to establish contacts through our agents in neutral countries with those he had wantonly provoked. His attempt to form a "Front of the Small Belligerents" (Rumania, Bulgaria, Croa-

[1] Tyranny was applied only against one group of Rumanians by Marshal Antonescu and by Hitler: the Legionaries. There were thousands of them in Rumanian concentration camps and hundreds in German ones, while conspiring politicians and enemy agents were moving about freely between Bucharest, Cairo, Stockholm, and Bern.

tia, Slovakia), and later a "Latin Axis" (Rumania, Italy, France, Spain, Portugal) were so many preliminaries to an intended coat-turning.

Marshal Antonescu could not have been ignorant of the action of his Minister of Foreign Affairs, nor of the contacts already established between the leaders of the opposition political parties and the enemy. It was certainly with his consent that Mihai Antonescu went to Rome in July 1943 to convince Mussolini of the necessity of establishing preliminary contacts with the Western Powers; and it was certainly with his consent also that our diplomatic agents in Stockholm had made contact with Mme. Kollontai. Nor could the Marshal have been ignorant of the activities of the agents of Maniu and Dinu Brătianu in Cairo to whom his administration had delivered the necessary passports, granted the necessary visas, and for whom they had procured the necessary foreign currency.

The result of all attempts behind the back of our fighting armies was nil and only hastened the final catastrophe. The "busybodies" had forgotten an ironclad law of clandestine negotiations in time of war: the enemy will always make the best of arrangements with would be traitors, but will never feel obliged to grant them any special considerations at the moment of the final settlement.

By November 1942, informed by the diplomatic grapevine and by the neutral press of the intensification of the activities of the Rumanian defeatists, I had resumed my sterile and unilateral correspondence with the German leaders. This correspondence explains, partly at least, the antipathy that those leaders have always manifested toward my humble person; very naturally this antipathy did not relent when my repeated warnings proved to have been justified.

It was only after Italy passed into the enemy camp that the alarm Horia Sima and I tried to spread among political and military circles in Germany was given some attention. "What are those diplomats of yours doing in Sweden?" Dr. Werner Best once asked me. "Exactly what all our diplomats in neutral countries are doing at this moment: trying to get in contact with the enemy," I answered.

On August 23, 1944, the saddest day in the life of many Rumanians, I was listening to the Bucharest radio in the home of friends, when I suddenly heard a young and rather uncertain voice saying words I had hoped never to hear in connection with our armies: *"our exhausted troops"* . . . *"our understanding with the Russian command"* . . . *"an armistice had been signed."* I finally understoood that it was King Michael who was announcing to his people that a convention of armistice had been signed between Rumania and Soviet Russia, ordering Rumanian troops to lay down their weapons.

I could not know that I had been fooled along with our army and twenty million Rumanians. No convention of armistice had been signed; the announcement was a deliberate lie meant to prevent any resistance to the advance of Russian troops. Those troops penetrated and surrounded almost everywhere Rumanian units that were conforming trustingly to the order of cease-fire. More than half of the Rumanian troops present on the front, Generals, officers and troops, hoodwinked and trapped, were taken prisoners, taken to Siberia where they were kept for several years and from which thousands of them never returned.

I left the home of my friends somewhat dazed, in the state of mind of a man who has persistently and accurately announced a disaster that in spite of all, he had hoped would not occur. The next day I received a phone call from Dr. Best asking me to call on him about urgent matters. I found him in the company of two Generals—one of the Wehrmacht, the other from the Schutzstaffel. Best's greeting was *Vor diesem haben Sie uns schon vor zwei Jahre gewarnt"* ("You warned us about this two years ago.")

I had the first news about what had occurred in Bucharest from my German interlocutors who were fully aware of what this breach, opened by King Michael's defection, meant not only for the Eastern Front but for the whole strategic picture. I heard the full story of that unbelievable betrayal only a few days later when I met Sima and my comrades.

It appeared that Marshal Antonescu, like Mussolini, had been invited to the Royal Palace where he was kidnapped by his royal host. Best and the Generals, impressed by the similarity of the two incidents, were asking themselves if the intention of the Palace conspirators did not go further than that sudden cease-fire. I understood better than they the moral and patriotic "qualities" of those who had advised the King in those circumstances, and my worries were even greater than theirs.

On Ribbentrop's behalf, Best asked me if I thought that it was possible to organize new Rumanian forces that would continue the fight against the common enemy, and if I were prepared to cooperate in this attempt. I answered that I had always been convinced that a Soviet victory would mean first Rumania's disappearance as an independent state, and then as a nation. I believed that our fight must continue at any price and with whatever means we could muster; I was therefore ready to cooperate. Best informed me that Horia Sima and the four hundred Legionaries had been liberated, that Sima would be soon in Vienna from where we would be able to operate. He assured me that in Berlin I would find Herr Ribbentrop. Once again we missed one another through no fault of mine.

My preparations were quickly made. Before leaving I tried to persuade

Schallburg's sister-in law to leave Copenhagen because we knew that her life was in danger there. She refused, but asked me to provide her with a handgun, which I did. Warnings and gun did not help much; half a dozen "resistant" heroes invaded her home a few days later and riddled her with their bullets. Here is a wreath on "Mäuschen's" grave.

CHAPTER

XXXIII

Posthumous Triumph

We mean here the posthumous triumph of the Barthou-Titu-lescu policy. Barthou and Titulescu were already dead; Beneš would soon be the same, helped through the pearly gates, or perhaps through more somber portals, by his Kremlin friends. It was the triumph of a betrayal not only of Rumania's most vital interests but also of Europe's and those of Western Civilization.

There is perhaps a difference between *betrayal* and *treason*. Treason always implies deliberate action whereas betrayal may also cover errors of judgment of such magnitude that treason has no difficulty in benefiting from them. We ask the reader, however, not to hold too much against us if in relating what occurred in Bucharest between 1942 and 1944 we do not feel always able, or obliged, to make a clearcut distinction between the two.

*   *   *   *

The Stalingrad disaster was exclusively the result of the stubbornness with which Hitler insisted on a frontal attack on the city, thereby giving up *a priori* any idea of maneuver. As soon as the retreat from Stalingrad began, a retreat in which the Rumanian Army lost four divisions, General Avramescu, Commander of our troops on the Crimean sector, forwarded a new plan of operation to the German command. What the General recommended was the systematic and timely evacuation of Bessarabia and Moldavia and the systematic and timely organization of the defense along the line of the Moldavian Carpathians, joined with the existing Nămoloasa-Galați line of fortifications and the Danube delta. Avramescu was certain of his ability to resist indefinitely behind such an organized barricade, and he offered two reasons in support of his recommendation: 1. The most effective utilization of the divisions still at our disposition; 2. The treasonable activities of the political cir-

250

cles, which would force him to devote a part of his attention to the security of the inner front. We do not think that General Avramescu exaggerated the possibilities of an almost unconquerable defense, under the circumstances he outlined. Indeed, at the time of the false armistice there was on Rumanian soil besides German troops the equivalent of thirty Rumanian divisions immediately available to the Rumanian command and twenty-one divisions in formation. Most important, the modern armament we had been promised by Germany and had expected from the beginning of the hostilities, had finally been delivered and was being distributed to our troops.

Let us pause a moment and observe that such a prolonged blockade of the advance of the Soviet armies toward Central and Southeast Europe would have changed impressively the general strategic picture not only on the Eastern Front but also *from the point of view of the Western Powers*. Of the two strategies that confronted one another since the landing in North Africa, the Churchill-Patton-Montgomery thesis and the Marshall-Hopkins-Stalin construction, it was the first that would have been strongly favored by a Russian setback in Rumania. In such circumstances it would have been the Western Powers that would have first reached Vienna, Budapest, Prague, Belgrade, Sofia, the Danube, and finally Bucharest.[1]

Alarmed by the Avramescu recommendations, Hitler asked his Envoy in Bucharest Baron Manfred von Killinger to report on the alleged defeatist activities of the political parties. Killinger denied vigorously General Avramescu's assertions, denouncing them as a part of *ein Legionares intrigen Nest*. The Avramescu recommendation was rejected, but the General sounded the alarm once more by resigning his command. He was to resume it a few months later in quite different circumstances, but in the same spirit.[2]

---

[1] Among the immediate possibilities there was also the bringing into line of the Bulgarian Army. The position of Bulgaria toward the Central Powers was that of a noncombatant ally; her tough and gallant soldiers had not seen action until then. The Prince-Regent and the Bulgarian Generals would certainly have preferred to fight than to be hanged. A Bulgarian contribution to the resistance against Communist advance would have greatly increased the chances of bringing the Western Allies to the Danube, and farther, before the Soviets.

[2] On July 24, 1944, Hitler ordered General Hans Friesner to take command of the army groups which were fighting in the southern Ukraine and which were composed of two Rumanian Armies and two German Armies. The General asked to be allowed to shorten the front by a retreat towards the Prut, and eventually towards the Moldavian Carpathians and the old line of fortifications. Nămoloasa-Galaţi. The arguments he put forward were identical to those used by General Avramescu: a better use of troops at his disposition, the uncertainty of the inner-front, and the demoralizing effect of the intrigues of the politicians upon the attitude of certain Rumanian Generals. Hitler, wrongly informed by his Envoy in Bucharest did not give enough importance to these intrigues, and ordered General Friesner to fight where he stood. After the resignation of Avramecsu, the command of the Army was taken over by Gen-

In Bucharest Marshal Antonescu, who like Carol had assumed or usurped the authority of the State, had like him abandoned it at the moment of greatest danger into the hands of whomever was there. It seemed that in Antonescu's tormented soul, willpower, power of decision and imagination had suddenly broken down; the stubborn, domineering, courageous and audacious man had given up any pretension to leadership. From Marshal Antonescu's hands, Rumania's destiny passed into those of the chiefs of the old political parties, Iuliu Maniu and Dinu Brătianu, later associated with Titel Petrescu, chief of a so-called Socialist Party, and with Lucrețiu Pătrăşcanu, representative of the Communist Party. Working directly with them was the flotsam of the Titulescu period that had again taken possession of the Foreign Office under the leadership of a certain Niculescu-Buzeşti. The clique that surrounded King Michael, among whom was another Titulescu waif, Savel Rădulescu, the man who tried to conceal the Göring proposals, and a small group of Generals like Sănătescu, Şteflea, and Racoviţă, were also keeping direct or indirect contact with the enemy. These were the politicians, diplomats and officers who had prepared the act of treason of August 23, 1944, taking advantage of the personal anti-Antonescu rancor and impressionability of young King Michael, and using him as chief protagonist in the drama of the false armistice.

Not only had no armistice been signed, but none had even been negotiated. The emissaries of Maniu, Brătianu, Petrescu, and Pătrăşcanu had received no answer to the demands presented to representatives of the Western Powers in Cairo and elsewhere, other than the information that those demands had been transmitted to the respective Governments, *and the repeated injunction to direct themselves to the Soviet authorities.* And it was in Moscow, three weeks after the misleading announcement, that the text of the armistice convention was presented to our delegation to be signed on the dotted line. In that three-week interval the Soviet Armies spilled over Rumanian territory, killing, raping, stealing, devastating, and capturing the deceived Rumanian troops.

Pamfil Şeicaru, a well known writer and an eyewitness of the catastrophe, commented as follows:

> This insane decision [announcing a non-existent armistice] has had as its first effect a dramatic confusion on the front. Conforming to the instruction of General Racoviţă, commander of the troops in operation, who was the chief element of the defeatist conspiracy, delegates of our military units

---

eral Şteflea, and General Racovitză took command of all Rumanian troops operating at that moment. Both belonged to the capitulation conspiracy. General Şteflea appeared as a witness for the prosecution at the trial of Marshal Antonescu, and accused his former chief of as much as he could. He also explained how he had, from the beginning, as Chief of the General Staff, sabotaged military operations.

made contact with the commanders of the respective Soviet sector. All the officers had heard on the radio the King's speech announcing the conclusion of an armistice. It is difficult to find in our vocabulary the word that could qualify such an act of deception directed against the army that had fought for more than three years, carrying its glorious standards as far as the Crimea, the Volga, and the Caucasus. An act of treason without precedent in the history of any country! A King betraying his army into the hands of the enemy!

After a moment of disorientation, the Russian commanders asked for Moscow's orders. Moscow's answer was in accordance with the truth: *No convention of armistice had been signed.* Consequently the Rumanian units must be surrounded, disarmed and captured. After two days the total number of prisoners was more than 175,000. . . .

And says Mr. Prost, also an eye-witness:

As long as the armistice was not signed the liberators kept on behaving like enemies. They surrounded and captured the Rumanian regiments, *which believed that they were facing friendly troops.* . . . The Russian armies lived on what they found on their way. They looted the farms, the stores, the warehouses. One of the first cars stolen was that of the Minister President. The looting did not cease with the armistice, and for months it was wise not to go home too late in order not to be robbed or left dead on the streets.

Concerning the execution of the clauses of the armistice, the governments of London and Washington relied entirely on the Soviets. Those clauses not only authorized but invited the Soviets to interfere in Rumania's inner affairs. . . . *An international instrument approved by the United States and Great Britain had abandoned Rumania to the whims and orders of the Soviet Union.* It was learned that this had been so decided in Teheran December 1943. And it explained why the Cairo conversations did not lead to any results. . . .

The Rumanians did not realize immediately the abyss to which they had been brought. Not even the text of the armistice convention opened the eyes of all. A decree of August 31 declared that the Constitution of 1923 was in effect again. *The old political parties believed that they would be able to start anew their usual pother.* In fact, the Teheran conference condemned Rumania to be a vassal state of the Soviet Union. A new history started for her as for all the countries of eastern Europe, abandoned, as she was, to the imperialistic ambitions of the Kremlin. *All those countries were to have the same fate, whatever their policy had been in the past, whatever their attitude had been in the recent conflict.*[3]

The public declaration of Niculescu-Buzeşti, who had meanwhile been appointed Foreign Minister by the defeatist clique, showed the indifference with which it considered the ordeal of the treacherously disarmed troops and of the Rumanian people:

---

[3] *Destin de la Roumanie,* p. 301. Italics added.

The Soviet Army has been received in Rumania in the most friendly spirit. We realize that in the period of the present military operations some unimportant incidents will necessarily occur. We do not intend to ascribe to them any significance. Those are episodic incidents without any importance. The Rumanian Government is convinced that all that has been agreed to with the USSR will be completely honored.

Those who witnessed with such imperturbability the capture and the deportation of hundreds of thousands of Rumanians, the murders, the rapes, and the plunders, had long before taken the necessary precautions in order to assure their own welfare in more peaceful surroundings when the moment of the unavoidable catastrophe, which they had provoked, arrived. Millions of dollars seized from the state treasury had been sent to their personal accounts in Switzerland and other places. We will soon find them in various Western countries, where they were allowed to take comfortable refuge by the Communist authorities, who had probably cleverly anticipated their disruptive activities among the Rumanian anti-Communist exiles.

It is easy to understand the indignation of General Chirnoagă expressed in a letter to Mme. Basdevant, a great admirer of the turncoat coterie, reproduced in his book *Un Chapitre d'Histoire Roumaine*:

Imagine, Madame, responsible French politicians asking the Germans to start a strong offensive in order to destroy the French Army! If such an act were possible, what would be the name by which it would be called by the laws for the defense of the French state?

In the night of August 23, King Michael announced on the radio that an armistice had been signed with the Russian Army. In fact the armistice was not signed until September 12, in Moscow, where King Michael's envoys were submitted to the greatest humiliations. They had to wait fifteen days before being allowed to learn the conditions imposed by the USSR, which they had to sign without any discussions.

During those fifteen days [in fact three weeks had passed since the time of King Michael's misleading information] the Soviet Armies occupied the whole of Rumania, preventing thereby any reaction to the conditions of the armistice before it was signed. As there was no armistice, all the Rumanian troops on the Moldavian and Bessarabian fronts, who had laid down their weapons in conforming to King Michael's order, were taken prisoner by the Russians and led into capitivity.

It was therefore a capitulation and not an armistice. Here is a King who hands over his Army to the enemy! In what country could be found such a chief of state? The Soviet Order of Victory was conferred on him by the Soviet Marshal Tolbukhin in Stalin's name. A sad honor, that of being honored by the mortal enemy of your own country.

YES, CONTRARY TO THE MEANING AND PURPOSE OF RUMANIA'S HISTORY, TO SAVE WESTERN CIVILIZATION FROM THE BARBARIC EASTERN HORDES, AND TO THE UNANIMOUS WILL OF HER PEOPLE, THE SOVIET TROOPS WERE ALLOWED

TO PASS ACROSS OUR TERRITORY, AS IN THE EARLY THIRTIES TITULESCU AND KING CAROL HAD PROMISED THEY WOULD BE ALLOWED TO DO. And since then, Europe is no more and will never again be allowed to be what it had been for three thousand years and more. Western Civilization in a new and degraded form, has shrunk in Europe to a few fringe states. It has disappeared almost completely from Asia and Africa with a rush and a swiftness no one could have imagined. As for America, from where the vanguard of the apocalyptical cavalry erupted in 1918, misinformation of the public and treacherous education of the youth are conditioning and preparing her for the biggest and final triumph of those dark forces which engineered both the Bolshevik Revolution and World War II.

When Only Honor Could Still Be Saved

On August 28, 1944, I left Copenhagen in a German military plane and arrived the same day amidst the rubble of what had been Berlin. Beholding the pulverized city, I thought of the loving care with which Hitler had started its embellishment and of his remarkable offer to reconstruct, at Germany's expense and according to foreign governments' wishes, all the embassies and legations, relocating them in a special residential district. That project, by the beginning of the war, had already reached substantial realization. I thought of how conflicting this was with Hitler's alleged premeditated aggressive intentions against the Western Powers.

At the Hotel Adlon, I yielded the room that had been reserved for me to the widow of a Danish volunteer who had been killed on the Eastern Front. This lady, wiser than Schallburg's sister-in-law, had left Copenhagen in time. From the hotel, with a heavy valise in my hand, I went groping through the total Berlin blackout, along the unrecognizable streets, seeking the Rumanian Legation. I was still far from my goal when a swarm of bombers, which I had heard so often passing nightly over our heads in Denmark, reached Berlin at the usual hour and started its routine carpet bombing. It revived my faith in modern ballistic accuracy since the last time I had seen the RAF operating. They had killed by mistake ninety-three children and some teachers in a girls' school in a Copenhagen suburb. While I was in Berlin the bombers visited us every night very punctually. With the same punctuality and with Germanic calm, men and women crawled out of their night caverns every morning and entered their day grottoes for their uninterrupted work.

At the Auswärtige Amt I was told the latest news from Bucharest. After the arrest of Marshal Antonescu and his delivery to the Communists, the new regime had immediately broken its relations with Germany and declared its alliance with Soviet Russia and the Western Powers. The German Army had started its retreat, pursued and leisurely harassed by Rumanian troops. General Gerstenberg, Commander of the German Air Force in that theater of operations, had taken in retaliation, the brutal and stupid initiative of bombing the center of Bucharest, with the foolhardy idea of destroying the Royal Palace and King Michael if he happened to be there. Michael and his worthy retinue, of course, had left days before for safer quarters.[1]

I found more complete information in Vienna, where with great emotion and after years of separation I met Horia Sima, the Legion's Commander, and the vanguard of the four hundred Legionaries liberated from the Dachau and Buchenwald concentration camps. The day the Legionaries in Buchenwald were informed that their internment had ended and while they were jubilantly preparing to leave, the camp was violently, for reasons unknown, bombarded by the RAF. Many inmates were wounded and killed; among the latter was the young and innocent Princess Mafalda of Italy.

From the moment Rumania entered the war, despite our justified resentment against the Antonescu regime, we had scrupulously avoided creating any difficulties for his Government. The Legionaries who entered the battle from the beginning, and those who were allowed to join it only later when the disciplinary battalions were formed with the inmates of the prisons, strived, as every unit commander could testify, to be models of spirit, endurance and courage. We had now to decide if Rumania's cause asked us to adopt the same attitude towards the new rulers in Bucharest. The information we had already received and that which we were receiving daily helped us to make up our minds rapidly.

For a long time, we in Vienna could not understand how entire Rumanian divisions were being captured and taken as prisoners to Russia and Siberia, seeing that a convention of armistice had been signed. It was not until September 13 when the signature of the real convention was announced from Moscow that we understood the treachery. The Soviet offensive against the Rumanian front, *urgently demanded by our political parties, by the Vișoianu-Buzești group of diplomats, and by King Michael himself,* had started August 14, 1944. Despite the felonious activities of one of two Generals like Racoviță and Șteflea, our troops kept fighting their retreat toward the country's boundaries with a stubbornness that did not correspond with the conspirators' computations.

[1] Truth forces me to mention that Gerstenberg had been provoked by a treacherous move by the new Rumanian Military Command—the Command of the false Armistice Convention. An understanding had been reached between the King and Gerstenberg concerning the date of the withdrawal of the German Air Force from Rumania. Twenty-four hours before the expiration of the agreed term, the Rumanian anti-aircraft artillery opened fire against the withdrawing German planes.

They had therefore asked King Michael himself to break their resistance.

The people and the army had been cheated; both abhorred the new masters that the betrayal of their leaders had given them. When in February 1945, under the protection of the Soviet bayonets, the Communist Party, which in Rumania had never numbered more than four hundred people, the majority of them of foreign origin, tried to parade in the streets of Bucharest, the demonstrators were forced to disperse under the angry jeers and the blows of the incensed public. In November of the same year on the occasion of Saint Michael's festivities, under a full fledged Communist Government and in similar circumstances, Communist manifestations were fought by the Rumanian people all over the country. The bloody scuffles ended with more than twenty dead in Bucharest alone.

The Soviet troops had reached Bucharest on August 28, 1944. Four days later the political parties in an acute crisis of euphoria went through the gesture of reinstating the Constitution of 1923. How could the leaders of these parties believe, even for a moment, unless they were complete fools, that the Communist masters of our country would ever abandon it again to a regime of liberty and justice? The true story of the Katyn carnage was public knowledge. What had occurred in the Baltic States in 1939–1940 was known to everybody: the whole of the intelligentsia, both civilian and military, and more than one-third of the peasantry, had disappeared, either liquidated on the spot or transported to extermination camps. The same thing had happened in Poland. Moreover, what nobody could have ignored or forgotten in Bucharest was the mass liquidation and the mass deportation of the Rumanian population of Bessarabia and Bucovina, which started immediately after the occupation of the two provinces by the Soviets in 1940.

Whether there were really some sincere illusions among the political leaders, we did not know. In any case, a sense of realization must have come very quickly when the same methods of annihilation started to be applied in conquered Rumania. Hundreds of thousands of inhabitants of Bessarabia, Transylvania, and Bucovina were herded like cattle, without any consideration for family bonds or other ties, and taken away. When, through emissaries and through British and American representatives in Bucharest, Maniu, and Brătianu complained to Roosevelt and Churchill about those inhuman methods, they received from the two Western leaders the answer that these matters had been agreed upon between them and Stalin, and that the Soviets had been authorized to use slavework as a part of the war indemnities to which they were entitled. *Vae victis!*

On September 25, 1944, Maniu and Brătianu abandoned the National Democratic Front they had formed with the Socialists and the Communists. General Sănătescu, a Palace man and the Minister President, under pressure from Soviet bayonets and menaced by the extremist members of his Government, was forced to complete it with still more Marxist elements. Terrified by the situation and by his responsibilities, he yielded the Presidency to the more forceful General Rădescu, who had himself played an important part in the complot that had put Rumania into Communist hands. Rădescu tried to adopt at least verbally a more energetic attitude before the growing exigencies of Andrei Vyshinsky and his Rumanian accomplices. After a speech in which he went so far as to talk about "people without God and without country," Rădescu felt the moment had come to take refuge in the British Legation. He appeared a few months later in Portugal. Rădescu once eliminated, Vyshinsky exploded into the Royal Palace, banged his fist, banged the doors, and forced subdued King Michael to appoint Communist Groza in lieu of the evanescent Generals.

The calvary of the Rumanian people was to increase in direct proportion to the Kremlin's triumphs in the diplomatic international arena. After Yalta and Potsdam: San Francisco, where Soviet Russia, by the very fact of her admission into a community of nations supposed to have been formed to defend the rights of men and of nations, was exculpated *ipso facto* of all her past, present and future crimes. After San Francisco: the Moscow conference of December 1945 and the Byrnes betrayal of Rumania by unfathomable stupidity, with the mock elections of 1946 as a consequence. After Moscow: the Paris Peace Conference where Rumania and ten other European countries were sentenced to lifetime penal servitude. Finally: King Michael's shotgun abdication.

A short time later Maniu, Brătianu, and many of those who had taken part in Rumania's affairs on the pro-Soviet side both before and after the capitulation, would be in Communist prisons. King Michael had long before handed over Marshal Antonescu to his Communist enemies and condoned his execution after Antonescu's condemnation by a Communist tribunal in Bucharest. King Michael could have prevented this execution if he had exercised his right of mercy—a thing we do not doubt he would have liked to do.

But in Vienna, by December 1944, we had already decided to consider the King and all those who surrounded him as the prisoners of the armed forces of an enemy government; to consider therefore that Rumania had neither King nor Government and that the persons who appeared in the successive Ministerial formations were, some of them, plain Communist agents, and the others terrorized or impotent Rumanians who were functioning in the various positions they occupied under the menace or even the fact of corporal coercion.

Faced with a situation without precedent in the history of the Rumanian people, we decided that it was our duty, as still free Rumanians, to try what we knew our enslaved compatriots would want us to try: to raise again the flag that their inept and terrorized leaders had dropped at the enemy's first bidding. On December 10, 1944, therefore, we gathered non-Legionaries and Legionaries in the Palace Lobkowitz in Vienna and formed the Rumanian National Government whose first act was to proclaim immediately the existence of the Corps of Rumanian Volunteers, the organization of which had actually started two months earlier, and which would continue the fight against the oppressors of our country.

In Vienna I had found an old acquaintance, Minister Altenburg, who had represented his Government on the committee investigating the Hungarian treatment of the Rumanians in Transylvania, and who now represented it before the Rumanian National Government in exile. It was Altenburg who informed me that three Rumanian officers had crossed the German line and wanted to reach Vienna. One of them bore my name, he said, and the commanding officer of the sector where those three persons had been held wanted to know what we knew about them.

We knew a lot. One of them was my son Elie-Vlad, who, I had always been certain, would do everything in his power to join our undertaking. His companions were Dr. Bulbuc, who was to be assassinated a year later in Italy, and a young lieutenant whom I shall call Lieutenant X, not knowing if he is still alive. Lieutenant X, modest, calm and valiant, crossed the lines several times on special missions. Constantin Stoică-nescu, another comrade whose confident, warm, and generous nature had so often comforted us in hours of greatest need, had already perished, victim of his courage and his spirit of initiative, on a mission similar to the missions of my son that, had it been successful, might have changed radically the course of events on that part of the Eastern Front.

The bombardment of Vienna was continuous and intense, although not to be compared with the similar fireworks in Berlin. The city was receiving two visitations a day, a British attack in the morning, an American one at night. The guests at the Hotel Imperial, where we were lodged, were consequently meeting twice a day in the hotel bunker, one of the most appreciated in the city, which for never quite explained reasons was called "Göring's bunker." As my son, for certain reasons, did not want to be recognized each time he returned from the front, with or without the news we were expecting, we generally chose the hour of the morning raids for our constitutional walks in the neighboring gardens. Once, while we were sitting there on a bench, we saw a lady with a heavy valise in her hands walking in our direction. Believing that she had just emerged from an underground station and did not know where to find shelter, we hastened to offer to take her into the hotel's catacombs, not failing to mention that they were among the best available. To our surprise she answered in good Rumanian and rather briskly: "I am not such a fool. I refuse, for the life of me, to bury myself in those rat traps. Each time those villains bomb us, I come out here with this valise and feel safer than anywhere else." How right she was was demonstrated that same morning when a more inquisitive missile penetrated as far as the Jockey Club cellar and killed nearly every person there, among whom were some of our friends from our Vienna heydays.

On October 25, 1944, our troops, following cautiously rather than pushing the retreating German divisions, had reached the location of our old borders as they existed before the Vienna Arbitration. The casualties on both sides had been extremely light up until then, none of the adversaries fighting with much conviction. What happened with our divisions afterwards, when they were asked to conquer Central Europe for the Soviets, is another story about which the Gafencu-Vişoianu clique boasted impudently in their memorandum to the Peace Conference in Paris.

> Our divisions participated in 16 big battles and 367 minor encounters, advancing for more than 1,000 kilometers as far as the center of Bohemia, crossing 12 chains of mountains in winter time, in regions completely devoid of lodgings and transportation. They liberated 2,832 localities, including 555 cities. They captured 103,243 prisoners. Their casualties were extremely heavy: 5,078 officers, 4,984 non-commissioned officers, 159,789 soldiers. A total of 169,882 casualties of which 111,379 were deaths.

The Rumanian National Government, on the other hand, was of the opinion that we ought to prevent, at any price, the sacrifice of Rumanian blood for the "liberation" of Mr. Beneš and of his country. If this blood were to be shed, it should be with one purpose only: in a last and desperate attempt to eject the Soviet troops from the national territory, to push them at least as far as possible toward their own borders in order to win as much time as possible, in the expectation of a political or military change that would be provoked or facilitated by just this attempt. If this project, which we had carefully studied and prepared, were to be abandoned because of the malfeasance of others—as was finally the case—we could at least try to save the honor of an army that until the time of Michael I had never broken its pledges and never turned its weapons against its own allies and battle comrades.

In no case would the division we were forming, from all the Legionaries who were in Germany and all the other Rumanian volunteers be brought to fight against Rumanian troops as happened tragically in North Africa and in Asia Minor with de Gaulle's soldiers. Therefore, our first project having been abandoned because of sabotage by some

Wehrmacht Generals (who saw in the possibility of an important victory on the Eastern Front only the occasion of a useless prolongation of a war that they considered already lost), we sent out troops, unit by unit as soon as their training permitted, to the northern part of the front in Pomerania, along the Oder. The remains of Gheorghe-Ştephan, the Wandering Prince of Moldavia who died in a Pomeranian castle, had been piously brought back to Moldavia by his granddaughter, Anna Sturdza, the wife of Prince John Gregory Ghyka of Walachia. What pious hands will ever bring back to their beloved country the bones of the Rumanian volunteers who died there, or who died in Siberian prison camps?

Our division was training in a camp northwest of Vienna, commanded, incidentally, by an old German officer named Colonel Ludwig, a man of strict military courtesy but with a grumpy nature acquired in a lifetime of soldiering, of which a good part had been spent exchanging blows with enemies of all descriptions. One night, in the room that he had put at my disposal, I heard a timid knock at my door. As it opened, I recognized the man entering as Petrea a private well over his forties, a mountaineer of Neamţ, one of the most picturesque of our Carpathian provinces.

"Petrea, how did you happen to land here with us?"

"Well, Sir, I saw others coming and I came with them."

"How do you pass the time of day when you are not drilling?"

"I sing, Sir, I sing."

"You sing, Petrea, in what way?"

"Just like this, Sir, just like this."

And Petrea drew from one of his pockets a nice oval piece of birch bark, not bigger than half of the heel of his hand, and started fixing it between his teeth.

Here I suppose I owe some explanation to my readers.

Those who have not partaken of the magic and the color of the sounds that our village virtuosos can conjure out of such a bit of bark can hardly believe it. As for the melodies produced and improvised, they are always of the nostalgic nature of our *doinas,* perennial accompaniments to the pastoral life which has been the fount of our folklore since the dawn of our history. These melodies are equally adapted to four fundamental themes: love, love of nature, legend, and heroism. Melodic *doinas* started to pour from Petrea's lips, who had knocked at my door just to shower them on some Rumanian's understanding ears.

Petrea stopped:

"Sir, I have another bit of birch that I have brought with me from Neamţ. It is from a thunderstruck birch, the best there is."

Then Petrea extracted another bit of bark from another pocket, and our dreams and longing absorbed us again. So entranced were we that we did not hear the door open. I was suddenly aware that the grumpy and irascible Colonel was sitting on the bunk near me, listening with the same rapture as I to Petrea's incantations.

Petrea, where are you now? Prisoner in Soviet Russia, back in your dear mountains, or in that other and happier world where your patron would not have, I am certain, any difficulty in admitting you? Wherever it is that you dwell, I am sure that you are not without that bit of bark in your pocket.

The atmosphere in Vienna grew more defeatist every day. The three *sancta sanctorum* of the Viennese, the opera house, Saint Stephan's Kirche, and Frau Sacher's hotel, had been seriously damaged by Allied bombing. And enough was enough. We could see the moment coming when we would be the only ones in the bunker of the Hotel Imperial who still believed in victory. Meanwhile our volunteers were fighting in Pomerania, and we saw with pride our soldiers and officers mentioned in the dispatches.

General Chirnoagă in his letter to Mme. Basdevant expresses his astonishment that in her book *Terres Roumaines contre Vents et Marées* this constant slanderer of the Legionary Movement fails even to mention the existence either of the Rumanian National Government in exile or of this last military effort of the Rumanian people against the conquerors of their country.

> In your book you do not mention at all the constitution and the activities of the Rumanian National Government presided over by Horia Sima. . . . From August 23, Rumania had ceased to be a sovereign and independent country; the Government's decisions were influenced or dictated by Moscow. No independent Rumanian Government would have incurred the dishonour of arresting Marshal Antonescu in the precinct of the Royal Palace and handing him over to Soviet agent Bodnăraş.
>
> Rumanians who happened to be in Germany and Austria formed therefore a Government, symbol of the aspirations of the Rumanian people . . . and formed an infantry division with which the Vienna Government continued the fight until Germany's capitulation.

General Chirnoagă's astonishment is worth some commentary. Mme. Basdevant kept very "good" company and their numbers were great. None of the Legionary Movement's professional slanderers who took the trouble to express themselves in books or newspapers—and they are not few—have ever mentioned the Rumanian National Government or the Rumanian Corps of Volunteers. The explanation of this silence is to be found in the facts of the situation: in what was occurring in Bucharest, and in what was occurring in Vienna at that time. In Bucharest there was a handful of usurpers, blind and deaf to the distress and aspiration of their nation; in Vienna, Rumanians who had forgotten any disagreement of political or other nature formed around a Legionary core, although far from their people, felt united with it and acted in full accord with their aspirations in trying to eradicate the shame of the capitulation, not by the customary and uncommendable methods of the "resistants," but by a last and heroic military effort.

How could even the most imaginative calumniator find in such a situation a weapon against Codreanu's Iron Guard, against the Legionaries?

Our enemy could have only one solution to this perplexing problem: to strike, through the *imposture of silence,* the story of this last and heroic military effort from the history of Rumania.

CHAPTER
XXXV

Hungarian Intermezzo

Vienna and the whole of Austria were slowly filling with Russian refugees who had followed the German Armies in their retreat. In Vienna I met some of General Andrei A. Vlasov's officers, leaders of a Russian anti-Communist Army of about 400,000 soldiers, men without any special sympathy for Germany and still less for the National Socialist regime, who for about two years had asked to be permitted to try to liberate their country from the odious Soviet tyranny without having been allowed by Hitler to do so. *All those soldiers and their officers were dishonorably handed over to Stalin by the British and United States Governments and High Commands, against the stipulations of the Geneva Convention and the laws and usages of war. They were victims of one of the greatest of war crimes, a crime about which all newspapers, magazines, historians, and commentators still keep a deep silence.* The soldiers were mowed down to the last man by Soviet machine guns. The officers were all hanged. Directly responsible for this atrocity were the President of the United States and the Prime Minister of Great Britain, without whose consent or orders such a violation of international, human and Divine laws would never have been possible.

While in Poland for a short trip, I had the opportunity to ascertain that the much talked about *Ostwall* (East Wall) was no more than an interminable moat, not very deep, over which any armored unit could have managed a prompt crossing in less than an hour.

The battle was every day moving nearer to Vienna. I found the front, on my return, at Sopron on the Austro-Hungarian border. Among those who formed or surrounded the Rumanian National Government, and among our fighting forces there, the possibility of defeat had not provoked any defections (with the exception of *one,* which we hasten to forget). General Chirnoagă and his officers maintained themselves in the position that, as soldiers and Rumanians, they felt compelled to adopt when they had seen their country abandoned to the enemy; their comrades and their troops betrayed to captivity; Marshal Antonescu, the Commander-in-Chief of the Army who had triumphantly carried our waving colors from the Prut to the Caucasus, handed over by his King and his Government to the Communists; and a Rumanian Prime Minister forced to take hasty refuge at the British Legation. General Chirnoagă is still with us, a cherished and venerated figure who occupies in our hearts the same place as did General Cantacuzene and General Petrovicescu.

We had decided that a visit to Baron Kemény, the Foreign Minister in the Hungarian Arrow Cross Government of Ferenc Szálasi, would give us an opportunity for a useful exchange of views now that our two countries had been totally engulfed in the poisonous Communist flood. I do not know why the German authorities, who arranged this interview for me, asked that a member of Altenburg's staff be present at the meeting. My intentions were definite: to consider with my Hungarian interlocutor the possibility of a radical revolutionary solution to the centuries-old rivalry between the two nations, whose quarrels throughout their history from Charles Robert and Neagoe Bassarab, from Ștefan the Great and Matthias Corvinus, from Michael the Valiant and Cardinal Báthory up to our times, had always hampered tragically their ability to resist the attacks of their common enemy: yesterday the Turks, today the Soviets.

Our trip from Vienna to Soviet-invaded Hungary recalled to my mind a relevant episode of the time I spent in Budapest as Secretary to our Legation. On that occasion, at dinner at Admiral Horthy's residence, Kanya, the Secretary General of the Hungarian Foreign Office, had rather tactlessly interrupted a discussion I was having with my neighbors about horses and horsemanship by declaring that there was now no reason to talk of horses in Hungary, as the Rumanian troops had taken them all with them when leaving Hungarian territory. The lady who was at my side kindly tried to restore the up to then prevailing harmony at our corner of the table by reminding Kanya that those troops had also cleaned Hungary of Béla Kun's Communist vermin. A young officer who was near at hand retorted immediately: "Yes, this is true, and we Hungarians are grateful people. We will not rest until we have rendered the Rumanians the same service."

After the official exchange of greetings, a visit to the troops and lunch with their officers, I spent within sound of the rumbling and rasping clamor of the nearby battle a night of unforgettable discussions with Baron Kemény, my Hungarian colleague. In the old mansion where we were lodged, everything, from the graceful elderly lady who was our hostess to the hunting trophies and family portraits hanging on the walls and the whiskers *à la François Joseph* of the elderly majordomo, was still an unscathed part of a world that was crumbling around us.

As if by a miracle, Kemény and I found ourselves thinking along the same lines, profoundly convinced of the same necessities, prepared, if in spite of all God gave us victory, to make the same decisions. It was Kemény who opened the way to this comforting exchange of ideas and dreams by telling me that after the Vienna Arbitration Ferenc Szálasi, Kemény's Prime Minister, who happened to be in Cluj—the capital of Transylvania, where years before I had, as Governor, tried to create even a minimum of understanding between Rumanians and Hungarians— asked an assembly of his partisans to observe with him a minute of silence in memory of Corneliu Codreanu, "with whom," he said, "we could perhaps have found another solution to the problem of our two countries."

Szálasi, Hungary's rightful Prime Minister, and Baron Kemény, Hungary's rightful Foreign Minister, were handed over by the British forces to the new Communist Hungarian Government. Both were hanged; and from those days when hangmen were the pets and bedfellows of newspaper men, columnists and press photographers, I had in my possession a picture of Szálasi's hanging. A priest is trying to reach Szálasi's lips with a cross; Szálasi leans as far forward as his position permits to kiss the sacred and beloved symbol. A crowd of unbelievably subhuman beings brutally pushes its way to separate the priest from the man who stands with the rope around his neck, trying to deprive Szálasi of this last consolation. What a fitting frontispiece to an epoch where we have seen the mention of God and the singing of Christmas carols banished by law from the public schools of powerful, formerly Christian countries.

CHAPTER

XXXVI

The End and After

Our still robust optimism was based on the spirit of discipline
and on the incomparable qualities of the German soldier, to whom
nothing seemed to be impossible as long as he was led by chiefs who
remained faithful to the old German tradition of military honor, of
fidelity to their Command, and of fighting to the last man. This optimism
was also based on the conviction deeply rooted in us, as it is still rooted,
that Divine Wisdom would not permit the ultimate triumph of the
diabolical forces that had seized Russia in their claws twenty-seven years
before, forces responsible for the greatest distress, the greatest massacres,
the greatest terror inflicted on the greatest number of victims known to
human history.

The battle of the Ardennes, the last clout of the dying lion, seemed
for a moment to bolster our hopes, but not even after the crossing of
the Rhine by the Allied Forces did we consider a German victory, a
German battle of the Marne, impossible.

Concerning the Eastern front, we had become accustomed to its
proximity and quasi-stability in the central Austrian sector, compared
to what was happening in its northern part where our troops were fighting. We were, therefore, painfully surprised when Altenburg informed
us that the Rumanian National Government was to be evacuated. We
left the Hotel Imperial in a big autobus en route for Alt-Aussee, a resort
in Tirol. I felt rather ashamed when taking leave, at the Schutzstaffel
center, of a young doctor in mathematics, an athlete with Iron Crosses
on his breast, who asked me half-jokingly, "Are you going? You leave
us to fight alone?" Some weeks later I read in the Western papers that
the last of that handful of heroes who defended Vienna to the end had
been executed by the enemy "because by a useless resistance they had
provoked considerable losses and destructions."

268

We spent Easter of 1945 in the bus on our way to Alt-Aussee, where we found that crowds of refugees had replaced the tourists of yore. From there we finally dispersed, each of us hurrying toward his destiny, to meet in Paris about two years later—except those who fell on the way, or those who, like my son, were fighting the same enemy on far-away battlefields. The second week in April I was in a train on my way to Berlin. Normally a ten-hour journey, it took us four days to cover the distance because of the detours and stops caused by enemy bombing. At the gates of Berlin there was a surprise for almost everybody. All able-bodied men were asked to leave the cars; each was given a rifle and sent to join the ranks of those who were defending the approaches of the capital. I was left with the women and the invalids.

There followed three nights at the Hotel Adlon. In the hotel's air raid shelter, where we spent a good part of our time, I regularly met Degrelle, the Commander of the heroic Légion Valonne, and the Grand Mufti of Jerusalem, a bright little chap who was always accompanied by two big Valkyries. Some months after, when the newspapers announced his escape from French captivity, they reported also that two ladies had left with him. I hoped that they were our two beauteous bunker companions.

I was taking my meals with a Rumanian officer who was waiting for an occasion, every day less probable, to pay a visit to our troops in Pomerania. The fourth day, via Warnemunde and Gesder, and by what could have been the last boat to make the crossing, I was on my way to Copenhagen. Between Gesder and the Danish capital we were forced to change trains; a party of "resistants" had blown up a culvert. I remembered the big bridge on the Drava, blown up by Yugoslav Partisans —the beginning and the end of a fragment of life, I thought.

But the real end was almost to come a little later. I did not find room at the pension in Copenhagen where I usually stayed; the landlady sent me to a hotel in a suburb of the city. When I returned to the pension a few days later, after the arrival of the British and American troops, when impromptu executions had been replaced by a more orderly settling of old accounts, I learned that as soon as I had left, the pension had been invaded by a gang of the worst sort of resistance people who, with pistols drawn, searched for me everywhere, even under the beds of all the guests. I wondered if a connection could be made between this daring "military expedition" and the friendly warning I had received a few months before from that thoughtful Director of the Press Department at the Danish Foreign Office.[1]

[1] As in other countries the "resistance" in Denmark was composed of about twenty-five percent young patriots concerned by foreign occupation and seventy-five percent Communists. As in other countries, it started its activities only after the beginning of

It was the "Funeral March" of *Die Götterdämmerung* that announced to us, the first of May 1945 the death of Hitler. Not being German, we do not feel qualified to decide if Admiral Dönitz was right or not when he declared on the radio that "the greatest hero of Germany's history has passed away." Nine words for which the justice of Nürnberg, the justice of Katyn and Yalta, punished him with fifteen years of prison. But we are very much afraid that it was not only the death of the German Führer that was broadcast to the world that evening but the crepuscule of the old German gods. These were the gods who, as far back in the past as the realm of legend, had been the defenders of Europe, this happy mote of land, this elected continent, father of all civilizations, against Asiatic predatory and slaughtering invasions, the defenders of this Europe already reduced today to a last stump unprotected and open to the onslaught of the barbarians.

The murderers of the last of Russia's Czars and of more than twenty million of his subjects had been entrusted with the undermining and destruction of all that three thousand years of pre-Christian and Christian Civilization had bestowed on the world. From the appearance of the diabolical Communist entity up to the beginning of the Eastern War in 1941, and from the end of this war until now, no government, no head of state, no statesman had made it his purpose and his duty to defend at whatever price this irretrievable, unexpendable legacy against the enterprises of the Beast. Germany alone undertook it, accepting the terrible risks implied in this attempt. She failed, but I am proud to remember that Rumania, my country, contributed with all her young forces, with all her faith and courage to this superhuman endeavour.

The day after the announced death of Hitler, I went to the seat of the German mission to shake hands for the last time with Dr. Werner Best. The building was surrounded by a pushing, menacing crowd through which I had to navigate with difficulty and a certain amount of risk. At the gates two German soldiers were mounting guard in statuesque immobility; a young officer was contemplating with melancholy the agitated landscape. I found Best in his office, gazing through the window with crossed arms at the frenzied crowds. "And now what will you do?" he asked me. "I will wait," I told him. And I am still waiting for the day of the resurrection of the civilized nations, to the consciousness of their mission, the pride in their past, and their will to live.

Dr. Best, like his predecessor Renthe-Fink, had done all that was in

---

the German-Soviet war. The whole idea was preposterous. The practical thing would have been to prepare, as secretly as possible and in cooperation with the army, a general insurrection. Nothing like that happened in Denmark. The minor sabotages and the reciprocal assassinations, generally between Danes, served only to keep the German authorities on the alert against a surprise similar to that organized militarily in Warsaw by the gallant Polish patriots.

his power to sweeten for the Danish people the bitter pill of a foreign occupation. It would have been much easier for him to do it without the countermeasures the British Government was able to take in Denmark, as in almost all other occupied countries. In order to spare the British population all the tragic and useless consequences of the so-called re-sistance, the British Government had given the strictest orders and ad-vice to the authorities and the population of the German occupied Channel Islands not to provoke in any way the German authorities, but to try even to establish friendly relations with them. The same Govern-ment had adopted a diametrically different policy wherever a British population was not concerned. British agents and British-supplied weapons formed the core of the terrorist organizations whose mission it was to provoke the chain reaction of sabotage, murder, retaliation and counter-retaliation, whose victims were so seldom, in Denmark as else-where, the perpetrators of those outrages.

My new Danish exile lasted two years. In this period of forced in-activity, when I could not obtain a visa for any other country, I watched with lacerating pangs the occurrence of all that I had foreseen and foretold in my reports to the King, to the Prime Ministers, and to the Ministers of Foreign Affairs, in my verbal and written interventions with so many of our political factors—a consequence of the foreign policy we were following, directed not by specific Rumanian interests but by the never-mentioned influence of never-named forces.

I watched, in this period, the disappearance of Rumania from the world of independent states. I saw the Rumanian nation submitted to a regime of physical and spiritual degradation without parallel in human history. While in Copenhagen I received the news of King Michael's decoration with the Soviet Order of Victory, and that of the execution of Marshal Antonescu with the consent of his King. I took note of the hypocritical maneuvers of Truman, Attlee, Bevin, and Byrnes, who under the appearance of an honest resistance to Soviet exigencies and the pretext of the pursuit of a one-world dream were doing all that they could to guarantee the continuity of the Teheran, Yalta, and Potsdam iniquities and to see this one-world "ideal" become finally a Communist empire. I heard there too, of the mock elections in Rumania, recognized as valid by the Western Powers; of the conferences in San Francisco and Paris where eleven European nations with 130 million inhabitants were fed to the Nameless Beast; of the unbelievable outrage of George C. Marshall's mission to China.

We have not been lenient in the preceding pages with Marshal Anto-nescu, with Iuliu Maniu or with Dinu Brătianu, the two latter the chiefs of the political parties, the National Peasant and the Liberal—the Con-servative Party had disappeared at the end of World War I, leaving in the moral structure of our political life a tragic emptiness—but we cannot refrain from manifesting our indignation for the way these three men were abandoned in the hour of danger by so many of those who were so evident at the time of the gratuities, the patronage, the pork barrel and the important appointments. Not only did these hangers-on not do anything for the defense of their chiefs and benefactors, but some of them were their accusers before the Communist courts.

We have hesitated a long while and we still are hesitant to place King Michael's case in the same category as that of the deserters and the traitors. We have withheld judgment on Michael not only in relation to the fate of the three statesmen, but also in relation to his attitude toward his people, to whom he owed everything, and who had the right to expect from him even the sacrifice so many crowned heads have made with majestic serenity. Even after the publication of the text of the King's abdication, a unique document to the best of our knowledge in the history of the downfall of monarchies, the Legionary Movement continued to admit that the King could still be a "flag" of convergence and union among Rumanian exiles, and a symbol for the day, much yearned for, of the fight for Rumania's liberation. We had decided to forget the past for the sake of union among Rumanians and the fight for Rumania's independence. Many Rumanians, including the writer of these pages, were prepared to forget the past also because they were convinced that the monarchic form of government that ruled the Rumanian nation without interruption for more than seven centuries was the best adapted to this nation's character and needs. The text of King Michael's abdication will show how much we had, and still have, to forget.

MIHAI [Michael] the FIRST
  by the Grace of God and the will of the people
KING OF RUMANIA
  To all those present and those to come: greetings.
  Deep political, economic and social changes have occurred in the life of the Rumanian State, which have created new relations between the principal factors of the life of the state.
  Those relations do not correspond anymore with the conditions established in the Fundamental Pact, the Country's Constitution. They demand a complete and fundamental change.
  In view of that situation, in perfect accord with the responsible element of the country, knowing also my responsibilities, *I consider that the monarchic institution no longer corresponds to the present conditions of our state's life; it represents a serious hindrance on the way to Rumania's progress.* [Italics added.]
  Consequently, fully conscious of the step I am taking for the benefit of the Rumanian people:

I ABDICATE

for Me and my followers to the throne, giving up for Me, and for them, all prerogatives I have exercised as King of Rumania.

I leave to the Rumanian people the liberty of choosing its new form of State.

Given in Bucharest
today December 30, 1947

MIHAI

History tells us of many emperors or kings who have been stripped of their crown or have been killed on the steps of their throne. We never read however of a monarch who, before leaving or dying, declared that the monarchic regime represented an obstacle to the progress of his country. After all, the right to decide about such matters belonged to the Rumanian people; all the more so since the hands into which Rumania was abandoned were those of the most cruel tyrants. The good and faithful Rumanian population had shown its feelings toward the grandson of King Ferdinand and Queen Marie in the September 1946 insurrection on Saint Michael's day, the King's own saint's day, which filled Bucharest's streets with dead and wounded.

Despite the act of abdication and all that had happened before, we decided to grant the young exiled King the chance for a future that might have permitted him to make up for past errors, the chance to promote and guarantee unity among the exiled Rumanians and between Rumanian and other national exiles, to work with them in their fight against the indifference and the ill will of powerful Western political factors, to prepare with them for the supreme effort, even at the risk of ending like the other Mihai of the Rumanian past, who after almost four hundred years is remembered by the Rumanian people as Mihai the Valiant.

It took us some time to understand that King Michael in his exile, as in his Palace, was the prisoner of the same camarilla, of the men who insisted that a powerful enemy offensive be directed against their own country; the men of the false armistice, of the unconditional surrender and of the filched millions deposited in advance in foreign banks to help them evade the gehenna into which their misdeeds would throw their country. It also took us some time to understand that the King neither could, nor probably wanted to, part with those who, usurping again the right to represent the interests of their country before the victorious powers, had entered the profitable service of the conspiracy.

In Paris I found Horia Sima with a great many of the Legionaries I had left in Austria. The majority of them were working in various factories and plants, especially at the Ripolin painting industry and at the Renault works, many carrying on their studies at the same time at the University of Paris.

My son was in Africa with the French Foreign Legion, and I went to see him before his departure for Indo-China, where he fought the Communist enemy for four more years. His wife and her father, General Avramescu, had been arrested in Rumania by the NKVD (the Russian secret police) and taken to Russia. The only news we had later was of their death in a Soviet prison. It was by mere chance that the same fate did not befall my wife.

Horia Sima and the exiled Legionaries were animated by my own instinctive and powerful obsessions: *union* between exiled Rumanians in view of the *fight* for the liberation of our country. In order to offer an example to those who were involving Rumanian exiles in an extension of the farce of former political life in Rumania, we announced the dissolution of the Legionary Movement as a political organization, involving its activities in exile; but not as a fighting factor abroad or in Rumania, where it represented the only organized resistance. Moreover, we invited all other groups of exiled Rumanians to join us in this fight.

In total contradiction to this attitude, the new leaders of the old political parties, who by some miracle of levitation had been transported from the streets and coffeehouses of Bucharest to those of New York, Paris, and London, had shamelessly organized themselves on the accursed pattern of their former political life. They even included the Marxist Socialist Party, which had never played any part in Rumanian politics except for the last obscure leaders who were functioning as auxiliary forces to the "gravediggers." This group, far from responding to our wise and friendly overtures, chose to be the instrument of a campaign of discord and disintegration among exiles, and its members applied themselves to their task with an assiduity and a consistency that could not have been greater if their disruptive activities were a condition *sine qua non* of their comfortable lot in New York and Washington.

I must however mention as a qualified exception the case of old General Rădescu, accepted reluctantly by the political swarm as President of the so-called Rumanian National Committee.

It was with the purpose of establishing the solidarity of all groups of Rumanians on this side of the Iron Curtain that I had written from Copenhagen to General Rădescu who was at that time in Lisbon. I had received a very encouraging answer that seemed to reflect my worries and my desires, with a few flattering words for our Movement, but also with a suggestion that I felt obliged to decline. The Movement could not take the responsibility for any individual violence against the persecutors of our people, since this would provoke only cruel retaliation and still more suffering for those left behind. Only a mass upheaval could offer us a possibility of victory. Such an upheaval could be organized, and the permanence of an eventual victory could not be guaranteed without the help of the Western Powers. Had the General the promise of such help? Well, he had not.

Rădescu arrived in Paris from New York and immediately let us know that he wanted to contact every group of Rumanian refugees of whatever political extraction. We could not disregard such an invitation, and I was sent with Professor Protopopescu to call on the General at his hotel. We found a true patriot, convinced as we were of the necessity of establishing an unanimous agreement of purpose and of effort among Rumanian exiles as a *first step toward the constitution of an organic, militant collaboration with the representatives of other enslaved nations for the liberation of our countries.* The reception was warm and cordial; we talked for a long time, and it was with real emotion, on both sides, and the satisfaction of work well done that we parted.

I met General Rădescu again a few days later at a reception given by a well-intentioned Rumanian in honor of this establishment of contact between the Legionary Movement and the President of the Rumanian National Committee. About fifty persons were present, and a circle had formed around the General and this writer as we engaged in an animated discussion. However, when an enthusiastic photographer came and pointed his camera at us, Rădescu, with a nimbleness astonishing for his age, bent almost double, as if it had been a bullet and not a Kodak that he had to dodge, and reappeared suddenly at the farthest corner of the room.

I understood! The President of the Rumanian National Committee was not a free agent either. He had less liberty to choose the way he believed best to defend the interests of his country than the poorest worker at Ripolin or at Renault. Before leaving, the General took me aside and told me: "You must forgive me, Sir. Imagine what *those people* in New York would have said if they had seen you and me photographed together!"

Post Scriptum

Early in April, 1943, Sikorski came to luncheon at No. 10. He told me that he had proofs that the Soviet Government had murdered the 15,000 Polish officers and other prisoners in their hands, and that they had been buried in vast graves in the forests, mainly around Katyn. He had a wealth of evidence. I said, "If they are dead nothing you can do can bring them back." [Roman added.]

Winston CHURCHILL

The Hinge of Fate

"Ten millions," he [Stalin] said, holding up his hands. "It was fearful. Four years it lasted." . . .

"These," [I said] "were what you called Kulaks?"

"Yes," he said, but he did not repeat the word. . . .

"Oh well . . . the great bulk were very unpopular and were wiped out by their labourers." . . .

I record as they come back to me these memories, and the strong impression I sustained at the moment of millions of men and women being blotted out or displaced for ever. A generation would no doubt come to whom their miseries will be unknown, but it would be sure of having more to eat and bless Stalin's name. [Roman added.]

Winston CHURCHILL

The Hinge of Fate

Yet when Mr. Churchill came to power, one of the first decisions of his Government was to extend bombing to the non-combatant area.

Captain Liddel HART

The Revolution in Warfare

We must not add needlessly to the weight of our task or the burden that our soldiers bear. Satellite States, suborned or overawed, may perhaps, if they can help to shorten the war, be allowed to work their passage home. But the twin roots of all our evils, Nazi tyranny and Prussian militarism, must be extirpated. Until this is achieved there are no sacrifices that we will not make and no lengths in violence to which we will not go.

Winston CHURCHILL

"The War: Past and Future"
A speech in the House of Commons
September 21, 1943

Let those who have hitherto not imbrued their hands with innocent blood beware lest they join the ranks of the guilty, for most assuredly the three Allied Powers will pursue them to the uttermost ends of the earth and will deliver them to their accusers in order that justice may be done.

Winston CHURCHILL

From the Allied Powers' "Declaration on German Atrocities" as quoted by Cordell Hull in his Memoirs.

Post Scriptum

The preceding pages might have provoked a certain perplexity in those who have had the patience to follow me all the way through: Was not the author horrified by the atrocities, attributed to the National Socialist regime, which he hardly mentions?

The author has indeed been horrified by the atrocities attributed to certain groups of the National Socialist organization, atrocities that were brought to public cognizance, even in Germany, only after the end of the war. My indignation did not need the fanciful figure of six and one-half million victims in order for it to be aroused. My indignation paralleled that of the many who had been equally horrified at the atrocities of the Communist regime in Russia and elsewhere and at those committed by governments, courts, and armies of the nations that were at war with Germany. My indignation was all the more intense as the immensity of the Soviet carnage was certified by the perpetrators themselves: by Stalin, for instance, when he confessed to Churchill that he had been obliged to liquidate ten million peasants, and by Molotov in his Odessa speech of 1933 when he boasted about the liquidation—up to that date—of more than twenty million "bourgeois." It was in American and British books, newspapers, and testimonies that I found further information regarding the atrocities that had been committed on the Western side of the barricade.

Has everybody the right to the same indignation and the same repulsion?

Roosevelt and Churchill knowingly handed over, at Teheran and Yalta, to the same Stalin and Molotov, and to the Kremlin gang of murderers and tormentors, one hundred and twenty million Europeans. They did this at the very time when, to their knowledge and with their tacit approbation, the Kremlin was inaugurating a new cycle of slaughters and massive deportations corresponding more than anything else in modern times to the definition of "genocide." At Teheran, when Stalin asked Roosevelt's consent to seize those doomed peoples, Roosevelt gave it without any hesitation, asking him only to keep this agreement secret until after the next presidential election in the United States.

When General Wladyslaw Sikorski, Prime Minister of the Polish Government-in-Exile, with indisputable proof in his hands, told Churchill that fifteen thousand Polish officers, the flower of Poland's heroic youth, had been butchered in Katyn and in the Arctic, the British Prime Minister shrugged his shoulders and answered coldly: "If they are dead nothing you can do will bring them back." [1] And on the same page of his memoirs that he relates Stalin's confession of the liquidation of ten million peasants Churchill informs us that future generations will bless the name of Stalin because they will have more to eat thanks to the collective farm system.[2] This not only indicates the imperturbable cynicism of the man who has been called by some "the conscience of the world," but also his supreme ignorance of agricultural, economic, social, and psychological matters. Furthermore, with the same astonishing amorality, Churchill boasts of the way he proposed to share the countries of Eastern Europe with Stalin, the mass-murderer:

> The moment was apt for business, so I said, "Let us settle about our affairs in the Balkans. Your armies are in Rumania and Bulgaria. We have interests, missions, and agents there. Don't let us get at cross-purposes in small ways. So far as Britain and Russia are concerned, how would it do for you to have ninety percent predominance in Rumania, for us to have ninety percent of the say in Greece, and go fifty-fifty about Yugoslavia?" While this was being translated I wrote out on a half-sheet of paper:

> | | |
> |---|---|
> | Rumania | |
> | Russia | 90% |
> | The others | 10% |
> | Greece | |
> | Great Britain | 90% |
> | (in accord with U.S.A.) | |
> | Russia | 10% |
> | Yugoslavia | 50–50% |
> | Hungary | 50–50% |
> | Bulgaria | |
> | Russia | 75% |
> | The others | 25% |

> I pushed this across to Stalin, who had by then heard the translation. There was a slight pause. Then he took his blue pencil and made a large tick upon it, and passed it back to us. It was all settled in no more time than it takes to set down. . . .

> After this there was a long silence. The pencilled paper lay in the centre of the table. At length I said, "Might it not be thought rather cynical if it seemed we had disposed of these issues, so fateful to millions of people, in such an offhand manner? Let us burn the paper." "No, you keep it," said Stalin.[3]

[1] Winston S. Churchill, *The Second World War: The Hinge of Fate* (Boston, Houghton Mifflin Company, 1950), p. 759.

[2] *The Hinge of Fate*, p. 499.

[3] Winston S. Churchill, *The Second World War: Triumph and Tragedy* (Boston, Houghton Mifflin Company, 1953), pp. 227–228.

President Truman, despite the fact that Japan had manifested the desire two months earlier to lay down its weapons, wantonly ordered that two atomic bombs be dropped on that country, killing or maiming more than two hundred thousand innocent beings.[4] For a long while the story of the bombardment of Dresden, contrary to that of other German cities, was tabu for chroniclers, historians, and newspaper people. Credible accounts place the total number of dead at 250,000. The number of casualties might have been still greater—according to certain reports—in a city crowded with refugees (there were up to one million permanent and temporary inhabitants), without any air raid shelters, which received in a few hours the full impact of 3250 heavy bombers. We read in the London *Times* of February 16, 1945, only three days after the Dresden air raid:

> Dresden which had been pounded on Tuesday night by 800 of the 1,400 heavies sent out by the R.A.F. and was the main object of 1,350 Fortresses and Liberators on the following day, yesterday received its third heavy attack in thirty-six hours. It was the principal target for more than 1,100 United States 8th Army Air Force bombers.[5]

We will let F. J. P. Veale further describe for us this brilliant aerial operation in his book *Advance to Barbarism* which everybody ought to have read and which few dare to open:

> The modern city of Dresden has grown up round the medieval town, now known as the Altstadt, which lies at the southern end of the bridge crossing the Elbe. In the eighteenth century Dresden became one of the great show cities of the world through the construction of a number of magnificent public buildings, all of which were erected in the Altstadt district of the city. Within a radius of half a mile from the southern end of the Augustus Bridge was built a unique group of palaces, art galleries, museums and churches—the Schloss, containing the famous Grünes Gewolbe with its priceless art treasures; the beautiful Brühl Terasse extending along the left bank of the Elbe; the beautiful Catholic Cathedral, the domed Frauen Kirche; the Opera House, the Johanneum Museum and, above all, the famous Zwinger Museum containing one of the finest collections of pictures in the world, including among its many treasures Raphael's Sistine Madonna, purchased by the Elector Augustus II, in 1745, for 20,000 ducats. Within this small area, so well known to British and American travellers on the continent, there were, and could be, no munition factories or, in fact,

[4] According to Edward Teller with Allen Brown, *The Legacy of Hiroshima* (Garden City, N.Y., 1962), p. 4, the "official statistics" for Hiroshima cite "78,150 people killed, 13,983, missing, 37,425, injured." For Nagasaki, according to Leslie R. Groves, *Now It Can Be Told* (New York, Harper & Brothers, 1962), p. 346, "the United States Strategic Bombing Survey later estimated the casualties at 35,000 killed and 60,000 injured."

[5] F. J. P. Veale, *Advance to Barbarism* (C. C. Nelson Publishing Company, Appleton, Wisc., 1953), p. 132.

industries of any kind. The resident population of this district was small. The main railway station of Dresden is situated a mile away to the South and the railway bridge which carries the main line to Berlin is half a mile down the river.[6]

This, then, was the target, and here are the details of this raid which might well count as one of the most illustrious instances of what have been called *war crimes,* and even of what has been called *genocide.*

On the morning of the fateful February 13, 1945, fast enemy reconnaissance planes were observed flying over the city. The inhabitants of Dresden had no experience with modern air warfare and the appearance of these planes aroused curiosity rather than apprehension. Having been for so long outside any theatre of war, the city lacked anti-aircraft defenses, and these planes were able to observe in complete safety all that they desired. No doubt, they observed and reported that all the roads through and around Dresden were filled with dense throngs moving westward. . . . It was common knowledge that a frantic orgy of murder, rape and arson was taking place in those districts of Silesia which had been overrun by the Soviet hordes. It should not have been difficult to deduce in these circumstances that many people in districts threatened by the Russian advance would decide to try to escape westwards.

Some hours after night had fallen, about 9:30 p.m., the first wave of attacking planes passed over Dresden. The focus of the attack was the Altstadt. Terrific fires soon broke out which were still blazing when the second wave of attackers arrived shortly after midnight. The resulting slaughter was appalling, since the normal population of the city of some 600,000 had been recently swollen by a multitude of refugees, mostly women and children, their menfolk having remained behind to defend their homes. Every house in Dresden was filled with these unfortunates, every public building was crowded with them, many were camping in the streets. Estimates of their number vary from 300,000 to 500,000. There were no air raid shelters of any kind, unless we so regard the enormous cloud of stifling black smoke which, after the first attack, covered the city and into which the second and third waves of attackers dropped their bombs. Adding a unique touch to the general horror, the wild animals in the zoölogical garden, rendered frantic by the noise and glare, broke loose: it is said that these animals and terrified groups of refugees were machine-gunned as they tried to escape across the Grosser Garden by low-flying planes and that many bodies riddled by bullets were found later in this part. . . .

The circumstances made it impossible for the authorities to undertake the task of trying to identify the victims. So enormous were the number of bodies that nothing could be done but to pile them on timber collected from the ruins and there to burn them. In the Altmarkt one funeral pyre after another disposed of 500 bodies, or parts of bodies, at a time. This gruesome work went on for weeks.[7]

[6] Veale, pp. 132–133.
[7] Veale, pp. 133–135.

Here are the commentaries of Howard Cowan, Associated Press correspondent at the Supreme Headquarters in Paris, reporting in *The People,* in the issue of February 18, 1945:

> Allied war chiefs have made the long-awaited decision to adopt deliberate terror bombing of German populated centers as a ruthless expedient to hasten Hitler's doom. . . .
>
> The all-out air war on Germany became obvious with the unprecedented assault on the refugee-crowded capital two weeks ago, and the subsequent attacks on other cities, jammed with civilians fleeing the Russian tide in the East.
>
> The decision may revive protests in some Allied quarters against "uncivilized warfare" *but it is likely to be balanced by satisfaction in certain parts of the Continent and Britain.*[8]

As Veale records it, a very unfortunately worded, semiofficial denial that the Dresden raid had been purely a terror-raid appeared in most newspapers: "The Dresden raid was designed to cripple communications. The fact that the city was crowded with refugees at the time of the attack was coincidental *and took the form of a bonus* (italics supplied)." [9]

We ask our readers: is any person, any group of persons, any public opinion which considers the killing of hundreds of thousands of women, children and other non-combatants as *a bonus* to an already barbarous military operation, entitled to express any indignation whatever at other acts of cruelty? On which side of the barricade must be sought the responsible factors for those unbelievable horrors? "It is one of the greatest triumphs of modern emotional engineering that, in spite of the plain facts of the case which could never be disguised or even materially distorted, the British public throughout the blitz period (1940–1941), remained convinced that the entire responsibility for the sufferings which it was undergoing rested on the German leaders," writes Veale.[10]

The strict censorship of any mention of the facts was lifted in April 1944 when the Luftwaffe was reduced almost to silence from lack of gasoline. It was Mr. J. M. Spaight, former Principal Secretary of the Air Ministry who was asked to publish a book entitled *Bombing Vindicated* from which we extract the following passage:

> Because we were doubtful about the psychological effect of propagandist distortion *of the truth that it was we who started the strategic bombing offensive,* we have shrunk from giving our great decision of May 11th, 1940,

[8] Veale, pp. 135–136. Italics added.
[9] Veale, p. 136.
[10] Veale, p. 120.

the publicity which it deserved. That, surely, was a mistake. *It was a splendid decision.*[11]

It is not the lack of frankness by the advocate of terror bombing that should be criticized. Mr. Spaight dismisses with justified contempt, the apology put forward that those bombings were only acts of reprisal for the German bombing of Warsaw and Rotterdam. "When Warsaw and Rotterdam were bombed German armies were at their gates. The air-bombing was an operation of the tactical offensive." [12] Captain Liddell Hart concurs. He writes: "Bombing did not take place until the German troops were fighting their way into these cities, and thus conformed to the old rules of siege bombardment." [13] Spaight agrees that Hitler was genuinely anxious to reach an agreement with Britain "confining the action of aircraft to the battle zones." [14] He recognizes also that Hitler undertook reluctantly the bombing of the British civilian population three months after the R.A.F. had commenced bombing the German civilian populations.

Air Marshal Sir Arthur Harris in his authoritative book, *Bomber Offensive,* agrees with Spaight and Captain Hart as to which government was responsible for the first terror bombings. In what concerns Dresden, especially, he writes: "I will only say that the attack on Dresden was at the time considered a military necessity by much more important people than myself." [15] When reproached for the inhumanity of indiscriminate bombing he always refers to a British Government White Paper. This document claims that the blockade of Europe by the British Navy between 1914 and 1918 "caused nearly 800,000 deaths, mainly women and children." [16] Indiscriminate bombing, argues the Air Marshal, did not kill as many people . . . so why make a fuss about it. Apart from the strangeness of this line of justification of a crime by another crime, the Air Marshal's statement provokes two questions: 1) Is he not aware that indiscriminate bombing killed many more than 800,000 people (the post-

[11] J. M. Spaight, *Bombing Vindicated* (London, Bles, 1944), p. 74; quoted in Veale, p. 121. If it is true that Mr. Leslie Hore-Belisha, British Secretary of State for War (1937–1940), initiated this "splendid decision," his coreligionists have no reason to congratulate him for it. Indeed, it was after the bombing of Hamburg and Bremen that the concentration camps in Germany started to be filled with the Jewish population whose homes and apartments were given to the hundreds of thousands of Germans left without a roof after the destruction of their cities—a fact generally forgotten by chroniclers and historians of those gruesome times. Italics added.

[12] Spaight, p. 43; quoted in Veale, p. 123.

[13] B. H. Liddell Hart, *The Revolution in Warfare* (London, Faber & Faber, 1946), p. 72; quoted in Veale, pp. 123–124.

[14] Spaight, p. 60; quoted in Veale, p. 124.

[15] Arthus Harris, *Bomber Offensive* (London, Collins, 1947), p. 242; quoted in Veale, p. 130.

[16] See Veale, p. 126.

war estimates bring the figure to 2,000,000), 2) Why does not the Air Marshal produce also the number of people who died in Germany during World War II, because of the Allied blockade—women, children, non-combatants, and inmates of the concentration camps?

It is only fair to observe that the French High Command was opposed to the use of the bombers otherwise than as an extension of the artillery fire on the battlefields. For motives only known to themselves—lack of bombers perhaps—the Red Army did not as a rule use terror bombings of enemy cities. The full responsibility of these atrocious crimes lies at the door of the British and United States Governments; in other words, on the shoulders of Prime Minister Churchill and Presidents Roosevelt and Truman.

It was President Truman who handed over to the same Communist murderers and lunatics to whom Roosevelt and Churchill had handed over eleven European nations, the whole of China, one-fourth of the population of the earth. As President of the United States, he shares with Clement Atlee and with the commanders of the American and British armies, the responsibilities of handing over to the Soviet executioners the four hundred thousand men and officers of the Vlasov Army, in contradiction to the Geneva Convention, to the traditional laws of war, and to elementary humanitarian considerations. Also under their orders and control, tens of thousands of Russian and East European refugees, including men who had fought as volunteers with the United States and British armies, were delivered to the Soviets and did not fare much better than the Vlasov soldiers.

Attlee refused to interfere to save the life of a young German boy of thirteen, sentenced to death by the military court of one of the "liberator" nations, for having kept a picture of Hitler in his room. This same Mr. Attlee paid a goodwill visit to Red China at the height of the barbarous terrors to which the humble and toiling Chinese people were submitted, and came back only with words of praise for the administration of Mao Tse-tung. He did not report any mass liquidation other than that of the Chinese flies, against which the Red Chinese sanitary authorities had declared, he assured us, a war to the finish.

President Eisenhower's Administration was an indifferent witness to the barbarous repression of the Hungarian insurrection by Khrushchev's Mongolian divisions; a repression that started only after Eisenhower assured Khrushchev, through his friend Tito, that the United States would never tolerate the establishment in Hungary, or in any other satellite country, of a government unfriendly to Soviet Russia. It was at the same time that the President mobilized the Eighth Fleet in the Mediterranean, not against a menacing Soviet Russia, but against her adversaries France and Great Britain. It was under this same Administration that half of the Korean and Indo-Chinese populations were fed, without consideration of their wishes, to the Communist Moloch.

It is not only the persons mentioned, their accomplices and partners-by-consent, who are directly responsible for the butchery and enslavement of whole populations, but also their political staffs and all those who by commission, omission or misinformation have helped, hidden or attenuated those atrocities. These people have lost the right to express, without hypocrisy, any indignation over what occurred in German concentration camps during the last two years of the war when, by the way, a great many of the lamented casualties occurred because of the system of starvation of the German civilian population provoked by illegal blockades—a system inaugurated by the British Government during World War I, in flagrant contradiction to the Geneva Convention and contrary to centuries of international practice.

We must not forget those either directly or indirectly responsible for the saturnalia of massacred civilians and for the uprooting of entire populations that followed the Allied victory. Most especially we must not forget the hundreds of judges, military or civilian who systematically sent to the gallows or to endless imprisonment enemy generals for the sole reason that they had been enemies. Let us remember that among those judges only two, to the best of our knowledge, kept their sense of honor and justice, condemning by their dissenting opinions, the crimes perpetrated by their colleagues: Justice Rahabinode Pal, the representative of India in the Tokyo trial, and Associate Justice Frank Murphy of the United States Supreme Court.[17] Lastly, we must remember the exhaustive massacre of Mussolini's soldiers and Black Shirts—last defenders of Italian territory—that accompanied the advance of the Allied armies along the peninsula.

Also deprived of the right to express indignation over German atroc-

---

[17] On page 176 Veale states: "In the war trials of Tokyo, in 1947–1948, the Indian representative, Mr. Justice Rahabinode Pal, delivered a brilliant dissenting judgment in which he laid down that 'the farce of a trial of vanquished leaders by the victors was in itself an offense against humanity,' and was, therefore, in itself a war-crime." On pages 224 and 225 Veale quotes Mr. Justice Frank Murphy of the United States Supreme Court, who "in his brilliant dissenting judgment declared that the charge against General Tomoyuki Yamashita amounted to this: 'We, the victorious American forces, have done everything possible to destroy and disorganize your lines of communication, your effective control of your personnel. . . . And now we charge and condemn you for having been inefficient in maintaining control of your troops. . . . We will judge the discharge of your duties by the disorganization that we have ourselves created. Our standards of judgment are whatever we wish to make them. . . . Yamashita was rushd to trial under an improper charge, given insufficient time to prepare an adequate defense, deprived of the benefits of some of the most elementary rules of evidence, and was summarily sentenced to be hanged.' " Veale then says that "on February 23, 1946, General Yamashita was hanged. Needless to say, he met his fate with stoical courage and dignity."

ities, in our opinion, are those who have accepted the participation of the Soviets and their stooges, the most constant and cruel violators of the rights of men and nations, as members of the United Nations, on the Committee of the Rights of Man, and in the International Court in The Hague; those also who with billions of dollars, with the most modern weapons, with the most modern industrial equipment, and with millions of tons of food have helped the Communist Governments to maintain their odious despotism and to prepare for further conquests; those who have received with open arms at Camp David, or elsewhere, Khrushchev and other Kremlin assassins even after the massacre in Budapest.

It was not the purpose of this book to recapitulate all the proofs of the complicity between the Kremlin and the Western capitals, or of all the misdeeds on a large or small scale for which the Soviet and Eastern leaders were directly or indirectly responsible during and after the last World War. That is why we have thought also that this is not the place to summarize the outrages of the National Socialist regime, which at least risked its existence in an attempt to wipe from this world of ours the Communist infamy, an attempt in which Rumania, we remember with pride, also valiantly participated.

I have examined in this book—and more elaborately in *La Bête sans Nom* now out of print—the responsibility for a war in which tens of millions perished; for a war which led to unbelievable brutalities and gruesome oppression; for a war that started under the pretext of saving Danzig for Poland and ended by handing over the whole of Poland to the mass murderers of Katyn. It was my conclusion, and it still is my conviction, that the responsibility for World War II, and therefore for all its horrors, lies chiefly with a certain international camorra that used the influence and control it had over Roosevelt and Churchill to apply irresistible pressure upon the Polish, the French and the British Governments, forcing them into a decision that was absolutely contrary to their genuine national interests and fatal to the destiny of Christian Civilization.

Appendix

Diplomatic Papers of the United States and Rumania's Capitulation

The *Diplomatic Papers* for 1944 issued in 1966 by the Historical Office of the United States Department of State include some interesting elucidations regarding Rumania's capitulation and the unprecedented betrayal of the Rumanian people and of the Rumanian Army at the hands of Rumania's politicians.

If we do not hesitate to call this betrayal unprecedented, it is because the Italian capitulation and coat-turning occurred in quite different circumstances. Indeed, the powers to which Italy surrendered were the United States and Great Britain and not the implacable, annihilating enemy that is Soviet Russia. The Italian people and the Italian Army were tired of a war that had never represented for them more than the personal ambitions of their leaders and their fanciful territorial pretensions. Rumania's war was an unavoidable one, for life or death, against a rapacious and never satiated enemy; her people, her army were fighting tirelessly and were prepared to fight to the last man and the last cartridge. A powerful opposition was bubbling in Italy under the Fascist superstructure. The whole of the Rumanian people formed a solid block behind the fighting troops, the State was functioning with eager and meticulous activity, the only opposition was the hidden one of the politician's conspiracy.

All the quotations in this chapter are from the official publication *Foreign Relations of the United States, Diplomatic Papers, 1944, Volume IV, Europe.*

Ambassador Lincoln MacVeagh in charge of United States–Rumanian affairs in Cairo wired the following to Secretary of State Cordell Hull on March 3, 1944:

I am informed that the Rumanian emissary has arrived in Ankara. He is Prince [Barbu] Ştirbei and is now staying with his nephew the Rumanian Ambassador until such time as he may be brought to Cairo secretly. . . .

According to a British secret document . . . Ştirbei is a relative of Cretzianu who has been representing Maniu in conversations with British agents and is father-in-law to a British officer Major Boxhall. He is not an emissary of the Government but Marshal Antonescu is said to be privy to his mission. . . .

Incidentally it would appear from the document referred to that the group behind Ştirbei does not yet realize the full seriousness of Rumania's position. When Cretzianu was informed that the sending of an emissary would be useless unless he were prepared to accept unconditional surrender or at least to discuss the details of accession to power of a government so prepared, he replied (1) that the Rumanians believe that Bulgaria may soon break with Germany and thus give the British the possibility of entering Bulgaria; (2) that under such conditions Rumania could surrender unconditionally to the British; and (3) *that Rumania would rather perish fighting than that "history should show that her present rulers surrendered unconditionally to Russia."* Yet it had been previously pointed out to him that there is no hope of British troops arriving in the vicinity of Rumania and that it would be better for the latter if the Russians should arrive at her borders and find her with arms turned against the Germans than that they should find her still fighting on Germany's side. [*Diplomatic Papers, 1944, Vol. IV*, p. 148. Italics added.]

Cretzianu's indignant declarations represented exactly the frame of mind of our Exile Government in Vienna and we have no reason to believe that *at that moment* Prince Ştirbei did not entertain the same categorical feelings. Soon, however, both would be obliged to recognize the trap into which they had fallen, to admit the Allied *non possumus,* and finally to yield the control of the Cairo discussion to another group of Maniu's emissaries who would hasten to comply and give over everything in return for a change of the political regime in Rumania of which they had hoped to be the beneficiaries.

The whole drama of betrayed Rumania unfolds between Cretzianu's violent outburst and Maniu's desperate confession to John Helier Le Rougetel and to Burton Y. Berry (the British and the United States representatives in Bucharest after the war), to the effect that *"if he [Maniu] had known the Soviets were to be given a free hand [in Rumania] he would not have advised the King to sign the armistice."* When we follow day by day the negotiations initiated in Ankara and Cairo by Maniu's emissaries, it is impossible to understand how he could have ignored the terms of surrender until it was too late to see that the Western Powers had entirely abandoned Rumania to the hands of the Soviets. One cannot help remembering the impression of many of those who had to deal with him, that behind an impenetrable mask Maniu was hiding a bottomless opacity, a total and carefully cultivated ignorance of history and of present political facts and contingencies. He discovered the tragic truth shortly before starting to expiate his errors in the Communist prison where, like Dinu Brătianu, he met his death. Maniu, Brătianu, and Ştirbei had at least the courage and the patriotism not to abandon their people in the hour of great misfortune and to share their calvary with them to the last day of their lives.

On January 8, 1944, Secretary of State Hull informed John Winant, U.S. Ambassador in the United Kingdom:

> Department was informed by British Embassy on November 21 that a message had been received from Maniu indicating his desire to send a special delegate or delegates out of Rumania for the purpose of discussing arrangements for a political changeover in that country. The British Government proposed to reply to Maniu's message by saying *that his emissary would be received on the understanding that his sole function would be to discuss "operational details" looking to the overthrow of the present regime in Rumania and its replacement by a Government prepared to offer unconditional surrender to the three principal allies.* It was stated that the Soviet Government had approved the proposed reply. . . . [This] Department gave its agreement to the proposed British reply already approved by the Soviet Government. [*D.P., 1944, IV,* pp. 133–134. Italics added.]

It was this reply, in which the three adversaries of Rumania concurred, which was communicated to Maniu before he decided—in secret agreement with Antonescu, obviously—to send Ştirbei to Ankara and Cairo. Here are some extracts of MacVeagh's report to the Secretary of State about the first conversations with Ştirbei in Cairo, dated March 17, 1944:

> Ştirbei stated that he represents Maniu and not Marshal Antonescu, though he "knows" what the latter thinks and that the Marshal has been in touch with the Allies both in Madrid and Stockholm. He said that the Government and the King as well as the opposition are desirous of making a change of front [Antonescu was "the Government," and Maniu and the other members of the conspiracy, belonging to the parties of Maniu and Brătianu, were the opposition] and that the Government is in a better position to do this than the opposition because it disposes of greater effectives and enjoying the confidence of the Germans could manage more adequate secret preparations. . . . On the other hand, should the Allies desire immediate action, the Maniu interests are willing to stage a *coup d'état*. . . .
> Further as regards the *coup d'état* he said that plans are prepared and that these include the participation by the King. . . . Immediate help from the Allies would be expected, consisting of air support *and debarkation at Constanza. When asked who would undertake this last operation he said that obviously only the Russians are in a position to do so.*
> In conclusion he was informed that what he had said would be reported to our respective Governments. [*D.P., 1944, IV,* p. 150. Italics added.]

On March 25 Ştirbei, who had received a message from Maniu, tried to communicate it to the American and the British delegates. MacVeagh informed the Secretary of State that:

> Lord Moyne [British Minister Resident in the Middle East] has informed Ştirbei that his message cannot be accepted because it is addressed only to the British and Americans and not to all three negotiating powers; and that negotiations will be resumed upon receipt of a message addressed jointly to the British, Russian and American representatives. [*D.P., 1944, IV*, p. 157.]

From the Joint Chiefs of Staff to the Secretary of State. Signed by Admiral U.S. Navy, William D. Leahy, dated from Washington, 28 March 1944:

> My Dear Mr. Secretary: The Joint Chiefs of Staff have considered your two undated memoranda forwarding a summary of a series of telegrams from Moscow to London [and] to Cairo, setting forth the views of the Soviet Government as to steps now to be taken if the surrender of the Rumanian army can be effected. The Joint Chiefs of Staff note that the Russian proposal in effect leaves the matter of Rumanian surrender exclusively in Russian hands but consider that, from a military viewpoint, this is only natural and to be expected since Russian forces are the only ones prepared to implement and to take advantage of the surrender terms. [*D.P., 1944, IV*, p. 161.]

The "Provisions for Imposition Upon Rumania at Time of Surrender," agreed upon in January 1944 between the American, the British, and the Soviet Governments, were never communicated officially until June 1944 to the Rumanian negotiators to whom the only information that was generally given was that Rumania had to surrender unconditionally. These provisions were enumerated *in extenso* by Mr. James Clement Dunn, the Director of the Office of European Affairs, in a communication to Ambassador Winant. Although space does not permit us to reproduce this lengthy document (*D.P., 1944, IV*, pp. 136–142), there is no difficulty however in recording it as the most humiliating, the most arbitrary, the most rigorous act of surrender enforced on a defeated country. Articles 2 and 3 read:

> 2. *Unconditional Surrender.* The Rumanian Government and the Rumanian High Command should be required to acknowledge the total defeat and unconditional surrender of Rumania's armed forces and to agree to submit to such terms and faithfully to execute such duties as may be imposed upon them by the occupation authorities.
> 3. *Additional Provisions to be Imposed upon Rumania.* The occupation authorities should be authorized to impose in addition to the terms stipu-

lated at the time of surrender, such further terms as they may from time to time deem necessary or appropriate.

The twenty-seven Articles, which provided for the projected act of surrender, gave the occupation authorities a right of interference and final decision in every branch of Rumania's national activity, not forgetting the judiciary or Article 23 which covered the conduct of educational and other cultural agencies. Article 18, "Undesirable Rumanian Organizations," which allowed that "such parts of these organizations as it may seem desirable may be retained or converted for the purpose of performing necessary economic or social functions" may or may not be interpreted as an invitation to organize slave labor. It is a fact, in any case, that several hundred thousand Rumanian citizens from Bessarabia, Bucovina, and Transylvania were forcible transported to Soviet Russia, with the consent of Washington and London, to the infamous labor camps of Stalin as a prelude to war reparations.

What were Rumanian soldiers doing while Marshal Antonescu, victim of a total breakdown, was permitting petty politicians, eager to return to their *dolce vita* of yore, to negotiate in secret the capitulation of Rumania's armies? Let Soviet Foreign Minister V. M. Molotov answer the question in this telegram from W. Averell Harriman, the American Ambassador in the Soviet Union, to Secretary of State Hull, dated April 18, 1944.

> For the President and the Secretary. In my talk with Molotov last evening he told me that the Rumanian troops were still fighting the Red Army and those who surrendered had done so only after battle. In the Crimea that resistance was particularly stubborn as the Rumanian divisions there consisted of better trained troops. He stated further that the Rumanian Government had not changed in any way its policy of cooperation with Germany. [*D.P., 1944, IV,* p. 175.]

It was about this time that the Soviets suddenly proposed to Maniu's emissaries, and asked them to transmit to Antonescu, armistice terms astonishingly more advantageous to Rumania than those elaborated by the United States and Great Britain, in fact drastically different from those proposed by the Western Powers. Here are those terms as they were transmitted by MacVeagh from Cairo, April 8, 1944, to the Secretary of State:

> 1. The Rumanian troops who are fighting with the Germans against the Red Army comprise seven divisions in Crimea, three or more divisions in the region of Odessa, three or more divisions in the region of Kichinev. These Rumanian divisions must surrender to the Red Army, or they must attack in the rear of the Germans and commence operations against the Germans together with the Red Army.

If this is done the Soviet Government agrees to complete the armament of all these divisions *and to place them immediately at the disposition of Marshal Antonescu and Mr. Maniu.*

2. The Soviet minimum conditions of armistice are the following:

(a) Rupture with the Germans and common operations of the Rumanian and the Allied troops including the Red Army against the Germans *for the purpose of restoring the independence and sovereignty of Rumania.*

(b) Reestablishment of the Rumanian-Soviet frontier in concordance with the agreement of 1940.

(c) Indemnity for the losses caused the Soviet Union by the hostilities and occupation by the Rumanians of its territory.

(d) Repatriation of the Soviet and Allied prisoners of war as well as the internees.

These minimum conditions can be changed for the worse if Rumania does not accept them soon.

3. *The Soviet Government does not ask that Rumanian territory be occupied for the duration of the armistice by the Soviet troops,* but the Soviet troops as well as those of the Allies must have unrestricted freedom of movement through Rumanian territory if the military situation makes it necessary. The Rumanian Government must contribute to this to the best of its ability. . . .

4. The Soviet Government considers unjust the decisions of the Vienna Award and it is ready to conduct operations in common with Rumania against the Hungarians and the Germans *with the object of restoring to Rumania all of Transylvania, or the major part thereof.*

5. If Rumania wishes to have for contact with the Soviet Union besides the general representative for military questions, also a political representative for political questions, the Soviet Government has no objections.
[*D.P., 1944, IV,* p. 170. Italics added.]

There is every reason to doubt the sincerity of the Kremlin's proposals. Nevertheless they offered the Antonescu Government two basic most important advantages: no change of regime, the command of the Rumanian Army in the Marshal's hands, two levers of action which he could have used ulteriorly, according to circumstances.

Both the United States and the British Governments immediately raised their objections, the chief of which were according to a memorandum of Mr. Cloyce Kenneth Huston, of the Division of Southern European Affairs, dated April 11, 1944:

1. Since the terms constitute a definite departure from the principle of unconditional surrender it would be important for the purposes of prestige and psychological warfare to protect ourselves as far as possible from charges of having deserted this loudly announced principle. . . .

3. The Russian proposals differ drastically from those prepared in the Department. . . . For example: The American draft was based on the principle of unconditional surrender, envisaged military occupation and carried detailed provisions regarding occupational organs, demobilization,

disarmament, communications facilities, *war criminals, repeal of discriminatory legislation* et cetera. . . .

5. Whereas we recognize the desirability of utilizing the Rumanian forces in the prosecution of the war against the Germans as well as against the Hungarians as long as they are fighting with and for the Germans, we feel it desirable to keep in mind the disadvantages of allowing Rumanian troops to operate or to serve as occupying forces in Hungary and disputed Transylvanian territory.

The foregoing considerations are not intended to combat our present disposition to endorse the Russian terms, but it may be well to keep them in mind.

Addendum: 6. *The Russian proposals place no term on the authority of the Antonescu regime, thus leaving open the question of whether we are to deal and collaborate with a government hitherto responsible for conducting war against the Allies alongside the Germans.* [D.P., 1944, IV, pp. 172–173. Italics added.]

The watchdogs in the State Department and the Foreign Office did not have to worry. The Soviet terms offered on April 8, 1944, which any *turncoat* ought to have accepted without further ado, were never seriously considered by Mr. Maniu and his new advisers; they had, for them, a prohibitive flaw. *They did not ask for a change of regime, they did not put Rumania back in the hands of the politicians.* We insist, there was, no doubt, some ulterior motive in Soviet Russia's relative leniency but the Kremlin terms represented the best possible price, at that moment, for the betrayal of the German ally. As an alternative Maniu suggested first to transfer himself to Russian occupied territory and to form there an exile Government. His proposal was neither made nor taken seriously:

Ambassador Harriman to the Secretary of State. Moscow, April 25.

In reply to my inquiry as to any developments in the Soviet-Rumanian situation Molotov informed me that Maniu's proposal made by Prince Ştirbei, to break away from Antonescu and to form a new Government in Soviet occupied Rumania, although acceptable to the Soviet Government, was not considered as having been made seriously. He said that there were yet no different [*definite?*] indications that Maniu would follow such a course. [D.P., 1944, IV, p. 177.]

It was on May 25 that a certain Constantin Vişoianu entered upon the scene. A derelict of Titulescu's clique he had been, along with his confederate Niculescu-Buzaşti, during those last weeks of negotiations and during the drama of capitulation and the false armistice, the true representative of the insane ambitions of the old political parties. Once in Cairo he took virtual control of the negotiations from the hands of Ştirbei, who had always been of the opinion that an understanding with Antonescu concerning an attack against the German Army offered more prospects than a *coup d'état* against him. The Soviet offers, which it seems at no time had been formally communicated to Antonescu either by Ankara or by the British secret DC station in Rumania, had momentarily to be bypassed. Therefore Vișoianu, who a few weeks later would be the warmest protagonist of the unconditional capitulation which treacherously disarmed our troops, came with irrelevant but irritant pretensions, including for instance the assurance "that Rumania's funds sequestered in Great Britain and the United States would be released." The result was communicated by MacVeagh to the Secretary of State on June 1, 1944:

> Lord Moyne, [N. V.] Novikov and I held conference this evening and agreed to hand the Rumanian emissaries a final statement in the following sense, provided our Governments approved:
> "In view of the situation created by the latest telegrams of Mr. Maniu the delegates of the three powers deem it necessary to declare to the Rumanian delegates that further negotiations would serve no purpose and the negotiations are considered ended.
> "If Mr. Maniu wishes to take advantage of the armistice terms offered by the three powers he should follow the advice already given him by sending an officer to make direct contact with the Red Army on the front." [*D.P., 1944, IV*, pp. 180–181.]

Marshal Antonescu had also established secret contacts with the enemies in Bern, in Madrid, in Stockholm. He was not adverse to the idea of turning his armies against his ally Germany, but was putting forward more matter of fact and less pointless exigencies than Maniu, as for instance that military operations against German troops by his armies would not imply the invasion of Rumania's territory by Russian forces. The fight between the two groups of would-be-turncoats had reached the form of a real auction sale with Antonescu keeping his price up and Maniu, or rather, the group of young adventurers he had chosen as advisers and executives, hastening to win the race by whatever means and whatever concessions. It is with the story of this sorry contest as told by the *Diplomatic Papers* that we will end this chapter:
MacVeagh to the Secretary of State. Cairo, June 13, 1944.

> Yesterday the Rumanian emissaries received from Maniu through Cretzianu a message in the following sense:
> "Maniu agrees to conclude an armistice upon conditions presented by the Allies. The means of putting the armistice into effect are in process of being established in agreement with those responsible and will be communicated to you in a few days.
> "The patriotic democratic bloc has been formed.
> "In view of the fact that the conditions of the armistice have been accepted, we are convinced that we shall obtain an amelioration of these

conditions when they are applied as repeatedly declared by the Allies."

The Allied representatives are at a loss to understand the last sentence above, since they have promised no amelioration of the armistice terms. . . .

Today the British received a radio message from Rumania asking for safe landing at Aleppo of a plane bearing three more Rumanians who wish to contact Prince Ştirbei. . . . [*D.P., 1944, IV*, p. 181.]

The Secretary of State [Hull] to MacVeagh. Washington, June 17, 1944.

. . . .

The Department knows of no basis in fact for statement in Maniu's message that Allies had repeatedly declared that Rumania could obtain amelioration of armistice conditions. Since Maniu accepts Allied terms as presented, however, his observation regarding their possible modification in Rumania's favor when applied would seem to be irrelevant. [*D.P., 1944, IV*, p. 182. Italics added.]

We remind the reader that no convention of armistice was ever signed in Cairo; that Maniu's agreement to conclude an armistice was in fact a blind agreement upon whatever conditions the Allied Powers would ask him to accept. When a Convention of Armistice was finally signed in Moscow on September 13, it was an aggravation not only of the Soviets' April proposals but even of the United States–United Kingdom draft of January 1944. The Rumanian delegates had to sign on the dotted line, and of all the Rumanian suggestions for redrafting only two were accepted by the Allied Powers. The first related to the amendment of the article requiring Rumania to intern all German and Hungarian citizens. The Rumanian delegates asked that an exception be made in favor of the Jews. The second was to the effect that the Control Commission would end its activities with the conclusion of peace; additional words with little significance, as the control of Rumania's affairs was soon to be firmly in the hands of a Vyshinsky-imposed government.

But the chief worry of the new emissaries of Maniu was how to push Antonescu out of the race for any sort of capitulation and out of the political field:

MacVeagh to the Secretary of State. Cairo, June 29, 1944.

. . . Maniu has sent Ştirbei and Vişoianu a telegram outlining his plan to *"get Rumania out of the war".* . . . For the Department's information, the plan provides the conclusion of the armistice *and the change of Government shall take place simultaneously with a "massive Soviet offensive." It also calls for Allied air bombardment and Allied provision of three airborne brigades and 2000 parachute troops inside Rumania. Whether these Allied contingents are to be Anglo-American or Russian is left to the decision of the Supreme Allied Command.* . . .

In a concluding paragraph Maniu states that having accepted the armistice terms and submitted "the precise plan of action," he would like to know what "immediate improvements" the Allies are prepared to accept in the armistice conditions. *He says that "definite information exists that so far as Antonescu is concerned modifications are agreed to"* and that the groups favorable to the Allies cannot undertake the grave responsibility of action on any terms less favorable than those accorded to him. [*D.P., 1944, IV*, pp. 182–183. Italics added.]

The United States Political Adviser [Murphy] Allied Force Headquarters to the Secretary of State. Algiers, July 2, 1944.

At the risk of possible repetition I report the following concerning negotiations now going on with Maniu: The main points of message received by AFHQ from Cairo are:

(A) As soon as the Allies confirm that they are ready to carry out their side of *the plan,* details of coordination of operations will be arranged. This can be done in a very short time. . . .

(C) In view of the fact that the armistice conditions have been accepted by the opposition, a plan of action submitted, and *that the armistice will only take effect following precise action by them,* the Allies are asked what immediate improved armistice conditions they are prepared to accept. In this connection, *it is asserted that better conditions were offered to Antonescu than to the opposition.*

(D) *The Allies are warned against the illusion that any understanding is possible with Antonescu.* [*D.P., 1944, IV*, pp. 183–184. Italics added.]

The *precise action,* the *plan* to which Maniu's messages were alluding were those which, with the complicity of four generals and the participation of the King, were to lead to the capture of Rumania's fighting forces, surprised and deluded by the announcement of a non-existent armistice agreement, and by a cease-fire order that did not bind the enemy.

Marshal Antonescu had also made contacts with the Allied powers, he was also prepared "to defend himself," to use his euphemism, against the German armies, but he would never have asked "for a massive Soviet offensive" against his own troops, for Soviet airborne brigades and parachutists to disorganize his command and his communications. He was blocking thereby the way of the political parties prepared to sacrifice everything for an ephemeral and tragicomic return to power. That is why he had to be eliminated, that is why he was trapped by his own King, upon the suggestion of Maniu and the politicians, and delivered to the Communist executioners.

On August 23 Cairo received a message from Maniu dated August 20, stating that he "has decided to take action" and asking if he can count on Allied bombing. A message from the King received by Ştirbei the same day states proclamation of break with Axis and requests massive bombardment of numerous special places. On August 25, Grigore Niculesco-Buzeşti, the new Minister of Rumanian Foreign Affairs, informed British, American, and Soviet Governments that the King had dismissed the Government of Marshal Antonescu and named General Constantin Sănătescu Premier of a Government of National Union comprising the National Peasant, the Liberal, the Communist, and the Socialist Parties.

The end was not very far away. Maniu understood it only in December of that tragic year when, crying on the shoulders of Le Rougetel and Berry, he said that if he could have known what was to happen he would not have advised the King to sign the armistice and would have been able to resist for a long time along the Focşani-Nămaloasa-Galaţi Line. Maniu was once more wide of the mark. He had forgotten that at the time of the signing of the Armistice Agreement, thanks to the unprecedented betrayal of the false armistice, the Rumanian troops fighting on the Eastern Front had already been captured by the enemy and sent to Russian and Siberian concentration camps.

A Selected Bibliography

Anders, General Vladislav, *Memoirs*. Paris, Éditions la Jeune Parque, 1948.

Auswärtige Amt (German Foreign Office), *Deutsche Weissbücher*. Berlin, 1939.

Basdevant, Denise, *Terres Roumaines contre Vents et Marées*. Paris, Éditiones de l'Epargne, 1961.

Bast, Jörgen, *Tva Krig, men inte ett Skott; Österrike och Tjeckoslovakien 1938*. Malmö, Dagens Böcker, 1940.

Bonnet, Georges, *Défense de la Paix de Washington ou Quai d'Orsay*. Geneva, Les Éditions du Cheval ailé, C. Bourquin, 1946.

———, *Fin d'une Europe*. Geneva, Les Éditions du Cheval ailé, C. Bourquin, 1953.

Borrego, Salvador, *Derrota Mundial*. Mexico City, 1965.

Botkin, Tatiana, *Vie, Martyre et Sacrifice de Tzars*.

British Foreign Office, *Documents Concerning German-Polish Relations and the Outbreak of Hostilities Between Great Britain and Germany on September 3, 1939*.

Caravilla, Mauricio, *Pearl Harbor, Traicion de Roosevelt*.

Charpeleu, *La Bête sans Nom*. Copenhagen, Les Éditions Diplomatiques, 1943.

Chennault, General Claire L., *Way of a Fighter; the Memoirs of Claire Lee Chennault*, Robert Hotz, ed. New York, G. P. Putnam's Sons, 1949.

Churchill, Winston, *The World Crisis—1918–1928: The Aftermath*, first ed. London, Thornton Butterworth, Ltd., 1929.

———, *The Second World War*, 6 vols. Boston, Houghton Mifflin Company, 1948–1953.

Ciano, Galeazzo, *The Ciano Diaries*, Hugh Gibson, ed. Garden City, New York, Doubleday & Company, Inc., 1946.

Ciuntu, Chirila, *Din Bucovina pe Oder*. Rio de Janeiro and Madrid, Editura Dacia, 1967.

Clauss, Max Walter, *Der Weg nach Jalta: Präsident Roosevelts Verantwortung*. Heidelberg, Vowinckel, 1952.

Crocker, George N., *Roosevelt's Road to Russia*. Chicago, Henry Regnery Company, 1959.

Codreanu, Corneliu, *Pentru Legionari*. Bucharest, 1936.

Conte, Arthur, *Yalta ou le Partage du Monde*. Paris, Laffont, 1964.

Dönitz, Admiral Karl, *Memoirs: Ten Years and Twenty Days*. New York, Hillary House Publishers, Ltd., 1958.

Dugan, James, and Stewart, Carroll, *Ploesti: Great Ground-Air Battle, 1 August, 1943*. New York, Random House, Inc., 1964. Also published as *Tidal Wave*.

Diewerge, Wolfgang, *Anschlag gegen den Frieden: Ein gelbbuch über Grunspan und seine Helfershelfer*. Munich, F. Eher nachf., 1939.

Easterman, Alexander L., *King Carol, Hitler and Lupescu*. London, V. Gollancz, Ltd., 1942.

Essén, Rütger, *Den Ryska Elvationen*. Stockholm, Fahlciantz and Gumaelius, 1941.

Fekete, Attila, *Hungary's Assassination*.

Fleming, Peter, *The Fate of Admiral Kolchak*. New York, Harcourt, Brace & World, Inc., 1963.

Flynn, John T., *The Roosevelt Myth*. New York, Devin-Adair Company, 1948.

——, *While You Slept*. New York, Devin-Adair Company, 1951.

Forrestal, James V., *Forrestal Diaries*, Walter Millis, ed., with the collaboration of E. S. Duffield. New York, Viking Press, Inc., 1951.

French Foreign Office, *French Yellow Book, 1939*.

Gafencu, Grigore, *Preliminaries de la Guerre de l'Est*. Geneva, 1945.

——, *Les derniers Jours de l'Europe*. Zurich, 1946.

Glaser, Kurt, *Czecho-Slovakia, A Critical History*. Caldwell, Idaho, The Caxton Printers, Ltd., 1961.

Groves, Leslie R., *Now It Can Be Told*. New York, Harper & Brothers, 1962.

Henderson, Nevile, *Final Report*. British Foreign Office, 1939.

——, *Failure of a Mission*. New York, G. P. Putnam's Sons, 1940.

Hillgruber, Andreas, *Hitler, König Carol und Marschall Antonescu*. Weisbaden, Steiner Verlag, 1954.

Hitler, Adolf, *Mein Kampf*. Munich, 1926.

Hull, Cordell, *The Memoirs of Cordell Hull*. 2 vols. New York, The Macmillan Company, 1948.

Irving, David, *The Destruction of Dresden*. London, William Kimber, 1963.

Jaksch, Wenzel, *Potsdam 1945: Histoire d'un Mensonge*. Paris, Éditions de la Table Ronde, 1967.

Jordan, George Racey, *From Major Jordan's Diaries*. Belmont, Massachusetts, Western Islands, 1965.

Lane, Arthur Bliss, *I Saw Poland Betrayed*. Belmont, Massachusetts, Western Islands, 1965.

Laurie, A. P., *The Case for Germany*. Berlin, Internationaler Verlag, 1939.

Markham, Reuben H., *Rumania under the Soviet Yoke*. Boston, Meador, 1949.

Montigny, Jean, *Le Complot contre la Paix, 1935–1939*. Paris, Éditiones de la Table Ronde, 1966.

Monzie, Anatole de, *Ci-devant*. Paris, Flammarion, 1941.

Noulens, Joseph, *Mon Ambassade en Russie Soviétique, 1917–1919*. Paris, Plon, 1933.

Oliver, George, *Roosevelt, The Man of Yalta*.

Petrescu-Comnen, Nicolas, *I Responsabili*. Verona, 1949.

——, *Preludi del grande dramma*. Roma, Edizioni Leonardo, 1947.

Polish Foreign Office, *Polish White Book: Official Documents Concerning Polish-German and Polish-Soviet Relations, 1933–1939*. London, 1940.

Poncins, Léon de, *Les Force Secrètes de la Revolution*. Paris, 1933.

Potemkin, Vladimir P., *Histoire de la Diplomatie*. Paris, Libraire de Medicis, 1946.

Price, George Ward, *Years of Reckoning*. London, Cassell & Company, Ltd., 1939.

Prost, Henri, *Destin de la Roumanie (1918–1954)*. Paris, Éditions Berger-Levrault, 1954.

Rassomer, Paul, *Les Responsables de la Seconde Guerre Mondiale*.

Rogger, Hans and Weber, Eugen, eds., *The European Right, a Historical Profile*. Berkeley, University of California Press, 1965.

Romanescu, Traian, *Traicion al Occidente*. Mexico City, 1961.

——, *La Internacional*. Mexico City, 1962.

Romier, Lucien, *Le Carrefeur des Empires Morts*.

Roosevelt, Elliott, *As He Saw It*. New York, Duell, Sloan and Pearce, 1946.

Sainte-Aulaire, Auguste Comte de, *Genève contre la Paix*. Paris, Plon, 1936.

Sima, Horia, *Destinée du Nationalisme*. Édition P.E.G. Paris, 1951.

——, *Europe at the Cross Roads*. Munich, 1955.

——, *Dos Movimientos Nationalistas*. Madrid, 1960.

——, *La Crisis del Munde Libre*. Ediciones Europa. Madrid, 1960.

——, *Cazul Iorga-Madgearu*. Madrid, 1961.

Sokolov, Nicholas, *Enquête Judiciaire sur l'Assassinat de la Famille Imperiale*. Paris, Payot, 1924.

Spengler, Oswald, *Yahre der Entscheidung*. Munich, Beck, 1933.

Sturdza, Michel, *La Roumanie Peut-elle Combattre sur Deux Fronts?* Lausanne, Payot, 1916.

——, *Avec l'Armée Roumaine*. Paris, Hachette, 1918.

——, Katanga. *El Occidente al Servicio del Comunismo*. San José, Costa Rica, Libr. Lehman, 1962.

——, *Open Letter to Their Excellencies*. San José, Lehman, 1962.

——, *World Government and International Assassination*. San José, Lehman, 1962. Reprinted by American Opinion, Belmont, Massachusetts, 1963.

Szembeck, Jean [Jan] Comte, *Journal 1933–1939*, translated from the Polish by J. Rzeweska and T. Zaleski. Paris, Plon, 1952.

Tharaud, Jean and Jérome, *L'Envoyé de l'Archange,* Paris, Plon, 1939.

Thompson, Warren S., *Danger Spots in World Population*. New York, Alfred A. Knopf, 1929.

Teller, Edward, with Brown, Allen, *The Legacy of Hiroshima*. Garden City, New York, Doubleday & Company, Inc., 1962.

United States Department of State, *Foreign Relations of the United States, Diplomatic Papers, 1944, Vol. IV, Europe*.

Veale, F. J. P., *Advance to Barbarism*. Appleton, Wisconsin, C. C. Nelson Publishing Company, 1953.

Weizsäcker, Ernst von, *The Memoirs of Ernst von Weizsäcker*.

Welch, Robert, *The Politician*. Belmont, Massachusetts, Belmont Publishing Company, 1963.

Xénopol, A. D., *Histoire des Roumains de la Dacie Trajane,* 2 vols. Paris, 1896.

Index of Persons

With Selected Biographical Sketches by the Author

Aldea, General Aurel, Rumanian General and Minister of Interior. Active in the Capitulation Conspiracy, lxii

Alexander I, Czar, 4

Alexander II, Czar, xv

Alexander John Cuza, Reigning Prince of the United Principalities of Moldavia and Walachia, xii, 5, 12

Alexander Karadjordjević, King of Yugoslavia. Assassinated in Marseilles. Irreconcilable enemy of Soviet Russia, xvi, xx, xxxix, 46, 47, 64–66, 77, 83, 89

Alexander Obrenović, King of Serbia. Assassinated with his wife, Queen Draga, by a military conspiracy led by Colonel Dimitrijević-Apis, the man who also organized the assassination of Archduke Francis Ferdinand and his wife in Sarajevo, 98n

Alexandri, Vasile, 5

Alphand, Hervé, French Ambassador to Moscow, 50

Altenburg, Dr. Gunther, German representative near the headquarters of the Rumanian Exile Government in Vienna, 176, 177, 260, 266, 268

Anastasia, the false Grand Duchess, 131, 132

Antonescu, Ion, General then Marshal, de facto Chief of State of Rumania during World War II. Delivered to the enemy by King Michael of Rumania and murdered by the Communist authorities. His *coup d'état* against his own government was impelled only by his own morbid ambition, xix, xxii, lv–lvix, lx, lxii, lxv, 31, 39, 55, 86–88, 104, 106, 111, 122, 153, 154, 163, 164, 167–170, 172, 173, 177, 179–181, 185–189, 200, 201, 204–221, 223–227, 235, 236, 242, 244–248, 252, 256, 259, 263, 266, 271, 291, 293–299

Antonescu, Mihai, Minister of Justice and Minister of Foreign Affairs in General Antonescu's government. Murdered with him, lv, lviii, lix, lx, 167, 179, 202, 205–210, 246, 247

Antonescu, Victor, Rumanian Minister of Foreign Affairs in Liberal Governments. Continuator of Titulescu's policy, 75, 86

Arciczewski, Miroslav, Polish Envoy in Riga and Bucharest and Undersecretary of State at the Polish Foreign Office, xlviii, 51, 56, 92, 97, 105, 112, 124

Argeşanu, Ion, General and Rumanian Prime Minister, responsible for the assassination of more than four hundred Legionaries, 149

Argetoianu, Constantin, Rumanian politician. Several times Minister of Finance and of Foreign Affairs. As Prime Minister he participated actively in the persecution of the Legionary Movement, 86–88, 149

Arion, Mişu, 67

Astor, Lord, 92

Attlee, Lord Clement R., 271, 285

Aurelian, Emperor, x

Averescu, General Alexander, 36, 86

Avramescu, General, Commander of Rumanian troops on the Crimean front. Advanced a vital strategy of defense along the line of the Moldavian Carpathians joined with the existing Focşani-Nămoloasa-Galaţi line and the Danube Delta. Ill-advised by his Envoy in Bucharest as to the political situation

China, but had taken previously the precaution of handing over the whole of China to the Communists. One of those unfathomable political mysteries with which the modern public mind has had to become accustomed, 271, 280, 285

Tukhachevski, Marshal Mikhail, Russian Marshal, partisan of a military Rapallo between Germany and Russia and secretly preparing a Russia of his making. This combination did not please the people he took into his confidence in London and Paris. That is how he ended in the Lubianka prison with the traditional bullet in his nape, xliii

Ureche, Great Vornic Nistor, Moldavian statesman and chronicler in the middle of the sixteenth century, 7

Vaida-Voevod, Alexandru, Rumanian Prime Minister. Member of the National Peasant Party. Sometimes opposed Maniu. Always totally devoted to King Carol, xxxvii

Vanger, 129

Vansittart, Lord Robert, as Permanent Secretary of the British Foreign Office always took great care to keep an open possibility for a British-German conflict. The probable inventor of the shrewd dismissing formula with which Great Britain answered Mussolini's last moment efforts to prevent a war between non-Communist powers, 145

Veale, F. J. P., author of *Advance to Barbarism*. One of those books, again, that few dare to open and still less dare to quote, 281, 283, 286

Victor Emmanuel, King of Italy. Whatever his feelings, did not oppose, or in any case did not oppose with enough energy, Mussolini's fatal decision for Italy to abandon the position of non-belligerency and attack an already beaten France. Finally put his Prime Minister *fuera di combatimiento*, and asked Marshal Badoglio to attack his former allies, lx, 179, 181

Victoria, Queen of Great Britain, 98

Vişoianu, Constantin, Maniu's emissary to Cairo where he brought the map of the lines of retreat of the Rumanian Army to help the enemy in his bombing and other operations. Rumanian Foreign Minister, December 1944–March 1945. Bearer of Maniu's acceptance of a conditional capitulation which opened the country to savage Soviet hordes. Fled from Rumania when the havoc he had helped to create seemed too hot for him. Presently head of the Rumanian National Committee with $1000 a month salary from the State Department, lxi, 110, 155, 244, 257, 295–297

Vlad the Impaler, xii, 150

Vlasov, General Andrei, prisoner of the Germans. Organized a Russian National Army in order to liberate Russia from the Communist yoke. Hitler never permitted him to fight. The United States and British Commands handed him over with all his soldiers, and all the Russian refugees who had followed the German armies in their retreat, in circumstances thoroughly described by P. J. Huxley-Blythe in his book *The East Came West*, a book whose reading we recommend only to adult males with strong stomachs. (The Caxton Printers Ltd., Caldwell, Idaho), 265

Vojen, Victor, 164, 209

Vorobchievici, Colonel, Rumanian Military Attaché in Berlin. Was warned by German military authorities of Soviet military preparations at the Bessarabian frontier. Tried to communicate his anxiety and that of his German colleagues to Gafencu, Rumania's Foreign Minister, but did not succeed, liv, 152, 153, 155

Vyshinsky, Andrei, Commissar for Foreign Affairs. Soviet Proconsul in Rumania. As Soviet Representative at the UN broadly popularized the Russian "Nyet!", lxiv, 222, 259, 297

Wales, Prince of, 81

Warburg, 23

Washington, George, Founding father and President of the United States. Knew about the danger from the *Illuminati*, 44

Weber, Eugen, 8, 25, 29–31, 33, 34, 36–40, 106, 222, 234, 236, 237

General Index